Confronting Captivity

Confronting Captivity

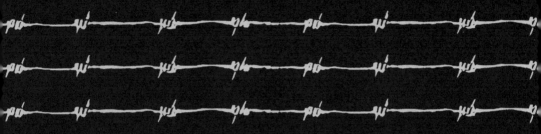

BRITAIN AND
THE UNITED STATES
AND THEIR POWS IN
NAZI GERMANY

ARIEH J. KOCHAVI

The University of North Carolina Press

Chapel Hill and London

© 2005 The University of North Carolina Press

All rights reserved

Set in Charter and The Serif

by Keystone Typesetting, Inc.

Manufactured in the United States of America

The paper in this book meets the guidelines for
permanence and durability of the Committee on
Production Guidelines for Book Longevity of the
Council on Library Resources.

Library of Congress Cataloging-in-Publication Data

Kochavi, Arieh J.

Confronting captivity : Britain and the United States
and their POWs in Nazi Germany / Arieh J. Kochavi.

    p. cm.

Includes bibliographical references and index.

ISBN 0-8078-2940-4 (cloth: alk. paper)

1. World War, 1939–1945—Prisoners and prisons,
German. 2. Prisoners of war—Germany. 3. Prisoners of
war—United States. 4. Prisoners of war—Great Britain.
5. Prisoners of war—Government policy—United States.
6. Prisoners of war—Government policy—Great Britain.
I. Title.

D805.G3K619   2005

940.54′7243—dc22   2004029708

09 08 07 06 05   5 4 3 2 1

CONTENTS

ILLUSTRATIONS AND MAP

Illustrations

Map

ACKNOWLEDGMENTS

For the research that went into this book I visited archives and libraries on both sides of the Atlantic, among them the National Archives, College Park, Maryland; the Franklin D. Roosevelt Library, Hyde Park, New York; the Public Record Office, Kew, England; the British Red Cross Archive, London; and the Imperial War Museum, London. While archivists in all places were invariably most helpful, I wish to single out Wilbert Mahoney of the Military Branch of the National Archives.

I owe a special debt of gratitude to my editor, Dick Bruggeman, for the insightful way we were able to discuss the theses at the heart of my study. I also wish to thank Asher Goldstein, who edited an early version of the manuscript, and Maya Dar, ever helpful as my research assistant. As always, I am grateful to my wife, Orna, and my three great kids, Talia, Uri, and Doron, who here have another chance to see their name in print.

ABBREVIATIONS

BMM	British Military Mission in Moscow
BRCS	British Red Cross Society
CAC	Combined Administrative Committee
CCS	Combined Chiefs of Staff
COS	British Chiefs of Staff Committee
DPW	Directorate of Prisoners of War, War Office
EAC	European Advisory Commission
ICRC	International Committee of the Red Cross
IPWC	Imperial Prisoners of War Committee
JCS	U.S. Joint Chiefs of Staff
JISC	Joint Intelligence Sub-Committee
JLC	Joint Logistics Committee
JPS	American Joint Planning Staff
JSM	British Joint Staff Mission
MMC	mixed medical commission
MOC	man of confidence
MP	member of Parliament
NCO	noncommissioned officer
OKW	Oberkommando der Wehrmacht
POW	prisoner of war
PWD	Prisoners of War Department, Foreign Office
RAF	Royal Air Force
SACMED	Supreme Allied Commander, Mediterranean
SAO	senior American officer
SAS	British Special Air Service
SBO	senior British officer

SCAEF	Supreme Commander, Allied Expeditionary Force
SHAEF	Supreme Headquarters of the Allied Expeditionary Force
SS	Schutzstaffel
UNWCC	United Nations War Crimes Commission
USAAF	U.S. Army Air Forces
USMMM	U.S. Military Mission in Moscow
YMCA	Young Men's Christian Association

INTRODUCTION

Sailing back from the Russian port city of Odessa on the Black Sea after having spent nearly five years as a British prisoner of war (POW) in German captivity, David Wild relates how "[a]fter four days the *Duchess*, which had so far carried no more than three hundred ex-prisoners, was filled to capacity with hundreds of homeward bound troops of various units which had been fighting their way northwards through Italy all through the winter. Confronted with this horde of battle-hardened professionals, we retreated into anonymous obscurity. They were mostly fairly exhausted, not to say suffering from delayed shock, and in no mind to be interested in our years of profitless inactivity."[1]

Back in England, Wild's sense of the futility of the way he and his fellow prisoners had spent the war years from the moment they had fallen into enemy hands deepened even further: "[W]hen I let on that I had just emerged from five years of useless incarceration, my disclosure was clearly an effective conversation-stopper. This was a reaction to be experienced many times in the coming months by me, and I suspect by many others. It was like letting on in public that one was suffering from an unmentionable terminal illness. Most people were quite sympathetic, but did not really want to know how we had filled up five years of enforced inactivity."[2]

Toward the end of World War II there were more than 2 million Allied prisoners of war in German captivity, among them close to 200,000 British Commonwealth and about 95,000 U.S. army troops.[3] Like Wild, tens of thousands of them had spent as long as five years in prison camps; others had been captured during later stages of the fighting in North Africa, in the Middle East, and of course in Europe. When he speaks of "years of profitless inactivity," Wild refers not only to the sense of waste POWs themselves had to come to grips with but also to the inescapable fact that for the home front these men were "lost" to the war effort. If we look at the memoirs leading British and American politicians and military commanders have published about the war, we find that the POW problem barely crops up in their pages.[4] More than a year into the war, Prime Minister Winston Churchill sent the following laconic message to British POWs in German captivity: "Keep yourselves fit in mind and body, so that you may the better serve our land, and when peace comes, play your part in establishing a happier, safer homeland."[5] Historians, too, on the whole have paid but scant attention to the measures and policies the British and U.S. governments discussed and adopted during the war in support of their own troops held prisoner in Nazi Germany.[6] Thus, one might come away with the impression that the overall attitude of the political and military leaders in London and Washington toward the plight of their own citizens in enemy hands was one of indifference, if not neglect.

The historical analysis I present in this book offers a more complicated picture. Throughout the war both London and Washington reveal a growing concern about how to ensure the health and safety of soldiers imprisoned in enemy territory. Ironically, they were helped to some extent by the racial policies of the Nazi leadership, whose horrific treatment of POWs belonging to "inferior" nations has been well documented: vis-à-vis British and American POWs the Germans tended—almost to the very last—to adhere to the 1929 Convention on Treatment of Prisoners of War (Geneva Convention).[7] Contacts with Berlin, through neutral Switzerland and the International Committee of the Red Cross (ICRC), testify to this. But—and this is one of the main findings of this book—when the collapse of Germany was imminent, apprehension over the safety of the POWs turned into anxiety for their very lives, yet the priorities the Allies decided on in the war theater precluded any operative steps on behalf of the POWs. With an Allied victory in sight, the collective fate of British Commonwealth and American POWs suddenly appeared to hang by a thread: To what extent would fear of retribution after the war effectively stop extremist groups in Germany—whose horrendous crimes were already a matter of international record—from committing one final act of horror out of vengeance at having lost the war?

This book is divided into four parts, each unfolding a major aspect of the POW issue. Together they aim at giving a comprehensive representation of the way British and American policies evolved in the course of the war with respect to Nazi Germany and, later, Soviet Russia. In particular, they try to assess the relative weight London and Washington—separately and together—would give over time to two factors that at one point near the end of the war seemed almost impossible to reconcile: the moral and practical concerns raised by the increasingly large numbers of troops that fell into German hands, and the political and military exigencies of obtaining victory in the total war they were fighting against a ruthless enemy.

Part I examines the life and fate of British and American prisoners in German POW camps and analyzes the circumstances behind the diverging attitudes the two governments developed in the way they dealt with the problem. As early as the spring of 1940, at Dunkirk, around 34,000 British Commonwealth troops fell into German hands. Moreover, following the fall of France, Britain stood alone in the immediate confrontation with Nazi Germany—only a year later did Hitler attack the Soviet Union, and the United States was not to enter the war until December 1941. By then, close to 70,000 British soldiers had become POWs in German captivity.

POWs were housed in main (or base) camps and in work camps that were detachments of these base camps. Some of the main camps accommodated several thousand POWs, others no more than a few hundred; in the work camps numbers ranged from a few dozen or even fewer to many hundreds, though sometimes we find detachments with several thousand prisoners. Conditions in the camps depended on their physical layout but also—and often crucially so—on the attitude of the German camp authorities or the civilian employer for whom they were put to work. The kind of work involved also played a role, of course—POWs working on a farm were likely to be better off than those sent down a salt mine. Vital furthermore for the prisoners' health from both a physical and a psychological point of view were the food and clothing packages that reached them from their home countries via the Red Cross. As the war progressed, the situation in the camps worsened perceptibly: developments in the battlefield meant a constant influx of POWs, which in turn led to overcrowding and a growing lack of basic materials. But these developments also had an impact on the morale of the German camp authorities: as the Allies intensified their air attacks on civilian German populations, reprisal acts by the Nazis against POWs became a frightening possibility.

Significantly, it was during the final year of the war that most American troops were captured. Two main aspects come to the fore here. First, Washington was largely spared the intensive political and public criticism concerning government treatment of the POW issue to which London had been subjected early on. Second, following D-Day, not only did the scope of the POW issue change dramatically, but the problems that needed a solution were by now far more severe.

As stipulated in the Geneva Convention, officials of the protecting power (i.e., Switzerland, after the United States joined the war) and of the ICRC had access to the POW camps for the purpose of inspection. Such officials visited the main camps on average once every three months; the systematic reports they filed enable us to reconstruct developments in the camps until the very end of the war. It was largely on these reports that London and Washington based their assessments. Though naturally they tend to highlight deficiencies and ill-treatment, the official protests the United States and Britain regularly addressed to Berlin also throw light on the situation inside the POW camps. In most cases the Germans' version of how they treated British and American POWs has here been distilled from Berlin's responses either to complaints and protests lodged by the Western Allies or to queries made by the protecting power's officials following their periodical inspections.[8] As these are all official reports, the language used is generally highly formal, and any sense of the day-to-day reality of prison life appears to be lacking. In order to arrive at some notion of what it meant to be an inmate in a German POW camp, I repeatedly turn to letters prisoners wrote home as well as to their personal diaries and memoirs and to reports of POWs repatriated during the war. Bulletins regularly put out by the Red Cross and various POW relatives' organizations also proved helpful.

At the same time, it remains difficult to paint a comprehensive picture spanning the six long years of the war period: the nearly 300,000 British and American POWs in Germany were kept in literally dozens of base camps and thousands of work camps spread out over vast distances. Contemporaries already recognized this problem. Following the repatriation in September 1944 of 234 seriously wounded and sick American POWs, the U.S. Red Cross's *Prisoners of War Bulletin* told its readers: "There was, quite naturally, much difference between one man's report on conditions at one camp and another's report on conditions at another. Even from the same camp, repatriates' reports did not always agree."[9] An intelligence report the U.S. War Department published after the war came to a similar conclusion: "Conditions in German prisoners of war camps holding Americans varied to such an extent that only by examination of individual camps can a clear picture be drawn."[10] Although there were different types of German POW camps, for the present study I decided to focus on those that held the largest number of British Commonwealth and American soldiers, as they encompass the experience of the majority of the POWs.

Part II examines the course of the negotiations the belligerents started early on over the mutual exchange of severely wounded and sick POWs. There were to be four such exchanges during the war, involving more than 10,000 British Commonwealth and American prisoners. Significantly, both the negotiations and the exchanges themselves continued as the Allies were carrying out devastating air raids over German cities. That Berlin never broke off contacts during this period underscores the conclusion I draw that, when it helped them secure their interests with regard to the West, the Nazis could set out and consistently follow an overtly pragmatic course of action. Similar negotiations, however, over the repatriation of long-term prisoners failed—partly because of Washington. Whitehall's persistence until the very last weeks of the war reflected, besides concern over the fate of its prisoners, growing worries about criticism at home of the way it had been handling the POW issue.

Inevitably, the Allied invasion of Normandy on 6 June 1944 brought a marked change for the worse. Conditions in the camps deteriorated rapidly, and as the ICRC was now facing enormous difficulties in making sure that supplies would reach their destination, malnutrition became widespread. What further exacerbated the plight of the prisoners was the transfer of the responsibility for the POW camps from the Wehrmacht and the Luftwaffe to the Schutzstaffel (SS) and the Gestapo. Part III outlines how the British and American governments confronted this situation, especially when, following the decisive Soviet offensive early in 1945, the Germans began evacuating tens of thousands of British and American POWs into the heart of Germany. This was done by forcing them to march hundreds of kilometers in harsh winter weather without adequate food, water, or shelter. For the overwhelming majority of the prisoners forced to take part in them, these marches proved to be their most traumatic experience as POWs—for some they meant their death. Still, London and Washington failed to bring a halt to them. What is more, when at the close of the war U.S. and British POWs were exposed to potentially life-threatening danger, their governments proved utterly ineffective in coming to the rescue. The disquieting conclusion this study arrives at is that both the British and U.S. civil and military leaders in the end decided to take a calculated risk by assuming that, as they pressed on with their final and devastating military operations, Berlin would not retaliate against British and American prisoners in German camps. They were well aware at the same time that if the Nazis did decide to retaliate, there was by then little they themselves could do to stop them.

Shortly after D-Day it became clear that the Red Army stood to liberate tens of thousands of British and American POWs in the east, prompting both Western Allies to expect them to be repatriated swiftly. The Kremlin, however, conditioned the return of U.S. and British POWs on the repatriation by London and Washington of all Soviet nationals they were holding, irrespective of whether these people themselves wanted to go back. The crux here, of course, was that among them were citizens of the Baltic countries, territories the Soviet Union had now de facto annexed. Part IV explores how this linkage emerged and was then fully exploited by Moscow as a lever in the negotiations it conducted—separately, to enhance their effectiveness— with London and Washington. Whitehall proved almost unreservedly amenable, Washington at first less so. At the same time, both the British and the Americans were eager to have contact officers check out the areas in the east liberated by the Red Army for POWs still scattered there. The power struggle that developed around the issue was soon bound up with the question of the future government of Poland, highlighting how complicated relations between the West and the Soviets already were before the end of World War II.

When the war broke out, no one could have foreseen how long it would last or what its outcome would be. The anxiety about the fate of British Commonwealth soldiers who early in the war had fallen into German hands was very real among their families and friends, but for the government concerns about their situation were pushed into the background by the immediate threat the war posed at home. In both London and Washington priorities were dictated by developments in the battlefield and the wider geopolitical ramifications of the need to defeat Nazi Germany.

As the war continued and the numbers of those killed and wounded multiplied, the question of the POWs injected itself into policy-making discussions on government level only—if at all—in times of sudden crisis in their overall plight or at crossroads in the war itself. As in almost any long conflict when political and military interests clash with human considerations, here, too, the latter were moved aside. Perhaps one of the reasons that British and U.S. government policy making regarding the POW issue has hardly been researched is that most of the nearly 300,000 British Commonwealth and U.S. POWs survived the war and were able to come home when it was over. But they might not have.

FACING THE CHALLENGE

I

Whitehall and British POWs

AFTER DUNKIRK

World War II broke out on 1 September 1939 with Germany's invasion of Poland. Turning westward after the winter, the German armies during May 1940 invaded the Low Countries, where they met little or no resistance. In effect, the thrust of the German attack was such that it forced British and French troops to beat a hasty retreat from southern Belgium and northern France. Between 26 May and 4 June, approximately 220,000 British and 120,000 French troops were hurriedly evacuated from the beaches near Dunkirk across the English Channel to Britain. About 34,000 British Commonwealth troops failed to make it and fell into German hands.[1]

By July the war had reached the British Isles, with the Germans attacking British coastal shipping and the country's southern ports. In the Battle of Britain the German air force (Luftwaffe) first tried to defeat the Royal Air Force so as to gain superiority in the air and prepare the way for an invasion by ground troops. Simultaneously, they began targeting small-scale urban centers and civilian populations. In late August, the city of Liverpool became the main target; on 7 September 1940, Berlin sent 300 German bombers and an escort of 600 fighter planes across the Channel in the first of a series of air raids that would strike London relentlessly for sixty-eight consecutive nights, killing 13,000 people. By then, more than 40,000 British troops were in German captivity as prisoners of war.[2]

The impact of the huge devastation of infrastructures and the severe loss of civilian life the Germans were able to inflict during these months heightened the awareness among all levels of the population that after the fall of France Britain stood alone in the fight against Nazi Germany. This helps explain why in the aftermath of Dunkirk we find Whitehall focusing all its energy on the struggle for survival at home, with little attention given to the fate of British troops in enemy hands. Moreover, until Dunkirk the total of British POWs in German camps had never been more than 3,000, all held under conditions representatives of the U.S. government—the protecting power under the Geneva Convention—generally reported "to be good."[3]

There was also the salient fact that the government appeared largely unprepared to deal with the issue. The official history of the Foreign Office's Prisoners of War Department (PWD), published in 1950, offers the following critical assessment: "The War Office was, like the Foreign Office, lacking in imagination, and for some months the care of prisoners of war was, in that Department, in the hands of a few individuals having also other duties."[4] The authors conclude: "If there had been in both Departments from the outbreak of the war special organizations, small though they might have been, various matters of detail having considerable importance in their bearing on the welfare of our prisoners might have been properly dealt with and settled."[5]

Initially, the Germans, too, lacked adequate facilities to absorb the large number of POWs who at this early stage had already fallen into their hands.[6] For example, about 18,000 of the British troops that had been caught at Dunkirk were taken to Thorn, in German-occupied Poland, where a small number of forts on the edge of the town dating from the previous century were hastily turned into a POW camp. Soon, however, the Germans had put in place a system of base camps and work units that was to serve them for the rest of the war. It divided prisoners and placed them in different camps according to their military rank and the force they had served in.[7]

There were three kinds of main camps. A *Stalag* (an abbreviation of *Stammlager*) was a permanent central army camp for noncommissioned officers (NCOS) or enlisted men; an *Oflag* (an abbreviation of *Offiziernlager*) was a permanent central camp for officers; and a *Stalag Luft* (short for *Stammlager Luftwaffe*) was a central camp for air force prisoners. There was one *Dulag* (short for *Durchgangslager*), literally a transit camp but in fact serving as an interrogation center for air force personnel, who were then sent on to Stalags, and one *Marlag* (short for *Marinelager*) for navy personnel. Then there were *Arbeitskommandos* (work camps) and *Lazarette* (military hospitals). The entire German POW system came under the control of the Oberkommando der Wehrmacht (OKW), the High Command of the German Armed Forces, which meant that the final say in all POW matters officially lay with Adolf Hitler (who himself never visited any of the camps). Within the OKW overall responsibility belonged to the Abt Kriegsgefangenenwesen im OKW (Office for POW Affairs), but this office delegated much of its authority over the camps to the chiefs of the Luftwaffe, the Wehrmacht, and the Kriegsmarine (the German navy). The main POW camps were numbered (in roman numerals) according to the military district in which they were located (Germany was divided into twenty-two such *Wehrkreise*.) The POWs themselves had their own internal organizations and hierarchy. The highest-ranking officer in an Oflag served as the senior British officer (SBO) or senior American officer (SAO), while the spokesman in Stalags was the "man of confidence" (MOC), usually a noncommissioned officer chosen for the job by his fellow POWs or sometimes appointed by the Germans.[8]

The POW camp on the outskirts of Thorn where the approximately 18,000 British Commonwealth troops had been taken was called Stalag XX A. Each of the forts that made up the main camp had an inside court (with or without a moat) and crescent-shaped concrete defense works two and a half stories high that were built into a hill and facing outward. The interior arrangements consisted of two kitchens at the center of the crescent and, between them, a hot-air delousing chamber and showers. The canteen was also located here, as was a room for food storage. The wings on either end held a dispensary, a room for tailors and shoemakers, and dormitories—all on the ground floor. Two galleries on the second floor had dormitories, each holding 30–35 men. Except for the sick, the men slept on the floor on burlap sacks filled with straw and had blankets. There were stoves in all rooms that were used as dormitories; as these rooms were built into the hill, daylight was faint, and electric lightbulbs had to be switched on most of the time. The forts were supplemented by wooden barracks, each of which had a small kitchen, washroom, and night toilet as well as windows. The number of occupants in these barracks ranged from 150–200 to as many as 800 in a large barrack. Noncommissioned officers were quartered at one end of each barrack. All forts offered showers with warm water and a section where prisoners could do their laundry.[9]

Medical attention consisted of a dispensary in each camp and fort; Fort XIV had been turned into a hospital. The latter was attractively surrounded by a moat with two neat, prefabricated wards on top of the hill for lung and isolation cases. When a U.S. inspector visited Fort XIV in late July 1940, 195 men were hospitalized. Light cases slept in two-tier bunks, but serious cases had proper beds. All had mattresses and covering. There were bathtubs and showers and a large toilet with separate seats for scabies and venereal cases. POWs needing special treatment or an operation were sent to a military hospital nearby.

The American inspector who reported these details added that there was a shortage of clergymen but that efforts were made to hold Sunday services. Authorities in Berlin refused to grant permission for American ministers from Dresden or Berlin to visit the Stalag.[10] Prisoners were offered no

GERMANY

NORTH SEA

Kiel

Barth

Lübeck ▲

Neu Brandenburg ▲△
                      II

HOLLAND

X
Hamburg

Bremen

VI

Hannover ▲

XI

Drewitz △

Berlin   Frankfurt
Luckenwalde
Altengrabow △

III   Fürstenberg △

Annaburg △

Sagan

Düsseldorf
Köln

Kassel ▲ Spangenberg

Halle
Leipzig   Mühlberg
          Colditz ▲

IV

Dresden

Görlitz △

Hadamar ▲ Wetzlar

IX
Obermassfeld

Hartmansdorf △

BELGIUM

Coblenz △
Limburg
Frankfurt

Hohnstein

XII

XIII
Nüremberg

Hammelburg △

Prague

BOHEMIA

LUXEMBOURG

FRANCE

Stuttgart

V

Eichstätt ▲
Moosburg △

XVII

Munich

VII   Salzburg
Memmingen

XVIII

Bern

SWITZERLAND

Graz
Wolfsberg △

ITALY   Marburg △

Location of POW camps by the end of 1944 (Based on map courtesy PRO, Kew, England)

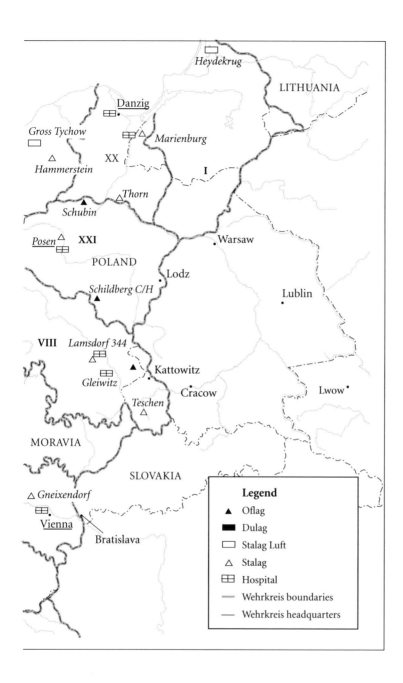

Heydekrug

LITHUANIA

Danzig

Gross Tychow

Marienburg

XX

Hammerstein

I

Thorn

Schubin

Posen   XXI

Warsaw

POLAND

Lodz

Lublin

Schildberg C/H

VIII   Lamsdorf 344

Kattowitz

Gleiwitz

Cracow

Lwow

Teschen

MORAVIA

SLOVAKIA

Gneixendorf

Legend

▲ Oflag

■ Dulag

▭ Stalag Luft

△ Stalag

⊞ Hospital

〰 Wehrkreis boundaries

— Wehrkreis headquarters

Vienna

Bratislava

recreation and thus relied on what they could come up with themselves. It was possible for prisoners to do work in these camps, which the inspector thought was a good thing. Saturday and Sunday were rest days. Mail had been sent, but none had yet been received. Neither had individual packages from England. Eight hundred Red Cross packages had just arrived from Switzerland—about one per twenty-five men. The American inspector discovered that the commandant, a Major Wittmer, had himself been a prisoner of war during World War I and described him as an efficient, energetic man, "stern but fair." Generally, "the impression was most favorable."[11]

For a description of what was in store for a POW entering Stalag XX A for the first time, we have the recollections of Private H. S. Bowers: "We seemed completely cut off from the world outside, wandering about down the dark corridors with water dripping eternally from the roof and down the walls, dimly lit with low wattage bulbs in places. The hollow echo of voices and food steps and a mournful dirge called 'Stalag Blues' that someone was playing on a trump, all . . . contributed to what seemed to be part of another world. One could almost imagine that one had already died."[12]

Oflag VII C/H was the main POW officers camp. It was actually an old castle located in the heart of a small village, Laufen, near Salzburg, which formerly had belonged to one of the archbishops of southern Germany. When one of the American inspectors visited the camp in mid-June 1940, it held 601 officers and 82 orderlies. The camp commandant, one Lieutenant Colonel Frei, told the American that he expected to receive another 1,600 officers within a few weeks' time but that the proportion of about 8 officers to 1 orderly would be maintained. All the prisoners were English. Among them were a brigadier, C. N. Nicholson, who had commanded British troops in Calais and was the camp's SBO; several colonels; and 17 chaplains. Most of the prisoners had the rank of lieutenant.[13]

Two recreational fields surrounded the castle, which also had an unroofed inner courtyard. The top three floors of the four-story building served as sleeping quarters. Most of the rooms were large and had ample ventilation and light. The smallest sleeping room measured approximately twenty by fifteen feet. Twelve of the seventeen chaplains slept in this room. Ninety people slept in the largest room, which contained double-tier bunks and five windows. For each person there were two blankets and one pillow, but there were no sheets. Cold running water was available for washing, and prisoners, who were given one cake of soap monthly, were allowed a hot shower once in two weeks. There was one toilet seat for approximately every fifty men.

The major complaint was about food, which "is provided with the purpose of sustaining life but with all luxuries eliminated and with certain necessities sharply reduced in quantity. Considering the fact that the prisoners have little opportunity for exercise the menu as a whole seemed little better than what could be called starvation rations." But there was no trace of diseases customarily associated with bad or too little food, and no one seemed to have been hospitalized. The younger officers chiefly complained that there was not enough bread, while others protested they had to do without jam and wanted more milk and sugar.[14] For his part, camp commandant Frei maintained that the prison rations were as good as—and for some items, better than—the fare German civilians were getting. German troops on reserve ate no better, and anyway this was the maximum allotment required by the Geneva Convention.[15]

Brigadier Nicholson thought that the attitude of the Germans toward the prisoners was courteous and that the camp was well organized and managed. Nicholson reiterated that there were no serious complaints and that suggestions for "greater comfort" should by no means be considered as a criticism of the camp or its discipline. Agreeing with Nicholson and describing Lieutenant Colonel Frei as "cultivated and conscientious," the American inspector concluded: "The irreproachable attitude of the camp commander and the senior officers and the fine morale of the prisoners together with the spirit of cooperation prevailing between captor and captured formed the major impressions obtained during this visit to Oflag VII C."[16]

Three months later, in September 1940, another American inspector by the name of Gordon Knox visited Oflag VII C/H. By now, the number of inmates had doubled: there were 1,240 officers and 220 orderlies. Although it had obviously improved somewhat, food continued to be the main source of complaint.[17] Chief British prisoner physician Lieutenant Colonel T. Samuel Rambuilds estimated that each prisoner consumed 1,500 calories a day, and he reported mild cases of edema because of malnutrition. Knox considered none of these cases to be serious enough to require hospitalization; though showing a prison pallor, captives were obviously not starving. Patients received milk, white bread, milk pudding, red wine, and butter in addition to their regular rations. At the time of the visit, ten prisoners were in the sick ward; serious cases had been transferred to a nearby local hospital. Six patients had fallen ill before being interned in the castle. No one had died since the camp had been established.

Whereas Brigadier Nicholson again had no serious complaints to make, other officers were less reticent: one blanket per man was not sufficient;

more electric lights were needed; mail from England was slow, particularly parcels (prisoners were allowed to send three letters and three postcards per month); provisions in the Geneva Convention pertaining to food were not being respected; clothing was needed; exercise fields were small, and there were no footballs; and prisoners were unable to buy hot coffee in the canteen. That treatment was overly strict was shown by an incident on 9 September 1940 in which three sentries had fired four shots into some windows of the camp at 1 P.M. The Germans explained to Knox that they had reason to suspect an impending escape because in the past two months six people had succeeded in escaping from the camp, only three of whom had been recaptured.[18]

Knox thought that the biggest shortcoming at Oflag VII C/H was over-crowding. He believed that many of the complaints would be dealt with and that the morale of the men, particularly what he called their "spirit of cooperation" with the Germans, would improve if a certain percentage of the prisoners were transferred to another Oflag. He agreed there was serious need for more clothing, particularly winter wear and shoes, but advised the British to bear in mind that the obvious hardships of POW life "must be expected and accepted and that a belligerent attitude and open distrust of the German authorities will not serve to ameliorate their condition."[19]

Letters from officers in Oflag VII C/H can help throw some more light on the internal situation of the prisoners. The shortage of clothes was pointedly brought up in a letter dated 24 September 1940 by a lieutenant, who wrote, "I have no overcoat, underclothes, pyjamas or shoes, only a tattered cotton shirt so am bitterly cold. I have bought a German blanket after weeks of economy and by borrowing." Food shortages featured in the following letter sent home by a captain: "We get up at 7 a.m. and have a mug of coffee, soup and potatoes at 11 and 5 o'clock, sometimes bread, so you understand that parcels of food are urgently needed. Some arrived today from Red Cross, they are to be shared one between ten officers. No parcels arrived yet for me, my clothes are worn out and in holes." Another officer penned this description: "There are 99 sleeping in our room and 1,000 of us in the barracks. Our soup ration is one tumbler a day, also one loaf of brown bread every 5 days. It is bitterly cold already, I have only the clothes I stand up in and they are in rags."[20]

By mid-October 1940, after a three-week tour of POW camps in Germany, Darius A. Davis, associate general secretary of the World Committee of the Young Men's Christian Association (YMCA)—which was already on hand to provide educational and recreational facilities for the prisoners—was able to present London with an overall assessment of the prisoners' situation. Davis estimated that there were more than 40,000 British prisoners, including about 1,600 officers. There were no complaints about the quality of the food they were given, but it was clear that the portions they received were rarely enough. The most pressing problem was warm clothing: most prisoners possessed only the summer uniforms in which they had been captured. Men who were sent out on working parties were provided with underwear and Polish army greatcoats, which they obviously disliked having to wear and which in any case were mostly worn out. Officers and men who were not called on to do manual labor had to stay indoors during the cold weather unless they could be given warm clothing: Davis claimed that he saw numerous parcels from England containing civilian clothes but the Germans prohibited the prisoners from wearing them. Officers and men who were unable to work clearly suffered from their enforced idleness. Every effort, though, was being made by the YMCA to provide them with interests of various kinds to help them pass the time.

What appeared to be the greatest cause for distress among the prisoners was the almost total lack of news from home. Many prisoners had not heard from their families since they had been captured and were afraid their own letters were not reaching Britain. The German authorities assured Davis that they were ready to do whatever they could to facilitate postal communication within prescribed limits. As Davis saw it, the German camp commandants carried out their duties conscientiously and in most cases even sympathetically. Conditions on the whole, he summed up, were satisfactory.[21]

For their visits to the camps American embassy personnel needed permits. When applying for a such permit, embassy representatives had to give their name, place, and date of birth, and passport number. The permit issued was valid for one calendar month and covered all prison camps in the Reich, including hospitals and work camps affiliated with such camps. The permits had to be returned before their expiry date. Once received, a permit could be used only after at least a week's advance notice had been given to the German High Command, which then notified local military commanders of approaching visits. Since permits were not always issued punctually on the first of a given month, visits were effectively prevented from taking place for as much as the first two or even three weeks of a particular month, thus diminishing by half or even two-thirds the time available for inspecting prison camps. These regulations limited flexibility in the program of camp visits. Still, embassy inspectors assessed that, however restricted these visits, their reports reflected the situation in the camps more or less realistically. Being able to talk to prisoners, particularly to the SBO, without German camp representatives being present enabled them to obtain as much of an authentic picture as possible.[22]

RESPONDING TO CRITICISM

With the outbreak of the war, the British government entrusted the War Office with the administration of and policy decisions vis-à-vis all British Commonwealth and enemy POWs. On 25 May 1940, the War Office created the Directorate of Prisoners of War (DPW), which from then on had direct responsibility for the administration of enemy POWs in the United Kingdom and for the general welfare of all British prisoners in enemy hands, in particular the safeguarding of their rights under the Geneva Convention. The DPW's first director, Major General Alan Hunter, was succeeded in late 1941 by Major General E. C. Gepp.[23] The Foreign Office retained the responsibility for all diplomatic contacts with Axis countries, which were handled by its Prisoners of War Department via the protecting power and with the ICRC. Here, too, the authors of the official history of the PWD are critical: "It is strange that, as at the time of the First World War, so also in the Second World War, the need of a Prisoners of War Department of the Foreign Office was not for some time realised." In 1914 "this lack of foresight," as they call it, was perhaps understandable, as "war came after a long period of peace and with little warning," but in 1939 "what was going to happen had long been clear, even though the exact date of the happening was not known."[24] The overall impression is that the experience gained during World War I in handling the POW issue was largely ignored.[25]

Given the potential overlap in their activities, the War Office and Foreign Office on the whole worked together smoothly. Sometimes disputes would arise between them—especially in the face of looming public criticism—as to who could be held responsible for a particular action that had (or had not) been taken.[26] For their part, the Admiralty and the Air Ministry watched over the interests of their own troops who had become prisoners of war and continually informed the War Office, which, of course, also dealt with them. The same was true for the Colonial Office and the Indian Office. With the prolongation of the war, the Dominion governments demanded a greater say in formulating policies concerning their captured men, and Whitehall recognized that it needed better coordination between government departments involved in the POW issue; as a result, in 1941 the Inter-Governmental Prisoners of War Committee was set up under the chairmanship of the secretary of state for war. Its name was soon changed to the Imperial Prisoners of War Committee (IPWC).[27]

Almost from the outset of the war, there was concern in Parliament over how food and clothing could be guaranteed to reach British POWs in Germany. For example, as early as mid-October 1939, two members of Parliament (MPs), Eleanor Rathbone and Sir Alexander Russel, asked the secretary of state for air what arrangements, if any, had been made for sending food, clothing, and medical supplies to Royal Air Force POWs.[28] The response came a few weeks later when, at the beginning of December, Secretary of State for War Leslie Hore-Belisha announced that, in consultation with the government departments concerned, the British Red Cross Society (BRCS) had set up the Prisoners of War, Wounded and Missing Department, which would also be the accredited authority for packing and dispatching parcels to British POWs.[29] The BRCS already had the important task of serving as a link between the POWs in Germany and their families at home, and beginning in May 1942 it published a periodical called the *Prisoners of War*.[30]

The government's transfer of the responsibility for dispatching parcels to the POWs to the BRCS was to become the object of much criticism from not only MPs but also relatives of POWs and members of the press, especially when the BRCS proved unable to keep up with the needs of increasing numbers of POWs as the war progressed.[31] The BRCS opened its first packing center in November 1939. The contents of the parcels, based on professional medical and dietetic advice, sought to offer the right proportions of starch, protein, and sugar as a supplement to the weekly rations for one prisoner as established by the Geneva Convention. An effort was made to include items for which prisoners themselves had expressed a liking. At least until the summer of 1942, the contents of the parcels differed from week to week.[32] With the dramatic increase in the numbers of British soldiers in German captivity by the spring of 1940, the speed and scope of dispatching parcels to the POWs already seemed inadequate. A total of 88,331 food parcels were packed and shipped between June and August 1940. By the beginning of September, ten packing centers were operating, with an output of approximately 27,000 parcels per week. Five more centers were opened between October and November, each turning out 22,500 parcels per week.[33] By now, Britain, and particularly London, were suffering mass bombing attacks by the German Luftwaffe that greatly disrupted all aspects of life.

In early November 1940, MP Major General A. Knox, Conservative, representing the Wycombe division of Buckinghamshire since 1924, asked Prime Minister Winston S. Churchill whether he was aware that "there is a great deal of dissatisfaction at the conduct of the Red Cross, and would it not be a good thing to have an inquiry to find out whether it is justified or not." As the Red Cross had been given sole responsibility for the dispatch of parcels to British POWs, Knox—who would become a major critic of Whitehall's handling of the POW problem—proposed that the government appoint one of its ministers to the council of the Red Cross. Rejecting the proposal, Churchill claimed that the influence and usefulness of the British Red Cross Society were largely due to its independence of government control and to its relationship with the International Red Cross in Geneva.[34] In actual practice, however, the BRCS was highly dependent on the government, particularly on the War Office, for obtaining supplies, for transporting and shipping the parcels, and even for advice on the desired composition of parcels.[35] That Churchill preferred to play down this interrelationship was partly because he realized this could serve to help deflect public criticism of the government.

Not all relatives of POWs, however, readily accepted Whitehall's explanations. Conspicuous among the protesters was a Mrs. Coombe-Tennant, whose son, Captain A. H. S. Coombe-Tennant, was being held in Oflag VI B (Warburg-Dossel). She constantly wrote critical letters to the War Office, to MPs, and even to Mrs. Churchill, to the extent that War Office officials internally began speaking of her as "a regular nuisance."[36] Accusing the government of leaving the POWs "to rot in starvation and rags," she argued that the government knew how the Germans treated Czech and Polish prisoners and that therefore "our men had little to expect from the enemy." Her main criticism was that the government had handed over to the Red Cross the responsibility for supplying food and clothing to the POWs without first ascertaining whether this body was indeed competent and able "to carry out an admittedly big undertaking."[37]

Recognizing the need to calm public anxiety over the welfare of the British POWs, Foreign Secretary Anthony Eden stated in the House of Commons on 26 November 1940 that the government aimed at ensuring that every prisoner would receive, along with standard parcels of clothing, one parcel of food each week through the British Red Cross. The latter would send once every three months personal parcels prepared by relatives of prisoners. All together, the BRCS had already sent more than 340,000 parcels; of these 86,000 had been individually acknowledged by prisoners. Many more, Eden estimated, by now would have reached their destination. In addition, 149 tons of food bought in Switzerland since 1 August had already arrived at five specified camps. It was known, Eden acknowledged, that the scale of rations the Germans furnished the POWs with was below that enjoyed by German depot troops (the reserve army guarding POWs) at certain camps, and strongest representations had been made through the proper channels.[38]

Not everybody was impressed by the praise Eden had for the British Red Cross. Mrs. Coombe-Tennant, quoting complaints by POWs in Oflag VII C/H, called on the House of Commons to press for an official inquiry into the way the Red Cross was functioning. She quoted a long "letter to the editor" in the *Sunday Express* of 24 November 1940 that carried the headline "Scandal of Our Men in Germany." The writer had praised the paper for being the first to call attention to the plight of British POWs in Germany and urged the editor "to continue the good work and keep on hammering the subject till real and lasting benefit results."[39] Two weeks later, the *Sunday Express* published an article headlined "The First Full Story of the Scandal of Our 44,000 Prisoners." The paper claimed that no adequate arrangements had been made in Britain to pack and dispatch parcels of food and clothing for the POWs and that the government had left everything to the Red Cross. Never once, the paper maintained, had the weekly total of food parcels sent amounted to even 37,000. Quoting a statement on 7 November by Lord Clarendon, director of the Prisoners of War Department of the Red Cross, that letters from prisoners showed that parcels from Britain were then being safely received in the camps, the story contended that even if each parcel had arrived safely, "nearly 20,000 prisoners must have gone short, because only 23,888 food parcels . . . [had been] dispatched that week."[40]

On 24 December 1940 the *Times* published a statement by Brigadier Nicholson—the BSO at Oflag VII—that except for three containing medical foods, no parcels had been received directly from the Red Cross in Britain since the beginning of August. There were still many prisoners in Oflag VII C/H who had received no parcels at all in six months of captivity.[41] As we saw earlier, Nicholson had no complaints about the treatment POWs were receiving from their German captors. Foreign Office officials rejected Nicholson's criticism, arguing that he was unaware of the fact that everything sent by the ICRC had either been shipped from England to them for distribution or been paid for by the British Red Cross.[42]

Captain H. David R. Margesson, who had become secretary of state for war in December 1940, explained in Parliament that parcels sent to British

POWS in Germany via Lisbon were now being seriously delayed in transit across the Iberian Peninsula and France. Ships had now been chartered to transport parcels directly to Marseilles or other convenient ports, from which they would then be forwarded to Switzerland and delivered to the prison camps in Germany under the direct supervision of the Red Cross. He added that during the four weeks between 19 December 1940 and 17 January 1941 the General Post Office had dispatched 228,658 parcels to Lisbon and that 99,592 parcels, in addition to 105 tons of food, had left Geneva for the camps in Germany during December.[43]

A number of MPS remained unconvinced. Knox pointed to the fact that these parcels had been accumulating between Lisbon and Geneva for four months and that no representative of the Red Cross had gone to Lisbon in this connection until December 1940. Member of Parliament Sir Annesley Somerville joined Knox in his criticism, and both referred to letters they had received from prisoners, including officers in Oflag VII C/H, complaining that they had received no parcels from the Red Cross. Angrily dismissing the contention that no Red Cross parcels had arrived, Margesson called this claim "misleading and calculated to cause needless anxiety to the families and friends of prisoners of war."[44]

Conditions in Oflag VII C/H, which held some 1,400 officers and orderlies, were now no worse than in any of the other camps, and there was evidence that a considerable number of parcels had arrived there. Heating, lighting, and sanitary conditions proved reasonably satisfactory, and improvements had recently been made in bedding, washing, clothing, and welfare.[45] These improvements had come on the heels of Foreign Secretary Eden's request to the Americans to bring home to the Germans the deficiencies the British knew about in Oflag VII C/H.[46]

Countering London's complaints that prisoners were not given enough food, the German Foreign Ministry reiterated that since the beginning of the war POWs in Germany had "received the same quantities of food as the German depot troops on the scale due German officers and married noncommissioned officers." These food rations corresponded to those of the German civil population and had remained the same ever since the war had broken out. Prisoners ordered to work received rations in accordance with the kind of labor they did. In addition, besides their rations, prisoners were now able to buy different kinds of seasonal foods, and menus were supervised daily by the camp physicians "in respect to the combination of the meals answering this purpose and the required number of calories." Given the reports from protecting power and Red Cross visitors and letters from the prisoners themselves expressing their appreciation, there was no reason to change the current regulations concerning food for POWs, all the more as they corresponded with Article XI of the Geneva Convention.[47] Similar arguments were given following British complaints about the clothing issued, or rather not issued, to British officer POWs.[48]

London was not convinced, and in a note to the U.S. chargé d'affaires in London, Herschell Johnson, Churchill—who signed the note—maintained that a comparison of the monthly rations supplied to British POWs with those of German civilians clearly showed that the former received appreciably less of a number of important items. In the case of meat, for example, the difference was as much as 25 percent. The rations supplied to German depot troops were similarly superior to those received by British POWs. As to Berlin's suggestion that POWs purchase unrationed food, reports from Oflag VII C/H stated that officers in this camp had been unable to purchase anything extra, as there were few supplies, if any at all, in the camp canteens. Reports from other camps indicated that although the canteens in some camps were somewhat better stocked than those in Oflag VII C/H, most of this consisted of potato starch. Johnson was asked to obtain from the German government a table showing the following: (1) rations issued to German depot troops when served from troop kitchens; (2) rations issued to German civilians in three cases: normal consumers, heavy workers, and very heavy workers; and (3) rations issued to British POWs when not working and when engaged in very heavy work. Churchill also asked for an assurance that British POWs would in the future be given rations on the same scale as those issued to German depot troops when fed from troop kitchens, with requisite additions in the case of those POWs engaged in heavy work.[49]

At the same time, in an effort to encourage the Germans to respond favorably to Britain's requests, Churchill added that he was interested in facilitating the shipment of parcels to German POWs in the United Kingdom. The Germans had claimed that only small parcels weighing no more than half a pound sent by letter post had been able to reach German POWs in Britain. This Churchill denied, and he then suggested that German authorities send parcels from Marseilles to Lisbon in one of the vessels the British Red Cross had specially chartered. The arrival of these vessels at Marseilles, he pointed out, was inevitably irregular, but details could be obtained through the ICRC. Still, Churchill maintained, the only really satisfactory way of ensuring a routine flow of parcels to both British and German POWs was to establish a regular steamship service between two agreed ports.

These did not need to be Channel ports, although this would offer the most practical solution.[50] What is perhaps most remarkable in this exchange is the fact that each side tried to convince the other that it was adhering—even pedantically so, as the argument over rations shows—to the stipulations of the Geneva Convention. As in World War I, both powers seemed to appreciate that the advantages reciprocity offered outweighed the disadvantages.[51] And even when, as we shall see later, both governments did resort to retaliation as a lever, they applied it only moderately.

Meanwhile, Whitehall failed to put an end to criticism at home of the way the Red Cross was functioning. Parliament learned that the ICRC had only four inspectors, who visited the sixteen camps one every three months. Knox reminded the secretary of state for war that only one in every twenty parcels dispatched by the Red Cross from the United Kingdom ever crossed the German border. Margesson countered by responding that he was "satisfied that the British Red Cross Society is doing everything possible to further the end which we all have in view. The society has had a very difficult task to perform and has from time to time come in for criticism, in my view often unmerited." However, he was further pressed by MP Garro Jones, who asked whether Margesson intended to take "steps to ensure that the staff of the Red Cross from top to bottom is re-organised to include people who have knowledge of business affairs rather than amateurs." As Margesson was so satisfied with the job the Red Cross was doing, Knox now ironically asked him if he was pleased, too, with the work that the government had done.[52] Member of Parliament Henry Morris-Jones questioned whether the BRCS was discriminating against POWs in Oflag VII on the grounds that some of them had been able to obtain occasional supplies from other sources. He also wanted to know whether it was true, as recent reports from the camp indicated, that under the present conditions the prisoners were showing signs of malnutrition. Margesson denied such reports, stating that the 1,320 officers currently in this camp had received more than 5,500 parcels from the ICRC in the last two weeks of December 1940.[53]

The ICRC had been established back in 1863 in Geneva as a nongovernmental humanitarian organization and operated successfully during World War I. However, when World War II started, not only was the organization still very small, but it also consisted mainly of volunteers.[54] With the dramatic extension of its tasks and responsibilities, the ICRC succeeded in gradually increasing the number of people it employed, first in its home base,

Switzerland, but then also in the organization's delegations in the warring countries. Yet the process of adjustment proved too slow for the ICRC to respond adequately to the growing needs of the POWs, the expectations of their kin, and the criticism of MPs.[55]

By early 1941, the parcels issue had turned into politically the most sensitive aspect of the POW situation, and thus it comes as no surprise that we find Whitehall periodically making efforts to convince MPs that the government was doing its utmost to stay abreast of the situation. For example, in March 1941, Richard Law reported to the House of Commons that receipts had been obtained for 78,345 food parcels and 3,172 clothing parcels that had reached POW camps in Germany. He insisted that Oflag VII C/H had received 8,341 and 1,129 of the respective parcels and another six and a half tons of bulk provisions. Law did admit, however, that up to 26 December 1940, British POWs in Stalag IX B (Hessen-Nassau), where there were two hospitals, had failed to receive any parcels at all except for half a pound of chocolate per man from the Red Cross. Law further noted that German POWs in the United Kingdom were receiving rations on the same scale as those given to British troops, with certain variations introduced at the prisoners' request to suit their national taste, but that the German government was not fulfilling its responsibility. Pressure was being put on Berlin to do so, however.[56]

Although in public critical of the Germans, British officials were not actually dissatisfied with the situation in the POW camps. A comprehensive report— based on a huge number of separate accounts, extracts from letters, and general information sources—that was presented to Churchill in early 1941 significantly concluded that British POWs were "well and humanely treated." Relationships between POWs and the German camp staffs seemed to be correct. Accommodations, though crowded at one time, were improving daily. Criticism focused on food as either inadequate or not up to the standard of depot troops as laid down in the Geneva Convention. Even if it were up to this standard, it was argued, it would take the POWs a long time before they felt satisfied with it. The Germans, who had been tightening their belt for years, had been living on a diet that, though it enabled them to do moderately heavy work, was basically unpalatable. British POWs, especially officers accustomed to a higher standard of living, naturally thought the food most inadequate. At the same time, the Germans had no excuse not to supply outerwear, especially as they had captured sufficient supplies in

France to clothe all British POWs. On the other hand, they could perhaps not be blamed for the shortage of boots and shoes, as there was a dearth of leather and leather substitutes throughout Europe.[57]

As to criticism at home, the report responded that "everything that can be done is being done, and as quickly as is humanly possible." The attacks on the Red Cross and the government in this regard were unjustified. If it were not for communication difficulties, the BRCS and ICRC scheme "would work as well as possible for an operation of the magnitude involved."[58] Whitehall officials tended to rely more on ICRC reports than on accounts of individual POWs, as the former were considered more balanced. That they strongly defended the ICRC may well have been because they feared that ongoing domestic public criticism of the organization would prove detrimental to its prestige in German eyes and, therefore, hamper its ability to operate. Acceding to criticism of the ICRC might, of course, be construed as an admission of failure on the part of the government for having delivered to the BRCS the responsibility for the overall care of the POWs.[59]

Nevertheless, the issue of food and parcels continued to attract the public's interest. In the summer of 1941, British requests via the protecting power for information regarding current food rations British POWs were given met with evasive responses from Berlin. In early August, Margesson was able to tell Parliament that rations for British POWs had been changed on 3 June 1941, as had those for German civilians. (This change was directly related to the invasion of the Soviet Union the Nazis were preparing for later that month.) The figures obtained indicated a reduction of the meat ration by one-fifth, a slight increase in the fat ration, small decreases in cereals and sugar, and an addition of skimmed milk to the diet. Quoting the Prisoners of War Convention, which said that food rations for POWs should equal those of depot troops, Margesson admitted that he had no information on how much and what kind of food was being issued to depot troops in Germany.[60]

From informal conversations with German military authorities American diplomats in Germany learned that the German government did not intend to feed Allied POWs better than it did its own citizens for political reasons, as the use of food had become a "weapon" in this war now that the Allies were trying to enforce a blockade around Germany. (Similar considerations had played a role during World War I.)[61] It could also be—although there was no true evidence for this—that official POW rations had been reduced on account of the food parcels POWs were receiving from abroad, especially since these food parcels often contained many articles that were unavailable to Germans themselves.

The Americans also pointed out that the basic food rations applied only to a minority of POWs, those detained in basic camps (Stalags and Oflags) and those receiving the basic diet in hospitals. The majority of nonofficer prisoners had been sent out to work camps, where they were given supplementary rations on a scale similar to that of the quantities of food given German civilians engaged in "long or night work" and "heavy work." Even though the Germans were not forthcoming with the information the Americans asked them for, the embassy thought that on the whole it seemed Berlin was following Article 11: "There is little if any evidence of an impairment of the health of British prisoners due to insufficient or otherwise unsatisfactory food," though the report immediately added: "[T]his is undoubtedly partly the result [also] of the supplementary food received in the parcels from abroad."[62]

HEALTH CONDITIONS

Food naturally played a major role in the lives of the POWs, largely of course for reasons of physical health. But there was a psychological aspect as well: punctuating their daily routine, meals gave POWs something to look forward to. The same can be said of the food parcels. In October 1941, Dr. Vance B. Murray, senior surgeon of the U.S. Public Health Service serving at the American embassy in Berlin, who had been inspecting POW camps in Germany for more than a year, presented the British with an overall picture of health conditions among the British POWs. He had based his report on the more than 100 visits he had been able to make to main and work camps where British, French, and Belgian POWs were confined. Although these represented only a fraction of all such camps, they were located throughout the Reich, including occupied Poland but with the exception of southern Germany and sections of Austria. Dr. Murray added that the German staff had been cooperative at all times and willing to give him access to all prisoners or all parts of the camp.[63]

Dr. Murray was generally satisfied with the functioning and behavior of the camps' administration. He told of a German instruction center for administrative officers that had been created at the model Stalag II D (Stargard), where they learned about improving the care of POWs. The officers had been selected according to particular qualifications; those who did not prove suitable for the positions they occupied had been gradually removed. Many chosen for this work had been POW themselves in World War I. Although this meant that some were embittered because of their past experience, the majority showed a sympathetic understanding of the lot of a

POW. The result had been a steady improvement in the organization of the camps and, consequently, better adjustment by the prisoners to their state of captivity.

As they arrived from the west, prisoners would be tired and dirty, their shoes worn out, and they would have trouble adapting to living not just with one another but as captives. Accommodations were overcrowded, and some of the collection camps proved highly insufficient. The principal illness was diarrhea, caused by utensils that were cleaned only with cold water, the presence of flies, inadequate and primitive latrines, and the—for the prisoners—often strange food they were given at the collection camps and temporary stops en route. Most of the cases of illness were nonmalignant, but many prisoners suffered bacillary dysentery. Dr. Murray believed that the mortality rate was quite low.[64] He may have been aware that during World War I epidemics in the camps had caused the deaths of thousands of prisoners of several nationalities, although the numbers of British among them had been relatively small.[65]

During the winter of 1940–41, the main diseases among POWs were respiratory illnesses, angina, and nephritis, all related to exposure and overcrowding. Delousing had to be performed constantly, especially when it was too cold to take a shower without hot water. Some facilities allowed only one warm shower a week. Furthermore, straw (or excelsior) mattresses harbored lice and had to be decontaminated as often as possible. After respiratory diseases, the most frequently occurring illness was open tuberculosis. Tuberculosis cases were sent to special Reserve Lazarette. For pneumonia cases, sulfanilamide compounds seemed to have been in sufficient supply at this stage. Nevertheless, paralysis occurred in many cases, and a number of carriers were discovered. Nephritis was either endemic or detected in patients having scanty urine containing albumin and blood and showing a rapid pulse and high blood pressure. In most of these cases, the prisoner promptly recovered after a period of rest in a warm bed and being given better food (milk, butter, eggs, and lemon). Because it was too uncomfortable to wash one's feet every night in cold water, many prisoners experienced itchy legs, which often led to infected scratch wounds and slow-healing ulcers. Wounded prisoners and others with chronic diseases received reasonably good treatment in special institutions. German physicians who were indifferent, Dr. Murray maintained, formed only a small minority, "about as might be expected in any other country with so many enemy prisoners." In general, the health situation among British POWs in the summer 1941 was "very satisfactory."[66]

The units established at each Stalag to provide prisoners with medical care were the base camp infirmary, for those who were only moderately ill, and the Reserve Lazarett, for serious cases or those who needed surgery. The infirmary (*Reviver*) had a small examining room and a minor surgical room and two wards, one with individual bunks for acute cases and another with two-tier bunks for convalescents. There were one or two prisoner physicians of the prisoners' nationality and a dentist, besides the supervising German *Stabsarzt* (medical captain). The Reserve Lazarett was located at some distance from the base camp, usually in the nearest small city. It might be in a civilian hospital, a converted school, or a country road house (*Schuetzenhaus*). The converted buildings had the surgical, X-ray, laboratory, and other equipment that could be found in all German war hospitals. Civilian hospitals, German-staffed and with female nurses, usually assigned a ward to POWs and set aside certain hours for them to enjoy the grounds when not used by civilians. The converted buildings had a German supervising staff; however, the active work was carried out by sanitary corpsmen of the same nationality as the prisoners. All hospital cots had mattresses, pillows, sheets, and pillow cases. Special hospitals were set aside for cases of TB, one hospital offered psychiatric treatment, and there was a special location where blind POWs could learn Braille.

As base camp planning improved, Dr. Murray found, the Reserve Lazarette were abandoned, and permanent pavilion-style Lazarette with 400 beds were being built about a kilometer away from the base camp. Again, the supervising staff was German, but physicians, surgeons, and dentists of various prisoner nationalities did the active work. Large work units had infirmaries identical to those of the base camps. Smaller work camps had first-aid kits managed by a sanitary corpsman. Prisoner physicians, and in some cases German supervisory medical officers, made weekly visits to medium-sized camps. Emergency POW cases were treated as civilians were. POWs requiring special study or treatment not locally available were sent to university hospitals.[67]

As for food, Dr. Murray found that the German High Command had given the subject careful consideration. The basic Stalag diet was intended for men who did little or no work. Its caloric value was around 2,400 a day.[68] Those in work camps who performed arduous labor were given more food, similar to German laborers doing heavy work. Prisoners who worked on farms fared better because food was more plentiful there. In hospitals, special diets were prescribed in appropriate cases (TB, diabetes, and postoperative). Dr. Murray pointed out that many thousands of prisoners had been kept well and strong for two years on this basic diet alone. He cited the results of the weighing of 400 British prisoners who worked in a mustard factory in Stalag XXI D (Posen). In February 1941, 61 percent of the captives showed some weight gain, 11 percent had neither gained nor lost weight, 23 percent had lost up to two kilos, and only 5 percent had lost two kilos or more. Some in this last group were ill in the infirmary. The basic diet may have been scientifically satisfactory, but it was monotonous. Some prisoners complained that the Stalag fare did not still their hunger and that they were glad to receive food packages.

Food and health conditions were best in the farm work units and next best in the base camps; they were likely to be poorest in industrial enterprises (e.g., factories). Captives worked the same number of hours as German laborers, which was excessive by most American standards, and food varied in quantity as it did with the German classes of "hard, harder, and hardest" workers. Summarizing his extensive report, Dr. Murray wrote: "Notwithstanding suffering caused by temporary overcrowding, exposures and isolated instances of injustice or assault, it is my belief that the treatment of prisoners of war in Germany has been as near in accord with provisions of the Geneva Convention as was humanly possible, particularly as regards safeguarding their health."[69]

Dr. Murray's report has been quoted here at some length because its many details confirmed Whitehall's stand that, in general, British POWs were treated fairly and that there was no immediate threat to their lives. It was above all the comprehensiveness of his survey and the systematic approach he had followed that convinced officials in London to adopt Dr. Murray's findings as a reliable source of information on the state of the prisoners. Reassuring, too, must have been Dr. Murray's conclusion that Berlin was indeed adhering to the 1929 Geneva Convention.[70]

INSIDE LARGE CAMPS

When Dr. Murray presented his report, the Germans held approximately 64,000 British Commonwealth POWs dispersed over forty-four camps. The largest number of British POWs, 14,814, was held in Stalag VIII B (Lamsdorf). Stalags XX A (Thorn Podgorz) and XX B (Marienburg) held more than 8,000 men each; Stalag XVIII A (Wolfsberg, Austria), 5,330 prisoners.[71] More than 3,000 POWs each were interned in Stalags IX C (Bad Sulza) and XVIII D (Marburg).[72] There were several more camps that held between 1,000 and 3,000 British POWs each. The largest officer camp was Oflag IV F, where 1,099 officers were held captive; 2,969 more officers were divided among six other Oflags.[73]

In an effort to reduce the level of anxiety among POWs' kin, the Soldiers, Sailors and Air Force Families Association, founded in 1885 to provide a link between serving men and their families, began publishing a regular newsletter on the state of British captives.[74] Newsletter No. 2 (May 1941), for example, focused on conditions in Stalag VIII B (Lamsdorf). Aware of the heightened concern of POW relatives following the difficult winter, the newsletter's editor stated that generally speaking, despite the intense cold and heavy snowstorms, "the men got through the winter fairly well." Work, in fact, had been suspended during snowstorms and wet weather, the men remaining in their heated quarters. The latest batch of letters showed that all prisoners were hearing from home regularly and that personal parcels had reached them safely and Red Cross parcels were arriving in greater volume.

The editor quoted extracts of an official report on Stalag VIII B submitted by U.S. inspectors: "New barracks, well built. New large hospital, well equipped. New showers. New disinfecting installation. Food good and sufficient. Discipline good. Uniform reserves sufficient. Shirts, socks, pullovers, and footwear lacking. Well treated." Seven detachments were dependent on Stalag VIII B, of which four were miners' camps. Conditions in the latter were good. "Prisoners are calm, satisfied, not tired, well treated. Billeted in heated barracks, well-lighted. Simple beds, two blankets, daily hot water. Canteen sells beer, cucumbers, toilet accessories, satisfactory food. Clothing satisfactory. Correspondence unsatisfactory. All wanting English tobacco. Books lacking." Relatives of POWs, the editor suggested, should not feel too worried at the mention of mining camps: apart from one or two veiled hints, no direct reference to mining work had been made in any of the letters.[75] As we shall see, the newsletter appears to have played down the difficulties and suffering of POWs who were employed in the mines.

The newsletter added that most of the approximately 3,000 British POWs attached to Stalag VIII B were dispersed in parties working many miles from one another, and this helped explain why some prisoners were worse off than others when it came to receiving Red Cross food parcels. All parcels first arrived at the main camp, and it took time for them to be distributed. The same applied to books. Extracts of letters were included to back up the editor's report.[76] Several weeks later, in the House of Commons, Margesson quoted the latest reports indicating that conditions in Stalag VIII B "are not on the whole unsatisfactory, although there is room for improvement on certain points, including the postal improvements at the camp."[77] In October 1941, the American embassy in Berlin reported that about 16,000 British prisoners were being held in the main camp and independent labor camps. Conditions were generally satisfactory, except for a lack of blankets and heating.[78]

R. E. Evans, who fell into German captivity in May 1940, spent five years as a POW in Stalag VIII B. Shortly after his arrival, he was assigned to a working party and moved to an Arbeitskommando near Ehrenforst building a plant that was to extract petrol from coal. The camp consisted of five long barracklike buildings and a wash place and latrine, surrounded by a double-wire fence; three similar buildings outside this stockade were for the use of the German guards and their officers. The barracks were divided into rooms with two-tier wooden bunks, a round cast-iron stove, and a table and chairs. "That first summer [1940] was very hot," Evans writes in his memoirs, "and after a twelve hour working day, we were absolutely exhausted when we returned to camp. After a wash with ersatz soap, which seemed to be made from sand and a coagulating medium, and which we could purchase with our few pence, we were then issued with our food." Meals consisted "of about a pint of watery vegetable soup, usually mangold or sauerkraut (pickled cabbage), three potatoes boiled in their jackets, and a loaf of black bread between twelve men, and sometimes a minute piece of ersatz margarine." Evans describes how the loaf of bread would be ceremoniously cut up into twelve equal pieces. "All twelve men crowded round the one who was dividing the loaf, to make certain that they received their due, and as the loaf sloped away at each end, he had a thankless task. There was always someone who felt that the next piece to his was slightly larger, but to ensure that justice was done, a playing card was placed on each portion and we drew lots. This may sound extremely uncomradely, but terrible hunger strips off all the veneer of civilisation, and it becomes a case of each man for himself, and devil take the hindmost." Occasionally, when the guards had finished their soup, which was much tastier than that given the POWs, they would put the almost-empty containers inside the main gate, after which some of the prisoners would rush and fight for the vestiges of soup left in the bottom: "It was not a very edifying sight, and most of us managed to preserve a modicum of dignity in front of the grinning guards."[79]

After a few weeks in this working camp, with no change of clothing, no decent soap to wash with, and no chance of drying one's clothes if one already had decided to wash them, the prisoners faced another problem: "[W]e became lousy—I am sure it was the most revolting thing that happened to us during the whole of our captivity." Matters became so bad that the prisoners had to discard the straw pallets on which they slept and to sleep on the bare boards of their bunks. "It became a nightly ritual, after we had eaten, to take off our clothes and search them for lice, which were usually in all the seams. The method was to crack them between the thumb nails, or if you were lucky enough to have a Polish cigarette, to run the lighted end down the seems, thus disposing of the eggs as well. It was particularly sickening when you realised that the blood that spurted from the lice was your own."[80] This state of affairs continued for about nine months when the POWs finally received a change of clothing from the Red Cross.

No less disturbing was the lack of adequate shoes. When prisoners' army boots disintegrated, the Germans issued wooden clogs. "We had no socks. The idea was to place your foot on [a piece of] cloth, and gather up the four corners round your foot, and put on the clog. The clogs were terribly uncomfortable and chafed the feet badly."[81] The real turning point in the lives of the POWs, Evans felt, was when they received their first Red Cross food parcels. "From then on, with the occasional gap, we received these parcels, from the British Red Cross society, until shortly before the end of the war, and I have no doubt that they were largely responsible for the fact that the vast majority of British and Commonwealth prisoners of war came through the war safe, and in reasonably good health."[82] Parcels began arriving regularly only in the second half of 1942.

In 1942, Stalag VIII B and the work camps dependent on it continued to house the largest number of British POWs. Now, however, Swiss government officials replaced the Americans in protecting the interests of both British and German prisoners. This followed the Japanese attack on Pearl Harbor on 7 December 1941 and Germany's declaration of war on the United States. Of the 18,997 British POWs in the Stalag in May 1942, a total of 5,678 were interned in the base camp, and 13,319 were dispersed among 272 work camps. Red Cross representatives who visited the base camp in early 1942 reported several shortcomings. Showers functioned irregularly—some prisoners had not had a shower in three months; paillasses (straw mattresses) had never been changed; and lice were still to be found. Medical supplies were inadequate, their use and distribution restricted by the German dispenser even when medical parcels arrived from the BRCS. In addition, because there were too many doctors in the main camp, many of them remained unemployed, as did medical orderlies; some of the work camps, in contrast, had no doctor at all.[83]

Reports on conditions in the work camps of Stalag VIII B were more disturbing. Many of these camps had received no food or other parcels for several weeks. The men of confidence had no control over the distribution of Red Cross clothing; uniforms and underclothes were given out by the various civilian German companies that controlled the work camps, and these companies frequently interpreted the official regulations in their own favor. In some work camps there was a rule that new clothes could be issued only in exchange for old ones, which meant, for example, that soldiers who had arrived from Crete without gloves or pullovers remained without them in the much colder climate they were in now. In various work camps, the POWs had to pay for clothes supplied by the Red Cross.[84]

Swiss inspectors thought that distribution was either wholly inefficient or even deliberately thrown into disarray in order to conceal the fact that supplies had been misappropriated. British Red Cross clothing parcels, for instance, had been issued to non-British POWs—as in the case of 4,000 sets of underwear that had gone to Croatian prisoners. As with clothes, payment was often exacted for boots and cigarettes sent by the BRCS. There was frequent theft of tobacco and food parcels, items that were immediately suspended as a collective punishment for small offenses by individual POWs. Blankets prisoners owned were described as worn out, small, filthy, and lousy. Worse, however, was that medical supplies had been withdrawn, and no skilled medical treatment was available in most localities.[85]

In mid-May, Swiss inspectors Gabriel Naville, who was also the head of the British Interests Division in Berlin, and Dr. Folke Malmquist paid a short visit to the Stalag VIII B base camp. Bathing facilities improved thereafter, as each man was given a chance to shower with hot water at least once every ten days. There were no complaints about the quality of the food, but there was hardly ever enough because Red Cross parcels were not arriving in sufficient numbers in the first few months of 1942; the average daily calories at this time amounted to only 1,666. (In this context it was calculated that a male person with little exercise and nine hours of sleep needed 2,150 calories.)[86] The MOC stated that he needed a stock of about 60,000 parcels to be able to supply each work camp regularly. At the time of the visit, there was no stock at all. Clothing improved but was still insufficient. A great need remained for battle dresses, shirts, greatcoats, and boots. The prisoners' main request was for more cigarettes, as they received no more than twenty-five per week each from the Red Cross and virtually none from the German camp authorities.[87] The Swiss inspectors visited eighteen of the Stalag's work camps, their assessments ranging from "not bad" to "very good."[88]

Complaints on the absence of parcels led James Grigg, who had become secretary of state for war in February 1942, to explain in Parliament in April the difficulties involved in getting Red Cross parcels to their destination:

> The dispatch of food parcels to British prisoners in Germany and Italy involves many difficult and complicated processes. After being packed by the British Red Cross Society, the parcels are handed over to General Post Office, who are responsible, in conjunction with the Ministry of War Transport, for their shipment to Lisbon. Between the United Kingdom and Portugal the ships carrying parcels are subject to all the normal war risks of Allied shipping on the high seas. From Lisbon they are conveyed to Marseilles in ships chartered by the British Red Cross Society, under the control of the International Red Cross Committee, with a safe conduct from the enemy Governments. The International Red Cross Committee arrange for transport onwards from Marseilles to Geneva by means of the French and Swiss railway and postal services. On reaching Geneva the parcels are stored by the International Red Cross Committee, who have also undertaken the task of dispatching them on to the various prison camps in the quantities needed. During the last part of the journey we are, of course, entirely dependent upon the transport facilities provided by the German and Italian authorities.[89]

Grigg emphasized that interruptions in the dispatch of food parcels were in many cases beyond the control of both the BRCS and the British government. He also expressed concern that at some point in the future the existing parcel route "may well become impracticable and the opening up of an alternative route is not likely to be easy," partially because the British were "doing [their] best to bomb communications in Germany."[90] In August, Grigg was able to tell MPs that there had been a satisfactory increase in the number of parcels sent on from Geneva, and he praised the Red Cross "for doing everything possible to cope with this work."[91]

Grigg's satisfaction certainly was in place. The significant improvement in the dispatching of parcels in the second half of 1942 was directly related to the increased involvement of the War Office after it became clear that the BRCS was not up to the task.[92] In September, Red Cross inspectors Dr. Otto Lehner and M. Friedrich, after still another visit to Stalag VIII B, thought that "this Stalag cannot be considered as bad on account of the collective parcels sent." Its main defect now was overcrowding, which made it difficult to maintain order and discipline.[93] Two months later, a representative of the Swiss legation in Berlin reported there was now a stock of about two months' worth of parcels. For their part, camp authorities had made a small cut in rations of German food, claiming that POWs were receiving so many parcels that they were wasting German food.[94] The constant flow of parcels certainly eased this major worry of relatives of prisoners and interested MPs and temporarily relieved the government of criticism. Still, there were other reasons for concern, no less disturbing.

In May 1942, Stalag XX B (Marienburg) in East Prussia held the second-largest group of British Commonwealth POWs, 9,555, all of them English except for 10 Canadians and 5 Australians. Only 742 prisoners were staying in the base camp itself, 90 in Lazarette, while 8,178 were spread among some 450 work camps. Delegates of the Red Cross who visited the camp early in 1942 had judged this Stalag "to be a bad Camp." Quarters and installations were inadequate, the infirmary was rudimentary, detention cells did not comply at all with international regulations, distribution of clothing was poorly organized, and treatment of prisoners in general was bad. When Dr. Jean-Maurice Rubli, one of the Swiss inspectors, visited the camp on 1 May 1942, he was able to report some progress. The men were better treated, and the order for guards to shoot without warning if a prisoner approached the barbed enclosure had been rescinded (since the summer of 1941, eight British prisoners had been killed in this way, and four had been wounded). Detention cells had been improved, and both the supply of clothing and the distribution of food from the collective consignments were better organized. Still, Dr. Rubli thought that there was room for many more improvements.

The barracks were in a very bad state. The beds were in three tiers and pushed up against one another along one of the walls; the beds in the bottom tier were so close to the ground that those who had to use them complained badly of the cold, since there was often no heating fuel. Most of the rooms looked dirty and messy, as the prisoners had practically nowhere to put their personal effects. There was no space for all of them to sit around the tables at the same time. Lighting was inadequate, during the day as well as at night, so at any given time only a small number of prisoners could do some reading or writing. That there was no recreation room made things worse. The infirmary was dirty, overcrowded, and in disarray. There were no paillasses, and the prisoners slept on bare boards without sheets and obviously with not enough ventilation.

There was only one washroom; it contained two sinks over which passed a pipe with holes enabling 100–150 prisoners to wash themselves simultaneously. In order to save water, however, camp authorities allowed this washroom to be open only for several hours a day. There were no special shower facilities for the 200 prisoners who worked at the camp—theoretically they could use the shower room for German soldiers, but actually the majority of the prisoners had not had a hot shower for several months. Vermin were abundant and tenacious. The latrines—no more than a hut of old boards constructed over a cement trench through which a current of water passed at regular intervals—were extremely dirty, giving off a stench that could be picked up a long distance away. There was no toilet paper.

All prisoners thought, and with justification according to Dr. Rubli, that the food rations they were given were extremely meager. Unlike the German population, they were not allowed to buy provisions that were not rationed, such as fish and vegetables. The prisoners claimed that they would have died of hunger without the consignments from the Red Cross. All prisoners in the main camp and in the work camps had an overcoat, a uniform, and a second tunic. A chief worry of the camp leaders was the boots—an order of the Stalag forbade issuing leather boots to prisoners during the summer; however, many of the prisoners had to work on slag stones for railways or in the field, where wooden clogs or shoes with wooden soles were a torture.

Approximately 70 percent of the British prisoners at Stalag XX B worked in agriculture; the remaining captives toiled in sugar factories, breweries, and machine factories. As was the case throughout Germany, in agriculture the workday was extremely long, from eleven to seventeen hours, depending on the season; Sunday was no exception. Far too often, Dr. Rubli pointed out, the prisoners were sent out to work while the local farmers were resting, especially on Sundays. Timetables were better regulated in industrial plants, but there were still a great many complaints here, too. In Arbeitskommando (Work Camp) 275, for example, the men had to put in ten hours of heavy labor every day, plus two hours of marching. In general, the Swiss inspector summed up, work conditions had improved to some extent in the industrial plants but not in agriculture. The prisoners received fifty pfennings per day for work in the main camp, while the basic salary in the work camps was seventy pfennings a day. Overtime—over eight hours a day—was counted and paid at a rate of thirty-three pfennings an hour. In the winter, the prisoners received only fifty-four pfennings a day for agricultural work, the excuse being that the work was not as hard during that season.[95]

As soon as this report had reached London, the British legation in Bern was instructed to urge Berlin (through the Swiss) to make sure British prisoners throughout Stalag XX B were properly and humanely treated and that all defects be remedied. It was especially intolerable, the Foreign Office stated, that British prisoners were not only roughed up by guards and punished by junior officers without permission from higher authority but also ill-treated and threatened by civilians with and for whom they worked. "This is not only in flagrant violation of convention," the Foreign Office wrote to Clifford Norton, the British minister in Bern, "but so entirely contrary to accepted military practice and tradition that it is hard to believe German High Command know what is happening." As the Foreign Office saw it, one single camp commandant, however capable and conscientious, could not hope to supervise the 23,000 prisoners (British and other Allies) distributed among more than 400 work units.[96]

When a Swiss inspector revisited Stalag XX B in August 1942, he reported that the main camp was still rat infested. The prisoners continued to work on Sundays in some of the agricultural work camps because harvesting was in full swing, and civilians were still beating prisoners. To prevent POWs from escaping, they were locked in their barracks at night and their trousers and shoes removed. The Swiss inspector also reported on several labor units individually. Prisoners in Arbeitskommando 283 worked from 6 A.M. to 8 or 9 P.M. on small farms and from 7 A.M. to 8 P.M. on larger ones. They received no extra free time as compensation for work on Sundays. In Arbeitskommando 81, the accommodation was unsatisfactory: leaking roof, smoking chimney, and insufficient toilets. Heavy workers' rations were not given regularly. When bad weather prevented work in the fields, prisoners had to work at night to make up for the "free" time. Prisoners in Arbeitskommando 54 had to work longer hours than did civilian agricultural workers. Guards sometimes struck prisoners and often threatened to shoot them. The good news was that the camp had a new commander who was doing his best, which resulted in improved conditions and higher prisoner morale.[97]

Although not always satisfied with conditions in the camps and the way British POWs were treated, Whitehall recognized that their overall situation appeared bearable. As the PWD itself put it in the summer of 1942, "[O]nce the prisoners are established in permanent camps their treatment has not given ground for serious criticism."[98] Whenever the British protested and demanded improvements through the protecting power and the Red Cross, the result generally was some amelioration. In the first nine months of 1941, for example, the Americans had presented the German government with forty-four protests on behalf of the British and had received twenty replies.[99] That Whitehall's main concern was largely with material issues—number of parcels dispatched and received, shortage of food and clothing, mail, over-crowding, and work conditions—also highlights that London was aware that prisoners were generally not subject to any physical threat. On the whole this assessment was shared by the MPs and POWs' relatives who were putting pressure on the government. Apprehension was further mitigated by the knowledge—repeatedly confirmed—that the Germans continued to abide by the Geneva Convention. Thus until mid-August 1942, with approximately 77,000 British POWs interned in German POW camps, the subject hardly ever reached the level of War Cabinet discussions.[100] This, however, was soon to change abruptly.

Years of Long Captivity

THE SHACKLING EPISODE

On 19 August 1942, a joint British-Canadian commando launched a major raid on the French port of Dieppe. Five thousand Canadians and 1,000 British troops took part in the operation, which ended disastrously with more than 1,000 of the Allied soldiers killed and about 2,000 taken prisoner, most of them Canadians. The Germans lost no more than 345 men; 4 Germans were taken prisoner and brought to Britain.[1] Two weeks later, on 2 September, the OKW ordered all British Commonwealth soldiers who had been taken prisoner at Dieppe to be shackled as of 2 P.M. the following day. This measure would be canceled only when the British government withdrew an operational order that the Germans had found on the British troops: "Wherever it is possible, the prisoners have their hands bound so that they cannot destroy their papers."[2]

Reacting quickly, the British War Office announced on the very same day that investigations were "being made as to whether in fact any such order was issued. It is categorically denied that any German had his hands tied. Any such order if it was issued, will be cancelled." The British War Cabinet recognized that although the Geneva Convention said nothing about shackling, tying the hands of prisoners, if only to prevent them from destroying documents, could be construed as running against the convention.[3] Declaring itself satisfied with the British assurance, the OKW had the reprisal measures lifted the following day, that is, even before they had been carried out.[4]

Matters might have rested here had it not been for a second incident one month later. On the night of 3 October a small British commando force raided the Channel island of Sark (Operation Basalt). After landing on the island, the commandos succeeded in making their way to the annex of a hotel building, from which they abducted five German engineers who were sleeping there. The prisoners' hands were tied so that their captors could link arms with them while moving past some barracks where German troops were quartered. At this point the five Germans tried to escape, and four of them were shot in the attempt; when the Germans later discovered the bodies, the prisoners' hands were tied behind their back.[5]

Again, the German response was unambiguous. Berlin informed London that as of twelve o'clock noon on 8 October, all British officers and soldiers captured at Dieppe were to be laid in irons until the British War Office ensured that German prisoners of war would not be fettered.[6] Taking these German threats seriously, the War Cabinet quickly issued a public statement explaining that the British force at Sark had been forced to kill the four Germans so as to prevent detection. The War Office reiterated that none of the German POWs brought back to Britain after the Dieppe raid had ever claimed that their hands had been tied, and the office suggested that representatives of the protecting power, that is, Switzerland, be invited to confirm this with the prisoners.[7]

In discussing the appropriate reaction to the German reprisal measures, the War Cabinet recognized the weight of the fact that the Germans were holding more British prisoners than vice versa. The total number of German POWs interned in the British Commonwealth at that time (excluding merchant seamen) amounted to 26,682. Of these, 16,540 were held in Canada, 7,843 in the Middle East, 1,398 in Australia, and 569 in the United Kingdom, and 332 were in transit to the United States.[8] At the same time, if Italian prisoners were taken into account, then the number of Axis POWs held by Britain was substantially higher than the number of British POWs held by both Germany and Italy. The War Cabinet thought that Berlin could ill afford to ignore the possibility of retaliation against Italian prisoners and therefore decided to adopt a firm stand. (As it turned out, the Italians refused to join the Germans in the shackling issue.)[9] Repeating that it did not and would not countenance any orders to tie up POWs taken in the field, the War Cabinet denounced the reprisals the Germans threatened as acts expressly forbidden by Article 2 of the Geneva Convention. Should the German government persist, the cabinet warned, the British government would see itself "compelled, in order to protect [its] own Prisoners of War, to take similar measures upon an equal number of enemy Prisoners of War in [its] hands."[10]

It appears that when, following Churchill's lead, the cabinet members first made their decision, they did not foresee (or they ignored) the possibility that it could bring about a string of reprisal acts with potentially great harm to the POWs. Questionable, too—in the end he was forced to yield—was the way Churchill allowed the issue to develop into a full-blown crisis. Seizing the opportunity to demonstrate the country's resolve and signal to Berlin that Britain would never surrender (Germany still had the upper hand in the battlefield at this time), the prime minister invested the matter with a significance that extended far beyond the issue at hand. As a result, what initially was no more than a minor incident turned into a conflict that lasted for more than a year. In the end it was public pressure at home—a factor Hitler did not have to contend with—and diplomatic friction with the Dominions that forced the cabinet to give in.

As of noon on 8 October, that is, five days after the raids on Sark, the Germans had tied up 107 British Commonwealth officers and 1,269 soldiers of other ranks who had been taken prisoner at Dieppe (protected personnel—chaplains, hospital personnel—as well as wounded and sick prisoners were spared). Furthermore, on 10 October they would start putting in chains three times the number of POWs that Britain threatened to put in manacles. On 9 October, the War Cabinet decided to shackle the same number of prisoners that the Germans had put in chains the day before. Significantly, in the discussion that had preceded the decision, some of the ministers said they believed that German military authorities would be glad if they were offered some pretext to put an end to these competitive reprisals.[11]

Although the majority of the German POWs captured thus far in the war were interned in Canada, the British cabinet had failed to involve the Canadian government when it made its decision. Wishing to avoid open confrontation, the Canadian government reluctantly decided to take the action requested. "We feel that we have been committed without proper consultation to a course of doubtful wisdom," Ottawa complained. "Not only are nearly all the Dieppe prisoners Canadians, but the task of applying reprisals to German prisoners falls mainly on Canada." More important, the Canadians feared that "a futile contest" might follow in an attempt to match the Germans with "an eye for an eye" and that the Germans were "certain to win" when it came to applying harshness to prisoners. In other words, more than London, Ottawa was aware that the issue at stake not only was a military one but had a psychological dimension as well. Prime Minister William L. Mackenzie King, therefore, suggested inviting the German government to submit its accusations to the protecting power for investigation and to suspend the shackling of POWs on a reciprocal basis, pending a report by neutral Switzerland.[12]

Meanwhile, the Canadians agreed to manacle 1,100 German POWs but urged London to pursue every opportunity for a settlement before seeking to match the number of prisoners placed in chains by the Germans. "If we keep pace with the Germans step by step the probable result will be the fettering of all German prisoners whom we hold, and of all commonwealth prisoners whom they hold."[13] Canada was not alone among the Dominions in expressing strong reservations at the reprisal policy decided on by London. The Australian government pointed to the potential danger it entailed for the large number of Australians already in Japanese hands.[14] The South African government warned that Britain could not compete with the Germans' "well known ruthlessness." As substantial numbers of Dominion troops were prisoners in enemy hands, the Dominion governments made it clear that they expected to be consulted before further actions were taken.[15]

Churchill strongly rejected what he called the Canadian government's "pusillanimous line." As he wrote to Clement R. Attlee, Labour Party leader and, as of February 1942, secretary of state for the Dominions, "For us to invite, at German dictation, a neutral state to examine the conduct of our troops in the field would be to accept humiliation which I am certain could arouse the deepest anger in Britain and also in Russia. Any such process is only a step to mediate peace." Churchill believed that the Germans had made a great tactical mistake when they threatened to chain a threefold number of British POWs, since not only would it expose them to considerable administrative difficulties, but it would also deprive them of much-needed labor in the fields and mines. The prime minister warned of stumbling into a position in which the Germans could blackmail Britain by threatening to maltreat British prisoners. He suggested that the government wait and see how matters evolved.[16] Behind Churchill's determination may well have been his knowledge of the imminent invasion by British and American forces of North Africa, Operation Torch.

The War Cabinet endorsed Churchill's stand and on 12 October called on the Swiss government to register with Berlin Britain's solemn protest against the breach of the Geneva Convention and to urge the Germans to desist from any such behavior.[17] Churchill, meanwhile, made Britain's stand on the issue clear in the House of Commons. His government had never countenanced any general order to tie up prisoners in battlefield, he stated, though he then argued that such a process "may be necessary from time to time under stress of circumstances." By throwing 1,370 British prisoners into chains, Churchill charged, the German government was attempting to use POWs "as if they were hostages upon whom reprisals can be taken for occurrences on the field of battle with which said prisoners can have had nothing to do." Churchill then told the House of the countermeasures the British government had decided to authorize.[18]

The Dominion governments were not alone in criticizing the decision to manacle an equivalent number of German prisoners. William Temple, archbishop of Canterbury, for example, wrote to Churchill that a large number of bishops had urged him to present their feelings on the issue. They shared the full indignation at the Germans' action; however, they did not see how this justified the government's decision to take reprisals against German prisoners. The bishops reported that this view was widely held by members of the British POW Relatives Association and also by others who had relatives or friends now held prisoner in Germany.[19] Churchill, however, refused to budge, citing reasons of a tactical nature. He told the cabinet that it was clear that by threatening to mistreat British POWs the Germans hoped to prevent British forces from carrying out commando raids on the coast of enemy-occupied territories and taking back German prisoners for intelligence purposes. The prime minister, though, agreed to cancel the orders to tie the hands of the 1,370 prisoners if the German government did likewise.[20]

Berlin, however, showed little sign of any willingness to compromise and accused the British of breaching international agreements, threatening more reprisals: "If German Prisoners of War are treated contrary to International Law or inhumanely in any theater of war, for instance also in Soviet Russia, all the Prisoners taken by Germany, without regard to their nationality, will from now on have to pay for it."[21] A few days later, on 18 October, Hitler issued an internal order instructing his troops to kill all enemy commandos that fell into their hands.[22] The Allies were to learn of this only two years later, but the order confirms that Churchill was close to the mark in his analysis of Hitler's motivation when he created the shackling crisis. Fear of severe retaliation by the Soviets against German POWs following the Germans' murderous treatment of Soviet POWs could also have played a part, as Berlin may have been trying to pressure London into restraining the Soviet Union.[23]

Discussing Germany's motives, some cabinet ministers thought that Berlin was deliberately trying to increase the tension during the winter months and to stir up hatred against Britain among ordinary Germans. Or, they suggested, the Germans sought to reduce the effectiveness of commando raids and of bombing attacks on Germany by threatening reprisals against captured air crews. The ministers agreed with Field Marshal J. C. Smuts, present at the meeting as South Africa's prime minister, who suggested that the protecting power ought to elicit an urgent response from Berlin to Britain's offer to mutually halt the manacling of POWs while in the meantime awaiting the German government's next move.[24]

Canada's Mackenzie King thought differently. Keenly aware from the outset of the repercussions the crisis might have, he now suggested simply unshackling the prisoners as of a certain date, preferably as soon as possible. King explained to Churchill that there were growing misgivings among the general public regarding Canada's participation in a policy of reprisal.[25] The Canadians also experienced serious difficulties in trying to enforce the shackling on the German prisoners who actively resisted any such action.[26] Seriously considering the Canadians' apprehension but also with an eye toward the criticism being voiced in Parliament of the way Whitehall was handling the issue, Foreign Secretary Eden suggested taking steps to end the deadlock as soon as possible.[27] Accordingly, on 9 November, the War Cabinet decided to urge Berlin to respond to Britain's approach and as a goodwill gesture reduced from twelve to eight hours the period during which German POWs were manacled.[28]

By then, the British had obtained some first bits of information on the state of the shackled prisoners. They knew, for example, that 1,253 warrant officers, NCOs, and men of other ranks in Oflag III C (Lübben) were being tied with rope for a total of eleven hours daily and that all entertainment, schools, and study groups had been suspended. In Oflag VII B (Eichstätt), 321 officers and 60 men of other ranks were being handcuffed for twelve hours daily, while in Stalag IX C (Bad Sulza), 29 POWs were tied with the strings from Red Cross parcels for a total of thirteen hours, with an hour's break in the middle of the day.[29]

One of the handcuffed officers in Oflag VII was Major E. Booth. His diary paints a seemingly paradoxical picture. For example, on 9 November 1942, he wrote, "I have been in handcuffs now for ten days and in many ways it has been a very enjoyable period. Common misfortune invariably leads to good temper and companionship." People in the "chain gang" were able to get out by "going sick," and their places were being filled by volunteers from the remainder of the camp. "The inconveniences were slight (one's hands get used very quickly to following each other round) and the advantages many, for the cookhouse prepare a supper for us every evening out of Red Cross supplies and it is a great blessing to have an evening meal brought to you without all the fuss and bother of preparing it." The handcuffs were put on at 8 A.M., came off for an hour at midday, and were removed at 9 P.M. for the night. Booth further noted: "I have yet to meet a pair of handcuffs that the average P.O.W. cannot open in under five minutes but on the other hand, German sentries are posted outside each room for the express purpose of preventing such removal." The handcuffed prisoners could go outside whenever they liked, but as they were not allowed to mix with the rest of the camp, they were cut off from camp entertainment and other attractions. Booth remained complacent. "We lead on the whole a more peaceful and quieter life."[30]

London's attempt at reducing the tension, however, met with an uncompromising response from Germany. German soldiers after their capture, the German Foreign Ministry wrote, "have been repeatedly robbed and brutally mal-treated by British troops. British Commandants have refused them food and medical attention in order to compel them to give information and in the course of interrogations have inflicted the most ignoble treatment on them." In order to justify its measures, the German accusation continued, London was trying to introduce a difference in the treatment of POWs between when they were still on the battlefield and after they had been transferred to enemy territory by rationalizing that the provisions of the Geneva Convention did not apply in the combat zone. This skewed interpretation of the convention regarding POWs was "characteristic of the conception of the British Government that soldiers immediately after their capture are handed over to the entirely arbitrary powers of their captors."[31]

Berlin further pointed to the contradictions in the British government's attitude. On the one hand, London denied that it had ever ordered the shackling of prisoners; on the other, it described such shackling as necessary on occasion and sought to justify it. Under these circumstances, "the German Government cannot consider further the question of removal of counter-measures it has ordered before it has received through Swiss Government an official intimation that British Government has issued to its troops an entire confession and general order forbidding under severe penalties any binding of prisoners and also the possession of bonds for this purpose." The German memorandum concluded with a threat: "Should it be proved that the British Government is still unwilling to desist from the methods it has hitherto adopted in its treatment of prisoners and that British troops continue to be guilty of abuses of the nature described, the German Government will for its part also be constrained to regard the corresponding provisions of the Hague and Geneva conventions as no longer binding."[32] In short, Berlin now threatened to depart from its commitment to international conventions that so far had effectively protected British POWs.[33]

Walter St. C. H. Roberts, head of the Prisoners of War Department in the Foreign Office, ascribed the German memorandum to Hitler himself. As he saw it, Hitler had no difficulties in refusing Britain's proposal because he knew that the British people were sensitive to such matters as the treatment of enemy captives and that British government "could never be as ruthless about prisoners as he himself will be prepared to be if necessary." Hitler further knew that if he was patient, public opinion among the British would compel their government to unchain the German prisoners. Roberts then rationalized that, from a political point of view, the recent Allied success in the invasion of North Africa enabled London to concede to the Germans that Hitler had beaten Britain in the matter of reprisals but to do so from a position of military strength.[34] Given such considerations, the War Cabinet decided to maintain its placatory tone, but without giving in to Germany's demands. Eden was asked to prepare a reply stressing Britain's humane treatment of German prisoners and rebutting the charges made. At the same time, the offer to unshackle German prisoners if the German government was prepared to do likewise was to be repeated.[35]

Meanwhile, there was increasing pressure at home. In the House of Commons, MP Knox asked whether the secretary of state for war was aware that a letter from Oflag VII B (Eichstätt) had described how 200 POWs there were being manacled for twelve hours a day and slept on the floor of a cold attic at night. Another member of Parliament, Frank Sanderson, asked whether Deputy Prime Minister Attlee was aware that POWs captured at Dunkirk three years earlier were being placed in chains in wire cages and separated from other prisoners. Attlee's efforts at evasion met with the MPs' insistence that the government immediately issue a statement on this matter.[36] For its part, Ottawa notified London of its intention to take independent action toward finding a solution. Two alternative courses were being considered: one, to inform the Swiss government of Ottawa's earlier proposal that shackling should cease at an agreed hour and day on both sides; second, to fix a date in the very near future on which Canada would cease the shackling of POWs on its territory, regardless of any action that the British or Germans might think advisable to take with respect to POWs in their custody.[37]

For Churchill, it was clear that the move proposed by Canada was very unlikely to prompt the Germans to unshackle British POWs. Still, London recognized that if the Canadians were to act independently, the consequences could be most unfortunate.[38] Under the circumstances, the Foreign Office informed Clifford Norton, the minister at Bern, of the cabinet's decision to unshackle German prisoners without waiting to hear what the Germans would do. He was asked to tell the Swiss, under strict confidence, that both the British and the Canadians would immediately take steps to unchain their prisoners upon receiving an invitation from the protecting power to do so.[39] Subsequently, on 7 December 1942, the Swiss government called on the British, Canadian, and German governments to untie the hands of all prisoners from shackles on 15 December 1942 at 10 A.M.[40] Taking this line of action was a tacit admission on the part of Whitehall that the cabinet's approach and tactics had failed.

A few days earlier, on 4 December, in an initiative of their own, the Germans told the IRCC that all prisoners would be unshackled during Christmas week. The War Cabinet took a positive view of the statement, believing— wrongly as it turned out—that the Germans would not resume shackling thereafter.[41] On 10 December Churchill duly went public with the Swiss government's suggestion as well as with his own instructions to unshackle German prisoners on 12 December. Canada's prime minister came out with a similar statement.[42] Berlin, however, was not impressed and reiterated through the Swiss that it was ready to cancel the reprisals as soon as it had been informed officially that the British government had issued a general order forbidding the tying of prisoners and the carrying of manacles for this purpose. The Germans made it clear that for them such an order was a sine qua non for settling the matter along the lines of the Swiss suggestion.[43]

Whitehall decided to free the German POWs of their chains but refused to cease manacling POWs while they were still on the battlefield.[44] Practically, that is, both London and Berlin stuck to their original positions. In their official reply, the British stated that orders had been issued to all commanders in the field to ensure that troops of all ranks were acquainted with and observed the terms of the Geneva Convention, particularly those that dealt with the treatment of POWs immediately after capture. These new orders strictly forbade the general binding of POWs. Yet London added that the binding "will only be countenanced when particular operational conditions make it essential in the interests of the safety of the prisoner and when any other action would be less humane."[45]

When the Germans responded one month later, Berlin, not unexpectedly, accused the two Allies of "continuing to adopt an attitude which is incompatible with the provisions of the Geneva Prisoners of War Convention and with the most elementary rules of humane and soldierly conduct of war."

The Germans again emphasized that unless both Whitehall and Ottawa issued a complete and categorical order forbidding, under severe penalty, all shackling of prisoners, reprisal measures would continue and both those governments alone bore responsibility.[46] London could find only little comfort in a report by the Swiss minister in charge of British interests in Berlin that showed that not only the German Foreign Ministry but also the German military authorities disfavored the instructions—which had come directly from Hitler's headquarters—to reject the British declaration on shackling.[47]

In many respects, however, Berlin's stand by now was more one of principle. On 17 March 1943, the Swiss minister in Berlin forwarded a special report to London in which German Foreign Ministry and army representatives were quoted as saying that shackling should be seen as a "symbolic act." The 4,040 prisoners shackled at the time were distributed as follows: 1,838 in Stalag VIII B (Lamsdorf), 1,853 in Oflag III C (Lübben), 320 in Oflag VII B (Eichstätt), and 29 in Stalag IX C (Bad Sulza). The practice was uniform: the shackles consisted of two handcuffs joined by a chain fifty to sixty centimeters long. Manacled prisoners suffered no other disabilities or disadvantages and were treated the same as other prisoners, which among other things meant that they continued to receive parcels. The Swiss minister pointed out that although no order had been issued to alleviate the measures, camp commandants were making an effort to treat manacled prisoners as well as they could within the given instructions.[48]

At Oflag VII B, where the situation of the prisoners was probably the most difficult, Major Booth, after he had been discovered without handcuffs, had been sentenced to seven days of close confinement with his hands tied behind his back for twelve hours a day.[49] Sounding as upbeat as in the entry quoted above, he wrote in his diary for 31 March 1943: "The tying of my hands behind the back is a farce, this much will appear from the writing of this diary." Booth actually saw some advantage to this temporary state: "On the credit side is the wonderful sense of privacy and quiet, all the more welcome in that I am not completely cut off—meals are taken al fresco in the passage way in company with other inmates, and moreover at night I return to the outer world and hear all about the current day's events." On the debit side, Booth missed the loss of exercise and some of his usual occupations, "particularly the gramophone and playing the recorder with Jimmy Dizer and his fiddle." He wrote further: "I suppose it is inevitable that, at times, the hours should seem to pass slowly."[50]

For all his resilience, Booth at one point hinted at the darker aspects of life in imprisonment: "Sometime, when I am depressed I feel that I have lost the art of being still in the constant hubbub of the last three years; it is not that I haven't done any silent thinking—only too often my mind goes racing away on some meteoric flight—but that even my thinking when walking alone or when lying wakefully on my bed, has been in a way a frenzied reaction from the pettiness of prison life. Sometime I feel that I have been so completely engulfed in this pettiness that the most important factor in my life has been reduced to the next meal or an extra cup of tea, and that gradually my power of affection has withered, leaving nothing but an ego-tistically centered shell." He then added: "Perhaps all of this is conjured up because now, for the first time in nearly three years, for a week on end I spend practically the whole day in a 'room' by myself."[51]

The continued shackling of British POWs confronted Whitehall with a di-lemma. On the one hand, it wanted to assuage the concern expressed by relatives of POWs; on the other, it could not publicly reveal that the Germans actually no longer strictly enforced their manacling policy. On 21 April 1943, Eden described to the House of Commons the series of events that had direct bearing on the shackling issue. He pointed out that since 12 December 1942, German prisoners were unshackled but the German government con-tinued to handcuff British prisoners. Questioned on this, Eden admitted that the shackling had been applied less rigorously of late.[52] In order to avoid further questions in the House, the foreign secretary confidentially told certain MPs that there was reliable evidence to show that special penal-ties inflicted on shackled men had been removed; that shackling was at present being carried out more leniently in two out of the four camps, involving half of all the men known to be shackled (2,713 out of 4,040); and that this leniency was unknown to higher Nazi authorities, who, if they learned of it, might order a reimposition of "full dress" shackling. He ex-pected the MPs to guarantee that no reference would be made to this matter in public.[53] That Eden was here presenting a realistic picture is corroborated by Booth, who a month later wrote in his diary: "We are still chained, but there is now no restriction on our moving freely about the camp and no action is being taken at the moment against those who unshackle them-selves. The affair seems to be dying out."[54]

In the spring of 1943, the Allies completed their victory in North Africa with the unconditional surrender of Axis forces in northeastern Tunisia on 9 May 1943. This meant the capture of large numbers of German troops in North Africa, which in turn led some officials in London to suggest that this might be used as a lever for securing an end to shackling.[55] Their assumption turned out to be reasonable. "We can no longer indulge in a prestige fight with the English in the matter of fettering," Joseph Goebbels, Germany's propaganda minister, wrote in his diary on 17 May, "since the English hold many more German prisoners in custody than we do English."[56] One day later, Secretary of State for War Grigg told the House of Commons that on 15 April 33,315 German and 284,776 Italian prisoners had been in British hands. Since then, about 109,000 Germans and some 63,000 Italians had been captured by Allied forces in North Africa. At the same time, there were about 80,000 British prisoners—from all the services as well as Dominion, colonial, and Indian troops—in German and about 70,000 in Italian hands.[57] However, toward the end of June the Swiss minister in Berlin had to report that, despite frequent representations, the German authorities refused to give in on the issue, especially, he added, since Hitler personally insisted on shackling and his foreign minister, Joachim von Ribbentrop, supported him.[58]

Annoyed by the stalemate, Churchill went so far as to suggest, in late July 1943, threatening the Germans by telling them that "a careful record will be kept of the total number of man-days on which British and Canadian prisoners are chained, and that [the Allies] will require double this number of man-days to be served in chains by the Officer Corps of the German Army after the defeat and surrender of Germany has been achieved."[59] Churchill may have been encouraged by the recent Allied victory in North Africa and the invasion, on 10 July, of Sicily, but he found himself out on a limb: War Office officials opposed the suggestion, highlighting that shackling was now merely symbolic in practice and was no longer causing any great hardship.[60]

Moreover, both the Swiss government and British POWs, who were in the best position to judge, had made it clear that they would deplore anything that might cause the German authorities to resume a more stringent practice of shackling measures. Churchill's proposal could benefit the prisoners only if the Germans yielded to the threat; on the other hand, if it caused the Germans to introduce harsher measures, "the effect on men who have been subject to this inhuman measure since October 1942 and the consequent reaction on public opinion here and in the Dominions might well be serious."[61] The War Office correctly appreciated that the Germans were unlikely to yield to the threat of the record Churchill had proposed because this could be interpreted as a palpable sign of weakness.

When the War Cabinet discussed the prime minister's proposal on 2 August, Eden suggested waiting for the results of an inquiry ordered through the British minister in Bern as to whether shackling had indeed become symbolic. Grigg said that his information led him to believe that this was the case. Moreover, Stanley M. Bruce, the Australian high commissioner in London, thought that both the Canadian and Australian governments would be strongly opposed to Churchill's suggestion. In view of the overwhelming doubts expressed, Churchill decided not to press his case.[62] The comprehensive report mentioned by Eden arrived in mid-September. All together, 4,128 prisoners were said to be shackled, 321 of them officers.[63] According to the Swiss inspectors, not only did the prisoners have no complaints or demands to make, but they asked the Swiss legation officials to treat the matter with the utmost discretion, since their present condition was bearable. Again, it was clear that further steps and representations to the German authorities might have an unfortunate effect.[64]

By now information was reaching London that Berlin gradually wanted to bring the controversy to an end. According to Swiss federal president and foreign minister Marcel Pilet-Golaz, not only Field Marshal Wilhelm Keitel, chief of staff of the OKW, but also Ribbentrop appeared in favor of abolishing shackling in early August 1943 and intended to approach Hitler on the matter.[65] Ironically, because of this the German Foreign Office refused a British request that shackling be carried out by rotation—given that handcuffing was now more symbolic in nature rather than systematically enforced, rotation would scarcely benefit the prisoners.[66] It took several more months, however, before the Germans finally agreed to do away with handcuffing, which they did as of 22 November 1943. What may have helped is that the first successful mutual exchange of seriously wounded and sick POWS in October had demonstrated the importance of reciprocity.[67] Berlin insisted that the decision be given a low profile, making it clear that the original order would not formally be rescinded.[68] On the advice of the protecting power, London decided not to give further publicity to the issue for fear that the highest political authorities in Germany might decide to resume the practice, and it asked the Dominion governments and the press not to publish any reports on the subject.[69]

Thus the crisis died down. In itself, Britain's act of shackling a number of German prisoners on the battlefield was too insignificant to have triggered a protracted series of mutual threats and reprisals of this kind. Churchill's insistence, however, on turning the quarrel into a power game with Berlin, or even between himself and Hitler, meant that approximately 4,000 British POWS had to endure being manacled for more than a year.

The episode allows us to draw a number of conclusions. First, while they were fighting each other in a brutal war, both sides made sure communication lines remained open so that negotiations between them could go on unhampered. This would continue until the end of the war, even at the height of the Allied bombing raids on German civilian population. In addition, Berlin revealed an undeniably pragmatic attitude throughout the shackling crisis vis-à-vis London when it wanted its own interest to prevail.

Whitehall came away from the conflict recognizing that it could not ignore public opinion—whether at home or in the Dominions—when it made policy decisions on the POW issue.[70] Moreover, the episode taught London to avoid creating situations that could serve as a pretext for retaliation by the Germans.

Finally, because of the shackling crisis both sides came to accept the importance of reciprocity as a guiding principle for the way they would settle other looming confrontations over the POW question. For example, as we shall see, reciprocity was at the heart of the negotiations the two sides held over the mutual exchanges of POWs.

Meanwhile, it is hard to escape the impression that for most politicians involved, certainly for Churchill, the POWs were mere pawns in a game that was largely played out over their heads. Even if in the way it was implemented shackling had become more or less symbolic after a few months, it meant further deprivation and, for many of the POWs, added to the psychological burden of imprisonment.

MENTAL HEALTH

As the war entered its fourth year, the Germans held 58,795 United Kingdom service personnel in captivity, together with 2,605 Canadians, 5,540 Australians, 4,044 New Zealanders, 7,893 troops of the Indian army, and 3,384 colonial and Southern Rhodesian troops—a total of 82,261 British Commonwealth POWs. These were official figures the Germans had given to the Swiss. London estimated the number of British Commonwealth POWs to stand at about 89,000. The total number of United Kingdom POWs at the time was 142,159, for in addition to those in German hands, 44,941 were captive in Italy and 38,242 in the Far East. There were also United Kingdom prisoners scattered in other countries: France, Greece, Hungary, and some neutral states.[71]

Following the Allied invasion of Italy in July 1943, the Germans began evacuating British POWs from Italy to Germany, their number ranging between 32,000 and 38,000 (by then Italians held about 74,000 British

POWs).[72] As a result, the capacity of several camps there had to be increased significantly. For example, by October 1943 in Stalag VIII B (Lamsdorf) the number of prisoners had reached nearly 30,000 (a year earlier it had been approximately 18,000).[73] A first group of about 2,300 captives arrived from Italy in the middle of August 1943, prior even to Italy's capitulation. During September, 2,789 more United Kingdom POWs were brought into the camp. "This terrific increase of the camp strength," wrote Gabriel Naville, one of the Swiss inspectors, "has brought about chaotic condition." Overcrowding was making sleeping conditions intolerable. Not only were all three tiers of beds occupied (until then only the two upper bunks had been used; the bottom bed was too close to the cement floor to be considered healthy), but many prisoners were now forced to sleep on pallets on the floor. Worse still, because in a number of cases there were only two for every three prisoners, 127 men had to share pallets. It also meant that little room was left for tables or benches, so that many men were taking their meals standing up. Owing to the overcrowding, washing and bathing facilities were worse than ever. No new wash barracks had been built, and at the present camp strength Naville estimated that prisoners would be able to get only one hot bath a month. The water supply was insufficient, the higher part of the camp being without water altogether, and there were far too few latrines. British medical officers feared that with winter approaching there would be an alarming number of bronchitis and pneumonia cases.[74]

Among the prisoners in Stalag VIII B, there were 76 cases of tuberculosis, mostly bed cases, as well as 92 psychiatric patients, 59 of them having been diagnosed as suffering from psychosis and 16 from neurosis. British medical officers were satisfied with conditions in the Lazarett and also thought that conditions for the TB cases were adequate. But they added that many of the sick POWs from Italy had arrived in a shocking medical state. Included among these were more than 20 who had lost limbs, were wholly or partially blind, or had been permanently maimed. In summarizing the situation, Naville stated that the camp in its present condition "makes a deplorable impression." Still, he insisted that the camp commander, who had always shown great interest in the fate of British POWs, could not be held responsible for the current state of affairs, as he had had to absorb thousands of prisoners from Italy on short notice.[75]

In October 1943 the first exchange of seriously wounded and sick prisoners between Britain and Germany took place through mediation by the ICRC. It gave British officials in London an opportunity to receive firsthand information on the situation in the POW camps.[76] From interviews with returned prisoners they learned that overcrowding appeared to be universal throughout both Oflags and Stalags. Moreover, many camps lacked a central mess room, which meant that prisoners had to cook, eat, and sleep in the same room, making it difficult, to say the least, to maintain a suitable degree of cleanliness and tidiness. The Germans appeared in many cases to recognize this but seemed unwilling to do something about it.[77]

As camp buildings were not uniform—varying from huts to solidly constructed buildings to old castles and forts—it was often difficult to get the necessary repairs done, which meant that prisoners' discomfort was exacerbated by broken windows and inadequate plumbing. Fuel for both heating and cooking was mostly in very short supply. In some camps, the POWs used the packaging of Red Cross parcels for these purposes, but in others the German authorities simply did not allow this. In a few camps POWs were able to supplement their fuel ration with wood collected by fatigue parties.

Repatriated medical officers reported that the food rations they had been issued were on the whole tasteless as well as meager—always less than those issued to German base troops. During most of 1943, Red Cross supplies had arrived on the regular basis of one parcel per man per week, unlike tobacco parcels, which came irregularly. There were no complaints about mail arriving from the United Kingdom, but the delivery of mail from Australia and New Zealand was unsatisfactory. One of the medical officers, Colonel Roney Dougal of Stalag VII B (Memmingen), thought that shackling had had a very considerable psychological effect on the officer POWs at the camp, as shown by a few attempted suicides. The treatment of tubercular as well as psychiatric patients appeared to have been reasonable. The officers also expressed satisfaction about a school for blind POWs the Germans had started. On the other hand, German authorities had made no attempt to supply the prostheses that were needed, and the Red Cross had also been slack in providing them.[78] As the above shows, repatriated POWs were actually adding little information to what London already had from the protecting power, thus corroborating for Whitehall that those reports had painted an accurate picture of the conditions in Germany.

Medical officers in Stalag Luft III (Sagan), where by May 1944 2,706 British and 2,078 Americans were being held, began expressing concern at the increasing number of POWs who were progressively becoming mentally unbalanced, particularly among those who had been interned for three or four years.[79] Some were suffering from insomnia and not only refused to get up but also stopped taking part in any entertainment activities and scarcely talked to anyone; they developed a growing antipathy toward fellow POWs with whom they shared quarters and began making life difficult for them. The medical officers warned that for some prisoners psychosis might prove permanent unless steps were taken quickly to provide them with treatment.[80]

One of the senior British medical officers in Stalag Luft III, Major G. B. Matthews, had made a thorough examination of the mental health of POWs in the camp. He listed four prominent factors he saw as responsible for the onset of mental instabilities: (1) Lack of privacy. Except when in solitary confinement, a prisoner never had a chance to be alone, to be free of intrusion. (2) Frustration. Prisoners not only were surrounded by barbed wire and guards but also had to endure an endless number of restrictive regulations. (3) Monotony. The almost continuous confinement within the boundaries of the camp—POWs seldom left the camps owing to the hostile attitude of the civilian population—subjected prisoners to a drab, unchanging environment. (4) Depressing surroundings. The necessity for prisoners to eat and sleep while herded together in a room equipped with only the barest necessities and often devoid of even the simplest amenities produced in many a state of a melancholy for which no immediate remedy was at hand.

Matthews divided the psychological disorders POWs suffered from into two classes: those that arose during the first two years of captivity and those that developed after two years. Disorders in the first category were the result of the numerous difficulties prisoners had to overcome when trying to adapt themselves to a life that was quite foreign to anything they had known until then. Manifestations here were transient; in most cases symptoms gradually disappeared. Although disorders in the second category were produced by the same factors, they tended to worsen steadily with the passage of time and thus could lead to permanent mental deterioration. According to Matthews, because the causative factors of such disorders were unlikely to change as long as POWs were kept within the borders of the detaining power or in territories occupied by it, POWs who had been interned for two years or more should be either repatriated or transferred without delay to a neutral country.[81]

British War Office officials thought that all those who had experienced more than four years of captivity (approximately 41,000 POWs) and the majority of those imprisoned for three to four years would need mental rehabilitation. In addition, 20 percent of the POWs interned for less than three years would also need mental rehabilitation to a greater or lesser degree.[82] In October 1943, a report by the Psychiatric Division of the War Office that was based on an experimental rehabilitation scheme for protected personnel who had been repatriated concluded: "[T]he difficulties of social readaptation on repatriation appear to be more severe in ex-prisoners of war than in any other body of men so far studied. . . . Emotional problems are disproportionately severe in men who have been prisoners for more than eighteen months."[83]

According to John A. Vietor, an American POW in Stalag Luft I (Barth), men who absorbed themselves in reading or games, were deeply religious, or even were engrossed in planning an escape were less likely to become psychotic. Others, "goaded by worries about their families and wives—it was distressing how many wives were unfaithful and wrote their prisoner husbands to that effect—would be prone to slip their moorings and start sailing 'round the bend.'" In general, Vietor wrote in his memoirs, breakdowns were characterized by inattentiveness and an inability to concentrate; those who suffered spent their days lying on their sacks daydreaming.[84]

Letters sent by POWs also made it increasingly clear that some of them were suffering from severe mental strain. Air force officials who censored these letters reported in July 1944 that "mental unbalance is apparently still a major problem."[85] In one such letter, Flight Lieutenant Lloyd S. Adams of Stalag Luft III wrote in February 1944: "I have felt terribly depressed and fed up the past few weeks, I hate to admit it . . . but the longer I am here the will to live is becoming less and less. At the moment I feel there is no future, I have forgotten the past and am just living in a dream from day to day."[86] Flight Lieutenant James Heber Ward, also in Stalag Luft III, told how a friend had suffered a complete nervous breakdown and had been taken away. "A lot of people have broken down under the strain," Heber continued, "but I think I can just about make it."[87] Warrant Officer M. C. Curties wrote in June 1944 that of one of his friends had "gone mad"; he added, "[W]e have one or two other interesting cases around the place [Stalag Luft III] as it seems to get some people down. We have even got one chap that practices Yogi and lived for a week on one raisin a day. He sunbathes in the shade covered up by a blanket. I am still all right, I think, so don't get alarmed."[88] That many writers seemed to play down their troubles in order to spare their families was another indication that the actual situation was even worse.[89]

Although nervous breakdowns generally had common causes, each POW had his own story. For example, Philip B. Miller, a bombardier on a B-24 who was shot down on 1 April 1944, recalled how "Frank R told us [that] when his ship was shot down, he had neglected to open the bomb bay doors which he thought caused two men to be trapped inside. In reality, those doors could be opened in several ways. There was a lever right in the bomb bay that would do it, or you could knock them open by just jumping on them. We told him this, but he insisted he had caused the death of these men. He brooded a lot. He once spent the entire day trying to write a letter to his parents. At the end of the day he had written only six words 'I am fine. Your son, Frank.'" Miller related that Frank then began to stay awake all night, constantly smoking cigarettes: "This made us all uneasy because those excelsior mattresses were flammable. We tried to get him to stop, but apparently he couldn't. He refused to go to the mess hall at the proper times, but went over when it was closed and locked and banged on the door." As Frank's condition deteriorated, he once tried to climb the barbed-wire fences in broad daylight and in full view of the tower guards. Although normally such an action would bring on a burst of rifle fire, in this case the Germans recognized the man was mentally disturbed and did not react. Finally, he was taken away from the camp.[90]

The last year of the war saw growing awareness and concern in London over the deterioration of the mental health of prisoners. More and more reports warned of a danger of permanent mental illness for long-term POWs.[91] Although several such prisoners were included in the exchanges of seriously wounded and sick POWs, London failed to conclude an agreement with Berlin on exchanging long-term prisoners during the war, which could have brought home more prisoners who had suffered nervous breakdown.[92] Still, even though after liberation many of the former POWs had difficulties accustoming themselves to routine civilian life, only a small number of the POWs had actually become mentally ill in the clinical sense.[93]

INSIDE WORK CAMPS

Among the causes that determined the mental condition of a POW was the strain of work he was forced to do. Private Elvet Williams, who was captured on 29 May 1941 on Crete, stressed in the introduction of his memoirs: "The normal conditions of captivity were not those of the Oflag, Luftlag or Stalag with which we have all been made familiar, but of the Arbeitskommando, of which there has been no sight." He then adds the following salient observation:

Where enforced idleness dictated the pattern of life and escape for officers, forced labour imposed a different, more strenuous, routine on other ranks. At first, like their separated officers, concentrated in large camps, they soon found they were not to be allowed to choose their bunks, lie on them, and plot. Even while [the] Stalag itself was still strange, inhospitable and bewildering, they were divided and despatched to Working Camps, often in very small groups; slave labourers hired out to civilian contractors. With hardly an unsupervised minute to call their own, they were left to sort things out for themselves, bereft of officers when they most needed them, and subject to both military guard and civilian bosses.[94]

Regarding labor by POWs, Article 27 of the Geneva Convention states: "Belligerents may utilize the labor of able prisoners of war, according to their rank and aptitude, officers and persons of equivalent status excepted." In case the latter themselves asked for suitable work, "it shall be secured for them so far as is possible." Noncommissioned officers "shall only be required to do supervisory work, unless they expressly request a remunerative occupation." Belligerents are supposed "to allow to POWs who are victims of accidents in connection with their work the enjoyment of the benefit of the provisions applicable to laborers of the same class according to the legislation of the detaining Power." According to Article 28, the detaining power has to take care of the maintenance, treatment, and wage payment of POWs who work for private enterprises. Article 29 establishes that no POW "may be employed at labors for which he is physically unfit." Article 30 rules that "the length of the work days of prisoners of war, including therein the trip going and returning, shall not be excessive and must not, in any case, exceed that allowed for the civil workers in the region employed at the same work." Every prisoner is to be allowed a rest of twenty-four consecutive hours every week, preferably on Sundays. Article 31 prohibits employing POWs in work that has a direct relationship with war operations, particularly the manufacturing and transporting of arms or munitions of any kind or transporting material intended for combat units. Article 32 forbids employing POWs in unhealthy or dangerous work.

The Geneva Convention also deals with labor detachments, that is, work camps. It rules that their system must be similar to that of POW camps, particularly with regard to sanitary conditions, food, attention in case of accident or sickness, correspondence, and the receipt of packages. Every labor detachment has to be dependent on a POW camp, and the camp commander is responsible for seeing to it that the labor detachments observe the Geneva Convention. Article 34 deals with the issue of wages for the prisoners.[95]

Numerous work camps, some of them with only a few prisoners, were spread all over Germany, Austria, and Poland. Unable to visit all of them, Swiss inspectors relied on interviewing spokesmen from different labor detachments as well as from the main Stalags on which these work camps were dependent. The picture they were able to draw of working POWs was, therefore, far from comprehensive. It was clear that the prisoners' situation was greatly affected by the behavior and attitude the German commanders happened to adopt, by that of the civilian employers, and by the type of work involved. Generally farmwork was considered to be the best alternative, while pit work counted as the worse. Chaplain David Wild was transferred to Stalag XX A in November 1941, and from there he visited smaller working parties. Some places he found satisfactory, as in the case of a large farm: "With great ingenuity this rude loft had been converted into a passable dwelling for thirty men. The walls were freshly colour-washed, the floor and tables were well scrubbed. Kit, eating utensils and ubiquitous Red Cross parcels were neatly stowed away, and within each bed-space personal treasures and photographs were cunningly arranged. Everywhere was evident cleanliness, tidiness and good order that could only have been achieved by a group of men who had shaken down well together."[96] In contrast, Wild describes the difficult conditions of twelve men who worked for a certain Frau Bratz: "Here we found a deplorable state of affairs. The men lived in one minute room; the ceiling was so low that in the upper bunk of each pair the men could not even sit up. Frau Bratz, a really mean woman, rarely gave them the rations to which they were entitled, although she had a large and prosperous farm."[97]

In the summer of 1943, Stalag VIII B (Lamsdorf) held the largest number of British POWs, 23,235, approximately 66 percent of whom (15,345) were employed in labor detachments. About 12,000 of the latter were English. Swiss inspector Gabriel Naville visited several of the Stalag VIII B detachments in early July 1943. In Arbeitskommando E 339 (Freudenthal), the prisoners worked on the railway. They were accommodated in a wooden barrack outside the small town of Freudenthal. There were two sleeping rooms for twenty men. The beds, of the wooden-tier type, came with two blankets each. Lighting and heating were adequate. Two of the prisoners cooked the food, about which there were no complaints. There was a four-week stock of Red Cross parcels. The POWs were free on Sundays. This was a good work camp, Naville concluded, and he thought the *Kommandoführer* strict but fair.[98]

A less favorable situation prevailed in Arbeitskommando E 249 (Kriegsdorf). At the time of the visit, seven of the thirty-eight British POWs there were each serving a seven-day sentence for attempting to escape. The prisoners received heavy-workers rations but complained that the meat they were given was mostly horse meat, which on two occasions had already turned bad and had to be sent back. In fact, many of the work camps in this district received horse meat. The Swiss inspector and the German control officer of all working camps agreed that there could be no objection to good-quality horse meat as long as it made up less than 50 percent of the weekly meat ration. The German army, it was pointed out, also received horse meat.[99]

At Arbeitskommando E 337 (Freudenthal), there were ninety British prisoners divided into three working parties. The largest party worked in an iron mine eight hours daily; the next largest was occupied in another part of the same mine but worked only six hours daily owing to the wetness that prevailed there and for which the men were provided with rubber boots and jackets. This kind of work, Naville pointed out, was unhealthy; however, as the men had volunteered and German civilians were doing the same work, no complaint was made. The third party did engineering work at Sternberg. The men left the camp at 6:15 A.M. and returned at 5:45 P.M. All the prisoners in this camp were free on Saturday afternoons and Sundays. This camp was also described as fairly good. Naville received a similar impression from his visit to fourteen of the other work camps belonging to Stalag VIII B.[100]

London's main concern was with the considerable increase in the number of British POWs who were being sent into coal and salt mines. In view of the long hours these men spent in the mines, it was feared that prisoners so employed, particularly those who had no previous mining experience or lacked the physical build for this kind of work, would suffer permanent damage to their health. London, accordingly, asked the Swiss legation in Berlin to find out in what way, if at all, British prisoners were medically examined to determine their fitness for such work and, in particular, whether those men the Germans wanted to send into the mines were asked about their past medical history.[101] Naville reported that, although many of the prisoners working in the coal mines were unfit, German doctors often passed them as qualifying.[102]

A comprehensive report on conditions in the coal mines followed at the end of 1943. Most British prisoners employed in coal mines, usually pit mines, worked in Upper Silesia, and all the coal-mining working parties there—some fifteen detachments with about 4,000 prisoners—depended on Stalag VIII B (Teschen).[103] Prisoners had undergone a medical examination before being "allowed" to work in a coal mine. This examination, performed by a civilian German doctor attached to the mine where the prisoners were supposed to work, took place either in the Stalag or on arrival in the labor detachment. In most cases, according to British medical officers, the examination was very superficial. There were no definite instructions as to what infirmities precluded mining. Up to the spring of 1943, such medical examinations had never taken place in the presence of a British medical officer, but they did since then, at least in the main camp. No inquiry was ever made into a person's past medical history, so that it could happen that even prisoners who had been seriously wounded in battle were sent to work in the mines.

British doctors told the Swiss inspectors that the sick rate was slowly increasing and recovery was taking longer, and there was a general state of fatigue. Few of the prisoners were professional miners, and many of them were unaccustomed to such heavy work. Tuberculosis cases were sent to Lazarette, but men suffering from ear troubles did not receive adequate treatment. According to the same doctors, prisoners needed to be withdrawn from mining work after two and a half years to prevent their health from deteriorating excessively. The German authorities had rejected this proposal and sufficed with X-raying prisoners after they had been working in mines for two years or more.[104]

Prisoners usually worked eight hours daily, but with the time journeying to and from the mine, they often were absent from camps for eleven or twelve hours, which left them very little time for taking care of personal matters and for rest. They were free but one Sunday in three. The example of one A. Sales is indicative. Sales had been captured by the Germans in May 1940 and taken to Stalag VIII B. After a few months in the main camp, he was sent to work in a cement factory in Upper Silesia, where he was assigned to a quarry. In the winter, the temperature often dropped to twenty to twenty-five degrees below zero. His group, he wrote in his memoirs, remained in this part of Germany for three years; he and some of his comrades were then sent to Poland to work in the coal mines of Sosnowice. "Here life was very hard—working every day for 12 hours in the damp, gas filled, pits which had none of the modern devices known to present-day miners. We had one free day every month to clean our billets and wash our clothes."[105]

British POWs who were professional miners told the Swiss inspectors that the mines in Upper Silesia were more difficult to work than British mines owing to the height and steepness of the coal seams: in England, seams were generally not more than two and a half to three meters high, but in Silesia they were five to six meters high. This meant that coal sometimes fell from a dangerous height and that, as miners were often unable to hear the coal "working" over their head, they could not always get away in time. Because of the steepness of the coal seams, miners often slipped on the ground, and pieces of coal constantly rolled down over them, causing all sorts of injuries. Although safety regulations were considered adequate, they were not always carried out. Adding to these difficulties was the lack of experience of most of the prisoners working in the pits. No one received proper instructions before starting to work in the mines; at most, the prisoners were sent down to the pit with an experienced German miner. The most dangerous mine was E51 (Klausberg), where three fatal accidents had already occurred. In addition, an average of about 20 men, out of 400, were absent daily as a result of minor accidents, the most frequent cases being smashed fingers that often had to be amputated.[106]

The Army Council rejected a claim made by German staff doctors to the effect that men found fit for war service were equally fit for work in the mines—these men had been living on a POW diet after their capture, and thus their physical condition was below the norm.[107] Prompted by the Army Council, the Foreign Office in December 1943 called upon the Swiss government to urge the Germans to remedy the detrimental labor conditions in the mines.[108] In May 1944, following a question in the House of Commons, Arthur Henderson, the financial secretary of the War Office, stated that about 20,000 British POWs, many of them miners by profession, were working in German coal mines. Henderson further admitted that there was nothing in the Geneva Convention that prevented the Germans from employing them.[109]

As time went on, however, it turned out that the difficult conditions were caused mainly by the German civilian authorities—the directors and staffs of the camps, the military authorities, and even the Labor Ministry appeared to have little say in the matter. The chief aim of the civilian authorities concerned, the Swiss now confirmed, seemed to be to increase the output of the POWs to the maximum. In most cases representations made by Swiss inspectors to the OKW and the German Foreign Office did bring about certain improvements in living conditions, but not in labor conditions. German authorities argued that they were entitled to subject British POWs to the same conditions as German civilian workmen. Moreover, they had no objection to the British authorities making German POWs work under similar conditions. In Berlin, the Swiss minister's attempts to convince the Germans to abolish Sunday work without adding hours of work during the week and to allow POWs a change of occupation after two and a half years spent in the mines bore no success.[110]

To back up the argument, the German Foreign Office pointed to Article 30 of the Geneva Convention, according to which the duration of the daily work for POWs should not be excessive and should in no case exceed that permitted for civil workers employed in the same work. The stipulation contained in the second sentence of Article 30, that a rest of twenty-four hours should be allowed, was to be understood in the light of the general rules laid down in the first sentence: the criterion was to be the amount of work demanded of a German civilian worker. If the latter was not accorded twenty-four hours' rest every week, then a POW could lay no claim to such rest. The provision of Article 30, sentence 2, the German Foreign Office stressed, merely precluded discrimination; it did not require the POW to "be placed in a more favorable position than the German civilian worker." These provisions were based on the general principle that POWs were not to receive less favorable treatment than the home troops or the civilian population of the detaining state. The Allies, the Germans maintained, also interpreted the convention in this sense. The German Foreign Office furthermore claimed that in Germany "only those prisoners of war are detailed for mining work, whose special physical aptitude has been established after conscientious medical examination."[111] Given the desperate labor shortage in Germany in the fall of 1944, there was little chance that the Germans would have changed their policy.[112]

Excessive working hours were soon taking their toll. Following inspection of Stalag IV A (Hohnstein) in September 1944, the Swiss inspector wrote: "The effects of long working hours over the past three or four years are becoming evident among British prisoners of war in this area. In many cases low-grade fever persisting for several days with listlessness, lack of appetite and headache is seen. Boils are very prevalent. During the recent hot weather many men suffered from heat exhaustion. Gastric complaints, abdominal pains, diarrhoea and vomiting are common." Prisoners at Arbeits-kommando 1135 of Stalag IV A, for example, were obliged to rise at 3 A.M. They left the camp at 4 A.M. to work on the railway and did not return to camp until 7:30 P.M. Similarly, the first shift of detachment T 2 of Stalag IV F (Hartmansdorf) had to get up at 2:30 A.M. and did not return till 6:45 P.M. Even if two hours of this period were devoted to meals or short rests, this still left a workday of fourteen hours. The prisoners of E. 44 of Stalag VIII B (Teschen) mined coal for eleven and a half hours a day. They were per-mitted a rest from work only one day in twenty. Detachment 1047/2 of Stalag XVII B (Gneixendorf) had to walk for two hours to reach its work site. After working throughout the day, the prisoners then faced the same long march back to their quarters. As the Foreign Office put it to the Swiss, these instances were "merely examples of present conditions in work camps and could be multiplied almost inexhaustibly."[113]

At a meeting between British officials and representatives of the Swiss government at the end of 1944, Naville told them that the worst conditions were found in the coal mines in Upper Silesia; next came the salt mines in Thuringia (Werkreis IX), and somewhat better conditions were offered by the surface mines in Saxony. Even the last, though, did not grant twenty-four hours of rest every week. The OKW was agreeable, but the civil work authority opposed any settlement, insisting that prisoners work the same hours as civilians. The protecting power's proposal to add 8 percent to the workforce in order to permit one day off in seven had so far not been accepted. Since the physicians whom most of these mines employed were company doctors, they would not easily let a man off from work for sickness. The only positive note in Naville's description of the situation was that these POWs received the civilian heavy workers' ration of food and that sleeping conditions (barracks) were good.[114] The British argued that the German government's practice of working its civilians for excessive hours did not justify its doing the same with POWs; these arguments, however, had no weight with the Germans, not the least because this policy fell in line with the Geneva Convention.[115]

CONTINUING CRITICISM OF WHITEHALL

The radicalization that had taken hold of the whole German government apparatus by the fall of 1944, including the reorganization of the control over POWs—commanders in charge of POWs were placed under the direct authority of the SS as of 1 October 1944—further diminished British ability to influence German treatment of the POWs.[116] The Swiss legation in Berlin told the British that it had failed to persuade the Germans to do something about overcrowding and to keep prisoners away from particularly vulnerable points, such as factories engaged in war production or located in large industrial centers or towns.[117] The Swiss also failed to influence the Germans to cancel an order of the German military authorities forbidding any accumulation of food reserves in POW camps. A high German official had told a member of the Swiss legation that this order was issued to prevent the possibility of large quantities of tinned foods falling into the hands of partisan groups. According to the ICRC, German authorities also feared that such stocks might prove valuable to British prisoners "when the time comes for them to follow broadcast instructions regarding collaboration with armies of occupation."[118]

The worsening conditions in the final months of the war also brought increased public criticism of the government for the way it was handling the POW issue. There had been several warning bells. In November 1944, for example, 150 MPs from across all parties signed a motion calling on the government to appoint a separate minister to deal with POW issues and put it on the Order Paper. It read: "That this House, being conscious of the disquiet felt by relatives of prisoners of war and believing that the present system of divided ministerial responsibility is unsatisfactory, urges that a senior minister should be designated to co-ordinate and be responsible for all action in connection with prisoners of war and to answer questions." When no action had been taken by November, MP Colonel Louis Halle Gluekstein (Nottingham, East) explained that the motion had been tabled because too many different departments were involved in the POW problem and then asked rhetorically, "Is the War Office really the Ministry which should be entrusted with the determination of policy and administration in the prisoner of war question?" The secretary of war, Gluekstein maintained, had no authority over the different departments that would enable him to issue a binding ruling in cases of dispute. The MP expected the proposed senior minister "to co-ordinate prisoners of war problems, and act as umpire and director." The minister should have responsibility for answering questions in the House, Gluekstein advised, unlike the present system, with different ministers "sometimes giving conflicting replies to the same sort of question."[119]

The War Office was the main but not the only target of the criticism in Parliament. Member of Parliament Geoffrey Hutchinson (Ifford), for example, blamed the foreign secretary's many duties for his failure to bring about an exchange of POWs who had been in captivity for more than three years.[120] Deputy Prime Minister and Lord President of the Council Clement Attlee denied that there was "very grave disquiet" at the way matters were handled by the government and refused to appoint a senior minister. "The indication that I and my colleagues have," Attlee stated, "is that the majority of the families of these men have confidence in the way these matters are being handled by the Government, by the Protecting Power, and the International Red Cross."[121] Another member of Parliament, Irene Mary Bewick Ward (Wallsend), called Attlee's attention to the very large number of MPs who had backed this motion, indicating that "the House felt progressively more strongly that the Government's attitude was not in fact representative of the views of the people and that the anxiety in the country had grown." Ward told the House that on her journeys abroad she had heard much criticism of the War Office's handling of POW matters from senior military officers.[122]

No separate minister was appointed, but Secretary of War Grigg was not indifferent to the House's demonstration of discontent. He thus decided to share with the House of Commons the difficulties Britain encountered in supplying food parcels and clothes to British POWs as the war progressed. Many of the issues that provoked much criticism in the first months after Dunkirk came up again. Toward the end of February 1945, Grigg told the House of the efforts the government and the British Red Cross were making to establish in the camps substantial reserves of Red Cross food parcels, medical supplies and comforts, clothing, and boots. At the same time, he expressed hope that the interruptions in delivering supplies to Geneva following the operations that had taken place in the south of France in the summer of 1944 would not cause a serious shortage of clothing. The ICRC had recently succeeded in getting the German authorities to agree that a limited reserve of food parcels be established outside the camps. But he added that this agreement had perhaps come too late because the disorganization within Germany had by now seriously reduced transport facilities for Red Cross supplies from Switzerland. "While everyone will welcome the results of this disorganisation," Grigg commented, "so far as the war effort is concerned, it has created increasing anxiety for the welfare of the British Commonwealth prisoners."[123]

The secretary of war further told the MPs that negotiations were under way between the ICRC and German authorities to permit 100 trucks with food parcels to enter Germany. He assured the House that there would be no difficulty with regard to the Supreme Headquarters of the Allied Expeditionary Force (SHAEF) providing trucks. The British Red Cross, furthermore, had authorized the ICRC to incur on its behalf any expenditure that the latter considered necessary in connection with the care of British POWs in German hands. It was only in Grigg's concluding statement that a third major concern came to the fore. "I hope that I have shown," he said, "that the Government in this country, the Supreme Allied Command, and the British Red Cross Society are doing all in their power to see that any request from the International Red Cross for vehicles, fuel or maintenance stores which can be effectively used to supply our prisoners is met, *subject only to the condition that such assistance will not weaken the attack on Germany and so delay the conclusion of hostilities.*"[124]

Conditions in Germany, in effect, were steadily deteriorating to the extent that both the British and the Americans realized some assistance had to be rendered to obviate large-scale starvation or even death among the POWs.[125] Major General Richard Howard Vyse, the chairman of the Prisoners of War Department, reported that the great majority of British prisoners, most of whom had been in captivity for more than two and a half years "and whose vitality has been recently lowered by half rations since September and by exceptionally cold weather, are now faced with the prospect of starvation."[126] The ICRC suggested establishing two main distributing centers, one in Stalag VII A (Moosburg) and one in Lübeck, from which parcels would be transported by road. This could be a suitable answer to the decision Berlin had taken in January 1945—threatened by rapidly advancing Soviet troops—to start evacuating all POWs to the center of Germany, where the Germans had established three principal camps: in the vicinity of Lübeck in the north, Altengrabow in the center, and around Moosburg in the south.[127] Following negotiations with the ICRC, German authorities permitted twenty-five American trucks driven by Swiss citizens and accompanied by ICRC delegates and fourteen members of the German army to enter Germany through Constance on 7 March; the Germans also allowed a fifty-wagon train carrying food and medicine to run from Switzerland to Moosburg. But the ICRC could not assure that the parcels would indeed be distributed to POWs of the nations that had sent them, that is, Britain and the United States. Thus, H. Wasmer, manager of the Relief Division of the ICRC, expressed his hope in mid-March that "all donors will understand that the method followed was *the only one possible* in the circumstances."[128]

At this stage of the war, however, both the British and the Americans set aside any altruistic motives, making it clear to the ICRC that their first duty was to protect their own nationals; in other words, British and American soldiers were to be the first beneficiaries if the ICRC got through with the parcels.[129] In his memoirs, John Vietor stressed the importance of the Red Cross parcels that arrived toward the end of April 1945. "If we had gone much longer on that diet," he wrote, "we would have suffered severe intestinal disorders and found ourselves in the predicament common to all inmates of concentration camps."[130] Although clearly an exaggeration, Vietor's words do reflect the great distress the POWs suffered during the final months of the war.

It could be argued—and officials in Whitehall certainly did so—that the hardships and deficiencies the POWs suffered during the first three years of the war were, on the whole, bearable, especially when taking into account that at the same time the British at home were living in constant anxiety and amidst widespread devastation. And, of course, none of this could compare with the savageries of war and the ubiquitous danger of death combat forces confronted on the battlefield. Furthermore, that there had been no severe incidents involving POWs and that as of mid-1942 food and clothing parcels had been arriving regularly in the camps greatly helped the government in keeping the POW issue on the back burner. It is true that during the height of the war Whitehall became the subject of some public censure, but attention was generally soon deflected by news of developments on the battlefield. Remarkably, even the shackling episode did not develop into a public and political crisis.

During the final months of the war, however, the situation changed dramatically for both British and American POWs. First, it became more and more difficult to ensure that POWs in German camps would receive the food parcels and medical supplies that helped keep them alive. Second, under the most grueling circumstances tens of thousands of POWs were sent on forced marches, while the threat of German reprisals against British and American POWs became more real than ever. Third, an exchange of long-term POWs failed to take place. Finally, with the collapse of the Third Reich, thousands of British and American POWs were now in Soviet hands, liberated by the Red Army's thrust into Nazi Germany. This required coming to terms with the political demands of an increasingly intransigent Kremlin.[131]

By the winter of 1945, when, on the one hand, winning the war seemed only a matter of weeks but, on the other, the prisoners' health and the overall situation in the camps began to deteriorate at an alarming pace, the government faced a double challenge: it had to justify the course of action it had been following on behalf of the prisoners and defend what it claimed were tangible results, and it had to find immediate and workable solutions to the practical and political problems that had thrust the POW question into the limelight. An added worry was that with the return of the prisoners the government could expect criticism of its past policies to become only more severe.

Washington and American POWs

THE DULAG LUFT INTERROGATION CAMP

Four days after Japan attacked the U.S. Pacific fleet at Pearl Harbor, on 7 December 1941, Germany declared war against the United States. "The long known and the long expected has thus taken place," President Franklin D. Roosevelt wrote in the message he sent to Congress the same day requesting it "to recognize a state of war between the United States and Germany, and between the United States and Italy."[1] As had happened in World War I, the responsibilities of the protecting power were transferred to Switzerland, which was to remain neutral also throughout World War II. The United States and Germany, now belligerent countries, agreed to adhere to the 1929 Geneva Convention, to which they were signatories.[2] As the Americans had mediated on behalf of London to protect the legal rights of British POWs in Germany from the start of the war, their experience gave them some measure of confidence that Berlin would continue to observe its obligations also toward American troops made captive.

The challenges facing the U.S. administration differed in a number of significant aspects from those that confronted Whitehall. The two main factors contributing to this divergence were the difference in the numbers of troops that ended up as POWs in German captivity and the timing of their capture. Dunkirk had left a large number of British Commonwealth troops in German hands, which created internal political pressure on the British government and compelled Whitehall to get a grip on the situation from the very outset. In the case of Washington, by the end of the war there were close to 100,000 American prisoners in German POW camps—during World War I this number had never been more than 3,550[3]—but, significantly, about three-quarters of them had been captured only during the last year of the war.[4] By then conditions in the camps had already begun deteriorating. As the war progressed and the collapse of Nazi Germany came closer, the main reality for the overwhelming majority of American POWs in German captivity was the threat of starvation and the looming possibility of reprisals on the part of their captors. In other words, when in the end Washington, too, came under some domestic pressure for the way it was handling the POW issue, the problems that had to be overcome were vastly more severe and the policy decisions that needed to be made by far more complex.

At first, as they numbered only a few dozen, American combatants who had fallen into German hands were held in the same camps as the British POWs. For example, when in early September 1942 a Swiss inspector visited Stalag VIII B (Lamsdorf), which had the largest number of British POWs, he also found 46 American prisoners there.[5] Three months later Swiss inspectors again mention American POWs, this time in Stalag Luft III (Sagan); of the 607 Allied officers interned there, 58 were Americans, as were 26 of the 1,578 NCOs.[6]

The American officers in Stalag Luft III had been placed in rooms of their own but could mix freely with their British counterparts in all activities. Neither the British nor the Americans liked this imposed segregation, but the camp commandant refused to allow them to share their sleeping quarters given the rule that different nationalities were to be kept separate. The senior American officer at the Stalag, Lieutenant Colonel Albert P. Clark Jr., on the whole was satisfied with the situation but mentioned that part of the officers' uniforms had been confiscated and were seen being worn by German guards.[7]

All air force personnel, both British and American, captured in German-occupied Europe passed through the Dulag Luft, which had three main components: (1) an interrogation center at Oberursel, (2) a transit camp also at Oberursel but later moved to Frankfurt am Main and from there to Wetzlar, and (3) a hospital at Hohemark (ground force officers were questioned in an interrogation center adjacent to Stalag III A, Luckenwalde).[8] The main part of the camp consisted of four large wooden barracks, two of which were divided into 200 cells. The latter were eight feet high, five feet wide, and twelve feet long and held a cot, a table, a chair, and an electric bell for inmates to call the guard. There were no mattresses or even blankets. Ventilation was poor, and there were no means to wash or shave. Lights were controlled by the interrogators. The entire camp was surrounded by a barbed-wire fence but had no perimeter floodlights or watchtowers. Upon arrival, POWs were stripped and searched and then given German coveralls, though they sometimes were allowed to keep the clothing in which they had been shot down. All were kept in solitary confinement cells and denied cigarettes, toilet articles, and Red Cross food.

Usually periods of confinement lasted four to five days. Occasionally a POW would be held in the "cooler"—a special corridor connecting the two barracks—for the full thirty days permitted by the Geneva Convention as a punitive measure.

All prisoners were required to fill out a form—deceptively made to look like a Red Cross form—asking for personal details as well as information referring to their military service.[9] Interrogators generally spoke excellent English and used friendly persuasion to achieve results (each interrogator had a daily supply of twenty cigarettes he could deal out for the purpose). Only in exceptional cases did interrogators, for example, slap the face of a POW in an effort to "refresh" his memory, but physical violence was not employed as policy. Interrogators had also been given all possible details of the POW's private and service background by the German Documents and Records Sections. Following a customary refusal—in accordance with service regulations—by the POW to supply information other than his service number, rank, and name, the interrogator would attempt to draw the POW into an ostensibly innocent chat in the course of which he assessed the POW's value as a potential source of information. Within a few days a second interrogation followed, more thorough because the interrogator now had at his disposal not only details from the Documents and Records Section and results from the previous interrogator but also information from other POWs of the same aircrew and squadron. POWs who the Germans decided could provide no valuable information were usually transferred within a few days to a Stalag; others could be kept a number of weeks, always in solitary confinement and without tobacco, books, or Red Cross parcels.[10]

In these latter cases, interrogators often resorted to intimidation and violent language, calling POWs "murderers of children" and threatening them with indefinitely prolonged solitary confinement on starvation rations unless they talked. Prisoners were also told that if they could not identify themselves as airmen by revealing technical information on, for example, radar equipment or air combat tactics, they would be considered enemy spies and thus could face the death sentence. Tactics further included confinement in an unbearably overheated cell and the mock shootings of "buddies." On the whole, intimidation tended to yield inferior results, and the Germans considered the "friendly approach" the more efficacious. Still, no amount of mental deprivation and psychological blackmail was considered excessive.[11] In general, German interrogators appear to have been successful in extracting valuable information from both American and British POWs.[12]

Daily food rations consisted of two slices of black bread and jam with ersatz coffee in the morning, watery soup at midday, two slices of bread at night. As a rule, men who needed serious medical treatment were sent to the Hohemark hospital. Hohemark had functioned since World War I as a health resort and as a clinic for all types of brain injuries and accommodated a large number of German soldiers wounded in the present war. The wards for POWs comprised one single room, two double rooms, and several rooms with four beds, with a total capacity of sixty-five. Discipline was mild. The doors of the wards were not always locked at night, and German medical orderlies were the only guards. Medical treatment was excellent, as was the food, which came from special Red Cross invalid parcels and from the hospital kitchen. Wounded men were sometimes interrogated even during their stay at the hospital, but generally this was postponed until they were sent to the main transit camp for convalescence. The comparatively luxurious single and double rooms at the Hohemark hospital were used to interrogate high-ranking Allied POWs in circumstances the Germans considered appropriate to their rank. Several British and American orderlies formed part of the hospital complement.[13]

When his interrogation had been concluded, the POW was sent to the Dulag's main camp, where he awaited transit to a permanent Stalag. On 10 September 1943, the transit camp was moved to Frankfurt am Main, close to the main railroad there. When, on 24 March 1944, it was destroyed in Allied air raids on Frankfurt, the Dulag Luft was moved again, this time to Wetzlar, a town some fifty kilometers north of Frankfurt. During the first nine months of 1943, approximately 1,000 POWs a month passed through the Dulag; in the last three months of the year the number increased to 1,500 a month, half of them British, the other half Americans.

Treatment at Wetzlar, according to a report prepared after the end of the war by the Military Intelligence Service, War Department, was better than at any other POW camp in Germany where Americans were held. German and American staffs seemed to work well together, resulting in favorable living conditions. The SAO was able to operate Wetzlar as a rest camp where POWs could regain their strength and morale after the harsh treatment at Oberursel before they were sent on to permanent camps. Significantly, no food shortage existed at Wetzlar. Moreover, before leaving for a permanent camp, each prisoner received from the Red Cross a suitcase that contained a toothbrush, socks, handkerchiefs, soap, a comb, razor, cigarettes, and sometimes also knitted gloves, sweaters, flannel pajamas, bedroom slippers, and suspenders.[14]

STALAG III B (FÜRSTENBERG)—CAMP FOR NCOS

The Allied invasion of North Africa in November 1942 (Operation Torch) culminated in the unconditional surrender, on 13 May 1943, of all Axis forces in northeastern Tunisia. During the months of fighting, American soldiers were inevitably captured by German and Italian forces and, of course, vice versa. In June 1943, 8,833 American POWs were in German captivity, distributed among sixteen camps.[15] Stalag III B (Fürstenberg) held the largest number of American prisoners. Among the 2,408 POWs imprisoned there in May, 1,667 were in the base camp, 711 were with labor detachments about forty to fifty miles away, and the remainder were hospitalized. Except for 118 air force personnel, all the Americans had been taken prisoner in Tunisia in February 1943 and arrived in Germany in fairly poor physical condition. Many of them were covered with vermin, and they were immediately given showers and had their clothing disinfected.[16]

Stalag III B was located in a valley about two kilometers from the railway station in Fürstenberg and about four kilometers from the glass factory in which POWs were put to work. Near the camp entrance stood the staff headquarters (*Kommandatur*) and the guards' quarters. The camp itself was large, allowing prisoners of different nationalities to be carefully separated from one another. The camp was well maintained and was surrounded by a double barbed-wire fence, as was each section with prisoners of the same nationality. Well-constructed buildings lined both sides of the long lane that ran down the center of the camp. These barracks measured about eighty meters in length, ten to fifteen meters in width, and five meters in height.

Barracks were divided into two sections, each lodging 150 to 190 men and separated by a washroom and a small room used as a kitchen; at each end, two flush toilets had been installed in an antechamber. Both day and night latrines were being disinfected with chloride of lime. On one side of the barrack were six rows of triple wooden bunks; usually only the two upper beds were occupied, while the bottom one was used as an open clothes locker. The other side of the barrack consisted of a central passageway with tables and stools arranged near the windows. Here prisoners took their meals when the weather was bad; otherwise they were allowed to eat outdoors. Each bunk was furnished with shavings, but there were no mattresses. Prisoners were issued two blankets, which were sufficient only in the spring and summer. Electric lights were installed everywhere, enabling the prisoners to read and write comfortably until 10 P.M., when the lights were turned off. The windows on both sides of the room could be opened, providing light and ventilation. A door led from the living quarters to two adjoining rooms, one a washroom containing five large cement basins, each with eight to ten faucets, and the second a laundry room that contained four long cement basins. Here prisoners could also prepare hot water in a boiler, and an extra stove allowed them to prepare their own food.

Fifteen American cooks and thirty-two kitchen helpers worked in the large camp kitchen, which had many modern appliances and was kept very clean. The foodstuff that the paymaster handed out to the cooks each day was prepared according to the wishes of the prisoners themselves.[17] On the other hand, many prisoners ate out of tin cans, for almost all the personal utensils the Germans were giving them proved to be rusty. The American POWs did not yet have their own canteen, but they could make purchases at the large camp canteen—in theory, that is, since most of them had no money. (According to the Geneva Convention, officers were given a salary; all other POWs were paid for the work they did in labor camps.)[18] At first, prisoners could take a shower only irregularly, but following a request by the Red Cross inspector, they were officially allowed a weekly hot shower. As long as the weather was fine, almost all of them performed their toilet with cold water, of which there was plenty.

Dr. Robert Schirmer, the Swiss inspector who visited the camp at the end of May 1943, was satisfied with the general state of the camp—when all buildings were finished, Stalag III B would be excellently equipped for American POWs. The camp commandant was a "remarkable man," in his opinion, and seemed on very good terms with the American prisoners' MOC. He had invited Dr. Schirmer to return some time later to witness the camp's progress.[19]

When another Swiss inspector, Rudolph E. Densler, visited the camp at the end of September, he confirmed that satisfactory improvements had been made. Most important was the regular arrival of American food parcels. The principal objection was the way NCOs were treated. In many instances, identity cards, disks, pay books, and badges had been taken away from them. Most of these prisoners belonged to mechanized units and had held noncommissioned ranks for several years; they were now being treated as privates and sent to work because they could not prove their rank. The camp commandant accepted the inspector's proposal that "every American non-commissioned officer, not in a position to furnish his identity card, shall be recognized by signing a sworn statement."[20]

Densler also visited one of the work camps at Trattendorf associated with Stalag III B, which held 716 men, including a medical officer and 4 "sanitaries" (medical orderlies). Since Stalag III B was primarily an internment camp for nonworking NCOs, Trattendorf was not as large as the work detachments attached to most other German POW base camps. It was mainly privates and unrecognized NCO officers who were sent to work here. The men were employed eight hours daily (some of them ten) in building a new turbo-electric power plant. The compound, situated in a pine wood, contained twelve barracks, including one for the kitchen, latrines, and the wash houses. Barracks were of the usual wooden type, each with two rooms. Rooms were spacious, light, and clean; beds were double tiered, and tables and benches were provided. The barbed-wire fence was a good distance away from the barracks so as to allow prisoners enough space to play various kinds of games or sports. Three showers with cold water were available in the camp itself, and once a week the men were taken to the factory for hot showers. Six men shared one basin in the wash house, and there were enough latrines (of the pit type). Food was prepared by American cooks under German supervision. The kitchen was well equipped and had a well-stocked store room. Red Cross food could be cooked in the prisoners' barracks. On the day of Densler's visit, 29 September 1943, the camp had a four-week store of food parcels.

There was a sick call every day, and it was up to the American medical officer in charge to decide whether a man was fit for work. Twenty-five men with mild illnesses were in the infirmary; Densler was told that they had been without medicine for several weeks. At the same time, prisoners lacked shoes, shirts, socks, and underclothing. The men did their own laundry, but facilities were inadequate, and there was a shortage of pails and tubs. The POWs' man of confidence also complained of how POWs at times had been maltreated. Densler thought relations would improve under the new commandant, Major Von Hausberger. The latter had spent seventeen years in the United States and spoke fluent English, and he had assured Densler that any further offenses or ill-treatment would be severely punished.[21]

When in February 1944 Dr. Roland Marti and Eric Mayer visited Stalag III B on behalf of the Red Cross, they learned from Master Sergeant Clyde M. Bennet, the MOC, that the general atmosphere at the camp was "not very pleasant." In discussing their findings with the camp authorities, the camp commandant refused the Red Cross inspectors' request that at least one new building be added in order to deal with the overcrowding. The commandant also declined to increase the number of stoves for individual cooking and refused to address complaints of insufficient electricity, stating that he was strictly following an OKW order that prescribed exactly how much light should be furnished. Moreover, from his point of view, the prisoners had enough time to read during the daylight hours, since they had nothing else to do anyway.[22]

Camp authorities did not deny that sugar and potato rations had been reduced, but they insisted that this was because prisoners were dismissive toward German food and often threw it away. Complaints that there was not enough hot water to wash clothes were rejected by countering that water could be heated in the kitchen and that if prisoners used less fuel for individual cooking more would be left for heating water. Camp authorities insisted that the overall condition of the POWs was fairly good. As the camp commandant saw it, far too many collective food parcels were being sent— one parcel every other week could easily suffice for men who were not doing any work, and one parcel per week for POWs who were working. He further made clear his irritation at the way the prisoners spent their time, the amount of poker they played, not to mention the cigarettes they smoked, and even the fact that they were gaining weight because of their complete inactivity. Ninety percent of the American prisoners, he ventured, were living much better in the camp than they had ever lived back home. Although the Red Cross inspectors partly agreed with the camp commandant vis-à-vis the behavior of the prisoners, they still thought that no distinction should be made between prisoners who were working and those who were not, since the latter had the right to remain idle.[23] At the same time, it is significant that neither the inspectors nor the POWs themselves mentioned any threat to their health or safety.

The tense relations that prevailed between camp authorities and the prisoners came to the fore over conditions in Arbeitskommando 1 (Trattendorf). Camp authorities claimed that they were meeting "passive resistance" on the part of the prisoners in regard to work; the men found fault with practically all the types of work in which they were engaged, creating "a most aggravating situation." What particularly disturbed the commandant was that the POWs had been backed up in their attitude by Bennet, the Stalag's MOC.[24] Bennet told Swiss inspector Dr. M. Meier that there was an absolute lack of cooperation between himself and the German authorities and that they no longer allowed him to visit the work detachments associated with Stalag III B. For his part, the camp commandant blamed Bennet for the fact that, after he had visited Arbeitskommando 1 (Trattendorf), many of the POWs there refused to work and had begun showing dissent. As a result, the commandant had decided to appoint a new MOC for Stalag III's main camp.[25]

This he did the day after Dr. Meier's visit, when Sergeant Arthur S. Taylor was chosen to replace Bennet. Albert A. Kadler, the Swiss inspector who visited the camp toward the end of July 1944, noticed that relations between the POWs and the Germans showed less strain and that Taylor and the Germans seemed to have reached some form of mutual understanding. American prisoners at the time, including those in work detachments, numbered 2,904. Taylor's main complaint was that the Germans would not allow the prisoners more than eight packs of cigarettes (twenty to a pack) per week even though there was a large stock of cigarettes and tobacco. The commandant told Kadler that the POWs used cigarettes for barter and that in any case smoking "would imperil the health of the men."[26] Complaints such as this one by Taylor may help explain the low level of anxiety in Washington at that time with regard to the fate of its men.

That same month, another Red Cross inspector, Dr. Luc Thusichum, visited Arbeitskommando 1 (Trattendorf), where the new MOC was Sergeant Harry J. Curry. From a material point of view, Dr. Thusichum reported, the situation was good. The main difficulty was the strict discipline. Workdays lasted from 6 A.M. to 5:30 P.M., with breaks of twenty minutes for breakfast and thirty minutes for lunch. Saturday afternoons were free after twelve noon, but the prisoners also worked on Sunday, again from six in the morning to twelve noon. Any prisoner the Germans deemed lazy was punished with extra work in the form of three hours of road building near the camp. The same applied to any prisoner who arrived late, even if only no more than two seconds. A POW who did not salute was punished with three days in the brig. Often prisoners who worked too slowly were sent to the brig for several days. Here, too, prisoners under arrest received only bread and water for the first three days and the usual food on the fourth day; all reading matter and tobacco were forbidden. But on the whole, Dr. Thusichum concluded, the prisoners in the labor camp worked under good conditions.[27]

That conditions in the Arbeitskommandos depended to a large extent on the attitude taken by the German commander as well as by the civilian employer became clear again in early September 1944 when Trattendorf's MOC, Sergeant Curry, informed the Swiss legation in Berlin that the situation in the work camp had seriously deteriorated following the appointment of a new camp commander. According to Article 30 of the Geneva Convention, work for POWS should not be excessive and should in no case exceed that permitted for local civilians employed in the same work. The new commander insisted that a number of men had to stay until they had finished the amount of work they had been ordered to do. This meant, Curry complained, that they were working two or three hours longer than the civilians employed in the same job, that is, from 6 A.M. until 8 P.M., with no time off for an evening meal. It was past 9 P.M. when they returned to camp, and only then could they wash up and prepare an evening meal.[28]

When the prisoners had protested, the camp commander not only said that this new routine would continue but added that if the specified amount of work was not finished daily the POWS would spend their nights in solitary confinement. The civilian workers, Curry pointed out, left the workplace at the usual hour, but a military guard forced the POWS to remain at work. These guards continuously attempted to intimidate and threaten the men with both words and action.[29] Sergeant William Kalway, who had been captured by the Germans on 19 February 1943 during the battle of the Kasserine Pass in Tunisia and sent to this Arbeitskommando, relates how he and nine of his friends decided to stop working after they found out that their names were on a list of NCOs at Stalag Luft III. When they refused the commandant's order to go back to work, Kalway recalls, the German ordered the guards to load their rifles. "One guard was standing right next to me and when I saw that brass cartridge going into the chamber, I knew that we had better move, even before the interpreter translated the orders. When we started moving towards the gate, one of the guards deliberately kicked one of our men in the small of the back, and he dropped unconscious to the ground. We later heard that he was paralyzed from the waist down, but I can't verify this. We never did see him again."[30] Kalway stated that the work the POWS were doing was hard and the food was bad. "If it were not for the Red Cross food parcels, we would have starved to death."[31]

In another letter to the Swiss, Curry complained that the camp commander had forced the prisoners on one occasion to remain at work for twenty-eight consecutive hours unloading large bundles of iron rods with no lights and with inadequate equipment. This was heavy and dangerous work. According to Curry, it had taken a group of civilian workers from 6 A.M. to 4:30 P.M. to unload a similar shipment: the POWS, who had been working on another job since 5:30 A.M., were expected to start the unloading work at 3:00 P.M. and to finish before dark.[32] When Washington learned of these letters, the Americans asked the Swiss government to make strong representations to the German government and to demand immediate assurances that no such methods would ever again be used at this work detachment.[33] At this stage of the war, January 1945, with the Germans evacuating prisoners because of the rapid advance of the Red Army, such complaints were mainly for the record.

STALAG II B (HAMMERSTEIN): CAMP FOR PRIVATES

Both Washington and London based their assessment of the state of their men in Germany mainly on reports of Swiss inspectors. There were two kinds of reports, those of the protecting power and those of the ICRC. Whereas reports of the latter inspectors were addressed to the committee in Geneva and from there to both the detaining power and the prisoners' governments, reports of the protecting power were confidential and were provided only to the prisoners' governments. Therefore they could be more straightforward.[34] The exchange of seriously wounded and sick POWs that had begun in October 1943 offered Washington and London an opportunity to judge the official reports against those of the POWs themselves. Naturally, differences were expected in the way the everyday conditions of the prisoners were perceived, but the main question, of course, was whether there was a considerable gap with regard to the health and safety of the prisoners. Some of the American POWs repatriated in the second exchange (May 1944) had been held at Stalag II B (Hammerstein).

This Stalag located north of Posen near the Polish border held in the beginning of 1944 the largest number of American POWs. All its 3,947 prisoners, including air force and navy personnel, were privates; 1,555 of them were in the camp, 40 in the infirmary, 41 in the hospital, and the rest spread out over about 140 labor detachments. Ninety percent of the last group was assigned to agriculture, the others to industry and handicrafts. Actually, Stalag II B was a clearing camp for American prisoners who at the end of two or three weeks would be sent on to labor detachments.

As they arrived in the camp, the POWs had their clothes taken away from them and were given uniforms from the collective shipments, one for each prisoner but two for those who worked in the detachments. These uniforms were in good condition. All the prisoners wore leather shoes. Everyone had a double set of linen. As a transit camp, Stalag II B had twenty shoemakers and sixteen tailors on hand to repair shoes and uniforms. The prisoners had one stove per barrack on which to heat water for washing their linen, but this was clearly insufficient for the approximately 500 prisoners housed in each barrack. Neither was there enough coal. The POWs received one piece

Inside a Lazarett, showing men liberated by the Seventy-fifth Infantry Division, Ninth U.S. Army. (Courtesy National Archives, College Park, Md.)

of soap that was expected to last for a month, but no laundry soap. There was also a disinfection room. Shower equipment was modern and well designed; prisoners were allowed to take three to four hot showers a month. Latrines were installed in a stone barrack, next to the three barracks used as living quarters. This barrack was not lit at night and had neither windows nor a door, but the latrines were disinfected almost every day. The washrooms in the center of each barrack consisted of a few dozen faucets and bowls, and there was running water throughout the day.[35]

In the large infirmary room that served the American POWs in the Stalag and its labor detachments, patients slept on straw mattresses on wooden, double-decker bunks. They were given two sheets apiece, a pillow with a pillow cover, and two or three woolen blankets. Heat and light were good. Next to the dormitory were two rooms, one for treatment and the other for dressings. Supplies and medicines were scarce and most of the instruments too old and rusty to be of any use. Only mild cases could be dealt with here; all others were transferred to the neighboring hospital, a military facility that had excellent equipment for X-rays and other special medical analyses and where any kind of operation could be performed.[36]

These details were reported by two Swiss inspectors, Dr. Schirmer and P. Wyss. At the time of their visit, early 1944, there were 40 patients in the infirmary, all indeed mild cases or victims of work accidents; many of them were suffering from furunculosis. Two American doctors and two medical orderlies cared for some 30 to 40 patients who came to the clinic each day. Half of the barrack accommodated a further 400 men who either had stomach trouble or were otherwise unfit for work. The latter numbered about 100, 20 of them with arrested tuberculosis. Stalag II B also served as a clearing camp for Americans who were unfit for work. Here quarters were even more crowded than those of the other POWs. Overall, the American prisoners who were working were in a good state of health. No epidemic had broken out, and no deaths had occurred yet. Medical treatment of the American prisoners in the various labor detachments was satisfactory; in particular, wounded prisoners were quickly evacuated to the various hospitals.[37]

As to entertainment for the prisoners and their intellectual and spiritual needs, the Swiss inspectors noted that the prisoners had sufficient books, playing cards, and other games at their disposal. They had formed their own theater troupe and even an orchestra and a jazz band. In addition, prisoners could play some sport every day thanks to the camp's spacious grounds; sports equipment was obtained from the YMCA. For one-half hour each afternoon music and news were played over the camp's loud speaker. The prisoners published their own camp newspaper, *Barbs and Gripes*. They also received copies of *Okay*, a German propaganda periodical published by the authorities in Berlin for POWs. Courses were given in economics, public speaking, and languages. A school had been organized, and classrooms made available for this purpose. Two chaplains practiced their ministry among the patients.[38] Finally, each prisoner was permitted to write two letters and four cards a month.

The Red Cross collective shipments were received by the MOC, who stored them himself; each prisoner received one package weekly. The MOC was also responsible for sending parcels on to the various work detachments. At the time of the inspectors' visit, the camp had a reserve of 22,031 parcels as well as 51,026 packs of cigarettes. Prisoners in the main camp performed routine tasks; those in the labor camps were assigned for the most part to agriculture. They worked the same number of hours a day as German civilians and had no complaints about the jobs they were given. Although some of these detachments offered very primitive quarters, prisoners on the whole felt that they were well treated. Here, too, the German authorities complained of bad discipline among the American POWs. The inspectors maintained that Stalag II B might be called satisfactory provided the Germans took care of various requests made by the American MOC.[39]

A somewhat different picture arises from contemporaneous testimonies by POWs themselves. As in the case of the British, the exchange of seriously wounded and sick American POWs that took place in May 1944 gave American authorities an opportunity to obtain firsthand information on conditions at Stalag II B.[40] The repatriated prisoners told of barracks badly overcrowded and of food that was invariably tasteless and always too little, certainly less than the German civilian food ration. For breakfast, prisoners were given only hot water; for lunch, barley and turnip soup, with black bread. This was also their dinner. Three times a week they enjoyed a small piece of sausage for dinner and every so often a bit of margarine. Private First Class James E. Patterson Jr., for example, claimed that he and the other men had subsisted principally on the food in the Red Cross parcels they were allotted once a week. Prisoners ate in the barracks, where they had tables and benches; they were not provided with knives, forks, or spoons, but these were obtained from Serb and Czech prisoners in exchange for items from the Red Cross parcels.[41]

Since all able-bodied American POWs who were not officers and NCOs were obliged to work, they were transferred to the Arbeitskommandos that lay some distance from the main camp. Only one of the repatriated POWs had spent time in such a camp, since all the other repatriates had been declared unfit for work. He had been held at Arbeitskommando 1536 and forced to do farm work for twelve to fourteen hours a day. There had been thirty men in this detachment. They slept in wooden bunks in part of a barn that was damp and barely heated, with a straw sack, two blankets of German issue, and one towel each. They had been given one pair of pants, two pairs of underwear, one shirt, and one pair of wooden shoes. Their own clothes had been taken away from them. Food was cooked in a nearby farmhouse and was not much different from that issued in the base camp, except that there was more of it. The repatriated POW had stayed several months at this work camp but had never been able to take a bath or shower. The detachment had no doctor; those who needed treatment or had fallen ill had to walk to a hospital located at an airport several miles away. The prisoners were also forced to work when it rained but were not supplied with raincoats or similar protective clothing. The former POW also claimed that no representative of the protecting power had ever visited this detachment.[42]

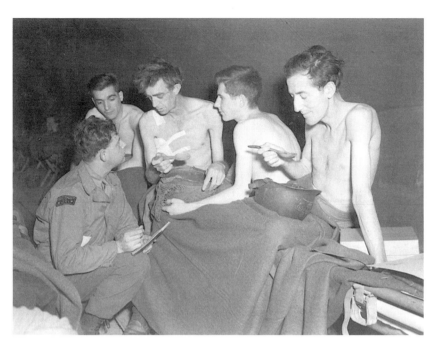

*Four American POWs at a field hospital in Germany awaiting
evacuation demonstrate how they had to eat with wooden spoons
from their helmets. (Courtesy National Archives, College Park, Md.)*

According to some of the repatriates, prisoners in the Stalag were sentenced to the guardhouse for the slightest infraction of regulations. Anybody trying to escape was given a sentence of three weeks in solitary confinement with a diet of bread and water. While in the guardhouse, prisoners were allowed to receive Red Cross parcels and to write letters. They were also given one hour a day to walk around outside. One of the repatriates recounted how, in late March 1944, he had seen six Americans being brought in after an escape attempt. The men had been badly beaten with rifle butts around the head, body, and legs but were forced to start their sentences immediately even though the physical condition they were in clearly required hospitalization first. About the activities of the protecting power, the repatriates all agreed that the attitude of the Swiss had been correct and that the Swiss inspectors, who had made thorough inspections of the camp, had stayed overnight during their visits. But, in their opinion, actual results of such visits were negligible.[43] However, in this case, also, none of them spoke of any serious danger to the physical or mental health of the POWs.[44]

U.S. reaction came in the form of a note that Secretary of State Cordell

Hull asked the Swiss legation in Berlin to convey to the German government regarding its failure to provide American POWs in Stalag II B with adequate treatment in accordance with the standards of the Geneva Convention. This failure was "parallel in many respects to the treatment accorded American prisoners of war at Stalag XVII B [Gneixendorf]," about which Hull had protested earlier.[45] The facilities used to accommodate large numbers of American POWs did not measure up to the accommodation enjoyed by German army depot troops. In contrast, German POWs in the United States "have been consistently provided with shelter, food, clothing, and medical care which is equivalent to the general high level enjoyed by members of the American armed forces." (In fact, several members of Congress did not approve of the favorable treatment given to German prisoners held in the United States.)[46] The German government was asked to give immediate assurances that steps were being taken to improve the standards of treatment.[47]

Hull generally was satisfied with the German response to his approaches, or at least he preferred to create an impression to that effect among members of Congress who had requested information concerning the treatment of American POWs in Germany. His customary response was that "as result of such representation improvements have been reported in the conditions under which prisoners of war are held by the German Government."[48] Actually, Washington's complaints had little effect partly because the United States refrained from threatening with reprisals. Officials in Washington knew that the German government "does not provide a ration comparable with the ration which the Geneva Convention demands," but they were satisfied they had succeeded in ensuring that through the American Red Cross and the ICRC every American prisoner would receive one parcel a week containing 14,000 calories. Similarly, they were content with the distribution of medical supplies and with the reports that "medical treatment accorded prisoners by Germany is excellent in most instances."[49] As long as the American prisoners were not subject to any serious physical threat, officials in Washington, as in London, were not wholly disturbed by their everyday difficulties and opted for a moderate course of action.[50]

THROUGH THE EYES OF A FORMER POW AIR FORCE OFFICER

Camp authorities at Stalag Luft I (Barth, Pomerania) also regarded conditions in their camp bearable. The camp, which was opened in May 1940, was the first permanent camp for air force prisoners. It was divided into an American and a British compound and held in May 1944 a total of 3,464

American prisoners. Sixteen of the Americans were higher-ranking officers, and 201 were NCOs. Compounds were open to each other during daytime, and British NCOs and men of other ranks acted as orderlies in both. Not only were these compounds administered under a joint command, but all resources and stocks were pooled. One of the main difficulties in the camp was overcrowding. Walter Braun, one of the Swiss inspectors, estimated that the two compounds were overcrowded by roughly 500 men and had calculated that every POW had an average living space of 2.72 square meters. The senior British medical officer lodged a strong complaint about the overall poor hygiene in the camp owing to the overcrowding but added that probably because of the fresh air from the nearby sea the prisoners' general state of health actually was amazingly good.

The prisoners themselves complained that the food ration handed out by the Germans was generally insufficient and of poor quality. Although it corresponded with the criterion laid down for POWs, its nutritional value, the Swiss inspector agreed, was not enough to maintain the health of POWs.[51] Here, too, it was argued that were it not for the food supplies of the Red Cross, the POWs' diet lacked substance. Disagreeing, camp authorities maintained that the prisoners had to adapt themselves to eating one hot meal a day, as did the German population, and accept the fact that there were no fruits and fresh vegetables. The camp commandant added that prisoners often wasted German food and in many instances also threw away some part of the Red Cross food articles, making it clear that as long as they continued doing so, "no improvements will be made to allow them a better preparation of their Red Cross food."[52]

Second Lieutenant John A. Vietor had been shot down by German fighters over Regensburg in February 1944 and spent more than a year in Stalag Luft I. Besides escape, he wrote in his memoirs, "food was our most important and pressing preoccupation, and eating engrossed the thought of every prisoner. In the early morning the first thought would be to check the gnawing feeling in our stomachs with hard German bread and coffee. At night our last thought were [sic] wistful vision of steaks, chops, eggs and milk." His food came from three sources: German rations, Red Cross parcels, and camp gardens. Vietor highlighted the importance of the Red Cross parcels: "If the Red Cross parcels didn't actually save our lives, they at least saved us from severe dietary disorders and kept us comparatively healthy." The American also mentioned that the Germans had grown very sensitive to food being thrown away: "Waste of food was severely frowned upon by the

Germans and anyone caught disposing of barley was sure to be sentenced to a week in the clink."[53]

Lieutenant Vietor relates how extremely important mail was to the prisoners. To illustrate how irregularly it arrived, he told of one man who had received a weekly letter from his family for a period of two years whereas another prisoner received all at once thirty-six letters that had been written on different dates. On the average a prisoner did not receive his first letter until eight months after he had been shot down. Because of the censorship, prisoners did not always know what to write. On the one hand, they wanted to encourage their families and friends by presenting a favorable report; on the other, they "hesitated to give the Germans the satisfaction of quoting these statements." Telling one's family that life was difficult and harsh might worry a prisoner's relatives, and in any event, the Germans might confiscate such letters. Although letters from home played a very important psychological role in strengthening prisoners' morale and will power, POWs sometimes had to face unpleasant news, such as the death of a relative, a girlfriend deciding to break off an engagement, or a wife wanting a divorce.[54]

What greatly disturbed the POWs in Stalag Luft I, according to Swiss inspector Braun, was an order the camp commandant had given on 27 April 1944 to the effect that prisoners who touched the main compound fences would be shot at. "If a prisoner of war crosses the warning wire in front of the compound fences, the guards will at once fire at him with the intention to kill after the first futile challenge. If he touches the main compound fences with his body or any object or if he tries to climb over it or had done so, so that the prisoner of war is already outside the compound fences, the guards will fire at him with the intention to kill him without any challenge. They will stop firing as soon as the prisoner of war comes to a standstill and has raised his hands." To the prisoners this meant willful killing. The order came against the background of the many attempts by POWs to escape from this Stalag as well as the actual escape of seventy-six Royal Air Force (RAF) officers from Stalag Luft III that had occurred several weeks earlier.[55] Summarizing his impressions, Braun stated that since his last visit, in January 1944, living conditions in general had changed largely for the worse. Most of the deficiencies could be blamed on the overcrowding, which, on orders of the OKW, could not be reduced in the near future.[56]

Overcrowding worsened following the capture of several thousand more American POWs in the weeks after the Normandy invasion. In mid-December 1944, the prison camp numbered 4,397 American POWs, 4,207 of whom were officers, and 897 British. The Germans were now turning down all suggestions concerning improvements, reiterating that the severe shortage of every kind of material throughout Germany made them impossible. Officer prisoners also complained that the German authorities were ignoring Article 18 of the Geneva Convention by insisting that all POWs had to salute German officers, regardless of rank, and by meting out several disciplinary punishments to prisoners who had failed to comply with the order.[57]

Vietor, in his memoirs, throws further light on relations between POWs and the German staff at Stalag Luft 1. In general, the policy of the POWs was to ignore the camp authorities except when they spoke to the POWs on official business, but not everyone stuck to this. There was a difference in attitude, for example, between young American airmen who had never seen any acts of Nazi brutality and veterans who had been in the hands of the Gestapo or had spent long spells in solitary. Many of the German guards were eager to be friendly toward the American prisoners in the hope of being given American cigarettes or American coffee. Since contacts ranged from mutual hatred and distrust to an occasional friendship and sympathy, Vietor found it difficult to assess the overall relationship between prisoners and guards, but on the whole he thought "the attitude of the Americans was more tolerant than that of the British."[58]

SWISS INSPECTORS CRITICIZED

Until the Allied invasion on D-Day, 6 June 1944, relief supplies generally reached POWs in Germany through the port of Marseilles. From here they were transported by train to Geneva and then on to the POW camps. Partisan groups had already been sabotaging rail communications, but with Allied forces sweeping through France, the entire route threatened to be disrupted. Given the almost complete breakdown of infrastructures within Germany during the final months of the war, the Red Cross was facing ever greater obstacles in ensuring that prisoners kept receiving the food and clothing parcels they now needed more than ever. By this time the Germans no longer allowed any buildup of stocks in the camps, fearful that well-stocked camps might provoke riots within or attract the attention of partisans on the outside. In August 1944 Berlin ordered an immediate reduction in such stocks and instructed the Red Cross to limit its shipments to one-day food supplies only.[59] This German decision, Secretary of War Henry L. Stimson wrote in his diary, "will have a fatal effect on the survival of the prisoners, for the German ration is not sufficient to carry them through the winter."[60] By then Germany held approximately 29,000 American POWs.[61]

In late September, Secretary of State Hull renewed efforts to convince the British to help set up a new, northern supply route between Sweden and one or more of the German ports on the Baltic Sea. This would involve providing safe-conducts for the Swedish ships carrying relief British and American supplies and mail for Allied POWs in German custody and vice versa. In July Britain had turned down a similar proposal by Hull because the Admiralty had objected to the idea for strategic reasons. But by September he wrote that with reserve stocks in Switzerland rapidly dwindling, the health and perhaps even the lives of Allied POWs might be at stake.[62]

It was only in early December that the Swiss were able to secure Berlin's consent for the renewed storage of reserve stocks, but this had to be in depots located next to each camp, that is, outside the barbed-wire enclosures. With transportation difficulties in Germany mounting by the day, the Red Cross could no longer rely on the railroads but had to resort entirely to moving goods around by truck.[63] By now, according to SHAEF information, the number of American POWs interned in Germany amounted to 49,114, the large majority divided over the following eight camps: Stalag Luft I (Barth), Stalag Luft III (Sagan), Stalag Luft IV (Gross Tychow), Stalag II B (Hammerstein), Stalag III B (Fürstenberg), Stalag VII A (Moosburg), Stalag XII A (Limburg), and Stalag XVII B (Gneixendorf). In addition, the Germans held 169,442 British prisoners, 784,395 Russians, and 740,472 French. Thus, all together, 2,330,190 Allied soldiers were held in POW camps in Germany at the end of 1944.[64]

As reports about the deterioration of the situation in the POW camps kept coming in, Secretary of State Edward R. Stettinius Jr. instructed the American legation in Bern in early January 1945 to keep his department fully informed not only about personnel changes at all camps but also about any changes at higher administrative levels that could have an impact on the overall control and supervision. The State Department also wanted the Swiss to step up their inspections of all camps in which there were more than 1,000 Americans; up to then these had taken place once every three months. Stettinius wanted the camps to be inspected monthly and reports to include information on how much and what kind of fuel was available and the amount and type of food rations the German authorities were providing. As for Americans who were lodged in tents, the secretary of state wanted information on the kind of heating, flooring, and lighting; the type and condition of the tents; and whether they were considered suitable for winter use.[65] When the camp commander of Stalag III C (Alt Drewitz), which held more than 1,700 American POWs, claimed he could not guarantee adequate winter heating unless a truck was provided by the Red Cross to transport firewood to this camp, Stettinius pointed Berlin's attention to Article 10 of the Geneva Convention, which obligated the detaining power to provide sufficient heating in POW camps.[66]

Vietor's memoirs clearly demonstrate the inexorable change for the worse when he describes the first few months of 1945: "Food became a complete obsession with all of us. . . . Ribs began to show and men lost between ten and fifty pounds. We had been thin before but had enough food and vitamins for minimum health requirements. It was impossible to talk in the room without mentioning food. At best, lack of food made men despondent and irritable; at worst, chiseling and greedy."[67] Like Vietor, Philip B. Miller, a bombardier who had been shot down in April 1944, spent most of his imprisonment in Stalag Luft I at Barth. Miller described the shortage of food toward the end of the war as follows:

> We began getting three meals a day, but soon that dropped to two with two loaves of bread for each room. During the battle of the Bulge [December 1944] we dropped to one loaf of bread at noon and one meal in the mess hall at night. There were approximately 1,200 men in our section of the north Compound, and breakfast, when we got it, consisted of six sacks of barley soaked overnight and heated early in the morning. This barley inevitably had a few grubs and insects boiled in, but we soon discovered they couldn't harm us. The noon bread ration was divided into sixteen parts and laid out on a table. A playing card was put on each piece of bread. Then the men drew matching cards from another deck to see who got which piece of bread. This bread was baked with sawdust as a partial filling and wood chips were sometimes found in loaves. . . . Supper consisted of potatoes and some kind of gravy. Sometimes animals killed in the war were cut up and mixed in the gravy. Occasionally we had pudding made of bread and chocolate with some prunes or raisins.[68]

As more information on the shortage of food and clothing in the camps became public, questions were raised in Washington about the way the protecting power and the ICRC were functioning. The catalyst was a letter by Colonel Thomas D. Drake, who had been a POW in Oflag VII B (Eichstätt) from February until June 1943, in Oflag 64 (Schubin) from June 1943 until July 1944, and in Stalag IV D/Z (Annaburg) until September 1944, when he was repatriated. Writing to John J. McCloy, assistant secretary of war, Drake stated that, along with many other American officers, he was of the opinion that the way the Swiss government represented American interests as a protecting power "was not neutral but pro Nazi." For example, two Swiss inspectors who had protested about the conditions of the American POWs and demanded improvement had been replaced by the Swiss authorities. Furthermore, the Swiss had never investigated numerous charges that had been made to the Swiss legation about German violations of articles of the Geneva Convention, accusations that ranged from petty and humiliating treatment to unprovoked murders. No Swiss inspector had visited Oflag 64 in six months, indicating that the Swiss were short of personnel. More serious, that the German government appeared to have asked for the recall of protecting power representatives who were too critical meant that the inspectors knew their jobs depended on their being agreeable to the Germans. Drake believed that the Germans wanted no unfavorable opinion to reach the neutral world, and therefore the mere notice of an impending visit by a Swiss delegation would have led to improvements in POWs' condition even if temporarily. He blamed the Swiss for a lack of aggressiveness in their conduct of investigations and in reporting violations of the Geneva Convention. Drake also accused the ICRC of failing "to properly carry out the intent and wishes of the American Red Cross for American Prisoners of War."[69]

Secretary of War Stimson, after he had personally talked with Drake, brought up the issues he had raised at a meeting with Secretary of State Stettinius and Secretary of the Navy James V. Forrestal. Stimson agreed that the Swiss were not taking as strong a position as one would have wanted in regard to the interests of American POWs and urged Stettinius to appoint "someone who would represent us vigorously in Switzerland on this subject."[70] But when, at the end of November, next of kin demanded that the State Department prompt the protecting power to make sure more food and clothing would reach the POWs, the War Department countered that there was an average surplus at the major German POW camps housing American prisoners of at least a fifteen-week supply of Red Cross parcels. The ICRC, the War Department continued, "has used every facility available to it to allocate the supply of such parcels, as well as the supply of clothing and medical articles for American prisoners of war." During 1944 alone, 50,000 complete sets of uniforms had been furnished by the U.S. government for shipment to American prisoners in Germany.[71]

Neither did officials in the State Department share Drake's criticism. A memorandum prepared for Stettinius commented that under very difficult conditions the Swiss were in general doing the best they could and in many cases had exceeded "what could normally be expected of the proper exercise of their protective functions." Many of the repatriated American nationals praised the Swiss people's energy and devotion in protecting Americans. Of course, there had also been contrasting reports, but adverse criticism had arisen largely from the inevitable differences in attitude between the American POWs and the Swiss officers who had filed the reports. Weight should be given to the fact that all male Swiss nationals were members of the Swiss military forces and were trained under such rigorous conditions that in comparison the normal routine of U.S. armed forces seemed a luxury to them. Their appraisal of detention facilities for POWs was likely to be "in the light of their own military experience rather than from an American point of view."[72]

The memo was also favorable toward the ICRC. Under generally acceptable international practice, the Swiss government could act in behalf of U.S. interests only to the extent that the German government permitted, and therefore the position of the ICRC was even more tenuous. The principal function of the Swiss representatives, it was pointed out, was that of observing, reporting, and acting as a channel of transmission of reports and messages. Their ability to achieve results depended much on their individual talents. Finally, the author of the memo reminded the secretary of state of the occasional criticism that had been leveled at them by the British when the United States had been the protecting power.[73] Judge Robert P. Patterson, undersecretary of war and Stimson's right-hand man in the War Department, thought differently, claiming that the State Department was "letting up on Switzerland on the ground that the Swiss represented the U.S. in the protection of American prisoners in Germany."[74]

As could be expected, Bern firmly rejected the criticism directed against it. The Swiss legation in Berlin was adamant that it had been defending the interests of American and British POWs energetically, explaining, however, that since the summer of 1944 it had become increasingly more difficult to deal with the German authorities. The Swiss disputed Colonel Drake's accusations that the two inspectors had been recalled because "they were particularly efficient in their work." The camps had been visited by inspectors "whose impartiality is beyond question," but the officials who had replaced them were better qualified for this particular work. Furthermore, prisoners were not always aware that more was needed than an inspector's report for improvements to be implemented.[75] This claim was not groundless—as Germany's overall situation deteriorated, the willingness of camp commanders to respond favorably to inspectors' requests perceptibly decreased.

Interviews the War Department conducted with repatriated POWs produced mixed reactions regarding the activities of the protecting power. Seven of the interrogated POWs said they were satisfied with Swiss efforts, whereas seven others felt that the protecting power was not carrying out its responsibilities properly; ten others were noncommittal. The War Department inspector general also learned that the prisoners in five of the camps were not satisfied with the activities of the protecting power on their behalf, an opposite view came from two other camps, and there was divergence of opinion among prisoners in three camps.[76] Memoirs by POWs also present a mixed picture. Many claimed that the Red Cross parcels had saved their life, but others were critical of the organization. Lieutenant Ross H. Calvert, who was held at Stalag XIII C (Hammelburg), told of his poor experience with the Red Cross. "A representative came to visit us occasionally and explained in great detail how our captors were doing all they could to keep us comfortable and that we shouldn't be complaining because it made the Germans nervous. Well, 900 calories a day made us nervous. We saw some Germans who obviously had quite a bit more. The Red Cross packages came in from Switzerland. When we asked why we weren't getting any, although the Serbs were, the Red Cross officials just changed the subject. I never did get a good feeling about the Red Cross."[77]

In contrast to the situation in London, where several MPs constantly asked questions in Parliament with regard to the POWs, members of the U.S. Congress hardly ever raised the issue, and when they did, they accepted the answer given. In the wake of Colonel Drake's criticism, Congressman Carl Vinson forwarded to Stimson copies of correspondence between unnamed American POWs in Germany and Colonel Drake containing allegations that services provided to American POWs in Germany by the ICRC had been inadequate, especially with regard to such vital items as food, clothing, and blankets. If the facts were as alleged, Vinson stated, the matter should be thoroughly investigated. In a particular case, the ICRC was accused of failing to supply enough heavy clothing and blankets to American prisoners in Oflag 64 (Schubin) during 1944, and not one weekly Red Cross food parcel had arrived there for a whole seven weeks during October and November of that year.[78]

In his reply, Stimson quoted information the War Department had received from the American Red Cross stating that adequate supplies of heavy clothing, blankets, and food both for current use and for reserve were being shipped to the ICRC in Switzerland and delivered to other transshipment points in Europe as well. Red Cross records further showed that American POWs in Oflag 64 had received adequate supplies of these goods during 1944. Then there was the fact that the Allied blockade command, acting for the Allied military command in the European war theater, had asked the American Red Cross to stop delivering blankets to American POWs in Germany during the summer of 1944 because the German authorities were expropriating American blankets for German use and instead issuing inferior German-made blankets to American prisoners. Shipment was resumed in the early fall of 1944. In the case of Oflag 64, 900 blankets had been delivered there in October and November 1944 and 600 in early January 1945, this in addition to the 820 that had arrived in the Oflag in September and November 1943. A substantial supply of heavy clothing furthermore had been delivered during September, October, and November 1944.

Stimson explained the shortage of Red Cross food parcels at Oflag 64 during October and November 1944 by pointing to the German military ruling that limited the reserve of food parcels stored in POW camps. Just then, Oflag 64, which during the first nine months of 1944 had averaged nearly 800 American POWs, had received a large influx of American prisoners; official reports spoke of approximately 1,200 by December 1944, but unofficially the figure was put at 1,400 or even 1,500.[79] Both the American Red Cross and the ICRC had made a number of vigorous efforts to persuade the German authorities to relax the new ruling, with the result that in December the OKW had agreed to reestablish reserve stocks of a four-week supply of Red Cross parcels for American POWs, which had done away with the shortage.

Stimson concluded his letter to Congressman Vinson by stating that the shortage of food or of blankets and clothing did not result from inefficiency or inactivity on the part of the ICRC. On the contrary, the committee had made every effort to get the needed supplies to American POWs in Germany and had functioned in an efficient manner under the circumstances, given the seriously disrupted transportation facilities and the substantial amount of administrative difficulties it faced within Germany. Stimson then expressed fears that the delivery of supplies and the maintenance of a reserve for American prisoners in Germany would become even more difficult as the war "progressed successfully."[80] As in the case of the British, by publicly complimenting the Red Cross, Stimson was also indirectly defending his own department, which was ultimately responsible for the welfare of American POWs. Moreover, Washington as well as London financially supported both the ICRC and Switzerland in order to help them carry on their activities.[81]

The *Prisoners of War Bulletin*, published free of charge by the American Red Cross for POWs' relatives, did not hold back, of course, in praising the activities of the ICRC. Moreover, the final decision on which items went into the *Bulletin* was with the State Department.[82] For example, in its November 1944 issue the *Bulletin* published a letter an American POW had sent to his apparently affluent parents from the Stalag Luft where he was being kept: "This is to let you know I am still well and to ask you to do something for me. Please donate $50,000 to the Red Cross for me. The Red Cross is doing a swell job for us and certainly deserves our help. We get Red Cross packages regularly containing all the little incidentals that are so important to men in my position."[83] Another letter an American POW held in Stalag III B had sent directly to the American Red Cross read as follows: "The humanitarian spirit in which your great organization and the International Red Cross in Geneva are extending aid in behalf of prisoners of war, of all creeds, colors, and nationalities, along with other subordinate relief agencies, is most inspirational, and a moral challenge to this war-embittered world." The *Bulletin* also told its readers that a new Red Cross ship, the *Henry Dunant*, had gone into service on 3 October 1944. The ninth ship in the service of the Red Cross, the *Henry Dunant* had sailed with a full cargo of more than 900,000 Red Cross packages.[84] The British similarly took advantage of Red Cross bulletins to highlight activities done on behalf of the prisoners.

As the overall worsening of the situation in Germany also brought a deterioration for Allied POWs in German camps, both Washington and the Red Cross readied themselves for further criticism of their handling of the POW question. The press, Stimson wrote in his diary, "have been giving out a lot of atrocity stories which are very true, but they must be very harassing to the relatives of the men who are still in prisons in camps."[85] As part of its campaign to forestall such criticism, the American Red Cross published a press release in February 1945 outlining the difficulties it encountered in delivering supplies to the prisoners and the great efforts it was making to overcome the obstacles. Because of the Russian advances on the eastern front in January 1945, the Germans had begun moving thousands of American and other Allied POWs westward on foot across Germany.[86]

A major problem was how to get relief supplies to these men in their new locations, as this depended primarily on whether the German authorities could and would provide the necessary transportation to move the goods that the American Red Cross and the ICRC had available. Lord Halifax, the British ambassador in Washington, informed London that the American Red Cross had "exercised every precaution in laying down large quantities of relief supplies not only at German frontiers but in Germany itself, more than one million food packages are today in charge of the International Red Cross representatives in Lübeck. Another two million packages can be moved to Lübeck within two days or to the Swedish port of Goteborg." A further four million packages were ready for shipment in Switzerland and southern Europe. This total of seven million available food parcels was said to be sufficient to meet the needs of American prisoners and of other Allied prisoners for a considerable period to come. Furthermore, more than twenty-five million dollars' (U.S.) worth of clothing was on hand in Switzerland ready for shipment to POWs. Representatives of the ICRC in Geneva, Berlin, and the port of Lübeck were struggling to obtain a sufficient number of railroad cars and trucks to keep the goods moving to the camps. "The American people," Halifax concluded, "must face the plain fact that the better the war goes for the allies in Germany the more difficult it will be to serve prisoners of war with essential supplies. Every possible step consistent with the primary aim of winning the war is being taken by the responsible governmental authorities and the American Red Cross with a view to improving the existing conditions among prisoners of war in Germany."[87]

Part of the anxiety American Red Cross officials felt over possible future criticism was voiced by Maurice Pate, director of the organization's Prisoners of War Relief section, at a hearing before the Special Committee of the Committee on Military Affairs of the House of Representatives. Pate feared that "in spite of several years of service [by the Red Cross] the average prisoner will return home with his last impression one of hardship." He hoped these men would understand the conditions in Germany with which the Red Cross had to contend in the last months of the war.[88] Reassuring Pate, acting committee chairman Sikes commended his organization "most highly for the way that it has assisted in this war and the great good it has done."[89]

DETERIORATION IN THE FINAL MONTHS

As Red Cross officials had feared, the capture of more than 21,000 American troops during the five-week-long Battle of the Bulge in December 1944, as well as the evacuations by the Germans of POWs to the center of the country in the face of the Red Army's rapid advance, indeed led to an acute worsening of the situation in the POW camps.[90] The camps were totally unprepared to absorb such a drastic increase in the number of American POWs. The result was that men had to sleep crowded together on the bare floor; washing and latrine facilities were inadequate; and rats, mice, lice, bed bugs, and fleas were prevalent throughout the camps. The lack of Red Cross parcels was deeply felt and had an adverse effect on the morale of the prisoners. Moreover, many of the newcomers were ill and in need of medical attention that was not available. In October 1944, for example, the number of American POWs in Stalag VII (Moosburg) had been 2,771, 972 of them in work detachments.[91] Three months later, this number had doubled to 5,989, and by February 1945 it doubled again, to 10,298, of whom 8,514 were in the camp and 1,784 in work detachments.[92] In mid-January 1944, Stalag Luft I held 508 U.S. Air Force officers. A year later, February 1945, 7,202 Americans, 4,949 of them officers, stayed in the camp.[93]

Swiss inspector Kadler, who visited Stalag III A (Luckenwalde) in February 1945, was able to highlight the situation of prisoners the Germans had begun evacuating from POW camps farther to the west. Like all standard camps in Germany, Stalag III A served POWs of various nationalities, each separated from the others. Recently evacuated American and British prisoners were kept separate from British POWs who were "veterans" in the British section of the Stalag.[94] Total evacuees in Stalag III A on 16 February thus numbered 4,361 American and 2,903 British prisoners.

The compounds were now excessively overcrowded. Rooms that had been designed to accommodate 200 men were holding 400 at the time of the inspection. All bunks were triple tiered, but still there were not enough beds for all men, and quite a number of them lacked wooden boards. About 100 men had to sleep on the floor. Some straw or wood wool had been provided, but a great many men simply had to sleep on bare boards or on the floor with one blanket underneath and another one as a cover. Conditions in the Oflag were somewhat better, but even there some of the officers had to sleep on the floor. All barracks were in a bad state; some had leaking roofs.[95] Sergeant William Kalway had arrived at the Stalag on 8 February 1945, one week before Kadler's visit: "This was by far the worst camp I had been in. . . . We were so crowded that it was absolutely impossible to maintain even the rudimentary conditions of cleanliness. We were about 3,000 men and there were absolutely no sanitary facilities and only one water tap. Every man became infested with lice. We would take our undershirts off and hang them on a line and try to burn off the lice with matches. This would work for a few hours, but it was impossible to get rid of them for good."[96]

Still, those who lived in these barracks were better off than those in tents. Each tent, measuring forty by twenty meters, accommodated 400 men. The 2,800 U.S. NCOs evacuated from Stalag III B were living in seven tents. A thin layer of straw covered the ground within these tents; there were no beds, chairs, or tables. At night, only a very narrow passage was left in the middle of the tent. There was no light or heating. Each POW had been provided with two or three German blankets. The men had no washing facilities; they washed in the barracks whenever they were free, but they mostly fetched water in buckets and washed and shaved in or outside the tents. No hot water or showers had been provided except on the day of their arrival, when each prisoner had been deloused.

Cooking and eating utensils were lacking in almost all quarters of this camp. There was an obvious shortage of food, the Swiss inspector stated, all the more acutely felt after the POWs had endured so much hardship during their long march and had been given so little to eat. As a result a large percentage of the evacuees were undernourished.[97] What made things even worse was the absence of any standard or diet Red Cross parcels at the Stalag. Heating was practically nonexistent in the barracks, since coal was no longer obtainable and wood-cutting parties had to bring in wood daily to help heat the barracks. Responding to a strongly worded protest on the part of the Swiss delegation, the camp commandant stated that arrangements had already been made with regard to supplying bed boards, more straw, wood wool, and eating utensils but that there was nothing he could do to ease the overcrowding. The Russian army was advancing so rapidly that evacuated POWs were arriving in the camp without prior warning, and he simply had to find room for them. The commandant assured the Swiss that he was doing everything in his power to improve the situation but that he could not expect any help from other quarters.

Even when the prisoners were not malnourished, their general state of health was very poor. About 60 percent of them suffered from dysentery, frostbite, or severe colds or had been severely weakened through the hardship of the march. All beds in the Lazarett at this Stalag were occupied; as a result, most of the sick were living among all the other men in the regular but much overcrowded quarters. Because they had practically no medicines or drugs, American and British medical officers were greatly hampered in helping the sick. About 5 percent of all POWs, besides those who were sick,

Starving American soldiers taken prisoner in the Battle of the Bulge after their release by Third U.S. Army troops in the German town of Fuchsmuehl. (Courtesy National Archives, College Park, Md.)

were too weak to appear for roll call. The Swiss warned that there was a great danger illness would spread among the POWs if no immediate action was taken to separate the sick. The camp commandant promised to study the question and, if possible, to have one or two barracks reserved only for the sick and to accommodate the others in tents, as no other rooms were available. Building additional barracks, Kadler explained, seemed to be out of the question; there was no construction material on hand, and none was to be had from elsewhere, given the present state of transportation in Germany.

The clothing situation was deplorable; most of the POWs had only the clothes they were wearing. They had been unable to carry most of their clothing with them when they were sent marching. Moreover, the POWs of Stalag III B had not been allowed to take along the store of items that had been kept in safe-keeping for them, which, according to the MOC, included about 500 pairs of boots, 2,000 shirts, and 1,000 undershirts, as well as parcels and cigarettes. Moreover, the cold and wet weather prevented POWs from washing their one set of garments.[98]

Sergeant Kalway writes poignantly of the psychological state of his fellow POWs:

> The mental condition of the men began to deteriorate rapidly. This deterioration took many forms. Mostly, the men would just sit and stare into space. If you asked a question, you received a blank stare for about a minute before the person realized you had asked him something. Then his answer was so disjointed, you wondered if he really understood the question. Some men refused to speak at all, and several times individuals had to be forcefully restrained from rushing the fence to commit suicide.[99]

Corporal Bob Engstrom, who was captured on 17 December 1944 during the second day of the Battle of the Bulge, reports a similar experience. He stayed at Stalag XIII D (Nuremberg, Bavaria) for about two months. From there he was moved to Stalag XIII C outside Hammelburg:

> Conditions were primitive at Hammelburg, at least for the enlisted men. We slept on the floor in a mule stable. We were so crowded no one could roll over at night unless everyone rolled over. There just wasn't enough room. We were stacked like sardines. The latrine was nothing more than a hole in the ground and a pail to sit on. The hole was periodically emptied by dipping the stuff with a steel helmet and dumping it into a horse-drawn wagon which was then taken out and dumped onto the surrounding fields as fertilizer. We called it the "honey wagon." Food was scarce. Each day we got one bowl of soup and a seventh of a loaf of bread. We became desperate for something to eat.[100]

Like Corporal Engstrom, most American POWs in German hands had fallen prisoner during the final months of the war, when conditions in the camps were deteriorating rapidly and starvation became a looming reality. Thus, the immediate fate of imprisonment hit them harder than it had the majority of their British Commonwealth counterparts taken captive when the Germans on the whole were still able to comply with the Geneva Convention. This helps explain why almost from the very outset of the war, certainly after Dunkirk, there were critical voices in Parliament taking Whitehall to task over the lack of attention British POWs were receiving whereas members of the U.S. Congress hardly ever questioned, let alone criticized, the administration over the way it handled the POW problem.[101]

When some members of Congress raised the matter of promotion for U.S. POWs while in captivity, Secretary of War Stimson allowed himself to respond to Congressman Andrew J. May, chairman of the Congressional Committee on Military Affairs, as follows: "Such action would not be in the national interest." While admitting that the misfortune of capture cut off a soldier's chances to earn the promotion he would otherwise have achieved, Stimson dryly added that this was equally true of an individual who had had the misfortune to suffer a prolonged illness or serious battle wounds.[102] Similarly, for many years after the war, U.S. military officials continued to oppose awarding World War II POWs a special medal in recognition of what they had gone through.[103] The attitude typically reflects the basic approach the War Department adhered to during the war: U.S. troops who had fallen into German hands ought to be looked after as any other soldier but did not deserve any form of preferential treatment.

REPATRIATION

II

Exchanging Seriously Wounded and Sick POWs

DISPARITY IN NUMBERS

Within a few weeks of the outbreak of World War II, the German government issued a proposal to ensure the repatriation of seriously wounded and seriously sick POWs.[1] Soon thereafter German Foreign Office officials informally advised the American embassy in Berlin that the German government had already appointed the people who would serve on the mixed medical commission (MMC) that was to help implement the agreement in Germany and had asked the ICRC to name the neutral physicians who were to be part of each commission.[2] The Germans were ready to place a hospital ship at the disposal of the MMC to transport those POWs whom the commission had certified as seriously injured or sick and to pay half of the running costs. The vessel was also to serve for the repatriation of medical army personnel, the exchange of civilians, and the carriage of letters and parcels for POWs.[3]

Berlin's move—somewhat surprising because there were as yet few POWs—may well have been meant to signal that it intended to follow the Geneva Convention, but a precedent set in World War I may also have played a part: negotiations between Germany and France on the exchange of severely wounded prisoners had begun almost immediately after the outbreak of the war and brought about the mutual repatriation of POWs as early as March 1915.[4] During World War II, however, the road to an agreement proved not only a good deal longer but also far more twisted.

The British Foreign Office reacted positively to the German proposal and agreed that finding a suitable method of transport was the main issue. In addition, the Foreign Office wanted to include in the exchanges a considerable number of German civilians, men as well as women, who were in bad health or above military age because, as an internal memo put it, "they are merely useless mouths."[5] Both sides were aware that the number of POWs would soon increase significantly. The first time this happened was in the summer of 1940 following the evacuation of Dunkirk, when, as we saw, the Germans captured approximately 34,000 British men. Although the Foreign

Office remained in favor, the Admiralty, at a time when the German navy was trying to block as much as possible merchant shipping to and from the British Isles in an effort to force Britain out of the war, turned against any exchange of POWs because submarine crews might be involved—their expertise was crucial to the German Naval Command.[6] Lord Halifax, until December 1940 the foreign secretary, countered, however, that as Britain was party to the 1929 Geneva Convention, the government had little choice but to let POWs selected by the MMC for repatriation "go back to Germany." In this he was supported by the Army Council and the Air Ministry.[7]

Accordingly, in November 1940, Whitehall suggested that the Red Cross charter a ship of about 1,500 tons to be manned by a neutral crew, which would sail on an agreed route between a British and a French port on the Channel and would be given safe-conduct by both sides, with expenses borne mutually in equal proportions.[8] Secretary of State for War Margesson stated in the House of Commons that "[a]s soon as it clear that the German Government are prepared to repatriate all seriously ill or seriously wounded British POWs of war whom the commission [MMC] decide to be entitled to repatriation, German POWs of war will be repatriated on the same basis."[9]

At this point, however, the German government reversed its stand, saying it could not assume responsibility because the waters around England were areas of operations and "even with all imaginable safety measures the safe passage of a boat cannot be taken for granted."[10] Two facts combine to explain this change of attitude: first, whereas Germany by now held more than 44,000 British POWs, the number of German POWs in British hands was negligible; second, as the Battle of Britain was at its height, the Germans had no intention of letting their military efforts be interrupted, however slightly, by a one-time safe-conduct across the English Channel.[11] Thus, Berlin also refused a British suggestion to have a vessel sail under the auspices of the protecting power—still the United States—between a port in Britain and either Marseilles or Lisbon.[12] On the other hand, the Germans agreed to allow British POWs who had been recommended for repatriation to be sent to Lisbon and from there by ship to Canada or, if their health made such a journey impossible, to either Sweden or Switzerland. German repatriables in Canada would be transported by ship to Lisbon and from there overland to Germany, while those in Britain would be sent to Ireland.[13] The British Joint Intelligence Committee thought the first suggestion unacceptable but welcomed the general idea contained in the second, provided the German Admiralty granted the ship safe-conduct.[14] London was eager to reach an agreement because by May 1941 more than 2,000 seriously sick and injured POWs and protected personnel (doctors, medical orderlies, and chaplains) had been recommended for repatriation.[15]

Although the German Admiralty continued to refuse to grant safe-conduct to any ship sailing from Britain to Lisbon,[16] Berlin did not entirely dismiss the idea of a reciprocal repatriation of the seriously sick and wounded. At the beginning of June, through the American representative, the German government recommended that, if a date could be fixed, all British POWs "entitled to repatriation be transferred to Spain and all German POWs of war entitled to repatriation to Ireland," implying that Ireland was a neutral country. The two governments might then repatriate their respective sick and wounded in sanitary planes.[17] This proposal was unacceptable to the British Foreign Office because it was clear that the Royal Air Force would never allow a special German aircraft free passage between France and Ireland. Moreover, Ireland's request for a formal recognition of its neutrality had been refused by Whitehall with the argument that a member of the British Commonwealth could not remain neutral and remain a member while the rest of the Commonwealth was at war.[18]

By now, however, Whitehall had to take into consideration the protests of relatives of POWs held in Germany who were openly blaming the government for the fact that, ten months into the war, none of the men had as yet been repatriated.[19] Thus, in early July 1941, London informed the Germans through the Swiss legation that it agreed to have eligible British POWs shipped to Spain. In view of the large numbers recommended for repatriation by the MMC in Germany, however, air transport had become impracticable, and from Spain the POWs would therefore have to be brought to the United Kingdom by sea after all: in its communication with the Swiss legation, London inquired whether the German government would "now waive its previous objections to granting a safe conduct to the ship selected for this purpose." In regard to German POWs, London proposed moving them to Sweden rather than to Ireland "in view of the short distance which separates Sweden from Germany."[20] The British had secured the consent of the Swedish government to provide the air transport needed to carry German POWs from the United Kingdom to Sweden in successive safe-conduct flights.[21]

When Germany rejected the idea of repatriating seriously sick and injured POWs via Swedish territory, British Foreign Office officials realistically recognized that this might be explained by the disparity in numbers—the British were to recover more than 1,100 men, but the Germans were to receive no more than 50.[22] British data for September 1941 reveal that the Germans held 63 British diplomatic personnel, approximately 1,000 POWs in protected categories, and 1,100 wounded and sick. At the same time, Britain held 14 German diplomatic personnel, 39 POWs in protected categories, and 44 wounded and sick.[23]

Nevertheless, at the end of August 1941, Berlin continued the negotiations and reiterated that it would not grant safe-conduct to transports by sea from Spain to Britain. The Germans suggested instead that sick and wounded British POWs be fetched by a British hospital ship from the French port of Fécamp, northeast of Le Havre, where it would first disembark German POWs from Britain. (By this time, the Germans had come to realize that invasion of Britain was a military impossibility.) The German government urged a speedy reply from London, "since repatriation would undoubtedly have to be effected in the daylight and the days are getting shorter." The high German Foreign Office official who handed this note to the American embassy added that all was ready for the repatriation of 1,200 seriously wounded British POWs and that a "speedy beginning with the seriously wounded could lead not only to the repatriation within the near future of all persons entitled to repatriation under both of the Geneva Conventions but also of seriously wounded British and German combatants from France, Ireland, Uruguay, and other neutral countries as well as of civilian internees not eligible for military service."[24]

The Germans indeed seemed serious for repatriation to begin as soon as possible after 1 October 1941. On 22 September, they informed the Americans that they had already begun assembling the people to be repatriated at convenient points and were making arrangements for hospital trains to carry all of them to a hospital in Rouen, from where they would be divided into smaller groups for embarkation at Fécamp. At the same time, the Germans were dissatisfied that only 150 to 200 Germans would be exchanged against more than 1,200 wounded British POWs. They suggested that perhaps not all German POWs in England had been examined or that "a standard was applied in the examinations other than that applied in the examination of POWs in Germany."[25]

The American embassy in Berlin was asked to ascertain whether all German POWs had been acquainted with the provisions of Article 70 of the 1929 Geneva Convention, which allowed them to present themselves to the MMC for examination, and whether all German POWs who wished to be examined had been brought before the MMC. Further, the Germans asked for the names of those German POWs in England who had been examined by the

MMC but whose right to repatriation had been denied or reserved for decision on the occasion of the next examination. The German authorities also expected the British to return sick and wounded German medical personnel not needed for the care of German POWs in Britain, and they wanted their names. For their part, the Germans planned to send home about 700 medical doctors and orderlies in the proposed October exchange. In addition, the Germans wanted assurance that arrangements would be made to transport Germans approved for repatriation by the MMC in Canada on American ships regularly plying the New York–Lisbon route or on other neutral ships. Finally, the Germans raised the question of soldiers interned in third countries who were entitled to repatriation. Specifically, the Germans wanted the British to recognize German captives in Ireland in this category and to bring them to an English Channel port for transport home along with the other German POWs.[26]

Berlin also quoted the agreement that had been reached with London in February 1940 about the repatriation of women, children, and men beyond military age. "As the space in the repatriation ships for the return of the German POWs entitled to repatriation and of the German sanitary personnel will be used to a small extent only," the Germans suggested that the available space be used "for the resumed return of interned or non-interned German women, children and men of non-military age who wish to go back to Germany."[27]

Quickly responding to Berlin's queries and expectations, London confirmed that all German POWs, both officers and men of other ranks, had been acquainted with Article 70 of the Geneva Convention and that all men of confidence at the permanent camps and in the hospitals in which German POWs were interned had been informed in advance of the tours of the MMC and asked to produce the names of any prisoner wishing to be examined by the commission. Moreover, any prisoner who had wanted to appear before the commission had been allowed to do so even if he had not previously made such a request through the MOC. The MMC had completed its fifth tour on 26 September 1941, and many POWs were being reexamined. Two lists were sent to the Swiss legation: a nominal roll of the German POWs in the United Kingdom who passed the repatriation requirement on the recommendation of the MMC, and a list containing the names of German POWs examined by the commission but not recommended for repatriation.[28]

Still, the reality was that the MMC had approved only forty-four Germans for repatriation. By way of encouragement, the British announced that in addition to the wounded POWs thirty-eight German medical personnel would also be returned. Although Foreign Secretary Eden declined in principle to accept the German demand to make up for the disparity in numbers of POWs with the repatriation of civilians, he stated that Whitehall was willing to facilitate the repatriation of those other than men of military age. The foreign secretary also gave no definite answer regarding seriously wounded German airmen in Ireland.[29]

The Germans called Eden's suggestion about the repatriation of German civilians equivocal and charged that the British Foreign Office attitude had led to "a new situation . . . which makes it impossible for the German Government to adhere to the date heretofore foreseen for the exchange." The Germans knew that the Geneva Convention did not allow the repatriation of wounded soldiers to be conditioned on a simultaneous repatriation of civilian internees, and they were therefore careful not to make a formal connection. They left no doubt, however, that they were determined "not to let repatriation of the wounded begin until they have definite assurance that concrete steps have been taken to begin the predicate of civil internees" and warned the British foreign secretary to issue a concrete statement on the issue.[30]

London recognized that if it wanted to get back seriously injured British POWs, it had to respond positively to the Germans' demands, including the return of German airmen in Ireland.[31] By 4 October, it seemed that all differences between the Germans and the British had been solved, as the German Foreign Office told the American embassy in Berlin of its satisfaction about the "willingness shown by the British government to begin the exchange of civilians and particularly with the British decision to send 60 women and children at the present time." The Germans hoped to be able to notify the British that the first ship could start from Newhaven during the present tidal period on 7 or 8 October and that the repatriation could continue during the next tidal period, beginning 18 October.[32]

As it turned out, the first repatriation of POWs was still far off. On 6 October, a broadcast by Bremen Radio referred to BBC reports that had mentioned a general agreement on POWs. These reports were considerably ahead of the facts, Bremen Radio stated, because so far only a partial exchange had been considered; through U.S. mediation Berlin had expressed its readiness to receive about 100 members of the German armed forces in exchange for a corresponding number of British POWs. The German POWs were to be sent in hospital ships from Newhaven; when the ships arrived at Dieppe, the 100 British POWs would be put on board those vessels. This particular exchange was to take place the next day, according to the German announcer, who ended by saying, "Diplomatic negotiations regarding an extension of this exchange and of the inclusion of further groups of German and British nationals are still in progress."[33] Following an oral inquiry by the American embassy, the German Foreign Office made it clear that the government of the Reich had agreed only "to a limited exchange," which meant that the Germans would return only the exact number received.[34]

Surprised by this last-minute reversal, the British reacted quickly and canceled the sailing of the ships. The sick and wounded Germans already on board were all disembarked and sent back to their hospitals and camps. On 7 October, Secretary of State for War Margesson claimed in the House of Commons that Berlin had been procrastinating and blamed the Germans for constantly raising new demands and not keeping their commitments. Britain, he said, had done its best to respond favorably to all German requests, including returning a first group of sixty German civilians with the sick and wounded POWs and accepting the German request in regard to POWs in a third country. Article 68 of the 1929 Geneva Convention, Margesson emphasized, stated that belligerents were required to send seriously ill and wounded POWs back to their own country without regard to rank or numbers. "Whilst His Majesty's Government were most reluctant to forgo any chance of bringing back to their homes the sick and severely wounded British POWs," Margesson concluded, "they were not prepared in view of the course of the negotiations in the last few days to risk being made the victims of a flagrant breach of faith on the part of the German Government, more especially as the bulk of the British sick and wounded would thereby clearly have lost all chance of repatriation."[35]

For Berlin, London's response, as reported on the BBC, was little more than an act of "propaganda." The German government had been the one to initiate negotiations on the repatriation of severely wounded POWs, which the British government was now simply obstructing through a "great public campaign" before any agreement as to the principles and modalities of the exchange had been reached.[36] Earlier BBC broadcasts that had hinted that it had made a "bad bargain" may also have influenced Berlin to change its mind.[37]

TOWARD A COMPROMISE

The Americans, who, still neutral, continued to serve as the channel of communication between the two warring sides, now stepped in and, as a way out of the deadlock, suggested that the British and German governments each put their conditions on the table as to how they wanted to proceed with the repatriation of POWs and civilians.[38]

The head of the PWD, Walter Roberts, suggested not renewing the negotiations because as long as the difference between the number of disabled POWs was so great, Britain's bargaining position would remain weak. He saw no choice, therefore, but to wait until Britain held more POWs. If the government was criticized for not taking up the matter again with Germany, "the answer must surely be that nothing short of compulsion will make Germany return our POWs, and that the only way in which we can help them is by pressing on with the war." Since the Germans had publicly committed themselves to a head-for-head exchange, he felt there was little chance that they would go back on that position. Moreover, even if Whitehall were prepared to yield to German blackmail, as he called it, and agree to such reciprocity, Britain would still not be able to get back all its wounded POWs. Of the 1,200 German civilian internees eligible for repatriation, only some 250 had indicated they were willing to be sent back to Germany. Even if this figure were doubled, a gap of more than 650 would remain.[39]

Other Foreign Office officials, however, were much more concerned about criticism that could be expected, if only on the part of relatives of non-repatriated prisoners, for not conducting any negotiations at all. The suggestion was thus to reaffirm Britain's adherence to the terms of the Geneva Convention and its willingness to proceed with the exchange of civilians in accordance with the agreement already reached. Eden adopted this latter recommendation and informed the Americans of London's readiness to resume negotiations on the basis of the 1929 convention, while Margesson told Parliament that the government wanted to continue negotiations with the Germans as quickly as possible.[40] A similar message was delivered to Switzerland's president, Marcel Pilet-Golaz, who had offered his good offices to mediate. Pilet-Golaz learned from a conversation with the counselor in the German legation, Dector Kordt, that German military circles had been angered by the last-minute intervention of Foreign Minister Joachim von Ribbentrop, as this had been responsible for the failure of the execution of the agreement.[41]

The German counteroffer was not long in coming. Forwarded to London on 24 November, it surprisingly went much beyond what had been suggested until then. The Germans now called for an exchange of POWs and civilian internees that was to take place "equally and in a uniform matter" and should include, in addition to severely wounded and sick POWs, all citizens of the Reich interned in the British Commonwealth and all British subjects interned in areas under German control who desired repatriation. Moreover, the Germans wanted the agreement also to apply "to men capable of bearing arms provided they make a declaration that they will not bear arms during the present war." Berlin also demanded that Germans who had been arrested in Persia by British and Soviet authorities and subsequently interned be part of the exchange. According to Berlin's calculation, when all these categories were taken together, each side would exchange about 15,000 individuals.[42] The offer came at a time when the Nazis were suffering great losses in the battle against the Soviet Union. The extremely severe winter of 1941–42 also cost the lives of many German soldiers. It may well have been these losses that prompted Berlin to seek the return of large numbers of POWs.[43]

British Foreign Office officials approached these new German proposals with suspicion.[44] In early January 1942, London told the Swiss government—which on the United States' entry into the war in December 1941 had become the protecting power—that it agreed in principle to the mutual repatriation but remained opposed to the release of men who were between the ages of eighteen and sixty and of German nationals apprehended in Persia or elsewhere. In addition, the British declined to take a stand regarding the figure of 15,000; they could "only entertain proposals for exchange made on the basis of categories of persons irrespective of numbers." As to the German suggestion that each side, as a general rule, not intern the nationals of the other party, Whitehall made it clear that it wanted to reserve the right to intern any person it thought could pose a threat to Britain's security.[45]

According to the data the British gave the Swiss at the beginning of February 1942 on the various categories of military personnel that both sides had accepted as being eligible for repatriation, there were 56 Germans in the United Kingdom and 1 in Ireland who qualified, compared with 1,144 members of the British Empire in Germany. It was pointed out that able-bodied German POWs were generally transferred to Canada and Australia. As for protected personnel, there were 39 Germans in the United Kingdom and between 20 and 30 in Canada; there was probably a considerable number in Egypt, but the exact figure could not yet be ascertained. The British further estimated the number of German civilians (men, women, and children) in the United Kingdom at 1,700 interned and 67,000 uninterned (men and women over sixteen), of whom 39,000 were women. The number of British Commonwealth civilians interned in Germany and German-occupied territory was estimated at 5,700, of whom 1,800 were women, children, and men not of military age. No figures were available on un-interned British Commonwealth citizens. The British agreed with the sug-gestion that the Swiss Foreign Ministry deal first with the sick and seriously wounded and protected personnel, as well as with the German plan that linked practical arrangements for repatriating POWs with those for the re-patriation of civilians.[46]

In June 1942, nearly five months after the British had signaled their willing-ness to continue negotiating with the Germans, Berlin finally authorized the Swiss to propose a tentative scheme to both sides. Besides their heavy losses in battle, another factor may have influenced the change in the Germans' stand: a first exchange of POWs had taken place between Britain and Italy in April 1942 in which the British had agreed to repatriate 344 sick and se-verely wounded Italian POWs and 575 protected personnel in return for 59 British sick and wounded soldiers and 69 British protected personnel.[47]

The Swiss subsequently tried to weave the interests of the warring sides together into one package deal. The Swiss proposal was based on the under-standing already reached between the two sides, namely, they were bound by the Geneva Convention of 27 July 1929 concerning the return of POWs of all ranks (Article 68), regardless of number, to their country if they were seriously sick or wounded and nominated for repatriation by the MMC. They had further agreed, in accordance with Article 12, that medical orderlies who had fallen into enemy hands would be sent back to their own country as soon as a route was available for their return. A third point agreed to was the repatriation of all civilians of the enemy power, even if interned, who confirmed they wanted to be repatriated. An exception would be made in two cases: those who were serving a jail sentence for an offense they had committed and those whose repatriation was considered harmful to the security of the detaining power. Able-bodied men between the ages of eighteen and sixty would be repatriated only if they gave a formal state-ment that they would not bear arms for the duration of the present war. In other words, the Swiss proposal officially linked the repatriation of sick and wounded POWs and medical orderlies, on the one hand, to the exchange of civilians, on the other.[48]

In its reaction, Britain's Combined Repatriation Committee, under the chairmanship of Major General Gepp, director of the DPW, decided that Britain should insist on a two-stage repatriation operation, not only because the Germans would have to be collected from different areas but also be-cause Britain should arrange matters in the first stage so as not to give the appearance of an exchange of equal numbers.[49] The committee also wanted each side to transfer its POWs to a neutral country in order "to insure ourselves as far as possible against German bad faith."[50] In their formal reply to the Swiss, the British rejected repatriation on a head-for-head basis but supported the inclusion of all civilians regardless of age or sex, so long as they expressed a wish to be repatriated.[51] This meant that the British accepted the principle of numerical equality de facto, though they continued to refuse to make an official linkage.

For their part, the Germans kept silent on the Swiss scheme throughout the winter of 1942–43 despite repeated reminders and representations made by the Swiss government.[52] Significantly, this lack of responsiveness coincided with the growing tension between the two sides over the issue of the shackling of POWs.[53] When the Germans finally presented their views of the Swiss plan of mid-June 1942, it was late March 1943. By that time the shackling crisis had subsided, at least from the German point of view, and negotiations between the British and the Italians had led to a second agreement on an exchange scheduled for 19 April 1943.[54] The Germans stuck to their demand for the return of all civilians regardless of age or sex, except those whose repatriation, as the Swiss proposal put it, was considered dangerous to the security of the detaining power. In the civilian category, too, were included civilian merchant seamen unless they had been on active military service when taken prisoner. The Germans further insisted that the exchange take place not only on the basis of numerical equality but even "without regard to the categories to which the different repatriated persons belong."[55] Here again the Germans' move had to do with their urgent need for extra troops, especially following the surrender at Stalingrad, on 31 January 1943, of Field Marshal Friedrich Paulus's Sixth Army.[56]

Foreign Secretary Eden wanted the War Cabinet to accept the German demands. In a memorandum circulated among the ministers he maintained that there was ample evidence to show that some of the severely sick and injured POWs in German hands were by now in a deplorable state, particularly blind or permanently crippled POWs and others who were suffering from TB. Eden advised his colleagues to agree that civilian men of military age also be included in the exchange, otherwise "the German Government will not make any agreement." As to the German demand regarding civilian merchant seamen, both Britain and Germany were holding them in POWs camps—if the question of their status was pursued any longer, it would inevitably involve protracted negotiations. Britain's aim, Eden concluded, "must be to bring matters now to a point at which either an agreement on the whole question is reached and put into effect, or negotiations break down."[57]

Eden was realistic enough to recognize that so long as the number of British POWs was larger than that of German POWs there was no possibility of Berlin's agreeing to any other basis of exchange. He put the option bluntly: "A choice must therefore be made between accepting this basis and waving our rights under the Conventions or leaving our sick and severely wounded indefinitely in Germany." He himself thought that Britain could compromise its position vis-à-vis the Geneva Convention, since the POWs' rights, as Eden put it, had "proved to be valueless" and Germany's attitude toward the convention "will be governed by self-interest and not by any action taken by us." Eden therefore favored accepting the German proposal that the exchange take place on the basis of numerical equality without regard to the categories to which the different repatriated persons belonged—with one exception: prompted by the views of the Admiralty, Britain could not agree that merchant seamen should count as civilians.

Eden's memo also informed the ministers that the total population of seriously wounded Germans and Axis medical personnel who were entitled to repatriation, and could be offered at once, numbered, respectively, 450 and between 800 and 900. In return, Britain could claim a corresponding number of its more seriously wounded. This would leave still in German hands approximately 1,600 severely injured British POWs, for whom Britain should propose transfer to Switzerland.[58] With ministers also troubled by questions in Parliament regarding the return of sick POWs, the general feeling at the War Cabinet's meeting of 19 April 1943 was that Whitehall should accept the offer of exchange on the basis of numerical equality.[59] Within a few weeks, however, Britain's position was to change dramatically.

AN ANGLO-AMERICAN PROPOSAL

It was the unconditional surrender of Axis forces in northeastern Tunisia and the capture of about 150,000 German soldiers in May 1943 that created the changed circumstances to which Eden had alluded.[60] Within days of the surrender, Berlin delivered to both the Americans and the British a proposal on repatriating wounded German POWs captured in Tunisia and appeared eager to conclude an agreement. This was also the first time the Germans had included the Americans in a POW exchange proposal. "In north Africa," the German note read, "there are a large number of wounded German soldiers of whom several thousands, according to the provisions of the Geneva Prisoner of War Convention, would appear to be entitled to repatria-tion." Worried by the difficulties involved in having a neutral medical com-mission rushed to North Africa to examine wounded POWs and to decide who qualified for repatriation, the Germans suggested that American and British medical corps personnel make the decision, with the proviso that a neutral medical commission conduct a later examination. Further, they sug-gested sending one German and three Italian hospital ships to collect the POWs. If the Americans and the British refused to allow these ships to enter ports in Africa, then the wounded should be evacuated in Allied hospital ships to a neutral exchange port, such as Barcelona. For its part, the German government was prepared to transfer to Barcelona all Allied POWs in Ger-man hands who were entitled to repatriation. Berlin added that it expected reciprocity from the British and Americans.[61]

Recognizing the significant opening the changing circumstances created, the Swiss immediately offered to dispatch physicians to check and choose the injured POWs who might be repatriated. In order to save time, the Swiss government suggested bringing the physicians, all Swiss, to Tunisia in Swiss airplanes.[62] The British were also aware that the German proposals offered an opportunity to recover all seriously sick and wounded British POWs, many of whom by now had been waiting nearly three years for this to happen. It would also relieve the North African Command of the burden of having to provide hospital accommodation and medical services for Ger-man POWs. Whitehall conditioned its agreement, however, on an assurance that if repatriation of all British and Americans captured by the Germans be-fore the end of the Tunisian campaign would be determined on the spot by German doctors, this would not mean that the POWs forfeited their right to a subsequent examination by the MMC. The British, in turn, were prepared to repatriate all eligible Germans held throughout the Commonwealth. The German proposal that Allied medical corps examine Germans in North Af-rica was acceptable. As to the port of exchange, the British considered Barcelona unsuitable and instead suggested Lisbon or, better, Gothenburg, as it was closer to Britain.[63]

Foreign Secretary Eden did not conceal from his American counterpart that Britain was eager to conclude an agreement. There were more than 3,000 disabled British POWs, many of whom had been in captivity since Dunkirk (May–June 1940), and, according to Eden, the "recovery of the blind and the permanently crippled cannot be carried any further until they leave Germany, [while] the reports of their mental and physical deteriora-tion which I have received are extremely bad." Up to now, Eden stated, the families of the POWs had shown great patience and understanding of the government's difficulties in arranging a mutual exchange, as the Germans had held many more POWs than the Allies. Now the imbalance was being redressed for the first time.[64] In order to coordinate positions, the British proposed that a small central Anglo-American organization be set up in London with authority to make rapid decisions when no major issues were involved. Eden thought that the Americans felt no urgency because, as he told Halifax, "in the main it is our wounded POWs who are suffering from this American delay."[65]

That Washington responded less quickly than the British would have wished was not because the Americans failed to give the German proposal serious consideration.[66] Major General Myron C. Cramer, the judge advocate general, told the U.S. Joint Chiefs of Staff (JCS) that United States was in principle bound to agree to the exchange requests of the German and Italian governments because of Article 68 of the Geneva Convention. Apart from the legal obligation, such a course seemed advisable because "it will relieve our Army of the feeding, guarding, medical care and transportation to the United States of a number of men, who, even if returned to their countries, will be of no military value to those countries during the rest of the present war."[67] The War Department strongly favored the mutual repatriation of seriously sick and injured POWs, regardless of their number, the operation in which they had fought, or their rank. Secretary of War Stimson agreed to coordinate replies and to set up a small central organization to this end. But, he thought, the organization should be based in Washington, "where coordination with the Combined Chiefs and similar combined groups will be most readily possible, and where there will be the least occasion for burdening the theater commanders with the problem." More problematic from the British point of view was that the War Department did not want to raise the question of repatriating protected personnel. Department officials felt that the introduction of the issue at this time might cause differences and delays, and, in fact, they were not certain that this "would be in the interest of the United States."[68]

British Foreign Office officials feared that the U.S. War Department had failed to grasp that Britain wanted protected personnel included because otherwise an agreement with the Germans was unlikely.[69] The German government would cooperate only when it was satisfied that it had a material advantage in doing so. Ambassador Halifax told Secretary of State Hull that the German offer to return to the Geneva Convention was "clearly prompted by the expectation that German repatriables in North Africa will amount to several thousands." In fact, there were no more than 400 sick and wounded Axis soldiers, including Italians, in that theater who were eligible for repatriation. Additionally, 602 Germans had already been passed by the MMC and were in various parts of the British Empire. The number of British POWs registered by the MCC as repatriable came to 2,952. This figure did not include American and British soldiers who had passed the most recent examination. The Allies, therefore, were to gain heavily in point of numbers.[70]

Halifax also reminded Hull that in October 1941, following the personal intervention of Ribbentrop, the Germans had reneged on an agreement with Britain and, ever since, had declined to negotiate except on the basis of numerical equality. London was worried that the German government "on learning the actual numbers may act as before." So that "everything possible should be done to obviate this risk," the British urged the Americans to reconsider the inclusion of the protected personnel, since the number in this category held captive by the Allies in North Africa probably exceeded that of those captured by the Germans.[71] Whitehall also did not favor the Americans' insistence on Washington instead of London as the headquarters of the proposed central organization.[72]

Again, the American response took time in arriving. "State Department, while professing eagerness for immediate agreement with enemy and prompt repatriation," Eden wrote to Halifax, "took more than a month to reply to our first suggestions and it is now [26 July 1943] three weeks since we made concrete suggestions in reply to their observations." In other words, ten weeks had passed since Germany's proposals had first been received, and no reply was yet forthcoming. Eden urged Halifax to press Hull again, stating that he was "most anxious to get [the POWs] back, especially the blind, before winter."[73]

A decision on the exchange issue rested with the JCS. Toward the end of July, Admiral William D. Leahy, Roosevelt's personal military representative and chief of staff to the commander in chief since July 1942, brought up the difficulties that the British had experienced up to now: "Should the United States join with the British in the negotiations for the exchange of POWs, we likewise might experience similar difficulties." General Joseph T. McNarney, the deputy army chief, saw considerable advantage if the United States proceeded unilaterally. He was in favor of collaborating with the British so long as they went along with the American proposals. The British provision to include protected personnel, for example, was beyond the scope of the Geneva Convention. Army chief of staff George C. Marshall, on the other hand, was not convinced it was advisable to deal with the Germans on a unilateral basis, as this ran counter to "our accepted idea of defeating the Germans as a British-American team." He also did not want to see a precedent established for other matters in regard to separate action.[74] In the end, however, it was decided that if the projected agreement would only work if it included protected personnel, "the United States must proceed with negotiations on a unilateral basis."[75]

Accordingly, the State Department conditioned concerted action by the Americans and the British on the acceptance by London of the following policy: "Seriously sick and seriously wounded shall be promptly mutually repatriated, regardless of the operation in which taken or of rank and number, as required by the terms of the Geneva Convention of 1929, without demands for safeguards or the inclusion of protected personnel in the projected agreement." The United States would join Britain in proposals for action on the repatriation of protected personnel at the earliest feasible date after the agreement for the repatriation of the sick and wounded had gone into operation. The Americans accepted the idea of a small central organization as proposed by the British, provided "the charter of the organization will not allow deviation from the basic policy set forth above but will limit the actions of the organization to the making of administrative arrangements for the carrying out of this policy." No mention was made of its location.[76]

The American stand, Roberts of the Foreign Office opined, "leaves us" with three alternatives. One: "We could act independently of the U.S.A. and reply to Germany offering to enlarge their proposal by adding doctors, medical orderlies etc. in accordance with what we all of us feel is most likely to lead to agreement with Germany with the least delay." That this alternative would greatly upset Washington was clear. Furthermore, as the larger number of German doctors and medical orderlies were in northwestern Africa, Britain needed the cooperation of General Dwight D. Eisenhower's headquarters. This would not be forthcoming without the approval of the U.S. government, whose permission would not be given until the badly wounded were actually on their way home.

The second alternative was to tell the Germans that Britain agreed to repatriating the severely injured, to communicate its plan for doing so, and to add that "the number of Germans badly wounded in North West Africa will be much smaller than was thought by the German Government but that as soon as the repatriation is under way we will make proposals for the mutual repatriation of the doctors, etc. of whom there is known to be a considerable number in North Africa in return for the repatriation of our doctors etc." This would also amount to acting independently of the United States. Since many of the German forces in North Africa were in American hands, Britain would in effect be committing the United States in advance without the Americans' consent. Britain could, of course, offer only those who were in British hands, but the objective of including protected personnel was to swell the numbers on the German side. The discrepancy with respect to severely injured was in the order of 3,000. To close the gap, London could add some 800 German protected personnel from Britain, Canada, and the Middle East—"not a sufficiently imposing figure," Roberts was forced to admit.

The third alternative was to accept the American view and reply to the Germans accordingly. By doing so, Roberts appreciated, "we shall please the Americans and avoid keeping the Germans waiting any longer for a reply." If, after learning of the numbers that Britain could offer, the German government decided to cancel the deal, Britain could then tell the Americans, "You cannot repatriate the badly wounded unless you offer at the same time to repatriate the doctors etc." If the Germans stuck to their proposal, Roberts wrote wistfully, "our troubles are over." He thought this alternative was the best course of action.[77]

Differences between the British and the Americans were solved in a meeting in Washington in August 1943. The American delegation, headed by General White, chief of G-1 (the personnel division) of the U.S. Army, acceded to the British request to include protected personnel in the current repatriation negotiations and to bring down Washington's assessment of the proportion of such personnel required in POW camps. It was also agreed that neither party would suggest in its replies any date for the proposed exchange, since there were still too many technical difficulties to be solved. The general feeling was that an earlier attempt by the British and Germans to exchange seriously sick and wounded POWs had been unsuccessful in part because a time limit had been set. The American delegation also agreed that the small central organization the British had proposed would be established in London to facilitate the completion of the necessary administrative arrangements.[78]

Almost three months passed from the moment the Germans had first proposed the repatriation of seriously sick and wounded POWs until both the British and the Americans were finally set to respond. The British reaffirmed their general attitude on the issue and agreed to the immediate repatriation of eligible German POWs via Axis ships to sail from a northwestern African port to an Axis-controlled port in the Mediterranean.[79] The British spoke of 171 sick and wounded German POWs who would be repatriated from the United Kingdom and 285 from the Middle East. The latter figure, it was pointed out, did not include the sick and wounded from northwestern Africa. The Germans were asked to convey information as to the approximate numbers of British and American seriously ill and wounded who would be sent to Izmir and Gothenburg, respectively. Further, the British were ready to repatriate on a reciprocal basis all surplus German protected personnel held in countries of the British Commonwealth. They also said that they had informed Washington of their agreement to the repatriation of all surplus German protected personnel in northwestern Africa.

To ensure adequate medical and spiritual care of German POWs, as they put it, the British suggested the release of 10 protected personnel—2 medical officers, 1 dental officer, 1 chaplain, and 6 medical orderlies—for every 1,000 POWs held, instead of 8 per 1,000 as proposed by the Germans. The number of surplus German protected personnel who would be repatriated according to the new proposal amounted to 684: 184 from the United Kingdom and approximately 500 from the Middle East. This latter figure, the British pointed out, did not include those from northwestern Africa, whose numbers would be considerable.[80]

The American note differed from the British mainly in regard to protected personnel. Although the Americans expressed a willingness for mutual and simultaneous repatriation using the same means to calculate surplus German and American protected personnel, the United States made it clear that its suggestion "is not a condition upon or a qualification of its agreement for the immediate repatriation of seriously sick and seriously wounded POWs of war."[81]

THE FIRST EXCHANGES

From here on matters proceeded smoothly. The Germans agreed both to include protected personnel in the exchange of seriously wounded and sick POWs and to increase from eight to ten the number of protected personnel per 1,000 POWs. As American POWs had not so far been brought before the MMC, they would be examined by German physicians until such time as the MMC could act. The Germans furthermore asked for assurance that seriously wounded and sick Germans in North Africa who were qualified for repatriation would be included in the exchange without exception even if they were not in British or U.S. custody. September 1943 was regarded as a suitable date for the exchange.[82]

This time, the Americans were quick to respond. Secretary of State Hull asked the Swiss to inform the Germans that his government was compiling a list of the German POWs and protected personnel held by U.S. armed forces in the United States and North Africa and eligible for repatriation. The Germans were also assured that German POWs and protected personnel in North Africa eligible for repatriation would include individuals not held by British or American authorities but captured by the Free French. Washington expected to receive a similar list of American POWs and protected personnel whom the German government considered eligible for repatriation.[83]

Although an agreement on exchange of POWs had been reached in principle, neither the British nor the Americans had any official information regarding the numbers involved. According to a British estimate, a total of 4,750 British and Americans were to be repatriated at Gothenburg, of them 2,750 sick and wounded and 2,000 protected personnel. In Izmir, the number of sick and wounded and protected personnel was estimated to total 1,500.[84] Toward the end of September, the British informed the Germans through the Swiss that the combined total of German repatriables would amount to 5,332.[85] For their part, the Germans planned to deliver via Gothenburg 3,053 British, 17 Americans, and 1,290 British medical personnel, a total of 4,360, which included about 50 civilians and 160 seamen; the number of British internees to be repatriated via Barcelona came to 456 sick and wounded POWs and 604 protected personnel, or 1,060 in all.[86]

After learning that no more than 17 Americans were to be repatriated, the War Department considered bringing this up but decided in the end not to approach the Germans on the matter. The Germans held only about 8,000 Americans captive, but there were 115,000 German POWs in the United States alone; thus, compared with the total number of prisoners held by each side, the proportion of Americans involved in the exchange operation was actually higher than that of Germans being returned by the United States. War Department officials also pointed out that the Americans in German hands were for the most part either downed airmen or troops that had been captured at the Kasserine Pass in North Africa. Since the latter had been in a very forward position, the proportion of protected personnel among them was certain to have been very low. Furthermore, no protected personnel accompanied airplane crews; it was believed that when planes were shot down, their occupants either parachuted out and landed in comparatively good condition or were killed. The department therefore accepted that, as low as it was, the German figure for American repatriables was "an honest one." Finally, it concluded that the establishment of the principle of the exchange of sick and wounded POWs and the process that had been worked out—in addition to the safeguard for future exchanges that was provided by the MMC—were "of such value that it is better not to risk the success of the current operation by engaging in dispute over numbers."[87]

The British, too, were to face a dilemma. The repatriation had begun in Gothenburg, according to plan. During the final stage of the operation, however, the British learned that the actual number of POWs who would be repatriated was smaller—by 185 men—than the number the Germans had promised to return. In London, the Combined Repatriation Committee debated whether to defer the sailings of the German POWs until the Germans had given a satisfactory explanation for the missing number. The committee chairman, Major General Gepp, warned against becoming caught in a position from which Britain could not back away, as might occur if the ships were to be held up pending a satisfactory explanation and the Germans then failed to provide one. If the sailings were suspended indefinitely, the Dominion repatriables assigned to Barcelona would remain in enemy hands as hostages for the Gothenburg party, he pointed out, adding that it "would be unfortunate if British, Canadians, and Americans were saved at the expense of the other Dominions." In the end, it was decided to ask the Germans for an explanation but not to hold up the sailings.[88] The deal remained in force.

The first exchange of POWs between the Allies and Germany took place at Gothenburg between 17 and 21 October and at Barcelona on 27 October. It saw the return of 1,426 seriously sick and wounded German POWs and 4,344 protected personnel; in turn, the Germans repatriated 3,945 sick and wounded Allied POWs (14 of whom were Americans) and 1,269 protected personnel.[89] When the operation was under way, Minister of State Richard Law, responding to a question in the House of Commons, stated that "the exchange has been conducted under the Geneva Convention without respect to the number of persons involved. The fact that the numbers [are] approximate is due to the fact that we and the Americans together have more German POWs than they have of ours." This statement did not wholly reflect the spirit of the negotiations with the Germans. Law himself indirectly hinted at the true circumstances when he stated that it was not "until after the end of the Tunisian campaign that proposals were received from the German Government which led to the present agreement."[90] Important for Whitehall was to highlight the principle that all wounded and sick POWs should be repatriated, regardless of numbers.

Finally, two telling features stand out in this first exchange. One is the fact that the negotiations and the exchange itself were carried through to their successful conclusion at a time when the Allies were conducting devastating air raids on German cities.[91] The second is that among the POWs the British returned were sixty Palestinian Jews serving in the British army.[92] In other words, when its own immediate interests were at stake, Nazi Germany proved capable of letting pragmatic reasons override ideological dictates. And it is the principle of reciprocity that emerges each time as the decisive factor: because Berlin was keen on retrieving as many of its POWs in British and American hands as possible, the Germans made sure they were seen to adhere to the Geneva Convention to secure their POWs' protection in Allied hands. One might even go further and conclude that the same reasoning was behind the fact that, on the whole, British and American Jewish POWs were treated by the Nazis no differently than their non-Jewish peers and like them survived captivity.[93]

THE SECOND BARCELONA EXCHANGE

At the beginning of November 1943, the German government assured the Swiss that the "British and American repatriables who, for technical reasons, were not repatriated during the recently effected exchange of seriously wounded will, in any case, be given priority in the next exchange of seriously wounded."[94] The British, meanwhile, had checked the lists of sick and wounded British POWs and protected personnel who had returned from Germany and had found that in fact 283 British POWs and protected personnel scheduled for repatriation via Gothenburg were still in German captivity. Moreover, a comparison with the lists compiled by the MMC up to its final examinations in May–June 1943 had shown that another 140 British POWs had not been repatriated. A further 55 were reported to have died in captivity. In addition, the transfer of 115 seriously sick and injured British POWs approved by the MMC in Italy for repatriation via Lisbon had been blocked by the German authorities.

The British now notified the Germans of these findings and, simply in order to save time, suggested for inclusion in the next exchange all those POWs who had been recommended for repatriation by doctors of the detaining power but who had not appeared before the MMC. On the other hand, men who had been rejected by the doctors of the detaining power would not be prevented from appearing for an MMC examination as soon as possible. The Germans were reminded that they themselves had proposed a procedure of this kind on a previous occasion. The British also expressed concern that a considerable number of protected personnel who had been in captivity for more than three years were still being retained by the German government. In the end, the British proposed that future exchanges be executed "with all feasible frequency in order that eligible prisoners of war and protected personnel whom it has not been possible to include in prior repatriation operations shall be returned in an early subsequent one."[95]

The Americans, too, did not receive all the seriously sick and injured POWs they had been expecting; seven of the seventeen American officers and men whose names appeared on the nominal roll that the German government had submitted were missing. Here again, the German government attributed the nondelivery to "technical reasons" and said it would give these men priority in the next repatriation movement. Washington was particularly embarrassed because these seven POWs had been passed by an MMC examination and their families had been told they would be coming home.[96] At the same time, twelve of the fourteen POWs actually repatriated had apparently been gathered together in a rather hurried fashion and had never gone before the MMC.[97]

Nevertheless, Washington regarded the first exchange of POWs a success to the extent that it expected further exchanges to take place in the near future. Secretary of War Stimson even suggested replacing the procedure of special negotiations for each exchange with a regular schedule of monthly exchanges covered by an overall agreement between the United States and the British Commonwealth, on the one hand, and Germany, on the other. To this end, a neutral ship was to be chartered to continuously ply—under safe-conduct—a route between the United States, Canada, the United Kingdom, Germany, and a European port. Once prisoners had been passed for repatriation by MMCs or German doctors, they were to be transferred at once to the selected ports of embarkation in order to avoid last-minute delays, since continental transportation difficulties were likely to grow worse.[98]

Stimson's ideas served as a basis for discussions among both State Department and Foreign Office officials. Barcelona was proposed as the most suitable exchange port, as mines had made the North Sea and Baltic Sea too dangerous. According to the American plan, American and British POWs awaiting exchange would be placed under the supervision of Spanish authorities, but the two Allies had the responsibility of furnishing the POWs with the necessary supplies. The Americans thought that the Germans should bear the cost of all land transport, while that of sea transport could be borne by the United States, the United Kingdom, and interested Dominions in equal shares. As the situation in Germany was deteriorating, reaching an agreement with the Germans was becoming urgent not only in order to recover personnel but also because it could help safeguard as far as possible against any hardening in the enemy's attitude toward POWs—the Allies were at this time stepping up their bombing campaigns on German cities. The War Department proposed discussing the matter directly with the Germans in Bern, as had been done in regard to the treatment of POWs toward the end of World War I.[99]

London supported the idea of regular exchanges at comparatively short intervals, though it was skeptical of monthly exchanges for technical reasons—a round trip made by a neutral ship could not be completed in less than eight weeks; more likely, three months were needed. Time also had to be allowed for tours by MMCs or doctors of the detaining powers themselves. For strategic reasons, the Admiralty preferred not to indicate to Germany which European port would be the most suitable for exchange. London strongly disliked the suggestion of direct discussions with the Germans in Bern or elsewhere for fear that "a meeting would most certainly give rise to every kind of rumour and suggestion about peace negotiations of which the Germans would take full advantage."[100] For Secretary of War Stimson, however, such a meeting "might well become a necessary step, particularly if the present negotiations for repatriation movements break down."[101]

Meanwhile, in early February 1944, the State Department informed the Foreign Office that arrangements had been made for an exchange of German and American officials to take place in Lisbon toward the end of the month. The Americans wanted to know whether the British would object if the United States suggested to the Germans that both sides also include in that exchange a number of sick and injured POWs eligible for repatriation. The Americans explained this by saying that it feared strong criticism by the public if it "missed completely this opportunity of repatriating some sick and wounded POWs, especially as for valid reasons, there will be far more Germans than Americans in this exchange and [the] ship will be comparatively empty on [the] homeward voyage."[102]

London recognized that it could not object to the American proposal but wondered why "it has been made at a time when we have been concerting with the United States Government a joint repatriation operation on a larger scale." If between 80 and 100 Germans were repatriated, the Foreign Office maintained, "the projected joint operation will inevitably be less attractive to the German Government whose attention may well be diverted from the study of the proposals which we had assumed would be made to them at an early date." The British especially regretted that the U.S. proposal spoke of an exchange on the basis of equal numbers even though Britain had consistently maintained that the repatriation of sick and wounded should be on the basis of Article 68 of the Geneva Convention, meaning without regard to rank or numbers.[103]

The Americans were not, in fact, led by any equal-numbers principle, and they told the Germans that the United States adhered firmly to the basic principle established by Geneva Convention. Washington expected, nevertheless, that the Germans would deliver to Lisbon all seriously sick and wounded whose eligibility for repatriation had already been determined. This included the seven American POWs who had been missing in the October 1943 exchange.[104]

Washington's proposal suited the Germans, as there were only about twenty American POWs who had been examined by the MMC and found eligible for repatriation. Although disappointed that so few American POWs in German custody had so far been singled out, the Americans did not renege on their proposal and told the Germans that all sick and wounded POWs who at the time of embarkation had been certified for repatriation would be returned.[105] Once again, the Germans would be receiving many more of their people. Whereas the American party totaled 307, consisting of 36 disabled POWs and the rest officials and other noncombatants, the German group numbered 917, made up of 131 disabled POWs (14 from Canada), 18 Vichy officials, and the rest German officials and other projected personnel.[106]

Simultaneous with American and German contacts over the exchange of officials, the British government, also acting on behalf of the other governments of the Commonwealth, asked the Swiss to forward to Berlin a message suggesting that, subject to the approval of the Portuguese government, another exchange of sick and wounded POWs take place in Lisbon on 12 April 1944. A safe-conduct passage would be arranged for a neutral ship, which would be employed by the Allies to transport to Lisbon the reported sick and wounded German POWs in custody in the United States, Canada, the United Kingdom, and northwestern Africa, including those transferred from Australia and the Middle East, and to return with American and British Commonwealth POWs delivered to Lisbon by the Germans. Similar exchanges, the British proposal continued, "shall occur without further negotiations at regular intervals of three months beginning with three months from the date of the exchange proposed above." Carrying out the present exchange on 12 April was not, it was made clear, conditional on acceptance of the idea of a regular series of exchanges.[107] The Germans agreed to one further exchange from 2 May onward but declined to reach an agreement concerning future exchanges.[108]

Differences of opinion now arose between the Americans and the British over the date of the exchange. The Americans wanted to defer the operation not just until after the MMC had completed its forthcoming tour of POW camps in Germany but for as long as it would take to transport POWs who had been approved for repatriation to the point or points of exchange. The MMC tour would take up both April and May. Foreign Secretary Eden opposed any postponement, arguing that the longer the delay the greater the disorganization in Germany and the risk of repatriables being left behind. In his opinion, "expectation of 100% return is illusory." It was better "to get most back now than none for a long time." Humanitarian considerations, reinforced by strong public opinion, the foreign secretary added, required that British Commonwealth repatriables who had been left behind in the last exchange in October 1943 be repatriated. London recognized that the United States was willing to postpone the operation because no more than thirty Americans were likely to be ready for repatriation by the beginning of May.[109] The British, however, were to give in.

Both Washington and Whitehall agreed that, because of military considerations, Gothenburg was out of the question as a place of exchange. Still, the Germans were not to be told of this, and discussions had to continue before gradually eliminating this port as an alternative. Since a considerable proportion of German repatriables were already assembled in northwestern Africa, it would be much more convenient "if those POWs could be exchanged in that area and in appreciation of the suggestion of the German Government that Lisbon involves an unnecessary long railway journey [the United States and Britain] suggest Barcelona as an alternative."[110] The Western Allies were concerned that the Germans "may be seeking a hint as to our future military intentions and plans" in their counterproposal with respect to the date and place of the exchange—preparations for the invasion of France, Operation Overlord, were at their peak.[111]

On 13 April, both the British Foreign Office and the U.S. State Department presented the Swiss with similar communications for transmission to Berlin the next day. Time pressure was now a major factor: the earliest date the Americans and the British were suggesting for the start of the exchange was 17 May; they had to give Germany notification of a safe passage route two weeks before the ship with German POWs was to leave New York, however, and 14 April was the last possible date for doing so if the ship was to arrive at Lisbon by 17 May. Following their plan, the Americans and British proposed Barcelona as the port of exchange.[112] The Germans accepted the proposal and notified the British and the Americans that the German forces would be ordered not to attack the *Gripsholm*, which the U.S. government had chartered for the purpose, on its planned journey from New York to the exchange port and back. This guarantee of safe-conduct was also given in the name of Germany's allies. During the ship's voyage within the Mediterranean, the Germans wanted the *Gripsholm*'s captain to announce his position every four hours, not once a day as had been proposed.[113]

Shortly after the agreement had been reached in principle, serious discord arose over the numbers of repatriables.[114] The British were adamant that Berlin stick to its promise to include in the next operation all those who for technical reasons had been left behind in the October 1943 exchange. In turn, the British assured Berlin that all members of the German armed forces who were eligible for repatriation, irrespective of nationality, would be included in the projected exchange.[115] Meanwhile, the British learned that the Germans did not intend to include in the coming exchange those POWs whose repatriation had been recommended by the MMC in its recent April tour because the lists for the exchange had already been established and could not be modified at such short notice.[116] The Foreign Office asked the Swiss to make urgent and strong protestations against this decision and to point out that in the October 1943 repatriation operation the number of Germans repatriated had exceeded by more than 500 the number of British; accordingly, "there can be no possible justification for reducing the number of British to be sent home in the present exchange."[117]

Washington was also upset when it learned that the list of Americans to be repatriated contained only eighteen names and that the Germans claimed it was impossible to include POWs who had been examined during the April 1944 tour of the MMC. A message from the German government dated 11 May assured the U.S. government that approximately 100 American POWs would be found eligible for repatriation on the basis of examinations by German camp doctors; however, no assurance was given that these POWs would in fact be ready for the May 1944 exchange.[118]

Apprehensive that the Germans might fail to get the POWs to Barcelona by 17 May, the Americans again wanted to delay the proposed exchange. Washington recognized that the great majority of repatriates would be British and that London might not welcome the idea of a further delay. Still, the Americans were determined to gain several days. They told the British that if nothing were to be done to postpone the exchange, "the United States Government would be very strongly criticised by the public for not taking obvious precautions to ensure the repatriation of Americans known to be eligible and ready." London was assured that if a week's delay proved insufficient, the Americans would not suggest postponement but would go on with the operation.[119]

By now there were overriding strategic reasons for the British to strongly oppose any delay. In coordination with General Eisenhower, General Henry Maitland Wilson, the commander in chief of the British forces in the Mediterranean, was carrying out an operation intended to simulate an attack on the southern coast of France. It was of paramount importance, therefore, that the western Mediterranean be kept clear. Any deferral of the exchange after 17 May, the British Joint Staff Mission (JSM) maintained, "would entail our POWs being detained at Marseilles in the target area, thereby preventing our carrying out preliminary air bombardment." In that case, the Germans were likely "to invent excuses for postponement in the hopes of studying our reactions and gaining information as to our intentions."[120]

Exchanging POWs involved complicated military arrangements, especially as D-Day was now only a few weeks away. By early May, the Western Allies still did not know whether the British and American repatriables would be taken directly by rail to Barcelona or to a port in German-occupied territory, such as Marseilles, and then transferred by ship to Barcelona. In either case, they would have to travel a considerable distance through France. The Swiss were asked to obtain as soon as possible a German decision as to whether ships would be used for part of the journey as well as the German train schedule for the POWs, including dates of the trains' departure, times, and routes.[121]

The British Chiefs of Staff Committee (COS) warned both Generals Eisenhower and Wilson that trains conveying these repatriables might risk being bombed during their passage through enemy-occupied territory—the Germans would not agree to have these trains carry any lights. Under the circumstances, the two generals were asked to take all possible precautions to ensure the safe passage of trains and ships conveying these repatriables without jeopardizing "Overlord."[122] On 12 May, five days before the scheduled date of exchange, the German government informed the British and the Americans that the repatriated POWs would be transported to Marseilles by four trains. Respective starting points would be Lammsdorf, Oflag IV B (Mühlberg), Danzig, and Posen. All four trains were to bypass Berlin and to reach Marseilles no later than the evening of 15 May and would return by the same routes. As assumed, the Germans stated that no trains would carry lights after nightfall.[123]

In the exchange that took place in Barcelona between 17 and 19 May, the Germans received 801 of their POWs and the Allies 1,001, of whom 65 were Americans and the remainder, with a dozen exceptions, British Commonwealth. Neither the Americans nor the British were satisfied with the outcome. The Americans were disappointed, as they had estimated the number of sick and wounded who had been passed by the MMC to be at least 340. The British found that 161 British personnel listed by the Germans in the past had still not been repatriated.[124]

THE SECOND GOTHENBURG EXCHANGE

On 9 June, three days after D-Day, the U.S. War Department suggested asking the Germans to send a ship to a port of their choice and at a date they could set to pick up the repatriables they had failed to deliver in earlier exchanges. The department realized that the proposal would have to be made in terms that would enable Washington and London to reject a port that was unacceptable for strategic reasons. The State Department thought that the Germans would inevitably turn down such an approach but that, if they did not, it would be necessary to offer to return all Germans who would prove eligible when the time came.[125] In London, the Combined Repatriation Committee wanted the Western powers to propose another exchange despite the possibility that it would not be completed because of military operations. The Supreme Headquarters of the Allied Expeditionary Force supported the committee's suggestion. According to information received in mid-May from Lieutenant Colonel Albert D'Erlach, the chairman of the MMC in Germany, the committee had passed for repatriation 2,298 of the 3,542 prisoners the MMC had examined in its April–May tour in Germany.[126]

Following consultations at the beginning of July 1944 with representatives of the British and Canadian embassies in Washington and of the British Army Staff and the U.S. State and War departments, it was agreed to propose another exchange to the Germans. The latter were to be told that the MMC had just completed its tour of POW camps in the United States and had qualified about 125 German POWs for direct repatriation or hospitalization in a neutral country. In addition, there were another 37 German POWs who had become eligible since the last repatriation. The United States was prepared to return all these POWs in exchange for the approximately 250 American POWs in German custody whom the MMC had found eligible prior to the Barcelona exchange. September 1 was suggested as the date for the proposed exchange.[127] Washington's decision to state the number of eligible German repatriables at the outset was made principally to avoid delay: past experience showed that the Germans would not complete the negotiations until they had received the list of relevant names.[128]

This time it was the British who insisted on delaying the exchange. Troubled by the fact that the Germans were holding 2,000 repatriable British POWs whereas the British had only approximately 100 Germans, London wanted to see whether it could enlarge that number. The British needed more time in order to examine German POWs captured in Normandy since D-Day.[129] Thus Berlin received a general, nonbinding statement to the effect that "substantial numbers of German prisoners of war will be available for exchange."[130] War Office officials estimated that a good proportion of the 2,539 wounded German POWs who had been evacuated up to 4 July from both the British and American sectors of Normandy were likely to be passed by the MMC.[131]

The Americans were very much against Britain's idea of examining German POWs captured in Normandy to secure eligibles for repatriation. The War Department even decided that "for the present it will not have any more USA owned German PWS qualified for repatriation by mixed Medical commission except on basis of reciprocal action by Germany." Moreover, the War Department had always been unhappy with the German policy of allowing the MMC only two tours a year in Germany, and it now hoped to induce the Germans to be more forthcoming in qualifying American POWs for repatriation.[132] As things stood, until the beginning of July 1944, the MMC had passed only 250 Americans for repatriation, compared with 2,000 Brits.[133]

The Americans' displeasure was well founded. According to a statement given by Major W. E. Tucker, Royal Army Medical Corps, who had spent three and one-half years in POW camps and hospitals in Poland and Germany as an orthopedic specialist and had been repatriated in October 1943, American POWs were being neglected by the MMC. Tucker said that while in Germany he had come into contact with a number of American POWs who, when they learned that he was to return to England, urged him to plead before the American military authorities in England for the official establishment of an MMC in Germany specifically for Americans. Tucker reported that the one MMC in Germany consisted of two Swiss and one German, "and it is generally accepted that such Commission is intended to present only the cases of British troops, including colonials and dominion troops." The British officer maintained that at the hospital at Obermassfeld where he had served, the Germans had given orders that no American case was to be presented as serious even though there were, at the very least, a dozen U.S. soldiers at this hospital who were suitable for repatriation. At the last meeting in a hospital that Tucker attended, two days before he was evacuated, there was some discussion as to whether Americans should appear before the MMC. A few Americans had been seen to receive certificates of eligibility for repatriation, and the Germans appeared to select at random six cases from his hospital and more from other hospitals so as to make up a total of seventeen Americans who were to be returned. Tucker thought that this was a token number, intended as a political gesture. Of the six selected at Obermassfeld, five were repatriated, whereas the sixth, an officer whose right arm, amputated at the shoulder girdle, had become badly abscessed, was turned down at the last moment because, Tucker believed, the Germans had found out this pilot had a special expertise. The British officer summed up his report with the observation that "the morale of American POWs of war would be improved, if there were a Mixed Medical Commission for Americans, or if the existing Commission were authorized by agreement to handle the cases of American as well as of British troops."[134]

The Americans blamed both the Germans and the Swiss for the situation. They now accused Lieutenant Colonel D'Erlach, the Swiss member of the MMC in Germany, of actually restricting tours of the MMC to only two a year, thereby allowing the Germans, at the time of both the October 1943 and the May 1944 exchanges, to use the excuse that certain men had not been passed by the commission in time to be included in the exchange. War Department officials wanted to notify the Swiss that D'Erlach's services were no longer required, but they accepted the State Department's proposal of making one further attempt to induce him to follow Washington's directions.[135] The Swiss, however, thought that the Americans also shared responsibility for the fact that so few Americans had been repatriated— whereas the British knew far more about the procedure of the MMC and, besides keeping records of the decisions, always had their cases very carefully prepared, the Americans knew very little and had presented very few POWs for examination by the MMC.[136]

On 21 July 1944, the German government agreed to another exchange and appeared ready to repatriate all British and Americans, officers included, in German custody who had so far been declared eligible for repatriation by the MMC. This group, the Germans pointed out, contained approximately 250 American POWs. The Germans expected the Americans to repatriate approximately 400 German medical officers, NCOs, and en-listed personnel who were considered in excess (i.e., of the number the other side was allowed to retain) in American POW camps in North Africa at the end of February 1944 and 700 German sanitary servicemen who were in excess in North America. The Germans also wanted 800 seriously wounded POWs who had been left behind in Italy, 150 of them in civilian hospitals in Rome and 650 in Civita Castellana. Further, Berlin expected that seriously wounded and excess protected personnel in camps in North Africa would also be repatriated even if they were not under immediate British or Ameri-can control. In the May 1944 exchange, the Germans maintained, only those repatriables who were under medical treatment near Oran had been given consideration, while a large number of men eligible for repatriation re-mained in other hospitals and camps. Early September was regarded as a reasonable date for the exchange, but the Germans avoided mentioning a specific place to effect the exchange and reserved the right to propose a location.[137]

The Allied invasion of Normandy, on 6 June 1944, appears not to have affected the negotiations on exchanging seriously wounded POWs in any significant way. One reason for this was that it was important for Berlin to retrieve as many medical personnel as possible so as to integrate them into an army that was suffering critical shortages. Another reason was the on-going concern in London and Washington for the fate of their wounded POWs combined with pressure from relatives of the POWs as well as the general public to keep the negotiations going.

Meanwhile, problems arose as to the number of protected German per-sonnel held in the United States. The total number of individuals in all ranks and categories claiming to be protected personnel was 2,989. The United States was entitled to hold 1,650 protected personnel, consisting of 330 medical doctors, 165 dentists, 165 chaplains, and 990 enlisted auxil-iaries. Actual claimants to such status amounted to 221 medical officers, 23 dental officers, and 23 chaplains. The remaining 2,722 were enlisted personnel who were claiming protected status for themselves but of whom only 395 had a genuine claim. Washington thought of asking the Germans for sample certificates that would enable status verification and to help determine who really were protected personnel. In the past, the United States had twice asked Germany for samples of authentic certificates, both times to no avail.[138]

After conferring with British and Canadian representatives in Washington, the State Department told the Germans that the U.S. government would repatriate 356 seriously sick and wounded German POWs. The Germans were asked to add to the approximately 250 existing repatriable American POWs any U.S. POWs whom German medical authorities could approve for repatriation in time for the exchange. As for the German request to include in this exchange the 800 wounded Germans left behind in Italy, the Americans explained that these POWs had been absorbed into U.S. and British POW camp and hospital systems and that therefore it was impossible to determine to which extent they were already included among those to be repatriated. The Americans also failed to give a definite response to Berlin's desire for the return of German POWs held by the French in North Africa. Beyond noting that the U.S. government was willing to put its facilities in North Africa at the service of the French authorities, the Americans were careful not to make any commitments, saying that they assumed no responsibility in this respect.

Berlin was also informed that the United States intended to use the *Gripsholm* to transport German repatriables from North America and the United Kingdom to Gothenburg, from where it was to return with Allied repatriates. The Germans were asked to notify the United States if they contemplated the use of a ship or ships to transport the repatriates to and from the exchange port, in which case Washington wanted to know fourteen days ahead what the characteristics of the vessels were, the approximate date of their departures and arrivals, and which routes they would follow so as to assure their safe passage.[139]

The British further confirmed that all seriously ill and wounded German POWs who were entitled to be repatriated would be included in this exchange, as would surplus protected personnel and, as on previous occasions, all merchant seamen passed by the MMC. Similar categories of German POWs in French custody in North Africa would also be included. The British blamed the German government for not living up to its agreement to take into account length of captivity as one of the factors when selecting protected personnel to be sent home. They also accused Germany of discriminating against Indian POWs—of the approximately 13,000 Indian POWs in German hands, only 94 had been repatriated in the October 1943 exchange and 34 in May 1944. Finally, the Germans were called on to adhere to the agreement to furnish complete lists of names showing the results of MMC tours no later than one month after the completion of a tour. The list of those who had passed the German MMC tour in October 1943 had been received in July 1944; no list had been received for May 1944.[140]

The German government accepted in mid-August the Anglo-U.S. proposals for a combined mutual exchange of seriously wounded and sick soldiers and excess medical orderlies to take place at Gothenburg on 8 September 1944 and for a simultaneous exchange of approximately 500 German civilians from Britain against a corresponding number of British civilians. Berlin, though, did not conceal its strong dissatisfaction with the number of protected personnel the United States intended to repatriate: "It must be observed that after effecting the Göteborg exchange the number of repatriated Americans will attain one and one half percent of total American POWs in German hands while United States Government with a total of 660 repatriated seriously sick and seriously wounded will represent only a small fraction of one percent to total number of German POWs in American custody." No American medical orderly had been included in the exchange transport, the Germans continued, because there were fewer than 200 members of such personnel in German hands; as this proportion was less than 10 in 1,000, all could be retained.[141]

While explaining their failure to return American medical orderlies, the Germans stated their own determination to receive in the September exchange 1,100 medical orderlies—700 from custody in the United States and 400 in North Africa—not just the 100 the Americans had in mind. The German government was "not prepared to accept American proposal that excess sanitary personnel in so far as they are not now repatriated be included in a future exchange."[142] This German communication, however, came too late. On the day it arrived in Washington, 23 August, the *Gripsholm* had already set sail. Hull now asked the Swiss to tell the Germans that since no reference to surplus protected personnel in American custody had previously been made, the U.S. government had proceeded with the repatriation on the assumption that Berlin fully understood the situation and comprehended the difficulties encountered by the American authorities in identifying German protected personnel. He added that an examination of those claiming protected status was in progress, based on the official identification documents the German government had furnished at the end of July, and reiterated "that protected personnel which the present survey may reveal in excess of the number this Government is permitted to retain, will be returned as soon as possible."[143]

With the date for the proposed exchange approaching, the Germans had informed neither the British nor the Americans as yet of the number of POWs and protected personnel they would repatriate. Apprehension in London increased when Whitehall learned via the Swedish Red Cross that Berlin expected a total of 1,500 to be exchanged in each direction. The British had counted on the return of more than 2,000 sick and wounded British and American POWs as well as an undetermined number of protected personnel and 575 civilians. They had based this figure on the report of the chairman of the MMC in Germany following the commission's tours in May 1944. They now wanted to know whether the information given out by the German legation in Stockholm had indeed been authorized by the German government,[144] while the State Department through its legation in Stockholm informed Count Folk Bernadotte, deputy head of the Swedish Red Cross, that the United States and Britain expected to receive at Gothenburg approximately 2,500 sick and wounded and protected personnel and about 500 civilians.[145]

There was good reason for the British and Americans to be anxious at this point: toward the end of August 1944, the Germans alleged that the MMC examinations of German wounded POWs had applied more stringent criteria than those of Allied POWs. There was a clear disparity between the percentages passed for repatriation, they claimed: only 0.3 percent of all German POWs in Allied hands versus 3 percent of all Allied POWs in German captivity. A German official of the Ministry of Foreign Affairs told the Swiss that following the September 1944 exchange the German government would bring up as a matter of principle the question of why, with regard to the total number of POWs, the proportion of German repatriables was smaller than that of Allied repatriables.[146] Clifford Norton, the British minister in Bern, thought he detected a "new tendency in the German Government circles to hark back to the old insistence on the approximate equality of numbers." The Germans were apparently waiting to learn how many German POWs would be repatriated in the September exchange "before making to the Swiss any communication which would bind the German Government to repatriate the given persons or groups."[147]

When the Combined Repatriation Committee debated the German complaints, its chairman, Major General Gepp, asked his colleagues to decide whether Britain and the United States should inform the Germans that they would both halt the exchange if Berlin was not prepared to repatriate all 2,200 to 2,300 Allied POWs announced to be eligible for repatriation. If they did so, Gepp thought that the Germans might then think it better to carry out the exchange as already agreed on in order to get their own men back. Brigadier General Edward C. Betts of the European Theater of Operations, U.S. Army, countered that if Britain and the United States refused to continue the negotiations "we might lose the 1,500 men that the Germans were prepared to send." He suggested emphasizing that the United Kingdom had always selected seriously sick and wounded POWs in accordance with its obligations under the Geneva Convention and regardless of relative numbers or percentages of total POWs. It, therefore, expected Germany to repatriate all those selected as eligible. Betts's proposal was accepted.[148]

The German Ministry of Foreign Affairs was quick to hand the Swiss legation in Berlin a list of 1,710 British POWs passed for repatriation on the latest MMC tour. At the same time, it again accused the British of not supplying the agreed-on lists of POWs examined by the MMC. The Germans did not stop at accusing the British but conditioned the proposed exchange at Gothenburg on the return of several hundred German protected personnel found in the United States and North Africa, in addition to 800 severely wounded POWs.[149] Again, the Germans' insistence on the return of all protected personnel had to do with the great losses they had suffered in the summer of 1944.[150]

London strongly denied the German allegations, particularly in regard to the so-called missing numbers of eligible protected personnel and severely wounded, and assured the Swiss that "[a]ll those passed by Mixed Medical Commissions everywhere have been or are now being repatriated."[151] The German government, the British insisted, "are not entitled to make any conditions except that all passed by Mixed Medical Commission and all surplus protected personnel should be included."[152] Following examination of the list of 1,710 names received from the Germans, the British learned that 6 had since died, 62 had already been exchanged in May 1944, and 9 had been deleted as Greek POWs, leaving a remainder of 1,633.[153]

What disturbed the British most, however, was the thought that the Germans might decide to revert to the principle of numerical equality.[154] The Americans, too, worried that Germany might want to make the exchange at Gothenburg on a head-per-head basis. Thus, Washington instructed the American legation in Stockholm to "ensur[e] that the full number of American repatriates are received in Sweden prior to the time when German POWs being repatriated from United States custody depart from Sweden."[155] At the same time, Hull assured the Germans that the U.S. government would return all surplus protected personnel soon after the survey of German personnel claiming protected status was concluded, "irrespective of further exchange operations."[156]

Even as late as twenty-four hours before the exchange at Gothenburg, the British were not yet officially informed of the names or number of British Commonwealth repatriables to be returned. They began suspecting that the Germans intended to hold back a considerable number of them in light of their allegations that the British government had been withholding lists of names.[157] These fears, however, did not materialize. "The result of the operation," a War Department memorandum summed up, "must be regarded as satisfactory, the numbers being considered higher than appeared probable during the latter phase of negotiations when the Germans seemed to be threatening exclusion on the wholly unjustified grounds that we were deliberately holding back Germans entitled to repatriation." A total of 1,816 POWs and protected personnel had been repatriated; the great majority, 1,210, belonged to United Kingdom forces, while 487 were British Commonwealth service personnel. In addition, 552 civilians were recovered on the basis of head-for-head exchange. The Germans also repatriated 234 U.S. Army officers and enlisted men. For their part, besides the 552 civilians, the Allies repatriated 1,787 German service and protected personnel.[158]

FINAL EXCHANGE

A few weeks after the Gothenburg exchange, Major General Gepp suggested initiating negotiations for a further repatriation. He feared that the German MMC, which had begun its fall tour on 9 October 1944, would not be able to examine the 1,400 wounded who had been left behind following the Allied defeat at Arnhem, Holland, in operation "Market Garden"; the strong probability was that they would not be examined until April 1945.[159] The defeat at Arnhem put an end to Anglo-American hopes to achieve victory over Germany before the end of 1944. London urged the Swiss government to take special measures to ensure that those captured at Arnhem were not passed over in the MMC tour. The Germans were also to be told that steps were being taken in the United Kingdom and Canada to examine all recent captives. Furthermore, all German sick and wounded in France would be examined, if necessary by British doctors. Everyone certified as eligible for repatriation no matter where held, the British stated, would be included in the next exchange.[160]

Meanwhile, in the fall of 1944 Joseph Goebbels, Germany's propaganda minister, announced that some 10,000 soldiers in the medical services of the German armed forces would be posted to the front for combat duty. This came at a time when Washington had intended to release the remaining surplus German medical personnel.[161] At an informal meeting toward the end of October 1944 attended by representatives of the U.S. War and State departments, the British Army Staff, and representatives of the Canadian and British embassies, the Americans reiterated their government's commitment to repatriate all surplus personnel—of whom there were about 2,000 in the United States alone—even before negotiating the next exchange of sick and wounded POWs. As this number was by no means insignificant, the Americans suggested that both London and Washington ask Berlin for assurances that, contrary to Goebbels's statement, repatriated surplus personnel would not be employed as combat troops. They also wanted every one of these captives to give their word that they would not take up arms after returning to Germany. This was not done out of a naive belief that the Germans would honor such assurances but rather with an eye to Moscow— the step was intended to prevent possible difficulties from arising with the Soviet government.[162]

British Foreign Office officials, too, were concerned about Soviet reactions. So far, they pointed out, the Soviets had been able to produce evidence of only very small numbers of repatriated Germans fighting on the Russian front. Even so, the Foreign Office officials had a very grave view of this situation and insisted that the greatest care be taken in the future to prevent any recurrence of the phenomenon. Roberts, the head of the PWD, who thought that Britain should not accept the American proposal, maintained that "to us and to the Russians, the idea of obtaining a German assurance against employment on combatant duties seems to be ingenuous." Roberts suggested that the British not "lecture to the Americans on the subject" but instead quote Moscow's pronouncements on the issue.[163] He referred to an aide-mémoire presented in September 1944 by the Soviet ambassador in London, Feodor T. Gusev, which maintained that more than eighty German repatriates had been sent to the German-Soviet front. Gusev wanted Britain to bear these violations of the Geneva Convention in mind when they exchanged German POWs, particularly "so-called" protected personnel, since "Hitlerite Germany is an enemy which shrinks from no breaches of the juridical provisions of international conventions."[164]

London's main concern, however, was the implications the exchange of protected personnel might have for the next exchange of sick and wounded POWs. The British wanted this exchange carried out after—not before— the exchange of sick and wounded. Negotiations over German assurances and protected personnel giving their word would inevitably be protracted, whereas an agreement on the exchange of sick and wounded alone could probably be concluded rapidly in view of the obvious anxiety that such exchanges produced for all parties.[165] Moreover, all German surplus protected personnel held in British custody had been repatriated in the September 1944 exchange, and therefore there was no accumulation such as existed in the United States.[166] Although they did not clearly state so, the British wanted to take advantage of the Germans' sense of urgency regarding the return of its protected personnel to press Berlin to conclude another POW exchange agreement.

The Americans were not prepared to accept the British stand but agreed to return surplus protected personnel as long as the Germans gave satisfactory assurances against employing them as combatants. The United States pointed out that it had succeeded in persuading the Germans to carry out the September 1944 exchange by assuring them that all protected personnel found to be surplus would be returned to Germany after a complete survey of all claimants to protected status. Several weeks after the exchange, furthermore, the Germans wanted to know the number of German medical personnel found to be surplus and the expected date of their return.[167]

Washington told the Germans that the survey of protected personnel had revealed a shortage of medical and dental officers as well as chaplains in the custody of the United States; on the other hand, there turned out to be a surplus of approximately 3,500 enlisted protected personnel, all of whom were held in Europe and North Africa. This number, though, was bound to change given the rising number of captured German combat troops. The State Department expressed its apprehension that the able-bodied among the surplus medical personnel repatriated might be diverted to other than medical duties. If this happened, "it would be contrary to the spirit of the Geneva Red Cross Convention which contemplates the return of sanitary personnel solely in order to enable them to resume their sanitary activities in their own armies." The German government was urged to give assurances that none of the repatriated German health personnel would be utilized in any military duties that contradicted their protected status. The United States wanted the written word of each repatriate not to engage in combat against the United States or any of its allies, the last sentence of the statement reading as follows: "I realize that in the event of my engaging in military operations contrary to the terms of this parole, I will be liable to be punished with death. I fully understand all the foregoing."[168]

Although the return of American protected personnel was not a prior condition for the repatriation of German protected personnel, the German government was asked to take advantage of the occasion and to return any surplus Americans in this category. According to American information, the German government was holding in custody a surplus of ninety-three U.S. enlisted protected personnel. Germany was assured that none of these returnees would be utilized for combat duty.[169] In early January 1945, the German High Command responded that "no member of the German Sanitary Service now to be repatriated by United States Government will be employed in military capacity other than that which his protection under the Geneva Convention justifies." The German government also stated that it had no objection to the delivery of individual assurances.[170] As it turned out, out of the approximately 3,500 German surplus protected personnel in the United States, only 144 agreed to sign the written statement; 400 German protected personnel in North Africa did so.[171]

At first, Washington was not greatly troubled by this refusal, as the tendency now was to avoid repatriating most of the German surplus protected personnel. But this changed following the great number of U.S. casualties in the fighting in the Ardennes, the Battle of the Bulge, in December 1944. Altogether, over a month and a half at the end of 1944, American units suffered 81,000 casualties, 19,000 of them killed and approximately 21,000 captured. It brought home the realization that the war was not over yet.[172] This led to a second thought about the assurance given to the Germans that all medical personnel found to be surplus would be repatriated, and Washington now decided to try to have the existing agreement with Germany changed. The Americans maintained that past experience in connection with handling and providing medical attention for the very large number of German POWs had demonstrated the inadequacy of the prevailing ratio of medical personnel that the United States was permitted to retain under the agreement between the two countries. Further, reports received of camp conditions in Germany indicated that the same inadequacy existed with respect to the U.S. and other Allied POW medical personnel. Accordingly, the Americans suggested changing the ratio: namely, to retain 3 medical officers, 2 dentists, 1 chaplain, and 14 enlisted men for each 1,000 POWs.[173]

Simultaneously, Washington negotiated for the exchange of wounded POWs to take place on or about 17 January 1945 at the port of Gothenburg. The German government was asked to employ the hospital ship *Gradisca* to collect German repatriables from Mediterranean ports and to deposit these sick and wounded at Trieste or another port to be agreed on. The number of seriously sick and wounded German POWs to be returned to Germany in this operation was expected to amount to about 2,800. The Americans took the occasion to ask the Germans for guarantees that there would be no interference with any U.S. vessel in this exchange. Washington recalled the incident that had occurred off Kristiansand, Norway, during the September 1944 exchange, when the *Gripsholm*, which was carrying back U.S. and British repatriates from the exchange port at Gothenburg, had been stopped and forced to put into Kristiansand, where two members of the crew had forcibly been taken off the vessel.[174]

In early December 1944, the British informed the Germans that the number of sick and wounded German repatriables throughout the British Commonwealth came to approximately 1,850; of these, 1,270 were held in the United Kingdom, 80 in Canada (including POWs transferred from Australia), 320 in the Middle East, and 180 in North Africa and Italy. The last figure was only an estimate, and correct figures would follow as soon as available. The British suggested including in this repatriation all eligible German merchant seamen and requested an assurance that the Germans would act in reciprocal fashion.[175]

The Germans agreed for the exchange to go ahead on 17 January 1945, but they were reluctant to use Gothenburg and instead proposed that the entire exchange be handled via Switzerland, which they thought would be in the interests of British and American repatriables interned in central and southern Germany. Washington and London decided to accept the German proposal but at the same time to reserve the use of Gothenburg as an additional point of exchange for those who could not be conveniently transported to Switzerland.[176] For their part, the Swiss agreed for the exchange to be carried out on Swiss territory and even offered to make available hospital trains that would travel between the German-Swiss frontier and a port in southern France.[177] All in all, a total of 1,932 British personnel were recovered in the January 1945 exchange. The Germans also returned 497 U.S. Army personnel, three U.S. sailors, and 807 U.S. civilians. The Germans received a total of 5,741 POWs, of whom 4,687 were military personnel, 191 protected personnel, and 863 civilians.[178]

LAST REPATRIATION ATTEMPTS

Given the deteriorating conditions in Germany during what was ostensibly the final stage of the war, and subject to pressure by POWs' kin and the public, both the Americans and the British were eager for another repatriation operation to be arranged at the earliest possible date.[179] They drew encouragement from the success of the operation via Switzerland. One of the obstacles that had to be overcome was the lack of an MMC in Germany at this time. Should the Germans decide again to establish an MMC, eight weeks might elapse before the commission could complete its task and before the repatriables could be transported to an exchange point. Thus, the Americans and the British thought of expanding the authority of military doctors, who up to then had been permitted to examine and determine the eligibility for repatriation only of POWs who were blind, had had an arm or leg amputation, or were suffering from open pulmonary or kidney tuberculosis. Since it had originally come from the German side, it was assumed that this suggestion would encounter no difficulties.[180]

In mid-March 1945, both the British and the Americans proposed to the Germans still another exchange of sick and wounded POWs, to take place on 25 April and once again via Switzerland. The whole transfer would be conducted through Marseilles, to which port the German repatriables would be brought. With the war nearing conclusion, the British wanted to safeguard as many POWs as possible. Accordingly, they suggested facilitating transportation by sending British and German repatriables to Switzerland from Germany and Allied territories, respectively, as opportunities offered themselves before the target date and holding them there until that date. In addition to sick and wounded POWs, the British proposed the inclusion of all eligible German and British seamen. The British were displeased that, despite the assurances the German government had given at the time of the exchange via Switzerland, approximately 127 seamen were known to be still in German hands. In an effort to encourage the Germans to accept the Allies' proposal, the British revealed that at this point approximately 2,460 sick and wounded repatriables were held in the British Commonwealth, 1,900 of them in the United Kingdom, 110 in Canada, and 450 in Mediterranean areas.[181]

The Americans, too, emphasized the relatively large number of POWs eligible for repatriation in U.S. custody. During a tour of POW camps the MMC had conducted since the January 1945 exchange in the United States, it had approved approximately 450 additional German POWs for repatriation, while American military medical authorities had found about 150 more eligible POWs. There were also approximately 1,500 German POWs who had already been examined and approved for repatriation overseas. Referring to the American prisoners who, with the Russian advance, were forced to march westward from German POW camps in eastern Germany, Washington let the Germans know it had received information about serious physical disabilities among these POWs. The Americans assumed that the physical deterioration a number of these POWs had suffered rendered them eligible for repatriation. Germany was asked for assurances that as many of these POWs as possible would be examined and that all of those found eligible for repatriation or accommodation in a neutral country would be repatriated to the United States.[182] With the dramatic developments in the final weeks of the war, concern among the Allies over the safety and health of their prisoners significantly increased.[183]

No official German reply was received. Although the German legation in Bern admitted that it had received no instructions, it expressed the view that, on principle, Berlin would find it difficult to agree to the temporary hospitalization in Switzerland of sick and wounded POWs. After rejecting the 25 April date, the legation reported that Germany would not undertake an exchange for at least two months after the necessary preparations had been completed and not less than one month after lists of names had been exchanged. General preference was for the next exchanges to take place via Gothenburg.[184]

By the end of March 1945, however, it had become doubtful that Germany would be able to implement any further exchanges.[185] They would have required that sick and injured Allied POWs be concentrated and moved in bearable condition and in relative safety between Germany and the Swiss border or Sweden.[186] According to SHAEF, "because of the fluid tactical situation, it will be difficult to guarantee that railways or other transportation facilities in Germany, used in the proposed repatriation, will not be subject to air attack." In any case, Germany was unlikely to control sufficient functioning transport means to ensure the delivery of repatriables. Moreover, the Allied advances in the next eight weeks "probably will uncover many of the sick and wounded which the Germans might consider for exchange."[187] Three weeks later, the war in Europe had been brought to an end.

In the four exchanges of seriously wounded and sick POWs that took place between October 1943 and January 1945, the British received approximately 10,000 of their men, the Americans about 800, and the Germans about 13,000. As remarkable as these figures undeniably are, their significance derives not just from the actual numbers involved but also from the wider repercussions they had, mainly in London. For Whitehall, the repatriation effort was a significant achievement first of all because of the humanitarian aspect involved—Britain was the first to lose large numbers of troops to the

Germans as early as Dunkirk—but also for reasons of domestic policy. As the first POWs arrived home, in October 1943, the government used the event to point out—for the benefit of its domestic critics—the success of its ongoing diplomatic activities on behalf of British Commonwealth prisoners in German camps.[188] That another three successful exchanges of seriously injured and sick POWs followed further worked in Whitehall's favor as negotiations with Germany over the repatriation of able-bodied long-term POWs kept running into difficulties.

Matters were different for the Americans. Of the approximately 96,000 U.S. troops who were in German POW camps by the end of hostilities, more than three-quarters had fallen into captivity after D-Day. In Washington, the ostensibly low figure of 800 POWs repatriated by January 1945 was more or less accepted as fair given the overall number of U.S. troops in German hands at this point. Moreover, Washington, in contrast to London, proved less anxious to come to an understanding with Berlin over the repatriation of POWs, particularly long-term ones.

One final aspect needs to be singled out. The four exchanges of seriously wounded and sick POWs highlight the nature and mode of contacts between Britain and the United States, on the one hand, and Nazi Germany, on the other. As we saw, in the midst of the most devastating air attacks on German cities by the Western Allies, lines of communication between the belligerent sides remained open, and the Germans never actually halted the negotiations or conditioned the exchanges themselves on a cessation of those bombing campaigns.

Long-Term POWs Kept in Abeyance

DISCORD WITHIN WHITEHALL

When, in October 1942, the Red Cross asked the British whether they would want to consider a mutual repatriation of POWs in long-term captivity, several months passed before London even reacted.[1] The Geneva Convention did not make such an exchange binding,[2] and Whitehall was pressed to first arrive at concrete arrangements for the repatriation of seriously injured and sick POWs (which the convention did oblige the two sides to effect).[3] It could also be reasoned that even for those who had fallen into enemy hands almost immediately, two years into the war made it too early to speak of a "long period of captivity." Certainly for the Americans the question did not come up at this time because the United States had joined the war only in December the year before. Thus, the first serious calls for the repatriation of long-term prisoners, especially older ones, came from the POWs themselves.

In April 1943, a Major General Fortune, writing from Oflag IX A/H (Spangenberg), pressed for the return, or at least for the transfer to neutral territory, of those POWs who had also been prisoners in World War I. A similar call came from twenty-one officers and ratings who had survived the sinking by the Germans of HMS *Rawalpindi* on 23 November 1939. They pointed out that some of the crew were considerably older than fifty "and naturally suffer deterioration much more rapidly than younger men."[4] The Red Cross joined these calls and encouraged the belligerents to conclude an agreement especially regarding older POWs. In early August 1943, Max Huber, president of the ICRC, reminded the British of an agreement that the French and Germans had concluded in May 1917 whereby POWs over the age of forty-eight who had been in captivity for at least eighteen months had been accommodated in Switzerland if they were of commissioned rank or repatriated outright if of lower rank. Huber suggested that negotiations be initiated toward a similar agreement.[5]

In fact, during World War I a first exchange of invalid French and German prisoners had taken place as early as March 1915, and by November 1916 more than 10,000 German and French prisoners had been repatriated. In January of that year, both sides had also started transferring POWs who were less seriously wounded to neutral Switzerland. In late May, following a British initiative to conclude a similar arrangement with the Germans, the first group of British prisoners arrived in Switzerland. The success of these agreements paved the way for the more comprehensive one mentioned by Huber. A month later, at a conference in The Hague, the British and the Germans agreed, among other things, on the internment of up to 16,000 men in neutral Holland. Finally, between 8 June and 14 July 1918, they agreed that all POWs interned in neutral countries could be released there.[6]

Huber's exchange proposal was received sympathetically in London, but there was immediate concern, particularly again within Admiralty circles, about the military implications of returning able-bodied men to Germany. In order to help overcome a crew shortage, Lord Leathers, the minister of war transport, had once before suggested an exchange of merchant seamen.[7] But the idea had greatly troubled Albert V. Alexander, first lord of the Admiralty, who explained that the Admiralty had always resisted the return of any merchant seamen to Germany on the grounds that they were potential submariners, a policy, he reminded his fellow ministers, that dated from the days when the prime minister himself had been first lord of the Admiralty. The Germans held 833 British merchant marine officers and 1,698 ratings, while 228 German merchant marine officers and 4,546 ratings were in British hands. Although the overall balance of numbers was weighted heavily in the enemy's favor should it come to an exchange, Alexander recognized that the figure for officers was to Britain's advantage. Still, he advised Lord Leathers that the proposal would in effect provide the Germans with "the equivalent of roughly a hundred U-boat crews." Even if not everyone repatriated was suitable for service in U-boats, the very release of captives unfit for submarine duty would free present merchant mariners for combat in U-boats.[8]

And it was exactly Britain's recent successes against U-boats, Alexander reasoned, that had intensified the German navy's need for personnel to operate them. According to Admiralty estimates, the Germans had lost about 7,000 submariners during the first seven months of 1943. As a result, German naval authorities had resorted to several extreme measures to supply fresh U-boat crews, going as far as to take personnel from main land units, although this meant withdrawing them from operational service. Even men who had been selected as air force pilots were transferred to U-boats. Furthermore, the general medical standard for submarine recruits had been lowered, as had been the age limit. Importantly, too, the training of future crews had been seriously harmed by the loss of experienced submariners, who would have provided the key personnel for these vessels. The Germans could not expect to compensate for these losses to any appreciable extent from either their navy or their merchant marine. Supplying crews for the German surface ships and auxiliary naval services was itself encountering problems, with the result that, despite their doubtful loyalty, foreigners—French, Dutch, Norwegians, and Danes—were invited to join the German navy.

Alexander concluded that despite the shortage of submariners and the fact that the German navy in general was stretched almost to the breaking point, the sea campaign still remained Germany's greatest potential for "weakening the offensive power of the United Nations sufficiently to secure a compromise peace." Accordingly, the Admiralty adhered to its longstanding policy of opposing exchanges of merchant seamen unless it could be shown that released captives would not materially help Germany alleviate its shortage of men for U-boat crews. "The eagerness recently shown by the Germans to promote exchanges of Merchant Seamen," Alexander maintained, "encourages me to believe that in this we are right."[9]

As Whitehall's officials saw it, however, the exchange of seriously sick and wounded POWs in October 1943 improved the chances for an agreement on the repatriation of POWs who had been in captivity for a long time. Admittedly, the numbers on either side were as yet small if one followed the criteria mentioned by the Red Cross. Still, the officials believed that "an attempt on their behalf [was] worth making. An exchange on a head for head basis should involve a good ship load." The number of United Kingdom officers and men of other ranks reported in German and Italian hands who would be at least forty-eight years old on 1 January 1944 and who had been in captivity for more than eighteen months amounted to approximately 625, of whom 345 were merchant seamen and approximately 280 army personnel. According to unverified information the British possessed, some 420 German POWs held in the United Kingdom and Canada were forty-eight years old or older on 31 October 1943; of these, 410 were merchant seamen, while 2 came from the army, 7 from the navy, and 1 from the air force.[10]

Admiralty officials persisted toward the end of 1943 in their categorical refusal to exchange long-term POWs, even if this stance ran counter to the consideration of making every effort to get POWs out of Germany. They argued that "allowing useful people to supplement the German man-power, particularly Merchant Seamen of experience in respect of which Germany is understood to be particularly short, could prolong the war." They feared that after the Germans had gotten back their merchant seamen, they would claim that Article 74 ("No repatriated person may be utilized in active military service") was not applicable to merchant seamen, since such prisoners were not strictly POWs. The Admiralty was certain that Britain's own POWs would be "of less value" to the war effort, since they had been in captivity for a longer period of time than the Germans.[11]

Whereas the Admiralty's stand derived primarily from obvious strategic considerations, the Air Council proved more directly concerned with the increasing danger of permanent mental deterioration suffered by long-term POWs. Risks likely to arise from repatriation were deemed small in comparison with the direct benefits to the repatriates. And, of course, there was a large, albeit indirect, psychological benefit to other POWs: the knowledge that their country was actively working toward their return. The council downplayed the security considerations, maintaining that any information that German repatriates might provide would "be more of a discouragement than of assistance to their compatriots." It also belittled the Admiralty's argument in regard to adding numbers to German troops, for "German prisoners may be as susceptible to the deleterious effects of long captivity as are those of other nationalities."[12]

As had been the case earlier vis-à-vis seriously wounded and sick POWs, domestic political considerations now also began playing a role in Whitehall's decision whether to exchange long-term POWs. Concern for the plight of these men and pressure exerted by families of POWs led to questions in the House of Commons, thus injecting a measure of political expediency into the discussion of military calculations. Responding to a question in mid-January 1944, Undersecretary of State George Hall announced that the investigations on which to base a proposal to the German government were nearing conclusion. German prisoners, he explained, were scattered in various parts of the Commonwealth, and thus more time was required to secure the figures relating to age and length of captivity.[13] A month later, MP Major General Alfred Knox wanted to know whether any progress had been made in negotiations with Germany on this issue. Richard Law, minister of state in the Foreign Office, was forced to admit that no such negotiations were as yet under way either with the German government or with other Axis governments.[14]

Following continuing pressure in the House of Commons, Whitehall decided that it had to set out some course of action. The Imperial Prisoners of War Committee agreed that negotiations should be initiated through the protecting power. It wanted to reach agreement on accommodating in neutral territory POWs who were forty-two years of age or older and who had been in captivity for eighteen months or longer. The suggestion of neutral territory was intended to prevent Germany from receiving merchant seamen. Sweden was regarded as the best possible alternative because of its geographical location and the fact that the Swedish government had indicated its readiness to assist generally in providing for the welfare of POWs. Switzerland was less favorable because large numbers of POWs who had succeeded in escaping were already accommodated there. The date proposed both for calculating the length of captivity and for determining the age qualification was 1 March 1944. This date had been especially favored by Canada so that its men captured at Dieppe in August 1942 could be included. Moreover, it was decided that negotiations should proceed without regard to numbers; all those qualifying on each side would be eligible for release, including merchant seamen.[15]

BRITISH PROPOSALS

In their official proposal to the Germans, delivered by the Swiss on 6 April 1944, the British stated that no individuals should be excluded on security grounds. Furthermore, the negotiations should proceed on the basis of nominal rolls: the British government would supply the German government with a list of all British Commonwealth POWs and merchant seamen in German hands who were qualified to be repatriated, and the German government would supply the British government with a list of all qualified German prisoners and merchant seamen in British hands throughout the Commonwealth.[16] Despite various reminders after the proposal was delivered, the British received no response from the Germans for several months.[17]

By this time the question of negotiating an agreement on exchanging able-bodied POWs who had undergone a long period of captivity was also being discussed in Washington, prompted by the report the Red Cross had sent in April 1944 on Stalag Luft III (Sagan), where 2,076 British and 2,078 American prisoners were being held. According to the report, as we already saw, medical officers were greatly concerned at the growing number of cases of psychosis, fearing that the "effect on some prisoners of war may prove permanent unless serious steps are taken soon." The best means of alleviating mental strain on POWs was the repatriation or internment in a neutral country of all prisoners held captive in excess of a certain period of time, such as two or three years.[18]

Taking up the finding of the report with Secretary of War Henry Stimson,

U.S. Secretary of State Cordell Hull first recalled how, in January 1944, the State Department had been against approaching the German government on the direct repatriation or accommodation in a neutral country of long-time able-bodied POWs, a recommendation that had come from Lieutenant Colonel D'Erlach, head of the MMC operating in Germany. But now, given the position London and the British Commonwealth were taking, Hull thought the War Department ought to reconsider the idea and initiate talks on the subject with the Germans.[19]

Stimson, however, insisted that the problem facing the British Commonwealth was "different from ours." The Germans by then held approximately 160,000 British Commonwealth prisoners, substantial numbers of whom had been in captivity since June 1940, whereas Germany reported a total of only about 12,000 American prisoners, the greater proportion of whom had been captured less than one year ago. Moreover, a large number of the American prisoners were members of the U.S. Army Air Force (USAAF), whose age bracket was considerably lower than that recommended by the IPWC. As a result of the limitations imposed by the U.S. Selective Service Act and War Department policies, which had tended to keep older men out of combat units, the average age of American soldiers on the front was well below the suggested forty-three years. In the present situation, Stimson concluded, very few American prisoners would profit by such an accord, "and the making of such an agreement at this time is not deemed advisable."[20] Naturally, the Americans did not advance this argument to the British but instead pointed to the strengthening of German combat forces that such a deal would produce and the need to prevent it. In the wake of the secretary of war's firm stand, Hull instructed the American legation in Bern to oppose any negotiations with the Germans on the issue. The legation was asked, however, to obtain information for the State Department on the number of cases of psychosis among American POWs who would not qualify for repatriation under the Geneva Convention but who might be qualified for transfer to a neutral country for hospitalization.[21]

In early May, Eden, pressed by questions in Parliament, tried to dissolve the issue in a general way by saying—equivocally—that the investigation into how many POWs could be repatriated had been completed and that "we have taken certain action regarding which I cannot properly make any statement."[22] But when no German response to his initial proposal was forthcoming, no statement followed. Once again it was Knox who, in early November 1944, reminded Eden that many of the POWs had been confined in Germany for four and a half years. In response, Eden told the MPs that the cabinet was examining alternative proposals that might have a better chance of acceptance by the Germans.[23]

By now, the British had learned from the Swiss that the Germans would never entertain any proposal that involved sending their prisoners to neutral territory; for them, moreover, Article 72 meant repatriation on a strictly head-for-head basis. Intelligence officials thought that this refusal had to do with the German government's opposition to exposing their soldiers to outside influences, in particular newspapers critical of German policy and Nazi principles.[24] The Swiss thought that the Germans' main concern was to replenish troops and that they would not primarily be influenced by humanitarian considerations. In order to break the deadlock, the War Office proposed that the agreement should cover a one-to-one exchange of British Commonwealth POWs in Germany for German POWs in northwestern Africa and the Middle East and that the numbers would depend on the transport available. The exchange would involve British soldiers captured before 14 April 1940, the date of the start of the Norway campaign, and Germans taken prisoner before 1 July 1943.

The War Office made it clear that its proposal was not designed to select German POWs from all British POW camps but simply to take repatriables from the Mediterranean area, where their selection, concentration, and transport could be effected with the least delay. A total of 8,776 German POWs captured before 1 July 1943 were in British custody in the Middle East. Of these, 132 were officers, and 11 were merchant seamen. According to the War Office proposal, the selection of those to be repatriated was to be left to the detaining power. The War Office thought that Britain should try to obviate the return of Germans who would ultimately be fit for further active service, such as U-boat crews, aircraft pilots, and other key men, and also, so far as possible, "rabid Nazis."[25]

Foreign Office officials were in a different quandary: whether London should first attempt to submit the project to the Soviets and the Americans, since it "clearly involves the return of able-bodied military men to Germany." So far as the Soviet Union was concerned, the dilemma was whether to consult Moscow at any stage of the negotiations. As we already saw, at the beginning of January 1945, Roberts, head of the Foreign Office's PWD, pointed to the Soviets' earlier strong protests against the repatriation of protected personnel because some of them had subsequently engaged in active military service against the Soviet Union in contravention of Article 74 of the Geneva Convention.[26] It seemed a safe assumption, then, that if Britain broached the subject of the repatriation of long-term POWs, the Soviets would almost certainly oppose any such proposal. Roberts suggested, therefore, that the Foreign Office begin negotiations with the Germans and only later "tell the Soviets what we are doing when it is too late to change our views." Other Foreign Office officials were of the same opinion, though one of them questioned "whether the advantage that we stand to gain from this outweighs the disadvantages of another cause of friction between ourselves and the Russians."[27]

As the Americans could not claim to have consulted Britain in all cases of repatriation, Roberts was much less concerned with their stand. He referred to a recent exchange involving 790 American airmen interned in Switzerland as against 1,500 Germans. Roberts supposed that the Americans would not oppose the British proposal "if put to them with determination." In any case, he believed that both humanitarian reasons and internal politics compelled Britain to proceed with the proposal. He pointed to the many letters arriving at the Foreign Office urging that something be done for long-term prisoners and to the questions being asked in the House of Commons on this subject. Pressure on the government would only increase, "especially when the new exchange of sick and wounded (now being organised) becomes known." Roberts was also well aware that by bringing back some of the long-term prisoners, the morale of the remaining POWs would improve and "so arm them against the extremely harmful mental effects suffered by prisoners long in captivity which would tend to decrease their value as post-war citizens."[28]

Roberts's concern about criticism of the government derived from, among other things, the House of Commons debate in mid-November 1944 during which several MPs had demanded the appointment of a senior minister to deal with the POW question. In the debate, MP Major Sir Jocelyn Lucas (Portsmouth, South), who for four years during World War I had been in German prisons and hospitals and an internee in a neutral country (Holland), urged the government to "get on with the job and do something without first waiting for the end of the war." Member of Parliament Geoffrey Hutchinson (Illford) spoke of prisoners who had already been in captivity three years and added, "I am bound to say it is very difficult to know which particular Department or Minister is responsible for initiating the necessary action to ensure that at the first opportunity these prisoners can be repatriated, either to this country or to a neutral country." He was quite sure that the secretary of state for foreign affairs had been most active in the matter, "but he has many other duties to perform": the House of Commons and the public would have been more confident "if there had been a single Minister to put this matter forward at every opportunity, and see that no opportunity was neglected to ensure that at the first possible occasion some relief should be brought to these men, who have been so long in captivity."[29]

Letters from British POWs that reached London and were scrutinized by British officials spoke clearly of their growing plight. Sergeant John V. Daly wrote from Stalag Luft III in June 1944:

> I am in better condition physically than I have been for the last five years. Mentally, however, the life is proving rather a strain—it's rather difficult at time to concentrate, and I often find my mind wandering towards past or imaginary scenes while I am reading. How long is all this going to last? By dint of a considerable amount of serious reading and deliberate optimism, I'm keeping my mind as alert as possible, but it is becoming increasingly difficult to avoid slipping into that apathy which is the hall-mark of long term prisoners. . . . I must keep my mind and nerves as steady as they were seven months ago, or it will be out of the question for good.[30]

Flight Lieutenant Fred Irvins, also in Stalag Luft III, wrote in December 1944: "Being in my fourth year now I am seriously wondering just how much more I can take of this life—this may sound a bit melodramatic to you at home—believe me this is a very serious question to me here." Another POW, of Stalag 344, told of two suicide attempts by a POW who had been a prisoner for four and a half years.[31] A report on the morale of Royal Air Force POWs in Germany based on their letters revealed that the nerves of numerous prisoners were obviously "on the edge" and that "people explode on the slightest verbal pin-prick." The psychological strain was increasing with the passage of time, and some of the POWs openly worried when they would reach the "breaking point." Many long-term prisoners wrote in a bitter terms alleging that nothing had been done to secure their repatriation. "There was no doubt whatever," the author of the report wrote, "that the burden of long captivity weighed extremely heavily upon them and that numbers of them were in a highly neurotic condition."[32]

Given the criticism in Parliament, the secretaries of state for foreign affairs and war circulated a memorandum among the War Cabinet members in mid-January 1945 that supported the mutual repatriation of able-bodied long-term POWs. The cabinet was informed that the Germans held about 40,000 British Commonwealth troops who had been POWs since 1 July 1940 and whose long captivity was causing them increasingly harmful effects, both physical and psychological. Eden and Grigg emphasized the need for improving the morale of the POWs so as to help them brace themselves against the cumulative effects of their incarceration and thus cope with the final phase of their captivity. The repatriation of even a small percentage of the long-term captives would have a good effect not only among this category but also among those who had been in enemy hands for shorter periods of time. Neither Eden nor Grigg concealed the fact that their initiative stemmed in part from the growing pressure being exerted by the families of the POWs, reflected in the eagerness of the press to publish news regarding captured British soldiers. The two ministers anticipated that the exchange of sick and wounded that was to take place later in January 1945 would result in fresh public pressure on the government to do something for long-term prisoners, particularly as by now Britain's proposals for their internment in a neutral country were known to have met with no response from the German government.

The cabinet was told that until the summer of 1943 it had proved impossible to reach agreement with the German government on the exchange of sick and wounded POWs. Britain's proposal of 5 April 1944 for the accommodation of long-term prisoners in neutral territory had resulted from the disparity in the numbers of long-term prisoners held by each side and from the assumption that this course, rather than direct repatriation, would appeal to the Germans. Despite frequent reminders, however, Germany had failed to reply. Both Grigg and Eden believed that the Germans would never agree to internment in a neutral country and that the exchange had to be on a one-to-one basis. Any initiative had to come from the British side, and, owing to the deterioration of German administration, the scheme had to be administratively simple. Accordingly, the ministers had suggested the exchange of 3,000 Germans (mainly soldiers) from among those taken prisoner in the Middle East before 1 July 1943 against a similar number of Commonwealth prisoners captured before 1 July 1940. The figure of 3,000 and the repatriation of Germans from the Middle East had been determined by the shipping situation. If agreement with the Germans was reached by March 1945 and the exchange succeeded, the hope was that further exchanges could then take place.

Both ministers were open about the greater advantage that would accrue to Germany in the proposed exchange as well as the probability that the Germans would not observe Article 72, which provided that no repatriated prisoner would be employed in active military service. Nevertheless, former

British prisoners "may, once they are restored to health, be employed in the United Kingdom with administrative, training, and non-operational units or, it is understood, after the defeat of Germany, on active military service against Japan." In other words, although Germany obtained an initial advantage from the point of view of service personnel, Britain would gain at a later stage. Eden and Grigg suggested that the U.S. administration be told at once of Britain's proposal to the Germans but that the cabinet await the Germans' reply before informing the Soviet government, which might raise objections, though "we should not allow these objections to interfere with our decision."[33]

The current proposal differed from the one presented to the Germans in April 1944 in several important aspects: it talked of direct repatriation, not of the internment of the POWs in a neutral country; it offered a one-to-one exchange; and no limitation was placed on the age of POWs or on years in captivity. The War Cabinet approved the proposals after the British Chiefs of Staff Committee had strongly supported them.[34] The decision to ignore the Soviets was also related to a stalemate with Moscow over an agreement between the two Allies on the mutual repatriation of liberated POWs.[35]

The cabinet's decision, however, raised anxiety within the Admiralty in regard to U-boat personnel. "The recrudescence of the U-boat threat has begun," the Admiralty stated, "and if the war against Germany should not be brought to an early conclusion the threat may become extremely serious and comparable to the black period of early 1943." Still, Admiralty officials were forced to admit that the present proposals contained little danger, as any U-boat prisoners captured in the Mediterranean before 1 July 1943 would have been brought to the United Kingdom, not interned in the Middle East. Alexander cautioned that the wording of the offer should avoid committing Britain to any formula or principle "which might seriously embarrass the withholding of U-boat personnel in future exchanges." The Admiralty advanced another argument—the possible reaction of the Free French. The French had seen many of their soldiers taken prisoner in 1940, and there would be strong political pressure in France to negotiate a similar exchange. In conclusion, the Admiralty explained that its concern resulted from the possibility that the war against Germany would "continue longer than we at present hope."[36] These apprehensions were not groundless. In March 1944 the Germans had begun investing much effort in building new types of U-boats in order to resume the submarine war; as a result, in February 1945 the German submarine force reached its overall peak with more than 400 ships.[37]

Despite the Admiralty's stand, Whitehall asked the Swiss government in mid-February to inform Berlin that London desired to reach an agreement for the direct repatriation, through Switzerland, of 3,000 long-term prisoners. (Three weeks earlier the belligerents had concluded their fourth exchange of seriously sick and wounded prisoners.) As all long-term prisoners were held in distant countries, they would be selected from among those in the nearest holding center, namely, the Middle East. These prisoners were almost all members of the German army who had been captured in the course of the North African campaigns. The British note explained that these conditions were meant to avoid shipping delays and difficulties on account of climate. As to British POWs, London proposed that they be selected from among members of the United Kingdom and Indian forces and that the qualifying date be 1 July 1940. Based on information supplied earlier by the Germans, this total included 36,077 (including 170 Indians) army, 426 navy, 396 merchant service, and 351 air force. The British also requested that "certain simple priority standards such as health, previous captivity and age be observed" when selecting individual POWs. It was further suggested that officers be repatriated in the ratio of 1 officer to 19 in the ranks.[38]

GERMAN PROPOSALS

Before the Swiss had had a chance to transmit the British proposal to the German government, the latter communicated, on 18 February 1945, a proposal for the mutual exchange of 25,000 men. Referring to the British proposal of 5 April the year before, it called for the repatriation of the prisoners rather than accommodating them in neutral countries and for the abandonment of the age limit. It also suggested that "no further limitations should be made than that prisoners of the same rank should be sent home in equal numbers." The exchange could take place immediately via Switzerland or Gothenburg, or both.[39] The proposal seems to have been derived directly from Germany's serious shortage of troops. From the beginning of June to mid-September 1944, German forces had lost approximately 1.5 million men who had either been killed or captured or were missing. This was followed by the failure of German offensives in the West at the end of 1944—about 100,000 Germans had been killed or wounded or were missing. The Allied invasion of Germany at the beginning of 1945 only deteriorated Germany's situation, as it meant the capture of hundreds of thousands of Germans.[40]

With many camps in Germany being broken up or moved, Swiss officials thought that POW exchanges should be large, rapidly conducted, and effected as simply as possible.[41] The Swiss suggested that nominal lists not be insisted on but that exchanges be carried out on a simple head-for-head basis. Gabriel Naville, a member of the Swiss embassy in Berlin and head of the British Interests Division, who was then on a visit to Bern, strongly recommended that as many Allied POWs as possible be gotten out of Germany at the earliest opportunity. This advice was strengthened by a confidential report from the Swiss legation in Berlin stating that recent Allied bombardments, especially of Nuremberg, had resulted in a large number of civilian casualties, inevitably creating "an ugly mood" that might develop dangerously for British prisoners.[42]

The British now withdrew their note of mid-February and instead proposed the repatriation of 5,000 POWs in good health on each side at the earliest possible date. Such an exchange, they pointed out, would give both sides the necessary time to consider additional numbers up to 25,000. London further suggested that 5 percent of those selected for repatriation be officers and 15 percent warrant and noncommissioned officers. For the sake of simplicity, the British stated, if these percentages did not correspond exactly to those selected by the other side, the discrepancy would be disregarded. London did insist, however, on obtaining assurance that British Commonwealth POWs and merchant seamen, irrespective of service or which part of British Commonwealth they were from, be included in the proposed exchange. The Germans were asked to select these POWs from those who were in captivity the longest and, so far as possible, from those captured before 1 July 1940. In return, German POWs and merchant seamen would be selected from among the longest-serving POWs in the United Kingdom. The British agreed that no age limit should be applied in the selection. Finally, London wanted the exchange to take place at Gothenburg on 27 March, provided it received an affirmative reply by 12 March 1945.[43]

The British preferred the Swedish port because it was the most convenient to both parties. In addition, a proposal for a further exchange of sick and wounded POWs through Switzerland was under consideration at that time, and London wanted to keep the two operations distinct. The proposal spoke of exchanging 5,000 German POWs from among those interned in the United Kingdom instead of Egypt because only in this way could the Ministry of War Transport transfer that many POWs to Gothenburg within the next four to six weeks and return an equal number of British POWs. This meant that the British would release not Germans captured in Africa in 1942–43 but Germans who had surrendered in France since D-Day, less than a year ago.[44]

That at the same time London wanted to hear from Bern whether the

Germans could be trusted to select not merely the most readily available POWs but indeed those who had been longest in captivity seems inconsistent.[45] But, as London saw it, Berlin was unlikely to object to receiving recently captured troops, as its main objective was to regain as many able-bodied men as possible, whereas Whitehall was responding to ongoing public pressure to secure the release of large numbers of the nearly 40,000 troops who had been in German hands for almost five years by now. This discrepancy in approach would not escape Washington.

The Swiss were confident that the Germans were genuinely anxious to execute exchanges of large numbers of prisoners. Naville agreed that large-scale movements would be operable more easily through Gothenburg than ports farther south. Naville also thought that the Germans were willing and able to select the longest-held prisoners. He again pressed for urgency in removing as many Allied prisoners as possible from Germany, not only in the interest of the repatriables but also in order to reduce overcrowding and the strain on whatever supplies it was possible to send into Germany.[46] Convinced by Naville's assessment, the British asked the Swiss on 7 March to suggest that the number of repatriates on each side be increased to 7,000.[47] Actually, London was close to accepting the full German proposal, that is, the exchange of 25,000 POWs from each side, as anxiety was growing day by day that the Nazis might start using British POWs as hostages or even begin liquidating them as Allied forces were advancing.[48]

War Office officials admitted that the returning Germans would be comparatively recent captures, in other words, fit fighting men, but this was offset, they thought, by the fact that "these Germans, who will have been specially selected, will know that the evils of captivity have been exaggerated by German propaganda and will have had opportunities to reflect on the prospects of defeat. They are unlikely to stiffen the German will to resist and may easily do the opposite." Possible accusations that Britain was trying to engineer an advantage for its own long-term prisoners at the expense of those of its Allies were brushed aside because, they argued, the Germans, "while taking care to hold on to British and American prisoners of war[,] are allowing French, Belgians, Dutch and other Allied prisoners of war to be overrun by the Red Army."[49]

DISSENSION BETWEEN LONDON AND WASHINGTON

London's agreement to exchange as many as 25,000 able-bodied POWs somewhat alarmed the U.S. Joint Chiefs of Staff, who thought the whole matter should be considered on a combined basis and suggested on 11 March that the proposal be referred to the Combined Administrative Committee (CAC).[50] The British Chiefs of Staff accepted their American colleagues' suggestion and explained to the British mission in Washington that Whitehall's support of such exchanges was influenced by constant political pressure being exerted on the government to obtain the release of 37,187 British POWs who had been in captivity for nearly five years and whose long confinement was causing more and more cases of mental illness among them. Moreover, the Germans were apparently making a genuine offer and were able and willing to select those who were in captivity the longest and to transport them to Gothenburg.

The COS did not deny that the Germans would recover troops, but it wondered whether indeed this would prove "an unmixed blessing to them" because, in making their selection, the British would exclude all POWs with qualifications of special value to the German war effort, such as Luftwaffe, U-boat personnel, and members of the SS. As far as possible, moreover, the group selected would consist of political "moderates." The COS assumed that since the Germans had not yet accepted 27 March as the date for the exchange of the first 7,000, it was unlikely that the remainder of the proposed figure, 18,000 POWs, would gain their freedom before late April. Anticipating objections by the United States, they added that the Americans might suggest that some of the 25,000 be U.S. prisoners but the British mission should remind the Americans of the large number of long-term British prisoners. As to the Soviet government, it was proposed not to inform Moscow until after the Germans had agreed to the exchange proposal.[51]

British fears of a negative American reaction proved well founded. A memorandum prepared by U.S. members of the CAC argued that the British proposal for an exchange of 7,000 able-bodied prisoners fell outside the provisions of Article 72 of the 1929 Geneva Convention "in that it contemplates the repatriation of recently captured able-bodied German POWs." Apprehension was also expressed that a successful exchange in this instance would open the door to similar transactions between Germany and other Allied governments, egged on by public opinion in those countries. In addition, if taken without Soviet agreement, the contemplated action "might result in unfortunate repercussions." Doubts were also expressed about the value of a pledge by Germany to abide by the provisions of Article 74 of the Geneva Convention. It would prove difficult to identify repatriated German soldiers who subsequently engaged in combat and were recaptured. Here, too, taking into account only military considerations, the U.S. members of the CAC concluded that the repatriation to Germany of combat-fit and

American POWs being marched along a road on the Western front.
(Courtesy National Archives, College Park, Md.)

trained personnel was inadvisable.[52] What may have strengthened the U.S. generals' opposition to any such exchange was the heavy losses the Americans had sustained in December 1944 during the German counteroffensive in the Ardennes: approximately 80,000 troops had been killed or wounded or were missing.[53]

Consequently, at the CAC meeting on 20 March, the U.S. and British members proved unable to resolve their basic disagreements. Major General A. W. Lee made it clear that to him and the other British members of the CAC humanitarian considerations overrode any objections. He wanted to know whether the American representatives were objecting to the exchange of the first 7,000 or only to any figure above that amount or whether they were objecting to any figure over the 5,000 that had originally been proposed. Brigadier General M. B. Bryan Jr., assistant provost marshal general, replied that the United States was mainly concerned with any figure over 5,000 because of fears that these 25,000 able-bodied German prisoners would be used in combat against U.S. forces. For his part, Lee doubted that they would get to Germany in time to participate in any fighting.[54]

Following the failure by the CAC to reach an agreement, the British Chiefs of Staff and the U.S. Joint Chiefs of Staff presented their views to the

Combined Chiefs of Staff (ccs). Repeating London's arguments for accepting the German proposal, the cos stressed the fact that the U.S. government itself had not long ago repatriated protected German personnel. "It will be recalled," the British pointed out, "that the U.S. Government exacted from the German Government an assurance that it would not use the repatriates in combat against any of the Allies, and further exacted from each individual, with the consent of the German Government, his signed commitment not to engage in such combat, under liability to penalty of death if recaptured." Because the American decision to return German personnel had been made despite firm British opposition, the British now accused the Americans of applying a double standard.[55]

As to the contention that this transaction would open the door to similar agreements between Germany and other Allied governments, the British chiefs pointed out that France was the only other Allied government whose nationals had been prisoners in Germany for as long as British prisoners and that held German POWs in its possession. There was, though, no need "for the French to know anything about this exchange at least until the end of April." By that time, the cos argued, the risk that the French would then desire to enter into a similar agreement with the German government could be accepted, since "unless there is some major change in the war situation, it is unlikely that they could complete an exchange of prisoners in time to be of any military value to either side." It was impossible, the cos summed up, on humanitarian grounds to refuse to accept the German proposal. The risks that the German prisoners to be exchanged would be of any value to the German war effort "are so slight that they can be accepted." The JCS were asked to confirm that they had no objection to the exchange of 7,000 POWs and to concur in the proposed exchange of a further 18,000, thus effectively accepting the German proposal of 25,000.[56]

Whereas the British were determined to carry out the exchange, the Americans were no less resolved to prevent it. The Joint Logistics Committee (JLC), in a report prepared for the JCS, who strongly opposed the proposed exchange, maintained that the operation did not guarantee that the returned British prisoners would necessarily be from among those who had been long in confinement.[57] In other words, the main British argument in favor of conducting the exchange was hollow, since no one could assure its implementation. In contrast to the British inclination to lessen the significance of the Soviets' reaction, the JLC warned that if the exchange was implemented without this ally's prior agreement, the Western Allies could expect serious repercussions, not the least of which would be difficulties in securing safe-conduct for the vessels transporting sick and wounded American POWs. The JLC also contradicted the British argument that all POWs in Germany were suffering increasing hardships and that the removal of 25,000 of them would reduce the overall problem of protection and supply for the remainder. If such an analysis was accepted, it was argued, it would "justify practically unlimited exchanges."

Impressed by neither the argument of domestic political pressure in Britain nor humanitarian arguments, the JLC warned of the military harm and the casualties that Allied forces would suffer as a result of returning trained combat personnel to Germany. For the JLC, this consideration wholly outweighed all others and made it "doubtful whether, on net balance, the proposed exchanges can be considered a humanitarian project." Accordingly, the committee advised that the U.S. government not concur in the exchange of more than 5,000 prisoners.[58] That humanitarian consideration played almost no role is demonstrated also in a letter Bryan sent to Judge Vincent A. Carroll, who was active with next of kin of American prisoners in Philadelphia. "To repatriate directly to Germany thousands of able-bodied prisoners of war would be in conflict with our purpose of the war" to defeat Germany by depleting every source of its strength, including its reserves. "In this respect," Bryan continued, "humanitarian desires to return American prisoners on this ground must be weighed and rejected in view of the benefits the enemy would gain by such an agreement."[59]

If one of London's main arguments in trying to influence Washington's stand had been the public pressure that was being applied on the government, for their part, the JCS now used a similar argument to undermine this British assertion. They pointed to the American public's great sensitivity to the casualties being suffered by U.S. forces in Europe. On the basis of prisoners captured since D-Day, the JCS calculated that "the U.S. troops suffered a loss of approximately 3,000 killed, 12,000 wounded, and 2,000 missing for every 25,000 German prisoners taken." If the exchange became a matter of public knowledge, they predicted, "the reaction in this country will be immediate and most unfortunate, whatever the merits of the case appear to be in the opinion of the British authorities." Accordingly, the JCS stated that they would refrain from any further participation in deliberations leading to a decision, since "this issue involves on the Allied side only troops of the British Commonwealth."[60] General Henry Maitland Wilson, who was in charge of the British Joint Staff Mission in Washington, told London following his talk with George Marshall that for the Americans "the question whether these Germans would ever be in time to join in the battle, or whether they would take the risks of recapture would not enter into public calculations, and was therefore beside the point." One way to overcome American opposition might be to propose that the 18,000 be exchanged in small batches.[61]

WHITEHALL GIVES IN

Just as the negotiations between the British and the Americans seemed to have reached a deadlock, military developments forced the British to re-evaluate their stand. In light of the advance of American forces into Germany, British officials recognized toward the end of March that it was "extremely improbable that the Germans could carry out any exchange, at least through Switzerland." Whether they could do so through Sweden depended on the state of the railways, roads, and telegraph communications. The German legation in Bern told the Swiss government on 27 March that the German High Command would require eight weeks to prepare an exchange. Under these circumstances, the Foreign Office thought that even if—hypothetically—the Allied land and air offensives were immediately halted, the exchange of 7,000 long-term prisoners could not take place before early May and that a second exchange could not occur until some weeks later.[62]

Roberts, who was a firm supporter of exchanging able-bodied POWs, now had to accept the inevitable conclusion that "there is in fact no prospect of the balance of 18,000 being exchanged, and that it would be stupid to antagonize the American Chiefs of Staff by pressing on with this plan." Well aware of Whitehall's sensitivity to public opinion in regard to the government's handling of the POW problem, Roberts believed that the recovery of large number of POWs in the near future would satisfy the public. Still, the moment was not ripe for the British government to state publicly that no more exchanges of POWs would take place. Instead, he suggested, Whitehall should take advantage of the imminent release of POWs to conceal its failure to repatriate long-term prisoners. Sounding both frustrated and as though wanting to exonerate his government, he added: "It is not our fault that our efforts of last year to get an agreement about long-term prisoners failed owing to the German Government's lack of interest in the question, or that when a month ago the Germans became interested internal conditions in Germany had deteriorated so far as to make any further exchange most unlikely."[63]

Meanwhile, at the beginning of April—when the Germans had largely recognized they had lost the war—the Swiss government learned from the

German legation that Berlin had declined the British offer of an initial exchange of 5,000 or 7,000 POWs, as it "fails to ensure requisite equality of treatment of British and German prisoners of war." Britain wanted the repatriation of British POWs who had fallen into German hands before 1 July 1940 but offered the repatriation only of German POWs who were in England. As it was a known fact that the mass of German POWs who had first fallen into British hands had been shipped overseas, especially to Canada, the German government "cannot declare their agreement to a proposal which does not apply equally on both sides to prisoners of war who have been longest in captivity." The Germans also declined the British request to include merchant seamen in this exchange, arguing—contrary to their actual practice—that London was well aware that Berlin did not regard merchant seamen as POWs.[64]

Given the circumstances, London realistically concluded that by now it was "too late to carry out any exchange."[65] Accordingly, the COS instructed General Wilson in April 1945 to inform the JCS that the negotiations with the Germans "are now unlikely to come to anything" and that Britain did not expect to reach agreement on the interim exchange of 7,000 POWs with the Germans, "who are probably incapable of making necessary arrangements." In any event, Britain was now abandoning the project. Wilson was also asked to tell Marshall that "we entirely understand the point of view of the U.S. Chiefs of Staff and appreciate their attitude to these negotiations."[66]

It was natural for Roberts, as head of the Foreign Office's PWD, to blame the Germans for the fact that none of Britain's long-term prisoners were repatriated during the war. But there were other reasons, closer to home. British efforts to negotiate with the Germans a mutual exchange of long-term POWs began as late as April 1944. Although acting out of concern for the growing distress these POWs were suffering, Whitehall was primarily prompted by the ongoing criticism leveled at it in the House of Commons, in the press, and on the part of the families of the POWs for the way it was handling the POW issue. Well aware of the lack of priority it had given the problem, the government was troubled by the unfavorable judgment of the wider public it could expect after hostilities had come to an end and by the political implications this might have. This may explain why Whitehall tried to reach an agreement with Berlin even when the war itself was already drawing to a close and the benefit for the POWs themselves was likely to be minor.

In the end, negotiations over the mutual exchange of long-term prisoners foundered for two main reasons. First, the Germans postponed reacting to

Britain's proposals for so long that when they finally did react, the situation on the battlefield made any exchange effectively impossible. At the same time, the British refrained from pressing the Germans when the time was ripe for such an exchange. Second, the Americans were opposed to the idea. Prompted by Secretary of War Henry Stimson, Washington refused to go along with any such exchange because the price—the strengthening of German combat forces—was deemed too high. Even more determining for Washington—though this was never openly stated—was that only a few American POWs were actually to benefit if an agreement were reached. For the sake of the partnership, however, Washington was reluctantly willing to agree to a total exchange of no more than 5,000 able-bodied POWs. Given the Americans' firm objection and the realization that by then such an exchange was no longer realistic, the British decided, in April 1945, to concede the issue and to concentrate on the quick repatriation of liberated British prisoners, including those held by the Soviets.[67]

THE FINAL STAGE OF THE WAR

Prisoners' Safety and the Collapse of Germany

ALLIED AIR RAIDS

Neither in London nor in Washington, until the end of 1943, did the physical safety of British and American troops who had fallen into German hands appear prominently on the agenda of government officials. Initial apprehension in Britain that the Germans might act against British prisoners in an openly brutal fashion gave way quite soon to the perception that Berlin would abide by the 1929 Geneva Convention and treat POWs in the manner to which the convention's signatories had committed themselves.[1] The Americans—until December 1941 the protecting power—had reached the same conclusion. Inevitably, some POWs were killed while in captivity, but the number of such incidents remained low. Between January 1941 and August 1943, according to German information, sixty-eight British POWs had been fatally shot (twenty-one in 1941, thirty-two in 1942, and fifteen in the first eight months of 1943). The periodical survey published by the German Ministry of Foreign Affairs, which contained these data, showed further that the average number per month had declined since the middle of 1942, until, in June 1943, a total of six POWs were fatally injured, four of them while attempting to escape. Proportionally, the number of German POWs fatally injured by the British during 1941 was more than double the number of British POWs shot in German camps, while for 1942 and 1943, the figures were just about even.[2]

Ironically, the one main form of organized retaliation the Germans carried out until the end of 1943—the shackling of several thousands of British POWs—only strengthened Whitehall in its belief that there was no likely threat to the prisoners' lives. The devastating air raids on German cities Britain and the United States carried out during the summer and fall of 1943, however, again raised the specter of German reprisals and renewed fears for the physical safety of British and U.S. POWs.

Goebbels's diaries clearly show the palpable shock and furious reactions Allied bombings caused. "During the night," Goebbels noted on 29 July, "we had the heaviest raid yet made on Hamburg." He quoted a report that spoke of "a catastrophe the extent of which simply staggers the imagination. A city of a million inhabitants has been destroyed in a manner unparalleled in history. We are faced with problems that are almost impossible of solution. Food must be found for this population of a million. Shelter must be secured. The people must be evacuated as far as possible."[3] More than 50 percent of Hamburg was entirely destroyed during the Allied raids between 24 and 30 July; approximately 30,000 people died, and more than half a million lost their homes.[4] A succession of raids on Berlin, also toward the end of July, killed about 40,000 civilians and caused as many injuries. The reaction of German leaders was not late in coming. On 10 August, for example, Himmler declared, "It is not the task of the police to intervene in altercations between Germans and landed English and American terrorist pilots who have bailed out."[5] As SS Reichsführer, Himmler was thereby in effect sanctioning the murder of people entitled to the protection of the Geneva Convention, while Wilhelm Keitel, chief of staff of the OKW, agreed to have captured enemy airmen be placed in camps in large cities threatened by Western air attacks.[6]

Allied raids continued, however, and on 5 September the RAF concentrated heavy bombing on the Mannheim-Ludwigshafen area, destroying both towns. A month later, on 4 October, large parts of the city of Frankfurt am Main were laid waste, and four days later most of the center of Hanover was destroyed. The raid on Kassel on 22 October created a huge firestorm, like the one that had ravaged Hamburg three months earlier. Returning from Kassel, Goebbels wrote in his diary on 6 November: "The impression is devastating. The entire center of the city and most of the outlying sections have been destroyed. A gruesome picture strikes the eye. The destruction here can be compared only to that in Hamburg. A catastrophic fire of vast extent has run its unhindered course."[7]

When, in November, the RAF renewed its focus on Berlin, Goebbels again witnessed the onslaught: "Bombs and land mines of notable size were dropped over the whole government quarter," he wrote on 24 November. "They destroyed everything around the Postdamer Platz [Berlin's busiest square]," and later on that day, "Devastation is again appalling in the government section as well as in the western and northern suburbs. . . . The government quarter is nothing short of an inferno. One can hardly recognize the Wilhelmplatz."[8] Two days later, Goebbels once again referred to the air raids and to Britain's role: "The English are achieving nothing with their attempts to unload the responsibility for air warfare on us. Everybody in

Germany knows that the English started it and that the blood guilt falls on them. The English now openly admit the terroristic intentions underlying their air raids. They talk with brutal cynicism about the block busters that were at work on the capital and that will continue to come."[9]

Apprehension in London and Washington about the possible fate of their POWs further deepened following the Kharkov trial in December 1943, when the Soviets hanged three Germans and a Russian collaborator who had been found guilty of executing thousands of Soviet citizens in specially constructed "gas cars," of destroying cities and towns, and of shooting wounded POWs.[10] Several days after the Kharkov proceedings, Paul Karl Schmidt, acting director of the Reich's news service, stated that if the reports of the Soviet prosecutor's declaration were true—that this trial had been carried out in accordance with certain principles laid down in a declaration signed in Moscow by Churchill, Roosevelt, and Stalin—then "this murder," as he called the sentence that was carried out, took on a different aspect: "Statesmen of the Anglo-Saxon nations then share the responsibility for this crime." German military courts, Schmidt warned, "will therefore shortly have to deal with those British and American prisoners who are accused of serious breaches of international law but who have not yet faced trial."[11]

Although it clearly seemed to be part of German tactics to try to take advantage of the Kharkov trial in the first place so as to create friction between the Western Allies and the Soviets, both the British and the Americans took the German threat seriously. Washington was particularly perturbed by Schmidt's warnings, since dispatches from Berlin connected his statements with the current German press campaign against American airmen, whose names and pictures were being published. The airmen had been charged with terrorist bombing and also accused of sporting "gangster squadron" insignia, such as "Murder Incorporated" and "Apartment Breakers." Leland Harrison, American minister in Switzerland, thought that the campaign was intended to pave the way either for Germany's use of terrorist weapons in reprisal or for punitive measures against captured Allied airmen.[12]

Given the intensification of German threats, Chief of Staff George Marshall wrote in a memorandum he handed to Roosevelt on 29 December 1943 that "as the effects of the bombing of Germany grew more seriously, desperate measures would probably be employed to discourage further attacks" and that the "recently announced intent of the Germans to try captive American and British airmen [was] concrete evidence of such intention." Marshall thought that from a military point of view it would be unwise to specify any particular form of retribution because "any mention of chemical attack, for example, or other specific measures might well play directly into German hands." That German propaganda had specifically excluded Russian airmen from the list published in the German press of POWs who might be put on trial meant that Berlin recognized that the Russians would retaliate immediately and in a manner that would be disastrous for German interests. On the other hand, public opinion in both the United States and Britain, the Germans assumed, would preclude them from adopting harsh measures. Marshall recommended issuing an official warning threatening the German people with retaliation if American and British prisoners were not treated according to the Geneva Convention.[13]

President Roosevelt believed that the United States should have a definite plan of action ready, though "such action need not be announced beforehand but . . . should be put into effect the minute the Germans start anything." The president drew encouragement from the fact that the Western Allies held more German prisoners than vice versa.[14] Secretary of State Cordell Hull found the situation after the Kharkov trial too tense to take any chances. He instructed the American minister in Bern to make it clear to the Germans that the U.S. administration was not taking any action against POWs as the Soviets had done but that the Americans were scrupulously adhering to the provisions of the Geneva Convention, to which both they and the Germans were bound.[15] Toward the end of March 1944, the Germans declared that "preparations for the trial of Allied soldiers charged with war crimes are now well advanced," but they added that these trials would not actually take place unless the Allies initiated new trials against German POWs.[16] Simultaneously, Nazi leaders continued to openly support violent measures against captured airmen, including lynching. Goebbels did so in two articles he published in the *Völkischer Beobachter* and *Das Reich* and Martin Bormann, Hitler's powerful secretary, in a meeting with all Gauleiters (district leaders).[17]

How serious the situation had become the British learned when, in the second half of March 1944, Dr. Carl Burckhardt, president of the ICRC, informed the British minister in Geneva, Clifford Norton, that the OKW was convinced that British and American airmen in the POW camps were making preparations to join in any revolt that might break out in Germany; in the event that this occurred, German authorities would be "compelled to take special measures." Burckhardt took this to mean that the prisoners' rights and privileges under the Geneva Convention might severely be curtailed in the near future.[18] The stark reality would only gradually become clear in the weeks that followed.

THE EXECUTION OF FIFTY RAF OFFICERS

When he arrived at Stalag Luft III (Sagan) on 17 April 1944 for one of his routine visits, Gabriel Naville, head of the British Interests Division at the Swiss legation in Berlin, was officially informed by the camp's commander, Colonel Friedrich-Wilhelm von Lindeiner-Wildau, that three weeks earlier, on 25 March, 76 RAF officers had escaped from the camp through a tunnel they had succeeded in digging. A subsequent investigation had led to 190 officers who in one way or another were implicated in the escape. Fifteen escapees had been recaptured immediately and brought back to the camp, where they received a punishment of twenty-one days in solitary confinement, but forty-seven others had been killed while resisting recapture or while trying to escape again after their capture.[19] Fourteen officers were still at large. When Naville pressed him for further details, von Lindeiner-Wildau insisted he could add nothing to the statement given out by his superiors concerning the death of the officers.[20]

According to senior British officers Naville interviewed in the camp, the German account did not tally with the facts because officers were well aware that resistance was quite useless, and no one who had previously escaped from this camp had ever resisted recapture. A few might have resisted this time, but it was absolutely impossible that such a large number had done so; and even then, not all would have been killed. Recaptured escapees also told him that thirty of their fellow escapees, handcuffed and under heavy civilian police escort, had been seen leaving Görlitz prison on a lorry. It was most improbable that any of these POWs would have made a further escape attempt and would have been killed then. Instead, they suspected that all forty-seven had been summarily executed by the Gestapo.[21]

It was only in mid-May that Norton could brief London. Outraged at the killing of the forty-seven air force officers, the War Cabinet asked the Swiss government to take the matter up with the highest German authorities and to demand a full and immediate report on the circumstances in which these officers had lost their lives. The suspicion that the recaptured men might have been murdered deepened for Whitehall because of the failure of the German authorities to notify the protecting power immediately of the

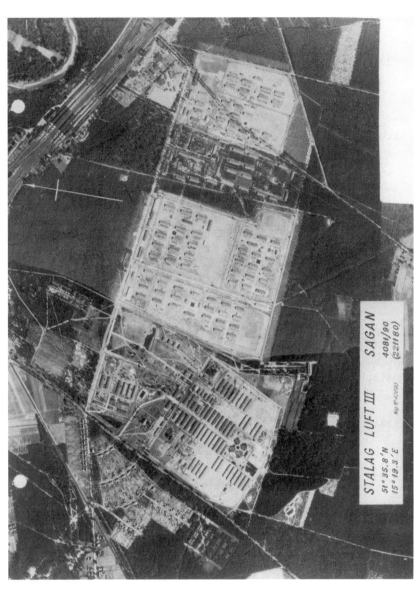

STALAG LUFT III SAGAN
4081/90
51° 35.8′ N
15° 19.3′ E
(22H80)
Neg N°42920

Air photograph of Stalag Luft III (Sagan). (Courtesy PRO, Kew, England)

deaths as required under the agreement Britain and German had concluded in August 1942.[22]

Within days, information about the killing of the officers began to appear in the British press, which made Eden decide to briefly inform the House of Commons.[23] The War Cabinet would have preferred to wait for further information from the protecting power, but this seemed no longer feasible.[24] On 24 May 1944, the *Daily Mail*'s correspondent in Stockholm, Walter Farr, quoted reports, "which appear to have good foundations," to the effect that of a total of 3,000 Allied prisoners 2,700, including 53 British servicemen, had died recently under suspicious circumstances at an unregistered prisoners camp near Bremen; further, 27 British and Dominion POWs had died at Graudenz, just south of Gdynia, on the banks of the Vistula. The Bremen "penitentiary" was reserved exclusively "for what are termed 'unruly' men who have either attempted escape or not submitted to the discipline demanded by their German guards." Normally, prisoners were not sent to Bremen from ordinary camps, the paper's readers were told, unless they had made five or six escape attempts.[25] The *Daily Mail* correspondent claimed that he had based his story on statements the British military attaché in Stockholm had made to him. The latter, however, strongly denied the attribution.[26]

Naville, who visited Stalag Luft III again at the beginning of June, could now tell the British that fifty (not forty-seven) of the seventy-six officers who had escaped had been killed, fifteen had been recaptured and brought back to Stalag Luft III, and eleven were still missing. The dead RAF officers were of the following nationalities: twenty-three English, six Canadians, four Australians, three South Africans, two New Zealanders, six Poles, two Norwegians, one Belgian, one Frenchman, one Greek, and one Lithuanian. One of the escapees who had been recaptured told Naville that the German interrogator had informed him that he was in the hands not of the military authorities but of the Gestapo and had warned him that he might never get back to his camp. The interrogator had added that any escapee found dressed in civilian clothes no longer had the protection of the Geneva Convention. The general atmosphere during the entire interrogation was marked by intimidation. Two of the returned prisoners had been told they would be shot, others that they would never again see their wives. One officer had been threatened that he would be shot if he did not sign his statement, another that he would be decapitated because he refused to answer questions.[27]

One of the returned escapees related how all nineteen in his party had been taken away by armed uniformed police in a motortruck with one car in front and one behind and brought to Görlitz. Any attempt to escape again must have been impossible in the case of at least one of the dead prisoners, Albert H. Hake: he had been so badly frostbitten that he could hardly stand. Several others had told Naville that they had no intention of trying to escape again because they were too exhausted and too hungry. There was too much snow. Another returned POW maintained that "if any at Goerlitz had been shown an open door and told they could walk out all would have refused. Everybody was very hungry, exhausted and the weather outside was hopeless." Other returned escapees made similar statements.[28]

In mid-June 1944, Berlin published its version of the chain of events that had led to the killing of the RAF officers. During the month of March, the Germans stated, there had been mass escapes of several thousand POWs of various nationalities from camps throughout Germany. These escapes had been systematically prepared, partly by general staffs in communication with foreign countries, and had military and political objectives. They were intended to undermine public security in Germany and to paralyze administrative and police authorities. In order to repress such subversive undertakings and in the interest of the security of commandos entrusted with searching out and recapturing escapees, severe orders had been given. As they carried out this large-scale search operation, commandos were to pursue at all costs anyone who failed to halt when challenged, offered resistance, or made renewed attempts to escape after capture. They were instructed to make use of their weapons to prevent fugitives from resisting capture or trying to flee again.

  With the exception of about one hundred POWs who had not yet been found, all other prisoners who had escaped in March had been recaptured and taken back to their camps. According to the German Ministry of Foreign Affairs, against a number of prisoners, including fifty from Stalag Luft III, firearms had to be used. The protecting power was further told that, as requested by the senior British officer at Stalag Luft III, the urns with the ashes of twenty-eight prisoners who had been shot and then cremated had been taken to that camp. The Germans also maintained that the large-scale search operation they had had to conduct throughout Germany had made it impossible to furnish precise data with the usual promptness. The exact clarification of individual cases, it was argued, was difficult and demanded much time, the more so since escapees often had no identity papers with them, carried false identity papers, or refused to disclose their identity. The search for POWs still on the run was not yet completed.[29]

By this time, the War Cabinet no longer doubted that the Gestapo had murdered the escaped officers. Foreign Secretary Eden thought that the motive had been the Germans' alarm over the high numbers of escapes that had taken place and the effect this was having on foreign laborers.[30] On 23 June 1944, Eden briefed the House of Commons and denied that there had been any further mass shooting of British POWs. After presenting the German explanation, which he saw as an attempt to justify the shootings, Eden summarized for the House what had been learned from statements made under oath by officers who had been in the camp at the time of the escape and who had recently been repatriated. One such statement came from Group Captain H. M. Massey, who had been the senior officer and had acted as the prisoners' representative.

On the night of 24–25 March, as Eden narrated it, some seventy-six POWs had exited a tunnel the POWs had excavated at night. Another four who followed the original group had been detected and arrested at the mouth of the tunnel; these had immediately been removed to camp cells. The next day the Gestapo arrived and took control of the camp. Except for one shot fired at the last of the seventy-six fleeing through the tunnel, no one in the camp heard any shooting at the time of the escape. The four captured prisoners were brought to the Gestapo prison at Görlitz, where they were put into cells containing five or six prisoners each. All of them were interrogated and kept in shocking conditions with very little food. The Gestapo's explicit threats included the following: "We have got you here. Nobody knows you are here. To all intents and purposes you are civilian. You are wearing civilian clothes and we can do with you what we like. You can disappear."

After their interrogation, all prisoners were taken back to their cells. Later some German officials entered and picked out a number of men who were seen from the prison to be driven away handcuffed and in the charge of Gestapo officials armed with tommy guns; the remainder were handed over to the Luftwaffe and brought back to the camp. Among those shot were all recaptured officers of European nationality. They had been taken away on different days in small parties, with one larger party of about twenty men. On 6 April, Eden stressed, the very day on which the commandant of the camp had informed Group Captain Massey that the number shot was

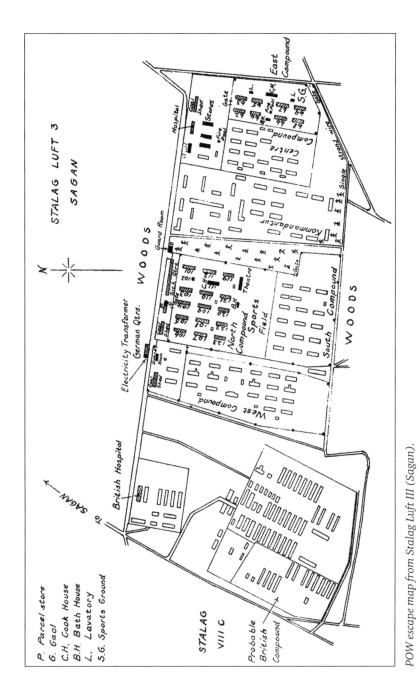

POW escape map from Stalag Luft III (Sagan).
(Courtesy PRO, Kew, England; PRO, AIR 40/229)

forty-one, the Gestapo took away another party of eight, six of whom were then later shot. The number of killed given to the Swiss inspector on 17 April had been forty-seven.

Eden then detailed a number of telling facts: first, no orders had at any time been given to British POWs, in the event of escape, to take part in any subversive action as alleged by the Germans. Second, all these officers knew the futility of trying to resist when recaptured. Third, owing to exhaustion and ill-treatment at Görlitz, the prisoners had been physically incapable of any renewed escape attempt. Fourth, whether these officers had escaped in small or large numbers—and here Eden was emphatic—there could be no justification for their execution. During the original escape the officers had been in pairs, and when last seen after leaving Görlitz prison, they were in comparatively small numbers, handcuffed and under heavy guard. Fifth, "there were no wounded [recaptured prisoners] as would have been inevitably if the shooting had taken place during an attempt to resist capture." Sixth, the German statement omitted all reference to Görlitz and contained no account of the circumstances that had led to the death of any single officer. Finally, the ashes of twenty-eight of the escaped prisoners had now been returned to Stalag Luft III—significantly the Germans had refused to send back the bodies for burial, and this was the only occasion on which British POWs who had died during captivity had been cremated.

It was abundantly clear, Eden concluded, that none of these officers had met their death while making their escape from Stalag Luft III or resisting capture. "These prisoners of war were murdered at some undefined place or places after their removal from the Gestapo prison at Görlitz, at some date or dates unknown." Denying the Gestapo's contention that the wearing of civilian clothes deprived an escaping POW of the protection of the Geneva Convention, Eden promised that the British government would never cease in its efforts to collect the evidence to identify all those responsible and to track down to the last these "foul criminals" who would "be brought to exemplary justice" once the war was over.[31]

Six of the fifty murdered officers were Canadians. On 23 June, Canadian prime minister Mackenzie King delivered a similar statement in the Canadian House of Commons. King argued that it was natural that men deprived of freedom should attempt to regain it. German prisoners in Canada occasionally escaped from the camps in which they were held, but neither the Canadian government nor the Canadian people were unduly perturbed by such escapes, as the military and police authorities were generally effective in recapturing them. Upon recapture, a German POW might be sentenced to confinement for a period of twenty-eight days but continued to receive full rations as well as opportunities for exercise and reading. This, King emphasized, was the only penalty for an attempted escape authorized by the international convention, which was binding on both the German and the Canadian governments.[32]

The German Foreign Ministry chose not to go into, let alone refute, the details of Eden's statement regarding the murder of the escaped officers. Instead, in a *note verbale* presented to the Swiss, the ministry claimed that the British government had lost all moral legitimacy to criticize Germany. "The Foreign Minister of a country which began bombing warfare against the civilian population, which has murdered tens of thousands of German women and children in terror attacks on dwellings, hospitals and cultural centers, which in an official 'Handbook of modern irregular warfare' written for 'His Majesty's Service' recommended verbally all English soldiers to adopt gangster methods, for example to put out the eyes of unarmed opponents lying on the ground and beat in their skulls with stones, has lost the moral right to touch this question in particular or to raise a complaint against anyone at all." As the behavior of the English foreign minister was unheard of, the German Foreign Office concluded, "the German Government refuse to make any further statements on this matter."[33]

The tone of the German response raised concerns in London as to whether the execution of the fifty RAF officers represented a shift in German policy vis-à-vis Allied POWs, all the more because German camp guards had now also been authorized to shoot without warning any prisoner whom they found touching the barbed wire of the camp fence or leaving his billets at night without permission.[34] It was around this time that the British started collecting evidence about Germans who were implicated in the murder of POWs so that cases could be brought against them at the United Nations War Crimes Commission (UNWCC), which the Allied nations had established in October 1943.[35]

DEEPENING CONCERNS

In both London and Washington, the Allied invasion of Normandy on 6 June 1944 augmented fears of German reprisals. With regard to the Germans' behavior toward Allied POWs upon Germany's collapse, the British Joint Intelligence Sub-Committee (JISC) examined two scenarios: in one, the defeated military leaders were still in effective control of Germany; in the other, there was complete chaos. It concluded that in the first case "wholesale planned atrocities against prisoners of war in German camps are highly improbable, although in isolated instances prisoners of war escaping from their camps might be in danger of being killed if they fell into the hands of the S.S. or Gestapo." In exceptional cases, however, fanatical ss troops in the field might shoot prisoners, particularly if they had already maltreated them. Broadly speaking, the JISC held that, unlike the SS, the Wehrmacht in general adhered to the provisions of the Geneva Convention of 1929; furthermore, one of the main aims of the Wehrmacht leaders in assuming control would be to establish an administration that the Allies might view with less disfavor than the present Nazi regime. Action taken against POWs at the moment of Allied victory, moreover, would destroy any hope that Britain and America could or would act as restraining influences on Russia, whose vengeance the Germans feared greatly. In sum, German military commanders, still in control, were not expected to allow action to be taken against Allied POWs.[36]

The JISC believed, however, that if there was chaos in Germany at the time of its defeat, the treatment of POWs was likely to vary from place to place. Most, if not all, Allied POWs, it was pointed out, were under the control of the German service authorities, and many of the camp commandants were "dug-out" officers of the old German army. In the hour of defeat, the thinking went, the inclination of these authorities would be to curry favor with the victors by considerate treatment of POWs. "At such a moment the camp guards would have everything to lose and nothing to gain by ill-treating Allied prisoners of war and it is in the highest degree unlikely that they would do so." These guards would be fully aware that very shortly they would have to account for the safety of the prisoners in their charge.

The only factions that might ill-treat POWs would be the SS and the Gestapo, some members of which had already done so, but the less fanatical and less deeply compromised members of these organizations, too, would more likely try to win favor by a last-minute show of moderation. It was the extremists among them who presented the danger. The JISC saw the possibility that Nazi die-hards would resist to the bitter end and that, fully armed, utterly ruthless, and totally indifferent to the consequences to either their country or themselves, they might try to revenge the defeat of their Führer and the Nazi cause, even at "five minutes past twelve." Their victims would be both prisoners of war and enslaved workers, whose killing might either appear as a delusionary act of heroic resistance or be resorted to as a means of eliminating dangerous witnesses. The JISC thought that camp commandants, guards, and other military Wehrmacht authorities might be persuaded to resist such action if they were clearly warned that the Allies would not entertain any excuses or attempts to shift responsibility to the ss or the Gestapo. The assessment was that with Germany in a state of chaos there would be local rather than general ss and Gestapo acts. Still, the possibility existed that the Nazi leaders might use prisoners as hostages in an attempt to bargain for their own immunity. This course, if adopted as a matter of policy, might in fact precede the breakdown of military resistance.[37]

Some information about an impending change in German attitudes toward the POWs also reached Washington and London through seriously ill and wounded POWs who had been returned home in the exchange that had taken place in September 1944. In a memorandum circulated in the War Cabinet in October 1944, James Grigg, the secretary of state for war, reported that interrogation of recently repatriated POWs from Germany revealed there was clear apprehension in the camps about the attitude that certain sections of the German community, in particular the ss and the Gestapo, would adopt toward POWs. Whereas the morale of the regular army guards was low, that of the ss had remained good, to the extent that attempts by civilians and guards to fraternize with the prisoners had ceased out of fear of the ss and the Gestapo. In some camps, German staff had hinted to the prisoners that there was a chance they would be used as hostages or even killed outright.[38]

The SBO in Oflag IX A/Z (Ratenburg), for example, reported that there was a very strong feeling in the Oflag that British POWs in Germany might be massacred by the more fanatical of the Germans when the collapse came. "It is felt that the Germans may either seize British Ps/W as hostages for their own lenient treatment by the Allies or alternatively may adopt the attitude that if they are themselves doomed they may as well 'take with them' all the Allied Ps/W available." Although the POWs in Oflag IX A/Z regarded this fate as a general possibility throughout Germany, they expressed particular fear for the fate of POWs in East Prussia, who might be massacred before the Allies reached that territory and before the more moderate Germans themselves could prevent the atrocities.[39]

In his report, Grigg highlighted the seriousness of the situation by including several instances of the murder of POWs who had been captured in the course of the fighting in France after the invasion. A party of twenty-four Canadians and two British soldiers captured at Chateau d'Audrieu, for example, had been shot by members of the Twelfth ss Reconnaissance Battalion of the Twelfth ss Panzer Division (Hitler Jugend). In another case, an ss officer had shot twenty-four American soldiers who had surrendered and thrown down their arms after being surrounded by ss troops. In still another case, eight POWs from the First SAS Regiment had been taken to a wood near Noailles by German soldiers, led by two ss officers and one Gestapo official; the death sentence had been read out, and the German escort had opened fire. Grigg, of course, also referred to the murder by the Gestapo of fifty of the RAF officers who had escaped from Stalag Luft III in March 1944.[40] Although all these murders had been perpetrated against POWs in the field, and not in camps themselves, the growing concern was that they reflected a new trend in Germany's policy.

The British cabinet shared its apprehension with Washington that Hitler and his associates might threaten to murder some or all of the prisoners unless the Allies agreed to come to terms with them. The object of such a maneuver, according to the British government, might "be either to avoid unconditional surrender or to save the lives of the most important Nazi gangsters and war criminals or to attempt to cause dissension among the Allies in the final stages of the war."[41] The Americans did not need the British warning. U.S. Army Air Forces planners had reached the conclusion in early November 1944 that recent developments indicated the possibility, if not the probability, of large-scale mistreatment of American POWs, particularly USAAF personnel, in Germany upon the cessation of hostilities in Europe. Their fears were based on, among other evidence, German propaganda, which consistently portrayed USAAF personnel as "Luftgangsters" and murderers; the lynching of American airmen by German civilians; the fact that many camps had suffered direct losses both in property and in the lives of guards as a result of Allied bombings; the fact that Hitler Jugend had been spotted, armed with rifles and machine guns, in the near vicinity of several POW camps holding Americans; and, of course, the murder of the fifty escapees from Stalag Luft III.[42]

Senior American POW officers, like their British counterparts, took advantage of their repatriation to prompt the War Department to come up with answers to the question of how to protect prisoners immediately after hostilities had come to an end. Colonel Thomas Drake, the SAO in Oflag 64 (Schubin), who had been repatriated in September 1944, declared that mass reprisals in his camp were almost a certainty. Prisoners in Stalag XVII B (Gneixendorf) related how they had heard from several different sources that the Nazi party leader of the district had promised vengeance against the POWs in the event of Germany's defeat. Senior American officer Colonel

Darr H. Alkire, of the West Compound of Stalag III (Sagan), delivered the message that men, arms, and food should be flown into his camp as soon as the war ended. He stressed that it was important to get the POWs out of the area as soon as possible because he was sure there would be an acute food shortage and feared attacks by civilians. For his part, Lieutenant John V. McGrath, repatriated from Stalag III, maintained that the Luftwaffe apparently had turned the running of the camp over to the Gestapo, which now seemed to be in complete charge.[43]

A letter dated 10 September 1944 and signed by Martin Bormann referred to a marked increase in resistance among POWs in the previous few weeks. Accordingly, those in charge of POWs were instructed to give their full attention "even to the slightest signs pointing toward the existence of illegal organizations, resistance groups, etc. Every suspicion must be followed up immediately and if results are obtained action must be taken in close collaboration with the Gestapo."[44] Several days later, Hitler issued an order stating that, as of 1 October 1944, the supervision of all POWs and internees as well as of POW camps and establishments with guard sections was to be transferred to the commander of the reserve army, Heinrich Himmler. Himmler, for his part, delegated the actual control of POW affairs to his right-hand man, SS lieutenant general Gottlob Berger, chief of staff of the Volkssturm, the last-ditch defenders of the Third Reich, formed in October 1944. Himmler further directed that the commanders in charge of POWs in each Wehrkreis (army district) would come under the authority of the higher SS and police leaders: "The strengthening of security measures in the control and handling of POWs to be assured by a coordination of effort between SS Lt. General Berger and Chief of the Security Police, SS Lt. General Dr. Kaltenbrunner." All POW camps and labor detachments were to be checked immediately and all suitable measures taken to effect greater security to prevent uprisings.[45]

After the war, in his testimony before the Nuremberg military tribunal, Berger mentioned four reasons Hitler had allegedly given for deciding to make these changes: "(1) The case of Sagan [Stalag Luft III], (2) the matter of the broadcasting station in the American prisoner-of-war camp Fuerstenberg [Stalag III B]; (3) the revolt in Warsaw [1 August–2 October 1944], and (4) the Allied plan concerning the landing of airborne troops and parachutists in the vicinity of prisoners-of-war camps." Berger further stated that Hitler told him he had lost confidence in the present administration of POW affairs and that "all people were lying to him and betraying him and that this Sagan affair would not have happened if the commander there had acted and undertaken suitable measures, in accordance with his duties."[46]

Official and confidential conversations that London held with representatives of the protecting power, members of the Swiss legation in Berlin, and the ICRC in Switzerland confirmed the reports that the SS and Gestapo were increasing their grip over POW camps and administration. The Swiss maintained that the Nazi authorities were obsessed with the possibility that POWs would act in conjunction with organized sabotage or uprisings, a situation that would constitute the greatest threat to their safety.[47] From Oflag VII B (Eichstätt) came reports of a plan, known as V. 15, that indicated how, during the final stages of the war, the Gestapo intended to murder POWs, especially those near the towns.[48] Intelligence reports revealed the likelihood of reprisals against British and American POWs in retaliation for British and U.S. air attacks.[49]

The interception of a two-year-old order from Hitler's headquarters when it was reissued with a supplementary order on 19 October 1944 further increased American and British apprehensions. The Germans clearly intended to exterminate all commandos, including airborne troops, who had been captured outside the limits of normal combat activities. Although neither order referred to prisoners in POW camps, Western Allies read into them a decision on the part of Germany to ignore the Geneva Convention and to begin implementing a truly ruthless policy. The earlier order, of 18 October 1942, stated that Germany's adversaries had been employing methods of warfare contrary to the provision of the Geneva Convention. It claimed that the so-called commandos were recruited in part among common criminals and released prisoners whose behavior was particularly brutal and underhanded—they had orders not to hesitate to kill unarmed prisoners if they were an obstacle to the completion of their mission. In fact, the captured enemy orders advocated killing prisoners as "standard practice." The reader may recall that the British had carried out a commando raid on the Channel island of Sark on 3 October in which they killed four shackled Germans who had tried to escape.[50] For these reasons, Hitler ordered that "[f]rom now on all enemies on so-called commando missions in Europe or Africa challenged by German troops, even if they are to all appearances soldiers in uniform or demolition troops, whether armed or unarmed, in battle or in flight, are to be slaughtered to the last man. It does not make any difference whether they are landed from ships or aeroplanes for their actions, or whether they are dropped by parachute. Even if these individuals when found should apparently be prepared to give themselves up, as a matter of principle, no pardon is to be granted them."[51]

These provisions, the order continued, did not apply to enemy soldiers who surrendered or were captured in actual combat within the limits of normal combat activities (large-scale offensive actions, landing and airborne operations). Nor did they apply to enemy troops captured during naval engagements or to aviators who had bailed out to save their life during aerial combat. "I will hold responsible under military law," Hitler concluded, "for failing to carry out this order, all commanders and officers who either have neglected their duty of instructing the troops about this order, or acted against this order where it was to be executed."[52]

The 1944 supplement to the earlier order confirmed that the latter remained valid and, following the Anglo-American landing in France, even extended it to enemy soldiers in uniform within the immediate combat zone of the beachhead (i.e., within the areas of the front-line divisions but including reserves as far back as corps headquarters). "Commencing tomorrow," the supplementary order read, "the Oberbefehlshaber will report daily the number of saboteurs thus liquidated. This measure is, above all, valid for operations conducted under direction of the Militärbefehlshaber. The number of executions must appear in the daily communique of the Wehrmacht to serve as a warning for potential terrorists."[53]

Eisenhower suspected that this policy was already being implemented against U.S., British, and French airborne troops. For example, one of the cases investigated and proved was that of thirty-one members of the First SAS Regiment who had been taken prisoner on 3 July 1944 and removed first to Poitiers for interrogation and then to an isolated area in a forest near Rom, where they had been executed by the Gestapo.[54] Secretary of State for War Grigg told the War Cabinet in mid-October 1944 that evidence was accumulating about prisoners being murdered, mostly close to the battlefield or on the way back from the battlefield, by SS elements in the German army.[55] The British further learned from the Swiss of another order the Germans had issued in an effort to prevent POWs from escaping. Constant escape attempts by British POWs had created considerable difficulties for the Germans, who believed that the escapees might incite foreigners forced to work in Germany. The Germans assumed that captured escapees had taken part in sabotage acts, and the onus was placed on them to prove the contrary. The Swiss also informed the British that escaping had now, at end of 1944, become extremely hazardous, as escapees who were caught were handed over to the Gestapo, which meant there was a good chance they would be shot. British intelligence interpreted Hitler's instructions as furnishing an authorization to shoot future escapees out of hand, whereby the execution of those who had escaped from Stalag Luft III showed how far the Gestapo was prepared to go.[56] Taking the German threats seriously, both the British and the Americans announced that escape was no longer considered a duty.[57]

SETTING PRIORITIES

The possibility that the Germans might begin to kill British and U.S. POWs without inhibition led Lieutenant General Archibald E. Nye, vice chief of the Imperial General Staff, to present the War Cabinet at the beginning of September 1944 with three alternatives for assisting or even giving some kind of protection to the POWs. Two were categorized as direct assistance, namely, the use of airborne troops and the dropping of arms into prison camps. The third alternative was to issue grave warnings, backed up, if necessary, by counterthreats. Significantly, Nye based his analysis on the fact that so far army intelligence had received no concrete indication that Hitler was likely to carry out his threat.

Nye's point of departure was that it would be militarily unacceptable to enter into any negotiations that might involve suspension of the fighting against Germany at the present time, and not only because this would create a dangerous precedent for the war against Japan. In examining the three options, Nye recognized that so long as German military resistance continued, no opportunity might arise for the tactical use of airborne troops immediately in front of the advancing Allied ground troops. In any case, the numerous camps were too widely dispersed, and many of the prisoners were not accommodated in camps at all. Ultimately, he did not want to divert troops required for current operations for the sole purpose of protecting Allied POWs, "whose safety would best be assured by the speedy occupation and control of Germany." In other words, airborne troops should be employed to protect POWs only when this did not conflict with the strategic interests of the battlefield.

Similarly, Nye ruled out dropping arms because this would be very difficult to execute and, even if partially successful, "would probably precipitate the action which we wish to avoid and which might not otherwise have taken place." Still, he agreed that in some cases where contact had already been made through agents and where guards were known to be sympathetic, the idea could work. In the final analysis, he came down in favor of the highest Anglo-American and Russian authorities issuing a general warning as the most promising way of assisting Allied POWs.[58] The War Cabinet suggested that Nye's proposal be taken up by Churchill and Roosevelt, who were to meet in Quebec during 11–16 September 1944. The latter, however, never came around to discussing the matter.[59]

U.S. Joint Chiefs of Staff thought differently than the British. Concerned that when hostilities had come to an end U.S. prisoners in German prison camps might be subjected to attack by the Gestapo or by German civilians, they believed direct action was needed to assure the safety of the POWs. One course was to dispatch protective units to German POW camps where Americans were imprisoned and evacuate them as quickly as possible. Initial protection, it was maintained, could be afforded by sending a small number of airborne units and evacuating all prisoners in a relatively short time, provided the Soviets raised no objection.

The American plan took advantage of the fact that about 35,000 of the then (October 1944) approximately 45,000 U.S. POWs in German camps were concentrated in seven camps located in the proposed Soviet zone of occupation in Germany and in Poland and that airfields capable of accommodating transports and bombers existed close to most of these camps. What was needed was to have one regimental combat team flown to or parachuted into the vicinity of each of these camps—if 400 heavy bombers were employed in a transport role, the prisoners in the Soviet zone could be evacuated within four or five days.

The JCS recognized that in order to carry out such an airborne expedition, the Russians had to be informed. But, although about 60 percent of the approximately 600,000 Soviet prisoners were being held in camps in the proposed British and American zones, Moscow had never shown much concern over the fate of its own POWs and might, therefore, be nonreceptive to an American plan for flying U.S. troops into the Soviet zone to protect American POWs. The JCS presumed that the British would agree to plans along the lines described because more than 65 percent of the approximately 180,000 British POWs were held in the proposed Soviet zone.[60]

The British Chiefs of Staff agreed that first priority should be given to making plans for the rescue of American and British POWs and preferred that the Supreme Commander, Allied Expeditionary Force (SCAEF), and the Supreme Allied Commander, Mediterranean (SACMED), examine only subsequently how they could help POWs of the other Allies. In contrast to the inclination of the JCS to present the proposal in terms of a simple operation,[61] the British stressed logistical difficulties: the majority of POWs were held in work detachments, in groups varying from single figures to several thousand, and were located at distances of up to 200 miles from the main camps. The COS thought it best to have the whole project appraised first by the commanders and then approach the Russians only after the plans were firm. They pointed out that the Russians had agreed to discuss the question of POWs at a meeting of the European Advisory Commission (EAC) with a view to preparing a directive to the Allied commanders in chief. The COS feared jeopardizing the success of these negotiations by raising a new issue, especially as the Russians were not expected to rate the offer of reciprocity very highly.[62]

The American Joint Planning Staff (JPS) accepted the British proposal to use troops and aircraft to assist POWs only when it would not interfere with battlefield operations, as the basic premise for action, in any case, was "upon the cessation of organized German resistance or of hostilities." They also agreed that the possible use of motorized columns should be considered. Neither did the Americans object to instructing SCAEF and SACMED to consider subsequent help to other Allies as the British wanted, but they pointed out how the intelligence reports on which the original JCS proposals were based had indicated the likelihood of German reprisal against U.S. and possibly British POWs in retaliation for Allied air attacks. Similar actions against other Allied POWs, it was argued, were not foreseen, and therefore the JCS proposals were intended as specific emergency measures to be used solely in the event of such attacks, not as a general method of returning all POWs. Consideration could be given to helping other Allied prisoners, but only as a precautionary measure to ensure their protection in the event of unforeseen attacks against them. ˙

With respect to the Russians, the JPS agreed that nothing should be done to prejudice Russia's participation in current negotiations within the EAC. The EAC was considering a directive on the broad subject of the repatriation of prisoners, but the particular problem of possible retaliation involved a plan that was purely operational and therefore neither necessary nor desirable if it jeopardized Soviet participation. Mention of this matter should be deferred until after Anglo-American plans had crystallized. Still, the JPS insisted that the Soviets be notified officially of the plans at an appropriate time, rather than risk having them learn of them by accident. The timing should be decided by the Combined Chiefs of Staff after recommendation from the heads of the U.S. and British military missions in Moscow.[63] The JCS adopted the JPS analysis and recommendations and presented them to the British.[64]

On 26 February 1945, the CCS asked both SCAEF and SACMED to prepare an appraisal and a broad outline plan "to dispatch troops by land or air in order to provide for the maximum initial security of such prisoners [U.S. and British POWs] in the European Theater and for [the] earliest possible evacuation of such prisoners using aircraft for this purpose wherever practicable." Both General Eisenhower and General Harold Alexander were instructed to give priority in their plan to the security of prisoners who had been captured while serving under U.S. and British command. Only when this plan had been fully carried out could they give consideration to the protection and evacuation of other Allied POWs within the Anglo-American zones. All plans were to be viewed as precautionary measures, to be employed only in the event that the safety of these prisoners was endangered. Eisenhower and Alexander were told that protective troops and aircraft were to be employed only "where their use does not conflict with gaining victory in the battle," but action was to commence at the earliest possible moment, consistent with the deterioration in Germany's resistance and evidence of its impending surrender. Furthermore, they were told to plan on the assumption that agreement to British and American forces' operating within the Russian zone would be obtained from the Soviet government at the proper time.[65]

The commanders in the field shared the priorities of the CCS. In total, Allied POWs in Austria at the end of 1944 numbered approximately 200,000, of whom approximately 14,000 came from the British Commonwealth, including more than 11,000 from the United Kingdom; there were approximately 5,000 Americans and 40,000 Russians.[66] Alexander was quick to stress how difficult it would be to execute these instructions. The safety of POWs, he argued, could be ensured only by the introduction of substantial forces into Austria, which the Allies were about to take over. If inadequate forces were introduced, "not only are they likely to be overwhelmed but the enemy may be provoked to action against Prisoners of War." According to Alexander's analysis, the cessation of organized German resistance would come about as a result of ongoing operations on both the western and eastern fronts while troops in his theater still remained outside Austria. He believed Austria would be the last part of Greater Germany to be overrun, particularly in view of terrain difficulties and the rumored formation of "Nazi Redoubts" in the Alps. Under these circumstances, the British commander anticipated that a high proportion of ss troops, fanatical Nazis, and war criminals might already have moved to Austria or were about to concentrate there at the time of the surrender. In addition to these elements, who operated either in organized formations or as guerrilla bands, he feared there might be resistance from enemy forces withdrawing into Austria from Italy and Yugoslavia.

Alexander went on to say that it would be impossible for him to introduce into Austria (and maintain there) a force on the order of two divisions in less than three weeks from the cessation of organized resistance. He doubted whether a smaller force could be set up in appreciably less time. Alexander also negated the possibility of parachuting forces from his theater, although he admitted that this was the best solution. His inevitable conclusion was that the quickest, most effective method of ensuring the safety of POWs was to move forces overland into Austria from Russian-occupied Hungary. Not only would the Russians be in the best position to send in adequate troops, but this would happen "in the normal course of their operations." Assuming that more than half of the POW camps were in Russian-held territory, Alexander insisted that obtaining the Soviets' fullest cooperation and support was of the utmost importance. He recommended obtaining their agreement for some Anglo-American missions to be attached to major Soviet formations. "Such Missions could be quickly flown into Russian held airfields and could be provided with adequate transport and wireless communications and some medical equipment. Their primary task would be to try and influence Russians to ensure protection and safety of Prisoners of War until Anglo-American Forces arrived overland and by air."

Alexander was quick to reject the idea of supplying the POWs with arms for their self-protection, as this step "might well provoke attack by such German Forces as are likely to be in Austria and it would not be possible to arm [the POWs] to make effective resistance." It would only, he feared, afford the enemy a pretext for declaring that POWs so armed had forfeited POW status, and so it should be used as a last resort. On the other hand, dropping supplies and medical equipment into POW camps seemed to him the only practical measure the Western powers could take. "In view of [the] probable failure of [the] enemy administrative machine," the British commander concluded, "this measure may well be of utmost importance."[67]

For his part, Eisenhower at the end of March 1945 called the War Department's attention to the fact that of the 257,000 British and U.S. POWs held by the Germans, approximately 97,000 were in the SHAEF sphere and some 70,000 more were believed to be moving into this area, as Russian advances were forcing the German army to retreat. Prisoners of war from other Allied countries numbered approximately 1 million. In most instances, British and U.S. soldiers were not in different camps than the POWs of other nationalities. As a result, Eisenhower stated, priority of security could be given to U.S. and British POWs only when they constituted the majority, as they were in thirty-five camps.

Eisenhower did not rule out the possibility that, under cover of the general disorder and instigated by SS troops or the Gestapo, atrocities might be committed against POWs. Nevertheless, he pointed out that the POW camps were well guarded and that German military forces might be in the vicinity; therefore, the protection of POWs had to be given in force rather than in small detachments. Army group commanders, he explained, would be prepared to dispatch relief columns only to a POW camp lying near their axis of advance, provided that such an action did not come at the expense of the success of the main operations.[68] Prisoner-of-war camps outside the reach of the advancing ground forces could be afforded protection only by dropping airborne forces. This protection, Eisenhower continued, might be extended to camps not yet covered in the Russian sphere and to camps in Austria. Eisenhower also mentioned the formation of three-man reconnaissance teams equipped with radio transmitters to be parachuted into Germany near known POW camps with the object of reporting on conditions at the camps and placing the POWs in wireless communication with SHAEF. These teams would also help to arrange the reception of supplies—plans had been made for dropping rations and medical supplies into camps before they were overrun.[69] However, determined not to give the Germans an excuse to retaliate against the POWs, Eisenhower had issued instructions not to drop arms, ammunition, and sabotage material within twenty-five miles of any known POW camp.[70]

When one further analyzes the approach taken by both Alexander and Eisenhower, it becomes clear that, while they were aware of the threat of German retaliations, they believed that operationally it proved too difficult to offer effective protection to British and American POWs in enemy territory during the final stages of the war. That is, in their assessment the best way to ensure the physical safety of the prisoners was to allow their military operations to unfold as planned. The order of priorities was clear, and there was no serious attempt to question it—the defeat of the enemy came first. Given that state of mind, only the third of Nye's alternatives was left open for the Allies. It had the generals' enthusiastic support.

TRIPARTITE WARNING

That alternative was for the highest Allied authorities to issue a general warning to all individual German commandants and guards, as well as military chiefs, so as to ensure they knew they would be held individually responsible for the safety of POWs in their charge and that no excuse or attempts to shift responsibility onto the SS or Gestapo would be entertained.[71] In London, the War Cabinet wanted the question of a joint warning with the U.S. and Soviet governments cleared as soon as possible and in mid-October 1944 presented them the following text:

> Governments of the United Kingdom, United States and U.S.S.R. hereby issue a solemn warning to all commandants and guards in charge of Allied prisoners of war in Germany and German occupied territory and to members of Gestapo and all other persons of whatsoever service or rank in whose charge Allied prisoners of war have been placed, whether in battle zones, on lines of communication or in rear areas. They declare that they will hold all such persons, no less than the German High Command and competent German military, naval and air authorities, individually responsible for the safety and welfare of all Allied prisoners of war in their charge. Any person guilty of maltreating or allowing any Allied prisoners of war to be maltreated, whether in battle zone, on lines of communication, in a camp, hospital, prison or elsewhere, will be ruthlessly pursued and brought to punishment. They give notice that they will regard this responsibility as binding in all circumstances and one which cannot be transferred to any other authorities or individuals whatsoever.[72]

Although it questioned the efficacy of the proposed statement, the State Department had no objection to issuing it; still, it requested the views of the JCS as to both the desirability of such a statement and its timing.[73] Meanwhile, in the winter of 1944–45, verified reports of increased cases of murder of American POWs seemed to indicate that the Germans indeed were beginning to carry out Hitler's threat. In a particularly dramatic case, on 17 December 1944 the First SS Panzer Regiment murdered some seventy American soldiers whom they had captured near the town of Malmédy in Belgium. News of the massacre spread quickly among American troops in the field and officials in Washington, causing much shock.[74] Alerted to the imminent danger facing captured American personnel, the JCS allowed no delay in publicizing the tripartite agreement. They now also suggested warning the Germans that for each Allied prisoner murdered, one thousand German prisoners or other German males would be employed "anywhere in the world that the interests of the various Allied nations dictate" for as long as the Allied governments "deem[ed] proper." They further recommended that the U.S. administration notify the British and the Soviets of its intention to issue such a warning at a fixed early date and invite the two to join in if they desired. Alternatively, if those governments could not proceed in concert with the United States by that date, they could add their names as soon as possible after the U.S. administration had issued the warning.[75]

Secretary of War Stimson and Secretary of the Navy Forrestal preferred to be more cautious. Both were of the opinion that the United States should not be the first country to abandon the principles of the Geneva Convention unless the evidence clearly indicated a deliberate decision by the German government or high military level to disregard its provisions. Up to now acts against POWs had not pointed in that direction. In the opinion of Stimson and Forrestal, "the reports of the incidents, including that of Malmedy, do not establish that uniform instructions have been given on a division or higher unit level, but indicate rather that the acts were those of relatively small SS or SS command units, and resulted from acts or instructions of subordinate unit commanders."[76] In his diary Stimson only briefly mentions the Malmédy massacre. When he informs British ambassador Halifax, he records that the latter "was greatly moved and horrified and kept reverting to it again and again."[77] Stimson also quotes Roosevelt's reaction on learning of the massacre: "Well, it will only serve to make our troops feel towards the Germans as they already have learned to feel about the Japs."[78]

Stimson and Forrestal pointed out that the proposed JCS warning had several disadvantages. If carried out, it was clearly a violation of the Geneva Convention, which not only expressly prohibited reprisals against POWs (Article 2) but also provided that their repatriation should be effected with the least possible delay the moment peace had been concluded. Furthermore, no warning had much promise of effectiveness as a deterrent, least of all one that proposed to penalize others than those specifically responsible. Finally, this threat of punishing very large numbers of relatively innocent Germans subsequent to peace was not especially conducive to creating an atmosphere favorable to capitulation within Germany. On the contrary, as Stimson and Forrestal saw it, such a warning placed an effective weapon in the hands of Germany's propaganda minister, Goebbels, who could interpret the threat as indicating that the Allies intended to enslave the German nation or to destroy the country by depriving it of necessary workforce. They were concerned, too, that the warning could lead to a reprisal race with the Germans, who held all the advantages because of their desperate situation and their willingness to discard normal humane considerations. The warning, Stimson and Forrestal concluded, only "lays down terms which would be almost unenforceable, from a practical standpoint, in the face of any widespread disregard of the warning."[79] This stand accorded with Stimson's overall position on how Germany ought to be treated after the war, as would come to the fore in the fight he put up against the plan proposed by Treasury Secretary Henry Morgenthau to deindustrialize Germany.[80]

On the other hand, Stimson and Forrestal believed that the United States had to take some action to protect the POWs if only to reassure the American public that the government was doing its utmost to defend them against violations of the Geneva Convention. They wanted the JCS to publish a warning along the lines of the former British proposal, that officers of the German High Command would be held accountable for atrocities committed against POWs in areas under their command, whether or not the abuses were perpetrated by or under the direction of political officials, political police, or special military units operating under political control. Such a warning would widen to the greatest possible extent whatever breach already existed between the Wehrmacht and the Nazi leadership. It might even help to have high-ranking officers of the German army now prisoners in Allied hands appeal to the honor code of the Wehrmacht. Further, Stimson and Forrestal suggested that full publicity be given to atrocities already committed, including naming individuals and units involved and details of the punishment meted out to those of the responsible who had been captured. Finally, vigorous protests were to be made to the German government through the protecting power about all atrocities, again giving full publicity to these protests and to whatever response was received.[81] What may have played a part here as well was that the two secretaries seemed to want to avoid taking steps that might encourage the Wehrmacht and the German people to persist in the war.

After careful deliberation of their joint letter, the JCS came around to the course of action Stimson and Forrestal had suggested, though they doubted the feasibility of requesting captured high-ranking German army officers to appeal to the Wehrmacht.[82] Following their recommendation, the War Department examined whether any of the thirty-seven German generals interned in Camp Clinton, Mississippi, would agree to make the suggested appeal—most of them had originally been interned in Britain, and the principal reason that the British had shipped them to the United States was their noncooperative attitude.[83] Interrogation revealed that none of the generals could be persuaded to make a plea before the cessation of organized German resistance.[84] Under the circumstances, Marshall advised dropping the proposal, quoting the conclusion of the War Department official who had explored the issue that even if a German general officer was willing to cooperate, "such a plea would have little or no effect in deterring further atrocities."[85]

On 14 March 1945, Stimson and Forrestal called Secretary of State Edward Stettinius's attention to a number of further recent incidents in which brutal atrocities had been committed against American POWs captured by the Germans. They thought vigorous action was needed on the part of the U.S. administration and asked Stettinius to call on the British and Soviet governments to join the United States in issuing a joint warning.[86] Coincidentally, on the same day in London, Foreign Secretary Eden urged Churchill to press both Roosevelt and Stalin on the matter of a warning to the Germans.[87] A few days earlier, the Swiss minister in Berlin had told the British of unconfirmed rumors that, as POW camps were about to be overrun by the advancing Allied forces, the Germans intended to kill all captives, rather than trying to remove prisoners or allowing them to fall into Allied hands. The Swiss diplomat also claimed that Hitler had threatened to take reprisals against Allied POWs after the bombing of Dresden but had been restrained from doing so by Himmler.[88] Crowded with refugees from the eastern front, Dresden had been devastated in a firestorm caused by massive British and American raids on the town between 13 and 15 February 1945. Approximately 30,000 people had been killed, and British and American POWs had been brought into the city to help dig out bodies buried beneath the ruins.[89]

Spurred by Eden, Churchill telegraphed Roosevelt on 22 March to outline the danger Allied POWs were facing now that Germany's imminent collapse was creating a chaotic situation. Britain had suggested back in October 1944 that Washington and Moscow publish an Anglo-American-Soviet warning to the Germans, but so far no reply had been received from either. Churchill then shared with Roosevelt the Swiss intelligence reports from early March 1945 indicating that the Germans might start liquidating POWs as Allied forces were advancing or, as a last resort, hold them as hostages.

Given the fact that an SS general (Gottlob Berger) was at present in charge of POW matters in the German Ministry of Defense and that the SS and the Gestapo were taking over control of the camps, Churchill recognized that a warning would have only limited effect, but he argued that "at the worst it can do no harm." On the other hand, on regular Wehrmacht officers still in place it might function as a deterrent: "We should surely miss no opportunity of exploiting any duality of control." A similar message was being sent to Stalin, and Roosevelt was urged to issue the warning at the appropriate moment.[90] Roosevelt replied the same day he received Churchill's telegram: "If Marshal Stalin agrees, I will go forward with you in our issuing the joint warning."[91] Stalin, however, was to take his time.

Reports coming in through Swiss diplomats only increased the confusion about Germany's intentions. In contrast to the Swiss minister in Berlin, Gabriel Naville, the head of the British Interests Division at the Swiss legation in Berlin, did not think Allied POWs would be massacred by the Germans or that any other aggressive action would be taken against them. Significantly, Naville had been the first outsider to report on the murder of the fifty POWs from Stalag Luft III. Although indeed there were rumors of revenge for the bombing of Dresden, in a discussion with the secretary of the American legation in Bern Naville maintained that his legation had received assurances that the Germans did not contemplate any such action. The Swiss diplomat also argued that if the condition of the POWs worsened in the future, this was not because of intentional mistreatment but because of overcrowding and a lack of supplies. Naville gave little credence to rumors that die-hard Nazis intended to take British and American POWs as hostages when making their last stand—the Germans did not wish to be hindered by large numbers of POWs, who might cause trouble and who would have to be guarded and fed. That is, the Germans might retain certain important or high-ranking Allied POWs, but the mass of POWs, especially ordinary soldiers, would not be considered valuable enough as hostages. Moreover, Naville did not believe that the Germans had intentionally placed POW camps near possible targets. However, work detachments were often located near the factories where the POWs worked and thus were close to targets likely to be attacked by the Allies. It rather seemed that the German leadership no longer concerned itself much with the POWs.[92]

Meanwhile, Eisenhower, in a radio broadcast on 24 March, cautioned the Wehrmacht and Waffen ss (the ss army) against carrying out "the Fuehrer's headquarters order of October 18, 1942, category 'Secret Military Matter' and its supplement issued in October, 1944, same category, ordering the execution of Allied airborne and parachute troops." Developments of the battle on German soil, he continued, "may bring you into contact with Allied airborne or parachute troops, large or small units. Such units may be landed or dropped deep behind your lines." These troops were not terrorists but soldiers carrying out legitimate military tasks, and executing captured airborne or parachute troops operating in uniform was entirely contrary to the accepted rules and practices of war. Consequently, "all persons—officers, other ranks or civilians—implicated in the issuing or the carrying out of the Fuehrer headquarters orders . . . or any other similar orders subsequently issued or to be issued," Eisenhower warned, "will be held to the strictest account and will be punished according to their deserts. The excuse of having carried out orders received from above will not be considered valid." Those who might carry out the orders, those who might have transmitted such orders, and those who might have issued them would be judged according to their conduct, "with strict justice, but without mercy."[93]

Eisenhower's warning, however, did not cover the soldiers in POW camps. In view of the rapid advance of the Allies across the Rhine, the British Chiefs of Staff Committee felt that the moment for issuing the warning in regard to those prisoners was imminent. On 4 April, they recommended that the U.S. administration be asked to consent to a joint warning, even without Soviet participation. Although he was prepared to go ahead with an Anglo-American warning, Eden preferred to give Stalin a last chance to join the Western Allies. The British foreign secretary thought that a tripartite statement would be more effective and therefore asked Churchill to send Stalin a short reminder.[94] This time Stalin responded quickly, raising no objection to the proposed text Churchill had submitted.[95]

Several days later, however, the Soviets asked to have the following words inserted in those parts of the text in which "prisoners of war" were mentioned: "and also internees and deported citizens of the United Nations."[96] Churchill thought there was no harm in the Russian amendment, but Stettinius objected, explaining that stories and pictures about German concentration camps in U.S. media were already causing distress in the United States to families of POWs, who mistakenly thought the scenes related to POW camps. Inevitable confusion and more distress, he maintained, would be accentuated if the warning dealt simultaneously with both POWs and civilian internees. If the Soviet government objected to the original statement, Stettinius advised, the United States should agree to its being issued in the name of the prime minister and the president alone.[97] Churchill, too, was determined to avoid any delay in publishing the warning, explaining to Stalin that by now instructions had already been given to drop the leaflets, which had already been printed.[98] Reports had been coming in that the Germans had removed a number of "prominent" British POWs from Oflag IV C at Colditz before the camp was liberated by Allied forces.[99]

Allied airplanes began distributing leaflets on the night of 23 April over those portions of German territory still in German control. These leaflets bore the facsimile signatures of Roosevelt, Churchill, and Stalin.[100] The text did not include the Russian amendment. The following night, a second edition incorporating the Soviet suggestion was not only dropped but also broadcast over the radio and published in the morning papers.[101] This form of cooperation came at a time when the Western powers and the Soviets were already effectively divided on a number of principal issues, including the mutual repatriation of POWs and, especially for the Soviets, that of civilians.

In the end, there were no organized acts of reprisal against British Commonwealth and American POWs in German hands. It is doubtful, however, that this was in any way due to the warnings the Allies broadcast to the enemy as late as April 1945. After all, during the early months of 1945 the possibility existed—both London and Washington accepted this—that certain groups might start killing prisoners as the demise of the Third Reich was inexorably approaching. U.S. secretary of war Stimson, for example, was well aware of this: "We are now afraid that there will be mass murders as the Russian troops and our troops converge on the present camps in Germany where our prisoners are being held."[102] As they were already deeply implicated in some of the most heinous war crimes ever committed, SS troops and the Gestapo knew they stood to gain little from an ostensible last-minute about-face. On the other hand, the top Nazi leaders might decide to use the POWs as hostages either to bargain their way out of unconditional surrender or to try to save their own skin.

When they discussed the options theoretically open to them to protect their men in German POW camps during the final months of the war, both the British and American civil and military leaders unanimously ruled out diverting troops from the overall war effort—winning the war came before anything else. Even when Berlin put SS troops in charge of the camps instead of the Wehrmacht and, later, forced tens of thousands of British Commonwealth and American POWs to march back into the German heartland, this still did not prompt the Allies to change their priorities. What perhaps may also have played a role—albeit a minor one and never openly uttered—was the consideration that POWs, though in German hands, never stopped being soldiers and thus, as every other soldier, might have to pay the ultimate sacrifice for the sake of their country.

When weighing the evidence, one ought to keep in mind that the Allies were well aware of the fact that, until the final weeks of the war, the Germans on the whole had refrained from killing British Commonwealth and American POWs as long as they were in camps and had generally continued to adhere to the Geneva Convention.[103] For the Nazis these POWs belonged to nations that, although Germany's bitter political enemies, ranked high in the Nazi hierarchy of races.[104] It is equally undeniable that in their ultimate fear of falling into Soviet hands some in the Nazi leadership made a desperate last-ditch effort to seek some form of settlement with the West.[105] Himmler himself, Stimson wrote in his diary on 2 March 1945, "was sending refugees to Switzerland apparently in the hope that he would thus get some credit and appeasement with the American Jews to soften punishment which he is expecting as a war criminal."[106]

In hindsight it may well be true that the lives of British and American POWs were saved by the Allies' decisive military victory. However, it is hard to escape the conclusion that when, in the face of the utter chaos into which Nazi Germany had descended, London and Washington decided against taking any direct and overt action on behalf of their men, reasoning that the operational difficulties were insurmountable, they were taking a calculated risk.

Forced Marches

SUFFERING AND HARDSHIP

It was general German policy to hold POWs in camps located as far away as possible from the front on which their compatriots were fighting so as to prevent prisoners who had succeeded in escaping from rejoining their own forces. Russian and Polish POWs were largely concentrated in western Germany, while British and U.S. prisoners were retained in the east.[1] On 12 January 1945, after months of preparations, the Soviets began a major offensive that stretched along the entire eastern front, from the Baltic in the north to the Carpathians in the south, and in which more than 6 million Soviet soldiers faced approximately 2 million German troops and 190,000 other Axis forces. By the end of the month, all of prewar Poland was under Soviet control.[2] The Red Army's rapid advance prompted the Germans to start evacuating POWs to Germany proper, where they established three principal centers: in the vicinity of Lübeck in the north, Altengrabow in the center, and around Moosburg in the south. Because of the heavy demands the German war machine was making on transportation, evacuation was mostly carried out on foot. These marches took place over long distances and under severe conditions with inadequate shelter and food and on the whole were organized in an atmosphere of panic; most POWs would later count them as their most traumatic experience during captivity.

At first, details about the forced marches of the POWs were sketchy. The British learned from a Swiss camp inspector who had visited Stalag VIII B (Teschen) on 17 January 1945 that the camp commandant there had received orders to move all prisoners to the Gleiwitz area. Of the approximately 72,000 POWs held in this Stalag, about 14,000 were British. On 19 January, a day before the Swiss inspector was to visit Arbeitskommando E 715 (Auschwitz), he was informed that all prisoners in the Sosnowitz and Auschwitz detachments had already been ordered to march westward to Stalag 344 (Lamsdorf). When the Swiss official arrived at Stalag 344, the newly appointed camp commandant there told him that POWs in this camp were being evacuated to Stalag VIII A (Görlitz) in order to make room for prisoners from Stalag VIII B and from some Stalag 344 detachments.[3]

In mid-February, Dr. Roland Marti, head of the ICRC delegation in Germany, confirmed that the evacuation toward the west was being carried out under very difficult conditions—on foot, without food, and in severely cold weather. The POWs were being assembled in transit camps where there were no food reserves.[4] Swedish YMCA Headquarters reported at the same time that Oflag 64 (Schubin) was marching westward to an unknown location. That the Germans had asked to borrow trucks in order to relieve the prisoners' hardship told them how harsh conditions must be under which they were moving.[5]

From the SBO in Stalag Luft III (Sagan), Group Captain D. E. L. Wilson, we learn in detail how British and American prisoners were marched from the North Compound of Stalag Luft III. The hardship these marchers underwent typically reflected the experience of most of the tens of thousands of British and American POWs who were being moved. Situated in eastern Germany, the camp was divided into six compounds: three compounds, South, Center, and West, held American prisoners; the East one held British POWs; the North and "Belaria" held both British and Americans. The approximate strength of the camp toward the end of January was 10,500 officers (more than 90 percent) and men of other ranks, about two-thirds of them Americans and the rest British.[6] Set aside for air force personnel, Stalag Luft III included some of the oldest prisoners in Germany. A few were in their sixth year of captivity, and many had been prisoners for three or more years. Since D-Day, 6 June 1944, prisoners at Sagan had been receiving only half a Red Cross parcel per week. This meant that their daily diet, which included German rations, was about 1,000 calories per head below the accepted norm and well below that necessary for a healthy standard. Mental health, too, was deteriorating, in particular following the summary execution of the fifty officers who had been recaptured after their escape from the North Compound in March 1944.[7] The psychological effect on the prisoners had been devastating and was further exacerbated by restrictive measures that included a limit on parole walks and the total suspension of intercompound communication, whether for sports or entertainment.[8]

By 19 January, the Russian advance had come within striking distance of Breslau and Posen, but when prisoners at Sagan asked the commandant, they were told that no move was being contemplated, as the German High Command was confident it could hold the Russians at the Oder River. Within a few days, however, Red Army troops had reached and crossed the

Oder south of Breslau. The commandant, though reiterating that no move would be necessary, gave qualified permission to let prisoners prepare rucksacks but refused to let them dig slip trenches for protection in case the camp came within the battle zone. Meanwhile, within the camp, the prisoners themselves were making preparations for either a march—whether under German or Russian command—or staying behind with German guards. Senior officers advised their men about the food and clothing they would need to carry in the event of a forced march and set a weight of between twenty and forty pounds for packs. Boots were overhauled, and the compound grounds were crowded throughout the day as the POWs trained for marching.

On the evening of 27 January, the commandant received a telephone call from Berlin instructing the camp at Sagan to march at once. Since many of the camp's administrative staff were in town at the time, the order was passed to the compounds at different times. Because of the preparations that the prisoners had already made at their own initiative, the sudden order caused less confusion than might have been expected. But there was no time to collect any of the prisoners' property—at least 25,000 Red Cross parcels were left behind unopened, as well as clothes, blankets, and literally millions of cigarettes.

The North Compound began to leave at 1 A.M. on 28 January. Each prisoner was given a Red Cross food parcel as he left the camp. In the course of the first mile, however, many POWs had to throw away part of their parcels because their packs proved too heavy. One small ambulance accompanied the column for the first stage of the march. Except for it and two horse-drawn wagons that carried German kits and some rations at the rear of the column, little effort was made to provide for stragglers or the sick. The guards, who were in the main elderly men, not only were insufficient to prevent individual prisoners from escaping but found conditions so severe throughout the march that it was all they could do to look after themselves. For the most part, they marched in groups, making little attempt to patrol the column. In several instances, prisoners even helped them by putting the kits into sledges and hauling them along with their own packs. Already by the second day, many of the guards, suffering from the increasing cold, intermittent snow, and the added difficulty of nighttime marching, were no longer fit for duty.

Given the circumstances, the organization of the march was, in effect, left to the prisoners themselves. The British officer in charge, according to Wilson, had no experience in handling a march. The attempt to lead about

2,000 men in one long line, without creating various sections, caused the column constantly to expand and then contract again, resulting in uncoordinated short halts and no recognized rest periods. Beyond the information that the first halt was to be at Halbau, a distance of seventeen kilometers from Sagan, the prisoners knew nothing about their route or destination. For the first few miles, the absence of any agreed rest halts caused trouble in the rear, where the guards forced at least four officers who were encountering difficulty with their packs to leave them behind.[9]

The Germans had made no provision for rations or water at Halbau but permitted a halt of one hour. Civilians, who throughout the march and with few exception proved friendly, provided hot water for a fair number of the POWs. This would become a regular phenomenon at main stops along the march. The German military authorities themselves never supplied water. Whatever food civilians made available was more or less negligible; still, in return for cigarettes or coffee and sometimes soap, it was possible to obtain bread, onions, and occasionally eggs and even beer. The guards in general did not interfere in these transactions, or even acted as willing intermediaries, although it also happened that guards tried to prevent civilians from giving food or water to POWs or held prisoners back and took the water or food civilians were offering for themselves.

At Halbau, the column was informed that it was to billet for the night at Freiwaldan, eleven kilometers farther down the road. The village was reached about noon, with the prisoners totally exhausted after a march of eleven hours without minimal meals or rest stops. Little attempt, though, had been made to actually find accommodations for them—the two halls allotted were totally inadequate. Half-frozen, prisoners began seeking their own billeting arrangements with civilians who were willing to take them in. However, objections were almost immediately raised to the prisoners' presence in the village—whether by its civilian or its military authorities is not clear—and the guards decided to resume the march.

By then the column had already covered twenty-eight kilometers. Despite frequent stationary periods, prisoners never took off their packs because no one knew in advance whether a halt would last long enough. Packs and clothes, of course, were soaked by now. The absence of bread and, for most of them, of any warm food was beginning to take a toll. The march to a small village called Leipp about six kilometers farther on offered a very grim sight. Prisoners were feeling the weight of their packs as they walked on with their backs slightly bent, stopping every now and then to raise the load higher or bending over double to rest their muscles. Many could barely keep going, particularly because aches that had plagued them during the day were now absorbed into a general weariness. Guards became indistinguishable from prisoners, some of them now helping to pull the sledges that carried their kits, others bartering for sledges themselves and, when possible, inducing children to pull them along. The column, which stretched for more than three miles, looked more like a string of refugees than military on the move.

The column reached Leippa at about 5 P.M., only to discover that just one single barn was available for billeting and it could hold no more than 600 men. Eventually about 700 prisoners were crowded in. Some of the prisoners had to wait almost four hours before they could be given a place to stay. Darkness fell shortly after the column's arrival, and that night was to be one of the coldest of the year; in addition, heavy snow was falling. Clothes and boots of prisoners waiting in the snow and slush on a country road were soon covered with ice, while darkness and numbed hands made it impossible to prepare even a bit of cold food. Following an assurance of parole by the SBO that no prisoner would try to escape during the night, more barns were found. Still, 60 officers had to spend the night lying on straw in the lee of a farmyard wall, and many of them as a result suffered frostbite and nausea. No medical assistance was forthcoming from the Germans, and the British medical staff was severely handicapped by the shortage of equipment and supplies.

Conditions inside the barns were not much better. There was no light and far from enough straw. The men were so cramped that it was almost impossible to move, and many had no choice but to urinate where they lay down. There were no meals to be had in the barns. The Germans tried to issue one-third of a loaf of bread per man, but few prisoners ever received theirs because of poor organization, the fact that they had no idea where their billets were, and the all-pervading darkness. Little water could be obtained.

The march was resumed on the morning of 29 January. Because the guards by now completely ignored their duties, certain groups of POWs received little or no notice of the resumption of the march, which meant that the rest of the column was subsequently kept waiting on the road. During the wait several officers collapsed unnoticed. A search party organized by the prisoners themselves later found them lying in a ditch. No guards were present. Had no search been made, these men would probably have died from hypothermia. Another long delay arose from an ineffectual attempt by the Germans to make a head count. That the full complement of prisoners was present was due entirely to the organization of the prisoners themselves.

They reached Muskau about 6 P.M. that same day. Billets were provided in a cinema (for about 300 men), a glass factory (about 600), a riding school (about 400), a stable (about 150), a laundry (about 80), a pottery (about 100), and a French POW camp (about 300). All billets were crowded, but except for the riding school, conditions were tolerable, and the civilians in charge endeavored to make the POWs feel as comfortable as the situation allowed. At the riding school, the earth of the floor was damp; there was little light, no heating, no sanitary arrangements, and no facilities for cooking. The majority of those in this billet ended up with a mild form of dysentery.

Part of about 1,500 Red Cross parcels that the Germans had taken with them from Sagan were now issued, as was about one-third of a loaf of bread per man. Again, not everyone received his portion of bread owing to poor organization on the part of the Germans. By this time, 523 officers and men of the USAAF left the North Compound's body to join a column of Americans already on the march. Orders were received in the late afternoon of 1 February that the North Compound and 566 British POWs of the East Compound who also had arrived at Muskau were to march together that night for Spremberg, where trains would be waiting for them. No marching rations were issued. Now, consisting of about 1,920 officers and men, the column moved out of the town in complete darkness, leaving behind 57 men from the North Compound who proved too sick to march. The prisoners had to carry both food and the remainder of the Red Cross parcels issued in Muskau. In addition, the effects of the previous marches—some officers had such severe frostbite that they could no longer wear boots and finished the march in socks—the darkness, the hilly topography, and the continued failure of the Germans to exercise normal march discipline turned this stretch into the most difficult part of the journey.

The guards, many of whom were loudly complaining about the conditions, soon abandoned any serious attempt to patrol, and they marched or straggled with the prisoners. The prisoners themselves marched in small companies; there was little conversation. Many of the sick dropped behind; when a halt was ordered, men soon fell asleep by the roadside and had to be rounded up by their friends when they continued again. Under such circumstances, incidents were bound to occur. One of the guards at one point fired at a group of prisoners who had dropped back with a sledge and had stopped to rearrange their kits. Another group, taking advantage of a halt to try to eat something by the roadside, was set upon with dogs by another guard.

The column reached the village of Graustein, seven kilometers from Spremberg, on 2 February and rested for a few hours. As it approached Spremberg, there was a noticeable stiffening among the guards, who became efficient for the first time since setting out. On arrival at the town, the prisoners were crowded into cattle cars for an upcoming train journey of at least 300 miles. None of the cars was clean; in many cases manure and even human excreta had to be removed first. The only possible way to sleep was in a sitting position or lying on one side wedged between two other prisoners. The journey continued like this for two nights and two days.

Before leaving, the British rations officer received a ration of two-thirds of a loaf of bread, 140 grams of sausage, and 80 grams of margarine per prisoner. What remained of the 1,500 Red Cross food parcels brought from Sagan was also issued. Water was another story. It was not until the morning of 4 February—when, thirty-six hours after it had left Spremberg, the train stopped on the outskirts of Hannover—that the prisoners obtained fresh drinking water. In the afternoon of the same day the train arrived in Tarmstadt. From there, the prisoners were marched approximately four kilometers to Marlag-Milag Nord. It was raining when they reached the camp. Nevertheless, each one of them was searched before being allowed to enter the barracks. As this took several hours, a number of prisoners collapsed and had to be taken to a hospital. More than 70 percent of the POWs suffered from gastritis, dysentery, colds, influenza, and other illnesses during their first week in the new camp.

On arrival, the strength of the column that had set out from Muskau was 1,916 officers and men of other ranks. The available accommodations consisted of twelve wooden huts, two kitchens, two wash houses, and two latrines. The camp had recently been evacuated by Royal Navy POWs. The huts had practically been gutted; there was neither light nor stoves in many rooms and no movable equipment in the kitchens. There were beds for only 460 people and a shortage of about 500 mattresses; in all, there were 165 small tables and 216 lockers. Wood shavings were provided for the POWs to sleep on. Wilson described the camp as scandalously ill equipped, though he mentioned that the authorities made efforts to supply the necessities. There was hardly any fuel, and a full two weeks after entering the camp the prisoners were still not able to dry their clothes and blankets properly. An added strain on the men's endurance was caused by the German Security Department, which, on the second and third days after their arrival, had kept the whole camp on parade in the rain and cold for prolonged and what seemed unnecessary periods in order to establish numbers.

Finishing his report on 20 February, Wilson concluded, "Without any exaggeration, it can be stated that neither the German High Command, which presumably gave the order for the move, nor the German Camp administration at Sagan, which had custody of the prisoners, nor the Camp authorities at Marlag-Milag Nord, who received the prisoners, gave any thought to the terms of the Geneva Convention in relation to the welfare of the prisoners moved."[10] The story of the POWs of the Northern Compound of Stalag III (Sagan) repeated itself with the five other compounds that had left the Stalag on the same date and, except for the Belaria POWs, had followed the same route from Sagan to Spremberg. From there, the prisoners were transported in different directions. Approximately 500 sick prisoners had been left behind in Stalag Luft III because they were too ill to march. On 6 February, they were removed by transport to a camp near Nuremberg, where they met the POWs who had been transferred from the West Compound of Stalag Luft III.[11]

As already noted, tens of thousands of prisoners from other camps underwent similar or much worse experiences. R. E. Harford, who was evacuated from Stalag 344 (Lamsdorf), stressed in particular the last four days of the march. The only food the prisoners received was one package of biscuits and some cheese each day, but there was an interval of thirty-six hours without any food at all.

> Many of my comrades fell down exhausted, but the Germans made watchdogs go after these sick men, sometimes without result, and [they] pushed and struck us with the butt of their rifles and with their bayonets. Most of us were in a state of exhaustion and starvation, many suffered from dysentery, bronchitis, and other chest complications. Although several of us were marked by the German doctor as unfit to continue the march, we were forced to go on by our sentries. I, myself, saw comrades kneeling down and begging the Germans with folded hands to let them behind and rest, but these pleas were ignored.

Harford concluded, "The treatment which we experienced for the whole of this journey was the worst we had for the whole length of our captivity."[12]

Harford was among 113 men who on 9 March were unable to continue the march and were then sent to by train to Meiningen. Swiss inspector Kadler, who interviewed the senior British medical officer at Meiningen,

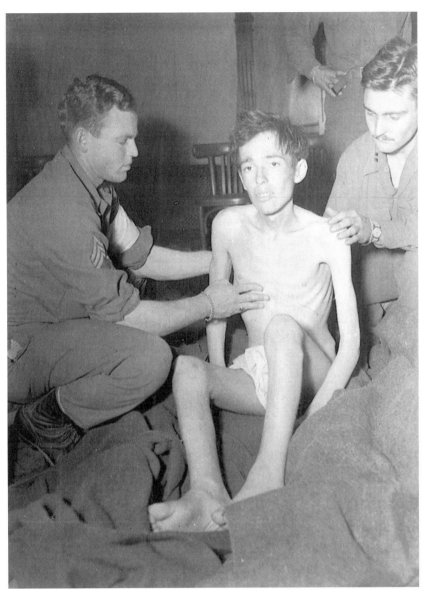

American prisoner after forced march from the Berga labor camp.
(Courtesy National Archives, College Park, Md.)

reported British fears that several of the men who were obviously suffering from severe dysentery, chest complications, and other diseases "might not survive this ordeal."[13] In an affidavit he gave to the UNWCC, Captain Turner McLardey, who had participated in the march from Stalag 344, stated that he knew of twelve men who had died from starvation during the march.[14] Kadler further reported that the way the guards treated the POWs was often "inconsiderate and brutal and there were innumerable occasions on which rifle butts were used on men known by guards to be sick or exhausted." Shooting, according to Kadler, was unnecessary and in all cases could have been avoided. Moreover, most of the men who were shot were blameless, and their injuries were occasioned by guards firing into crowded billets.[15] This is confirmed by the testimonies collected by the UNWCC: "The guards were brutal in the extreme, beating, firing upon and setting dogs on the exhausted and starving men."[16] The UNWCC also collected evidence against seven of the German guards who had been in charge of a march of roughly 2,000 prisoners of Stalag VIII C between 7 February and 10 March in which about 50 POWs lost their lives.[17] Sargent Thomas S. C. Aitken, from Scotland, testified in his affidavit that the march had taken about three months, during which his column of 560 British and 1,200 Russians had covered 1,050 miles. Between 18 February and 24 March 30 men in the British column (whom he lists by names) had died, either from malnutrition or dysentery, and in 3 isolated cases through beatings by the guards. Although he had not personally witnessed any of these beatings, he had seen the bruises on the dead men's bodies.[18]

POWERLESS TO HELP

Early reports about the marches of the POWs reached London and Washington only gradually.[19] In mid-February 1945, Major General Ray W. Barker, assistant chief of staff, SHAEF, suggested asking the Germans to allow POW camps to be overrun by the advancing Red Army instead of evacuating the prisoners.[20] As head of the PWD, Roberts argued that the Germans were unlikely to accept such a proposal because it contained no particular advantage for them, except for not having to supply food for the prisoners and for being able to use the guards elsewhere. On the other hand, it would deprive them of a possible bargaining chip—the Germans attached great value to reciprocity, and Barker's proposal contained none. Roberts further speculated that the SS might object for the sinister motive of retaining British and U.S. POWs as a protective shield.

Roberts was concerned, too, about Soviet reaction to the proposal because it referred only to the eastern front and made no mention of Soviet prisoners who were in camps on the western front. There was no certainty either that the Soviets would agree to the stipulation that prisoners recovered in this way would not be used against the Germans. Roberts, however, was in the minority, as the representatives of the Dominions, India, the Air Ministry, and the Admiralty at Sub-Committee A of the IPWC all expressed themselves in favor of the proposal.[21] Accordingly, Major General Barker called the U.S. Joint Chiefs of Staff to approve the proposal for dispatch to the CCS. He informed the JCS that the Germans were moving some 70,000 British and American POWs over long distances from POW camps in eastern Germany under severe conditions. He told of one instance in which 200 American officers who had been unable to continue walking had simply been abandoned. "It seems inevitable," Barker warned, "that great suffering, with probable heavy loss of life, will be incurred by these men."[22]

General Eisenhower supported Barker's proposal and urged the CCS to come up with specific suggestions that the United States and Britain could then offer to the Germans. Where evacuating U.S. POWs under provision of Article 9 of the Geneva Convention would prove more dangerous than leaving them behind in camps,[23] Eisenhower suggested that prisoners should be released in the following manner on the withdrawal of the German forces: (a) Whenever it was apparent that the fighting zone would involve areas in which U.S. POWs were held, they should be concentrated in camps or other suitable accommodations and left behind on the withdrawal of the German troops. (b) The German authorities should notify the appropriate Allied commander of these places of concentration, and this notification should be issued before the particular area was exposed to Allied shelling. (c) On their withdrawal, the Germans should leave the POWs with adequate supplies. (d) A nominal roll or sufficient description of those released should be left with the camp leader and a duplicate transmitted to the protecting power. For its part, the U.S. government would give its assurance that no U.S. POW left behind in accordance with the proposal would be employed in active military service for the duration of hostilities against Germany. "This is a matter of extreme urgency," Eisenhower ended his message to the CCS, adding that the suggested course of action could be of value only if action was taken promptly. Still, it was important to receive the agreement of the Russian government or the Soviet High Command before offering the Germans such a proposal.[24] Secretary of War Stimson strongly supported Eisenhower's proposal and urged the JCS to respond quickly.[25]

The JCS concurred that it would be better for the prisoners concerned to run the risk of remaining in an active combat zone than to be evacuated to the rear. This was contingent, however, on the German government's agreeing to concentrate the prisoners as rapidly as possible in suitable accommodations nearest to the points where they were currently encamped and to leave the POWs with adequate supplies. The JCS also believed that this proposal would have better prospects of acceptance by Berlin if SHAEF agreed not to make military use of POWs left behind by the German forces and if assurances were given to the Germans that these prisoners, while at the points of concentration, would make no escape attempts or commit acts of hostility against the German state. The JCS concurred that the agreement of the Soviet authorities needed to be obtained before this proposal could be offered to the Germans and that the most expeditious way to procure their assent would be through the heads of the U.S. and British military missions in Moscow.[26]

Whereas the War Office, the Air Ministry, and the Admiralty strongly supported approaching the Germans, Foreign Office officials thought that the proposal was useless, even dangerous, and therefore should be rejected. Not only were they certain that the German government would turn the proposal down, but they also had serious political objections to even putting it before the Germans. As Deputy Undersecretary Orme Sargent phrased it, "It would most certainly create in the minds of the Germans an impression of weakness at the very moment when it is so vital to drive home the overwhelming superiority of the Allies." Sargent was also certain that the Soviet government would regard such a move "as a weak concession to the threat of further German brutalities."[27] All considered, Foreign Office officials appeared more concerned with the political fallout of the proposal than with the plight of the POWs.[28]

The British Chiefs of Staff Committee on the whole backed up the American proposal but suggested one main change. This related to the U.S. administration's promise to instruct "the prisoners referred to, through the Protecting Power, immediately upon receipt of acceptance of this proposal by the German Government, that they are not to *escape from the concentration points at which they are held for the purpose of this agreement, and shall not* commit any acts of hostility against the German State" (italics added). The COS wanted to delete the italicized words, since they effectively meant that no prisoner would be entitled to escape. "We cannot ensure that this order would reach all prisoners or be carried out by them when held under intolerable conditions," the COS maintained, adding that it would give the Germans "a good excuse for shooting escapees."[29] The JCS accepted the British amendments, and the proposals were submitted to the Soviet government.[30]

Soviet foreign minister Vycheslav Molotov understood the motives of the British and American governments for wanting to ease the lot of their POWs, but he explained that the Soviet command considered it inexpedient to make a proposal to the German government to have American and British POWs concentrated at specified points on the eastern front because this was where Soviet offensive operations were being conducted. "It cannot be excluded," Molotov cautioned, "that the German authorities, for purposes of provocation, might dispose such prisoners of war at points especially dangerous in a military sense."[31]

Unimpressed by the Soviets' stand, Eisenhower believed it carried too little weight to warrant abandoning the proposal. Thus far, he observed, the Germans had shown no tendency to act according to the Soviet scenario.[32] General John Deane, head of the U.S. Military Mission in Moscow (USMMM), thought that the Red Army General Staff assumed that if the Germans accepted the proposals, they would live up to the agreement only when it furthered their own ends. The Soviets feared that the Germans would locate Allied prisoners at strategic points to prevent them from being attacked and to cover German withdrawals. In an extreme case, the Germans might inform the Soviet command of POW concentrations that did not in fact exist in order to prevent strategic areas from being bombarded by the Soviets. According to Deane, Moscow was convinced that unless some benefits accrued to the Germans, they would not live up to the agreement. The Red Army General Staff would also be reluctant to agree not to attack certain areas because subordinate commanders might fail to make distinctions in the heat of battle.

Deane anticipated a period of stabilization on the Russian-German front that could last until after the spring thaw and, with it, the possibility of a few hurried evacuations of American POWs from eastern Germany in April and May. When the next big Russian offensive got under way, however, more such evacuations could probably be expected. Under the circumstances, both Deane and the U.S. ambassador in Moscow, Averell W. Harriman, thought that only a direct appeal to Marshal Stalin by President Roosevelt and Prime Minister Churchill could yield the Soviets' approval of the Anglo-American proposal.[33] Secretary of War Stimson agreed and recommended that Roosevelt send a message telling Stalin that the U.S. and British governments appreciated the dangers mentioned by the Soviet government and the Red Army General Staff but that the Soviet leader, for humanitarian reasons, should consent to have these proposals forwarded to the Germans.[34] At the time, though, Roosevelt and Stalin were conducting an already tense correspondence over the question of the evacuation of American POWs liberated by the Soviets, and the U.S. president preferred not to raise another thorny issue.[35]

While the big powers debated the question of approaching the German government, more information came in about the movements of the prisoners. Toward the end of February, Dr. Robert Schirmer, of the Red Cross delegation in northern Germany, reported that the marches could be divided into three distinct lines: southern, central, and northern. The last consisted of approximately 100,000 POWs, who were moving west along the northern German coast. Eighty percent of these POWs were suffering from dysentery, which was clearly contagious. Their daily ration consisted of three potatoes and one quart of hot water daily, plus 200 grams of bread, if available, every four to five days. The POWs were trying to sell anything they had for food, but with little success. Dr. Schirmer mentioned 800 officers from Oflag 64 (Schubin) who were "in a worse condition yet seen" because they had never worked while in camp and were totally unprepared physically for the hardships of the journey. Some of them had lost between fifteen and twenty kilos and were unable even to carry the eleven-pound food parcels they had been handed.[36]

The central line of marchers numbered approximately 60,000 POWs, who were moving west in a region bounded by Leipzig, Dresden, and Berlin. Thanks to a more gentle climate, Dr. Schirmer thought, these POWs were in relatively good condition. He also mentioned 300 severely wounded American officers who had been abandoned in a camp Lazarett (probably at Stalag Luft III) that was subsequently overrun by the Russians. Finally, approximately 80,000 POWs made up the southern line of marchers. This group was said to include 25,000 Americans, though the American Red Cross in Geneva and the legation in Bern had doubts this figure was correct. This line was marching through the Sudetenland. It had suffered on account of bad weather while crossing the Czech mountains, little food, and, particularly, repeated strafing by Allied aircraft.[37]

Information obtained by the British War Office at the beginning of March indicated that about 60,000 British Commonwealth POWs had been moved westward from camps situated in East Prussia, Poland, and Silesia.[38] The prisoners were moved on foot, in stages of eighteen to twenty kilometers a day, and suffered considerable hardships. The War Office pointed out that the mass movement of POWS from camps in eastern Germany and the dislocation of the German railway system had created serious problems for the supply of Red Cross parcels for British POWS. The situation had been aggravated further when in the fall of 1944 the OKW ordered all camps to start consuming reserve stocks. For the immediate relief of prisoners who had been transferred from eastern Germany, SHAEF had placed at the disposal of the ICRC in Geneva a number of lorries and the necessary petrol and lubricants. The lorries had been loaded with food parcels and medical supplies and were to be driven into Germany by Swiss drivers. It was hoped that supply centers might be established in this way in the areas with the largest concentrations of POWS at the time.[39]

The difficulties in supplying food to both the marching POWS and prisoners in camps became one of the main concerns of U.S. and British authorities in the final months of the war. On 21 February, Chief of Staff Marshall highlighted the "critical situation of prisoners of war being moved westward in Germany" and authorized General Eisenhower to take all immediate relief measures such "as you deem necessary."[40] Following a representation made by the Swiss legation in Berlin to the OKW concerning the bad conditions under which British and American prisoners were being evacuated, the OKW admitted that the course of events had taken it by surprise and promised to take steps to improve the food and accommodations of the prisoners not only during the transfer but also in the camps where they would stay. The Swiss minister in Berlin, Feldscher, received assurances that from now on sick and weak prisoners would be transported by train or lorry.[41]

In mid-March, the German authorities gave permission for food and medicines to be brought into Germany. In order to distribute these supplies to POWS, SHAEF decided to create two transport services. For this purpose, it divided Germany into two zones: (a) south of a line from Berlin-Kassel, to be supplied from reserves in Switzerland; (b) north of that line, to be supplied from reserves in Lübeck. In the southern zone, a train consisting of forty-eight cars of food and two of medicines soon arrived with the agreement of the German government, at a point near Moosburg, where an advance base was to be set up. Twenty-five lorries had also left Switzerland in order to distribute supplies to the camps. In the north, a reserve of some 5,000 tons of food supplies was stored in Lübeck; however, the German railway system no longer functioned in this region, and no local means existed to ensure their distribution. Accordingly, the American and British Red Cross each bought fifty lorries in Sweden to send to Lübeck.[42]

Meanwhile, in Britain there was growing apprehension among the general public, and particularly among relatives of prisoners, about the state of the British POWs who were being evacuated. Toward the end of February, Secretary of State for War Grigg told Parliament: "The House is already aware that the progress of Allied attacks on Germany, by land and from the air, has resulted in mass movements of prisoners and civilians from the perimeter towards the central districts, particularly from the eastern side of Germany. The conditions under which such movements must take place have, largely, been created by the military success of the Allies. But, inevitably, these conditions involve for large numbers of our prisoners in Germany movement on foot under difficult conditions with inadequate provision on the road for accommodations at night and for food, and eventually overcrowding in the camps to which they are moved back." Grigg further mentioned the efforts the government and the British Red Cross were making to deliver supplies to British POWs.[43] On 20 March, he reported to the House that the first lorry convoy from Switzerland had reached its destination and had distributed food parcels to some 18,000 British and U.S. prisoners in Bohemia and that further convoys were now on the way from Geneva.[44]

LAST-MINUTE HALT

In the second week of April, after several weeks of stalemate, the German government agreed "to leave Allied POWs who are now in camps in areas close to the present Western front, and will not remove prisoners into the interior, on condition that Allied Governments furnish an official assurance that such prisoners will not participate further in the war." The Swiss legation in Berlin, which relayed this message from the German Ministry of Foreign Affairs, added that the German government wanted an immediate reply.[45]

The German proposal sparked intensive deliberations in both London and Washington. Foreign Office officials thought that the Germans were unlikely to move large concentrations into the "fortress" area in the south, since this would mean allocating extra guard troops and at least more food—neither of which could easily be spared there. In the north, the Germans might continue to move prisoners "out of sheer malice." Others speculated that the German offer might be designed to claim, when hostilities had come to an end, that the German government had actually done its best for Allied prisoners.[46]

The British government decided to accept the German proposal.[47] As the

Swiss communication had been unclear whether Berlin would apply the same conditions to Soviet prisoners if the Soviet government accepted the proposal, the British suggested that the two Western governments simultaneously inform Moscow of both the German proposal and their acceptance, so as to make it clear that both London and Washington assumed that similar conditions were being offered to the Soviets. Should Moscow's reply be unfavorable, the British suggested further, the two Western Allies should still go ahead and accept the German proposal for regions liberated by Anglo-American armies and in regard to British and American prisoners. The Soviets should then be told that this action had been adopted "on the grounds that the western theatre of war was the responsibility of His Majesty's Government and the United States Government."[48]

Fearing procrastination by the Kremlin, Washington instructed Harriman, the U.S. ambassador in Moscow, to impress upon the Soviet authorities that the United States attached great importance to the matter and to allow them no more than three days to consider their reply. In the event of either an unfavorable reply or no reply at all after this period, Harriman was to make it clear that Washington would accept the German proposal at least insofar as it related to American POWs.[49] For his part, Eden preferred not to give the Soviet government a deadline. If no reply was received by either the British or the American ambassador in Moscow within forty-eight hours of delivery of their communications, he thought, then the British and American representatives in Bern would convey their replies to the German offer to the Swiss government without Moscow's concurrence.[50]

Whitehall by now was facing constant pressure in Parliament regarding the plight of the POWs. Following a question, on 17 April, by Major General Alfred Knox whether the cases of ill-treatment of British POWs in camps in Silesia had been investigated, Secretary of War Grigg gave details of the British prisoners who had been marched 450 miles from Silesia in the depth of winter. The Germans had prevented them from making any preparations for the move and had failed to make any adequate provision for food and accommodations. No arrangements had been made for those who fell ill on the way. There was no sanitation, and there was insufficient food and water for the sick, who were moved by train. Grigg stated that a protest against these deplorable conditions had been dispatched through the protecting power.[51]

On 19 April 1945, the Swiss were asked to inform the German government that the United States had accepted the offer to leave all POWs in their camps as the Allies advanced. For its part, Washington agreed not to return to active duty American POWs whom the Allies recovered under this arrangement.[52] As the Soviets refused to have any direct communication with the Germans, they requested their Western Allies to accept the proposal on the Soviets' behalf.[53] On 28 April, the Swiss legation in Germany reported by telephone that representatives of the German government in southern Germany had issued the following communication:

> All transfers of prisoners of war have ceased. Prisoners of war are collected as far as possible in large Stalags. Reich Government has requested I.R.C.C. to send representatives to large Stalags and also requests Swiss Legation as representative of Protecting Power to delegate agents to these camps. On approach of enemy, camp guards will withdraw and only Commandant and administrative personnel will remain in camps which should under control of I.R.C.C. and representative of Protecting Power be handed over in good order to new authorities. Representative of German Government hopes that delegates of I.R.C.C. and Protecting Power will endeavour to ensure that German personnel remaining in camps will not be treated as prisoners of war.[54]

On 1 May, the British and the Americans received final assurances from the protecting power that all prisoner movements had ceased in areas still under German control. The POWs had been collected in large Stalags, and the German government had asked the ICRC and the protecting power to send representatives to these camps. Grigg stated in Parliament that the advancing Allied armies were continuing to liberate large numbers of British prisoners and that so far 43,000 prisoners from British Commonwealth countries had already arrived in Britain from northwestern Europe; further large numbers were likely to have been recovered by the Soviet army in the vicinity of Berlin and Dresden and by the Americans on their way to Munich and the Austrian frontier.[55] In a release to the press on 1 May, the State and War departments reported that the Germans were still holding 45,000 to 50,000 American soldiers and that Allied armies had overrun sixty-four of the seventy-eight POW camps and hospitals where American soldiers were interned.[56]

Long after the war the experiences they lived through during the forced marches remained for many of the POWs a recurring nightmare. "I am still suffering from the effects of the horrors of this march," Private Frank Norbury wrote in his affidavit. "My memory is very bad for names, even of my own friends. I have great difficulty in sleeping at night and I suffer severe pains in the head."[57] In the face of the total collapse of Germany, the fate of the marching POWs was largely in the hands of the guards who were taking them to the camps inside Germany to which they were relocated. Fear of reprisal acts by those guards must have been palpable among British and American POWs as London and Washington continued their devastating bombing raids on German towns. At the same time, the British and American governments stood by almost completely helpless—the most they could do was to try to ensure that food parcels would be waiting at the central points the POWs were led to. An agreement with Berlin to halt the marches and let the camps in the east to be overrun by the advancing Soviet troops came too late.

In the final analysis, besides the fear on the part of their guards of retribution after the war, what saved the British Commonwealth and the American POWs when they were sent on these marches was the same racist ideology that had caused their lives to be spared while they were in the camps—unlike POWs from the Soviet Union or concentration camp inmates, for the Nazis British and U.S. prisoners belonged to a "superior" race. How significant this was for the Germans is tellingly illustrated by the "death marches" of about 750,000 concentration camp prisoners (about half of them Jews) the Nazis conducted at the same time and ostensibly for the same reason—to avoid capture by the Red Army.[58] But whereas more than one-third of these prisoners either froze or starved to death or were killed outright by the guards, almost all POWs physically survived the ordeal and soon after were repatriated to their home countries.

LIBERATED BY THE SOVIETS

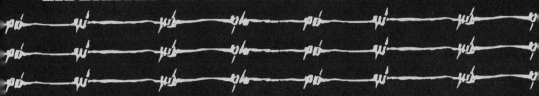

An Anglo-Soviet Bargain

EQUAL TREATMENT

Within a few days of D-Day, 6 June 1944, British and American military commanders discovered that among the German troops they were capturing there were unexpectedly large numbers of men who had originated from the Soviet Union proper but also from the Baltic republics, which Moscow had annexed in 1940, and eastern Poland. For the Kremlin, these men were all Soviet citizens whom it expected London and Washington to repatriate without delay. Some of these men had actively served in the German army out of choice—fearing for their very lives if sent back, they now demanded that the Allies recognize them as German POWs, while nationals from Baltic countries and eastern Poland objected to being repatriated because they refused to become Soviet citizens.

Washington at first appeared responsive to those demands and in its negotiations with Moscow tried to circumvent the problem through a formula that spoke of "claimants to Soviet citizenship." In London, however, Foreign Secretary Eden sensed that the matter was liable to jeopardize a swift exchange of POWs and early on opted to go along with the deal Moscow put in front of him. As negotiations with Germany over the return of long-term prisoners had bogged down, Eden counted on bringing home large numbers of newly liberated POWs via Russia to stave off the mounting criticism the government faced in Parliament and in the press.

Given their divergent attitudes, Moscow realized it stood to gain if negotiations with London and Washington were kept separate, including on issues in which both Western powers had an obvious common interest, such as access for British and American officers into parts of Poland that were now under Soviet control to ensure the safe return of their POWs there. Conducting separate negotiations enabled Moscow to maneuver in much the same way as it had done, for example, at the Teheran Conference to obtain advantages for the wider geopolitical interests the Soviets harbored.[1] In particular, the Kremlin used the repatriation issue as a lever against the Western Allies to lead them to recognize the provisional government the

Russians were backing in Poland. This raised new problems for Whitehall because, with the outbreak of the war, the British had claimed a moral commitment to the future of Poland—it was Hitler's invasion of the country in September 1939 that had led Britain to declare war against Germany, and London had become the refuge of the Polish government in exile. Moreover, Churchill at this time already had set his mind on blocking the pattern of Soviet expansionist moves he saw emerging.

By mid-July 1944 about 1,500 Soviet nationals fighting with the Germans had been captured by the British in France. Foreign Secretary Eden thought that Britain should hand them back to the Russians, but, in order not to discourage others whom the Germans had pressed into service from giving themselves up, he suggested requesting Moscow to take no steps against these Russians until after hostilities had ceased.[2] When he approached Feodor T. Gusev, the Soviet ambassador in London, on the matter, Eden stated that it was clear the captured Soviet citizens had served in German military and paramilitary formations, such as the Todt Organization, the major constructive unit for the German army. A large percentage of the prisoners had formerly served in the Soviet army, and most showed themselves to be hostile to Germany. Many of them had joined these German units or performed other work of a military or quasi-military character on behalf of the enemy because of the harsh conditions they had experienced as Germany's POWs. Gusev was also told that 1,114 of these Soviet citizens had been brought to the United Kingdom as POWs. Eden suggested that Soviet authorities in the United Kingdom contact these Soviet nationals so as to make arrangements for them to return as soon as possible. In the meantime, they would be employed in agricultural work. Eden added that a few of the captured Soviet citizens had been sent to Canada and the United States—given the lack of suitable accommodations, all POWs brought to the United Kingdom from France were quickly sent across the Atlantic. Britain would from now on make every effort to avoid transferring any more Soviet nationals overseas pending a reply from the Soviet government. In an effort to urge Moscow not to delay its answer, Eden emphasized that it would be very difficult to keep large numbers of POWs in transit camps in Britain.[3]

On 17 July, the cabinet decided to send back all Soviet prisoners irrespective of their own wishes, though some cabinet ministers had their reservations. Concerned about the likely fate awaiting Soviet nationals, the War Office suggested not insisting on sending back POWs who did not wish to return even if the Soviet authorities had selected them for repatriation.[4]

Lord Selborne, the minister of economic warfare, thought that they should not be blamed for having joined German labor units because it had been a matter of life or death for them, not just because of the appalling maltreatment they had suffered—"such starvation that cannibalism was not uncommon in their camps"—but also because anyone who refused to join was immediately killed. He warned the prime minister that all those sent back to Russia were likely to be shot and their families disgraced and maltreated.[5]

Eden, not untypically, approached the problem more in terms of political expediency. In a memorandum to the prime minister, he maintained that from the standpoint of relations with the Soviet government, there were very strong arguments in favor of allowing the cabinet decision to stand, with the proviso that the men should not be put on trial or become subject to punitive action so long as the risk of German reprisals remained. Unlike Lord Selborne, and in an effort to undercut the humane argument, he stressed the fact that these men had served in German military or paramilitary formations in France and that their behavior had allegedly often been revolting. (In his letter to Gusev, Eden had refrained from criticizing these men for joining German formations and even tended to defend their move.) In any case, Eden had no reservations about handing them over to the Soviets: "Provided that we protect Britain and American prisoners from all risk of reprisals, it is no concern of ours what measures any Allied Governments, including the Soviet Government, take as regards their own nationals, and we should be in an indefensible position if we tried to dictate to the Soviet or any other Allied Government what steps they should or should not take in dealing with their own nationals who may have committed offences against their own law by serving in the German formations." Britain, he concluded, "cannot afford to be sentimental about this."[6]

Eden also put forth a practical argument: Britain did not wish to be permanently saddled with a number of these men whether in Britain or in the Middle East. He then reminded Churchill that many of the British prisoners in Germany and Poland were likely to be released by the Russians in the course of their advance, which meant that, to a great extent, Britain was dependent on Soviet goodwill. "If we make difficulty over returning to them their own nationals," Eden cautioned, "I feel sure it will react adversely upon their willingness to help in restoring to us as soon as possible our own prisoners whom they release."[7]

After several weeks had passed without any response from Moscow, Eden hinted to the Soviet ambassador that the War Office might have to reconsider not shipping Russian prisoners to the Western Hemisphere.[8] This probably helped, and on 23 August 1944, the Soviets finally replied to Eden's note of 20 July. The message was clear: all Soviet prisoners had to be sent back to the Soviet Union at the earliest opportunity. The Soviet embassy ignored the fact that these prisoners had been captured while serving in the German army and advanced the argument that most of them had been "forcibly deported to Germany by the German aggressors." In other words, what counted was the fact that they were Soviet nationals. The British government was asked to supply a list of all Soviet nationals in British POW camps and the necessary transport for repatriating them from the United Kingdom as well as to assist in repatriating those Soviet citizens who had already been sent to Canada or the United States.[9]

The Kremlin's message only confirmed Eden's views. He now had to overcome Secretary of War Grigg's concern over the fate awaiting these Soviet nationals on returning to the Soviet Union. Grigg acknowledged there was a risk that the Soviets might delay returning British POWs, but he was not convinced that the Russians would deal with them in any special manner. In any case, Grigg wanted a cabinet ruling: "If we hand the Russian prisoners back to their death," he wrote to Eden, "it will be the military authorities who will do so on my instructions, and I am entitled to have behind me in this very unpleasant business the considered view of the Government."[10] Under the circumstances, the foreign secretary had no choice but to raise the issue again with the War Cabinet. He warned of the undesirable consequences for both Anglo-Soviet relations and the Soviets' future treatment of British POWs should Britain decide to refuse to hand back these prisoners.[11] When after a short discussion on 4 September 1944 the War Cabinet approved Eden's proposals, it was clear that the exigencies of realpolitik had won out over considerations of a humanitarian nature.[12]

Meanwhile, the status of the Soviet nationals held in Britain needed to be settled. The Soviet Military Mission in London requested at the end of September that all 12,000 Soviet nationals who had been captured in German uniform or had served in the Todt Organization and were held as POWs in the United Kingdom be released from POW status and instead be treated as members of the Soviet forces, pending their repatriation to the Soviet Union.[13] The British government was prepared to meet the Soviet Military Mission's requirements in full but insisted that Britain's goodwill depended on the Soviet government's willingness to come to some mutually satisfactory agreement regarding British Commonwealth troops in German POW camps about to be liberated by Russian forces. London expected to receive assurances that freed British prisoners would be properly looked after and a consent in principle that British officers could be dispatched to take charge of British POWs.[14] Negotiations with the Soviets were far from simple, however, and reciprocity was not easily attained.[15] London found it had to contend with continuing complaints about the way it was treating Soviet nationals (e.g., that Britain was feeding them anti-Soviet propaganda) and generally encountered an uncooperative attitude in regard to the British proposals. Nevertheless, the Foreign Office was most anxious to reach an agreement with the Soviets, if only because there were insufficient accommodations in the United Kingdom to hold the Soviet prisoners under British guard. Foreign Office officials also feared that their presence might become a source of "political and legal embarrassment."[16]

An opportunity to discuss the issue on the highest political level came about in October 1944, when Prime Minister Churchill and Foreign Secretary Eden visited Moscow. The initiative for meeting with Stalin had come from Churchill and derived from the British prime minister's wish to reach an agreement with the Soviet leader on what would be their respective spheres of influence in the Balkans and eastern Europe. Relations between London and Moscow had grown tense in the preceding weeks, not least because of differences over the future of Poland. The Soviets' refusal to offer assistance to the Polish uprising in Warsaw that had begun on 1 August—in particular by not allowing American aircraft to use Soviet airfields as takeoff points to drop supplies for the insurgents—had brought about a further deterioration in relations. On 4 October, the Warsaw uprising ended with terrible losses for the insurgents and an irreversible political defeat for London Poles.[17]

In a conversation with Eden during a dinner on 11 October, Stalin raised the question of Soviet troops in England and professed that he would be extremely grateful if any arrangements could be made to bring them back to Russia. After assuring Stalin that Britain would do all it could to help, Eden brought up the question of British POWs in German prison camps about to be liberated by the Red Army. Stalin gave Eden his personal word that his government would do everything it could to help the British prisoners.[18] Eden's assurance was apparently not enough for Molotov, who wanted to know whether the British government agreed to return all Soviet citizens to the Soviet Union as soon as possible without reference to the wishes of the individuals concerned. The Soviet government, Molotov stated, demanded this as its right. Eden replied that he had no objection, explaining that the British government "merely wanted these men, within the limitations of British law, to be placed under Soviet administration and discipline until they could be repatriated." On the understanding that the Soviet government was fully justified in demanding the return of all its citizens, Molotov agreed with him that this was the right way to proceed.[19]

Eden's cooperative attitude did not prevent the Soviets from accusing Britain of ill-treatment of Soviet citizens, claiming that despite assurances that they would not be regarded as POWs and that their living conditions in the camps would be improved, Soviet citizens were still being kept in British camps in intolerable conditions. The Soviets gave as example the Otley Works camp, where Soviet citizens were housed together with Germans and the internal camp administration was entirely composed of Germans. Similarly, Soviet citizens were often placed under German command personnel. Eden rejected these criticisms, reiterating that the entire problem could be settled on the basis of the principle that all these Soviet citizens should be repatriated to the Soviet Union.[20]

With the overall schedule of the Moscow ("Tolstoy") Conference the issue of British and Soviet POWs and nationals remained, of course, marginal and was only briefly discussed. For Churchill and Stalin, the main achievement of the meeting was the well-known "percentage agreement," about the division of spheres of influence between the Soviet Union and Britain in the Balkans and which among other things gave Britain 90 percent influence in Greece.[21] Nevertheless, the principles agreed on with respect to mutual repatriation of POWs and civilians were far reaching, particularly for Soviet nationals. Both sides, however, refrained from delving into the latter question, and thus several important issues were left open. Stalin was satisfied with Eden's agreement to return all Soviet citizens, while Eden was greatly pleased with Stalin's personal assurance regarding British POWs. Still, the Moscow Conference did not bring an end to disputes between the sides, and mutual accusations continued to be made.

A few weeks after the meeting in Moscow, London put forward a reciprocal agreement that would govern the treatment of Soviet prisoners in enemy-controlled camps in western Europe when liberated by the Allied armies and of British Commonwealth prisoners liberated by the Red Army during the period before the actual surrender of Germany. According to this proposal, all necessary arrangements had to be made for the rapid evacuation of all Soviet and British Commonwealth POWs whether they were in the main camps, in work detachments dependent on those camps, in hospitals, in prisons, billeted among the civilian population, or at large. Every effort had to be made to take advantage of all facilities the military situation allowed for the evacuation and repatriation of Soviet and British Commonwealth POWs.[22]

While waiting for Moscow's reply, William Strang, the British representative on the European Advisory Commission, urged Soviet ambassador Gusev to appoint his representatives to the committee the EAC had set up to deal with the question of the repatriation of United Nations POWs in Germany. Britain, the United States, and France had already appointed their representatives. Gusev explained that the problem was not so much the appointment of the representatives, which he had already made, as the British government's policy of treating both Soviet military personnel and civilians found in liberated territories as POWs. The Soviet government, he stated, resented this attitude, and there could be no common ground so long as the British government maintained this stance.[23]

Strang's efforts to influence Gusev to agree to join the committee's discussions bore no fruit. For the Soviet ambassador the question at stake was clearly not a technical but a political one. Not only had the Germans forced Soviet POWs and deported civilians to work either in their armed forces or in their Todt organization, but the Allies now treated these people as POWs after they had suffered for up to three years in German hands prior to being liberated. Neither the Soviet government nor the Soviet citizens concerned could understand why the British decided to act this way. The Soviet Union and the United Kingdom, Gusev reminded his counterpart, had a treaty of alliance and were fighting the same enemy: How could Soviet citizens be made POWs by their Allies? The Soviet ambassador explained that what primarily concerned his government was not a matter of the actual treatment these people received—about this the Soviet authorities had no complaints—but one of the utmost political importance: the status of Soviet citizens.[24]

Toward the end of January 1945, nearly two months after the British had presented the Soviets with a draft text, the Soviets finally issued a counterdraft. It differed little from the British one, except that it emphasized that all Soviet citizens liberated by Allied armies, whether POWs or civilians, were free citizens of an Allied power and should be treated accordingly.[25] Foreign Secretary Eden had no difficulty with this position. By now, the number of Russian civilians in German hands likely to be liberated by SHAEF and SACMED ran into the hundreds of thousands. If Britain wanted to secure Moscow's consent to an agreement on POWs, Eden forcefully argued vis-à-vis his colleagues, it had to be extended to civilians. The foreign secretary also wanted the Big Three to reach an agreement on this issue at the forthcoming Yalta Conference.

The main difficulty in the Soviet draft proposal, according to Eden, was a clause that read: "Ex-prisoners of war (with the exception of officers) and civilians of each of the parties may, until their repatriation, be employed on work in furtherance of the common war effort in accordance with agreements to be reached between the competent Soviet and British authorities. The question of payment and conditions of work shall be determined by agreement between those authorities." Prompted by Grigg, Eden was opposed to having British POWs awaiting repatriation work for the Soviets in Russia. He also feared public criticism "if our men were made to work in harsh conditions when they are not yet physically fit." Still, he thought it important to meet the Russians as far as possible on this point. Eden reminded his colleagues of the War Cabinet's decision of 17 July 1944 to propose—in nearly the same words—to the Kremlin that Russian POWs in the United Kingdom be employed in agricultural work ("These Soviet citizens shall, pending their return to the Soviet Union, be employed on such work in furtherance of the common war effort as may be agreed between the competent British and Soviet military authorities"). In other words, it was Britain, Eden pointed out, that had first formulated the idea that liberated nationals might be put to work. If London wanted to implement such a policy, then Moscow could justifiably insist on strict reciprocity. Moreover, SHAEF had experienced serious difficulty in maintaining proper control over the large number of liberated Russians for whom it was responsible. It wanted the right to put to work not only these captives but also the much larger number of Russians who might in the near future be recovered. Seeing no alternative, Eden concluded, "[I]t appears to me that, having laid down the principle, we should concentrate upon protecting our men from abuses by ensuring that the conditions of work are tolerable and upon taking all practicable steps to bring about their repatriation with the least possible delay."[26]

The general view at the cabinet meeting was that the Soviet draft should be accepted, subject to provisions ensuring that British POWs liberated by the Russians would, on release, automatically resume their status as members of His Majesty's Forces under the command of British officers; pending repatriation, they might be employed in work beneficial to the war effort in the environs of the camps where they were situated. Arrangement would also be made for the dispatch of officers to take command of the POWs on liberation in the case of Stalags that had no officer prisoners. Furthermore, the cabinet decided that the earliest possible repatriation of all British subjects liberated by the Russians should be the sole consideration dictating the POWs' subsequent movements and that they should not be moved to suit Moscow's labor requirements.[27]

AT YALTA

The War Cabinet discussion took place four days before the Yalta Conference (4–12 February 1945) and thus without the prime minister and the foreign secretary, who were already on their way. Given the top-ranking policy issues at stake, Eden was worried that the whole POW issue would be pushed aside. Thus, on the second day of the conference, he urged U.S. secretary of state Stettinius to recognize the need to get a reciprocal agreement wrapped up with the Soviets on the treatment of the respective nationals liberated by Allied armies.[28] On the very same day, 5 February, Eden approached Molotov and recalled the conversations they had had during the Moscow Conference the previous October on the question of caring for and repatriating Soviet citizens and British subjects; he also reminded Molotov of the draft agreements the two governments had exchanged on the subject. Eden pointed out that given the integrated character of the Allied commands in western and southern Europe, it was essential that any agreement be tripartite and therefore include the U.S. Command, too.[29] It now became clear, however, that the Soviets preferred separate bilateral agreements with the British and the Americans, possibly because this would enhance the probability of quickly reaching an agreement that suited their demands, at least with the British, who at the Moscow Conference had already accepted the Kremlin's viewpoint. The Soviets knew that, unlike the British, the Americans were reluctant to return to the Soviet Union nationals of Baltic states and Poles whose homes were east of the 1939 demarcation line and who had been captured in German uniform.[30]

At the same time, Eden impressed on Churchill that they needed to have an agreement before the conference was concluded. The camps the Soviet forces had already overrun, he pointed out, might contain as many as 50,000 British Commonwealth POWs. The Soviet authorities had made it plain that until an agreement was reached, they would not grant permission to British liaison officers to enter the Soviet Union in order to look after British POWs. Up to then, the Soviets had told the British ambassador about having released some British prisoners in the course of their advance but refrained from giving any further details.

Eden gave Churchill a copy of the draft he wanted to negotiate with the Soviets. This new British draft, which was based on the earlier Soviet draft and amendments, provided that work would be voluntary and that British POWs would be made to work only if British liaison officers agreed and that such work be located in the vicinity of the camps and for the period during which they were awaiting transport for repatriation. Work conditions, moreover, had to be agreed on. Finally, repatriation would in no way be delayed or impeded because of the POWs' temporary employment, and the same provisions would apply to the more than 1 million Soviet citizens whom Britain was expected to liberate in western Europe. Eden added that as Britain was already employing Soviet citizens in the United Kingdom and SHAEF was using them on the Continent, London could hardly object to the principle. But, the foreign secretary warned, "unless an agreement can be concluded, there is nothing to stop the Russians employing our men wherever and under what conditions they might think fit." Eden wanted Churchill to stress in his meetings with Stalin that the British were eager to receive all available information about liberated POWs and civilians in Soviet hands and to allow British officers to enter Soviet territory at the earliest possible moment. Eden also wanted the Soviets to agree that the ships that transported repatriated Soviet citizens would be used to bring back British Commonwealth POWs and civilians.[31]

The following day, Eden received a report that some liberated British POWs and civilians had reached Lublin. He called on Churchill to request the Soviets' consent to admit British liaison officers immediately to Soviet territories and, pending their arrival, to allow officers of the British Military Mission in Moscow (BMM) to proceed to those places where British prisoners could be found. So far, he stressed, the Soviets had refrained from giving visas to British repatriation missions.[32] Eden also wanted the Soviets to provide facilities for British Red Cross supplies stocked in Moscow to be forwarded to the British POWs and to arrange for the transfer of 7,000 POWs to Odessa in time to board the ships that were to arrive at that Black Sea Port with 7,000 repatriated Soviet citizens toward the end of February 1945.[33]

The question of Allied POWs was not among the main topics discussed at Yalta. Nevertheless, Churchill raised the issue with Stalin on 10 February when he spoke of Britain's "embarrassment" at the large number of Russian prisoners in the west, about 100,000 of them held by the British alone. After telling the Soviet leader that 11,000 Soviet POWs had already been transported back home and that 7,000 more would leave in February, Churchill wanted to know what arrangement Stalin had in mind for the rest. Stalin expressed the hope that they could be sent to Russia as quickly as possible and asked that they be segregated from German POWs. He left no doubt that the Kremlin looked on all of them as Soviet citizens. He hoped there would be no attempt to induce any of them to refuse repatriation. Those who had agreed to fight for the Germans, the Soviet leader stated, "could be dealt with" on their return to Russia. That is to say, they should not be regarded as enemy POWs.

Although he knew of the personal danger awaiting Soviet repatriates, Churchill chose not to raise the point. Instead, he told Stalin that Britain was anxious to have all these prisoners repatriated and that the only difficulty was lack of shipping space. After having established Britain's goodwill, Churchill brought up the question of British POWs. Stalin stated that very few British prisoners had been released by the Red Army and that those had been handed over to British liaison officers in Romania or Bulgaria. The Soviet leader agreed to send British liaison officers to the Red Army to look after British POWs and, meanwhile, to allow the BMM to perform the necessary liaison duties.[34]

Churchill's talk with Stalin paved the road for the signing, on 11 February, of the "Agreement Relating to POWs and Civilians Liberated by Forces Operating under Soviet Command and Forces Operating under British Command." It contained nine articles. Article 2 covered the question that particularly worried the British, that of contact with their POWs. "Soviet and British repatriation representatives will have the right of immediate access into the camps and points of concentration where their citizens or subjects are located." Facilities were to be provided for the dispatch or transfer of officers to camps or assembly points where liberated members of the forces of their own nationality were located and where there were insufficient officers. Shortly afterward, this provision would become a source of serious tensions between Britain and the Soviet Union. Article 6 answered British concerns regarding the sensitive question of the prisoners' employment.[35]

For their part, the Soviets were assured that all Soviet citizens liberated "will, without delay after their liberation, be separated from enemy prisoners of war and will be maintained separately from them in camps or points of concentration." The agreement did not mention the highly sensitive matter of the repatriation of citizens who were unwilling to return. Article 7 dealt only in a general way with the question of repatriation, stating merely that the contracting parties would use all practicable means available to transport liberated citizens or subjects to places to be agreed on where they could be handed over to the respective authorities.[36]

The issue of Soviet citizens in the United Kingdom was dealt with in a different agreement. Again, the possibility that Soviet citizens might refuse to return to the Soviet Union was not referred to at all. More significant, the agreement refrained from defining who was a Soviet citizen. Under the circumstances, both the British and the Soviets preferred not to touch on such a thorny issue as, for example, the citizenship of eastern Poland and Baltic nationals. Eden clearly recognized the problematic nature of this agreement and, whereas he instructed the Foreign Office to publish the full text relating to POWs and civilians liberated by forces operating under other Allied commands, he withheld the publication of the joint agreement on Soviet citizens in the United Kingdom.[37]

In contrast to negotiations at Yalta on geopolitical topics, the agreements regarding POWs and civilians were not hard to reach because both sides were in general accordance as to their goals. The British wanted to protect and quickly repatriate British POWs who would be liberated by the Soviets as well as to evacuate as fast as possible Soviet citizens captured by British forces. Whitehall was driven by a general concern for the safety of British POWs, but no less by apprehension at the growing interest in and criticism of the government's handling of the POW question coming from MPs, relatives of the prisoners, the press, and the wider public.[38] For its part, Moscow was determined to repatriate all Soviet citizens. The Soviets were mainly motivated by political considerations—given the ideological struggle between East and West, any large-scale preference on the part of the POWs to stay in the West would have serious adverse political and propaganda repercussions for the Soviet Union.[39] None of the parties was asked to make any substantial concessions. Humane considerations played almost no role with the Kremlin, and British officials preferred not to raise any in order not to put British interests at risk.[40] Even those cabinet ministers who admittedly felt uncomfortable with the forced repatriation decision resigned themselves to the realpolitik behind the agreements after considering the possible hardship the alternative could bring to British POWs. Concern for the fate of British prisoners, of course, played an important role, but it also served as a convenient pretext.

ACCESS TO POLAND

Within days after the agreement on POWs was signed at Yalta, the British found that the Soviets were refusing to allow British officers access to British POWs liberated by the Red Army. Reports reaching the British Military Mission in Moscow by mid-February 1945 told of 1,400 British and 600 American officers and men who had been freed by Red Army troops. According to information received from the Soviet-dominated Polish Committee of National Liberation, the former POWs were quartered in various Polish towns where they were being looked after by local organizations. The members of the BMM asked the Soviets to inform them immediately of the whereabouts of all British POWs, their numbers, and everything in connection with their general welfare as well as to permit British officers to visit them without delay. The team that was to deal with the liberated POWs was still in London awaiting visas to Poland. Rear Admiral E. R. Archer, who headed the BMM, also requested that the Soviet High Command provide the necessary transportation to the camps and give the BMM any available information with regard to permits that officers who were going to visit the camps might need.[41]

Lieutenant General K. D. Golubev, head of the POW directorate, which had recently been formed as the result of the agreement reached at the Yalta Conference, assured Archer that the Russians would soon start releasing British POWs according to rank; that protection would be given where necessary; that the Red Army General Staff was already engaged in moving about 40 British officers and 2,000 men of other ranks by rail to Odessa; and that the Soviets were building a transit camp at Odessa to accommodate 5,000 POWs, to be completed by 27 February. Pressed to give permission for British officers to enter the Soviet Union in order to contact POW camps and places of concentration, however, Golubev suddenly proved less cooperative, accusing the British of putting obstacles in the way of granting diplomatic visas to members of a Soviet mission that had arrived in London to deal with Soviet nationals. Golubev further gave the impression that the Red Army General Staff would not permit British officers to visit points behind Russian lines. For now, at least, they would be allowed to visit only the transit camp at Odessa.[42]

In response, Eden, the moving spirit behind the Yalta agreements on POWs and Soviet citizens, prepared an angry message to Molotov. The foreign secretary reminded his Soviet counterpart that at the conclusion of the Yalta Conference he had asked for his help in obtaining certain immediate facilities connected with the care of British POWs and civilians liberated by the Soviet forces, in particular in ensuring that visas be granted without further delay to the members of the British Combined Repatriation Committee—all requests that were covered by the agreement signed on

11 February and by the conversation between Churchill and Stalin on the subject. "I am both grievously disappointed and surprised," a frustrated Eden wrote, "to learn on my return here that no progress has yet been made with any of the points mentioned in my letter." The foreign secretary was especially incensed that the visas had not still been granted and that no information been received from the Soviet authorities on the numbers, names, or whereabouts of the British subjects already liberated, although reports reaching Britain indicated that their total was considerable. "I am at a loss to understand the reasons for this continued delay," Eden complained. He also pointed out that long before the signing of the agreements in Yalta, Soviet citizens liberated by Anglo-American armies had enjoyed every possible facility both in London and on the Continent. Furthermore, Britain, with the greatest difficulty, had already provided shipping from its limited resources for the repatriation of nearly 17,000 Soviet citizens from the United Kingdom alone and was about to repatriate 6,000 more. The British public, he wrote, manifested great interest in the fate of British POWs. Eden then requested the Soviet commissar to issue the visas immediately and also to provide full information about British subjects already liberated.[43]

As it happened, before Archibald Clark Kerr, the British ambassador to the Soviet Union, could convey Eden's message of remonstrance, he received from Molotov assurances that the terms of the agreement would be adhered to, that there would be no delay in issuing visas, and that British subjects at large in Poland would be gathered together at once.[44] The People's Commissariat for Foreign Affairs further told Clark Kerr that the Soviet embassy in London had been instructed to give entry visas to twenty-two officers and eight men of other ranks.[45] Eden thereupon decided to withhold his letter, but its angry tone clearly revealed the foreign secretary's state of mind at the time.

Secretary of State for War Grigg, however, had his suspicions and did not think the Russians were going to let British liaison officers, whether from the BMM or from Britain, behind Russian lines. "We shall therefore know nothing about what is happening to our prisoners until some of them arrive at Odessa." If the POWs would bring back stories of hardship and even maltreatment, Grigg warned, "we shall be responsible for not having done more for them, and public opinion may well be inflamed against the Russians." Grigg suggested putting pressure on the Russians, such as holding up the repatriation of the second batch of Russian prisoners from the United Kingdom early in March 1945.[46]

Grigg's firm stand was influenced also by continued pressure from MPs. On 22 February, for example, MP Knox asked the secretary of state for war about the most recent number of British POWs who had been liberated with the Russian advance, where they were being assembled, and whether all names had been communicated to their next of kin. Knox expressed dissatisfaction with the statement Grigg had given two days earlier that there had been no official information yet from the Soviet authorities on the recent situation. In response, Arthur Henderson, the financial secretary to the War Office, repeated figures Britain had received earlier from the Soviets: 2,661 British Commonwealth POWs (70 of whom were officers) recovered from German camps were on their way by rail to Odessa, where a transit camp was under construction. There all British prisoners recovered would be assembled until ships arrived to bring them home. So far, Henderson added, no list of names had been received, but it seemed likely that the Soviet authorities were providing British POWs with food, clothing, and the necessary medical attention in view of the agreement concluded in Yalta. Henderson's reply, too, failed to satisfy the MPs, who kept pressing the government for more detailed information.[47]

Foreign Office officials, too, continued to be suspicious about Soviets' intentions. Orme Sargent, deputy undersecretary of state in the Foreign Office, wrote to Clark Kerr that unless the Soviet authorities were prepared to enable British officers to travel freely to Soviet and Soviet-occupied territories and visit all the places where liberated British subjects were located, "the grant of visas alone will not be worth very much." Sargent was particularly irked by Golubev's attitude. The Soviet authorities had made a good beginning by sending more than 2,000 liberated British subjects to Odessa; however, Sargent insisted, what really mattered was whether British officers would be allowed to visit forward areas and then to evacuate and repatriate British subjects, many of whom were allegedly wandering aimlessly behind Marshal Ivan S. Konev's armies without any proper arrangements being made for them. "We need have no hesitation about pressing the Soviet authorities on this," Sargent concluded, "since they have enjoyed full facilities in our forward areas for the last four months or more and have made frequent representations to the Allied authorities about the conditions and treatment of liberated Soviet citizens." Clark Kerr was instructed to maintain constant pressure on the Soviet authorities.[48]

Once again, though, Clark Kerr was able to reassure the Foreign Office. He told Eden that Admiral Archer was satisfied that the Russians were not evading their obligations and were anxious to get British POWs out of the

Soviet Union as soon as possible. The ambassador recommended that the Foreign Office make do with the strongly worded memorandum he had handed Molotov demanding that facilities be provided to officers from the BMM to visit areas in which prisoners were collected by Soviet authorities pending dispatch to Odessa.[49] While Clark Kerr's cautious optimism was not without foundation, he was soon to learn that Soviet assurances were fluid. On 24 February 1945, Molotov sent a letter to Eden stating that in accordance with the Yalta agreement, information about all groups of British POWs liberated by the Red Army would be supplied regularly to the BMM and that instructions had been given to the Soviet embassy in London to issue visas to repatriated British officers. In the meantime, the Soviet foreign minister continued, the BMM might make use of its officers as liaison personnel, and he would take the required measures so that they could travel to Polish territory. He also told Eden that the Soviet authorities had made the necessary arrangements to send back all liberated British POWs on the ship that was bringing the Soviet POWs to Odessa.[50]

Following Molotov's assurances, BMM officers visited the transit camp that had been set up at Odessa, and another British team went to Lublin. Several days later, Golubev named Lwow and Volkvysk as two other assembly points for former British POWs and consented to the arrival of British repatriation teams there by 20 March, when camps at these locations would be ready. But when the Soviets supplied the BMM with a list of recovered British POWs, it turned out to contain names of men who had arrived at Odessa and whose details had already been reported to British officers there. The BMM was also dissatisfied with the rate at which the liberated British POWs were arriving at Odessa. Of the original list of 2,661 names that Golubev presented on 17 February as being en route to Odessa, no more than 1,847 had arrived by 12 March. Only 12 of these were reported as sick cases, whereas Archer had received numerous reports of many sick soldiers who had been left behind in Poland. The slow pace of the evacuation of the British POWs prevented Britain from filling the ships with British and American POWs—the first two ships that sailed from Odessa also had on board 826 French citizens, mostly civilians.[51] Moreover, on 12 March Golubev stated that no British soldiers remained in Poland and that he therefore refused to give permission for a British team, including a medical officer, to proceed into Poland to investigate the situation. Following pressure from Archer, Golubev admitted that sending British missions to Poland was outside his authority and required the concurrence of Poland's provisional government.

He therefore recommended that the British approach the People's Commissariat for Foreign Affairs.[52]

Recognizing that high politics was involved, Clark Kerr sent a letter to Molotov in mid-March pointing out that the only definite information the embassy had been able to send to London so far was the names of 1,200 liberated POWs who were already on their way to the United Kingdom from Odessa. "Although we knew of large numbers of our men scattered in various parts of Silesia and Poland," Clark Kerr complained, "the repeated requests from the military mission for permission to send British representatives there had been refused." The ambassador reiterated that the British public was greatly interested in the matter, and he pressed Molotov to take the necessary measures that would allow the British repatriation commission to perform the duties for which they had been sent from Britain. Moscow was not convinced and continued to deny British officers entry into Poland. Vladimir G. Dekanozov of the People's Commissariat for Foreign Affairs told Clark Kerr that there were difficulties in settling such matters with the Polish authorities and that there were also objections on the part of Soviet military authorities.[53]

Clark Kerr thought that either Molotov had been unable to overcome the objections of Soviet military authorities and to keep his assurances or he was using this issue as blackmail in order to force Britain into some relationship with the Polish Provisional Government. The ambassador believed that much of the trouble arose from the Kremlin's disinclination to have British officials witness too much of the chaotic conditions near the front line in Poland. He advised Eden to send a personal message to Molotov emphasizing the expected public reaction in Britain—according to Clark Kerr, the Soviets were sensitive to any suggestions of neglect or ill-treatment on their part. Eden's note should point out that as the agreement at Yalta was made with the Soviet government, which was in military control of all territory concerned, Britain could not accept the argument that difficulties were being raised by the Polish Provisional Government. Nor could Britain understand how Soviet military authorities could raise objections at this time to the full execution of the agreement.[54]

Clark Kerr's analysis and recommendations should be viewed against the background of the negotiations he was conducting at the time with Molotov and U.S. ambassador Harriman over the future government of Poland. The three formed the Moscow Commission, which had been established by the

Yalta Conference to discuss the reorganization of Poland's government. The question of Poland, particularly the nature of the country's future government, greatly preoccupied the Big Three at Yalta, where, following exhaustive negotiations, they had agreed that "the Provisional Government which is now functioning in Poland should . . . be reorganized on a broader democratic basis with the inclusion of democratic leaders from Poland itself and from Poles abroad. This new Government should then be called the Polish Provisional Government of National Unity" and "shall be pledged to the holding of free and unaffected elections as soon as possible on the basis of universal suffrage and secret ballot." When such a government was properly formed, the governments of the Soviet Union, the United States, and Britain would commit themselves to recognizing it and establishing diplomatic relations with it.[55]

When, in December 1944, the Soviets formally recognized the provisional government, known also as the Lublin Government, the British and the Americans had refused to follow suit. "I am very sorry that I have not succeeded in convincing you of the correctness of the Soviet Government's stand on the Polish question," Stalin had written to Churchill on 1 January 1945; "nevertheless, I hope events will convince you that the National Committee has always given important help to the Allies, and continues to do so, particularly to the Red Army, in the struggle against Hitler Germany, while the émigré Government in London is disorganising that struggle, thereby helping the Germans."[56]

The negotiations conducted by the Moscow Commission now demonstrated that the Western powers and the Soviet Union had differing interpretations of the Yalta agreement, particularly on the matter of reorganizing the Polish government. Heated debates developed between the two sides. Analyzing Soviet policy at the end of March 1945, Clark Kerr stated angrily that the Russians had to "be blind" if they did not see that Poland might become a test case of their relations with the West; "their attempt to twist the Yalta communiqué to the exclusive benefit of the provisional authorities at Warsaw is . . . disquieting." As Clark Kerr saw it, the Soviets were determined to have a comfortable neighbor but failed to understand Britain's moral commitment to Poland. He thought that Stalin and Molotov might have come away from Yalta with the impression that Britain would be satisfied with their interpretation of the Yalta agreement "as a means of cleansing ourselves of our commitments to Poland" and therefore, Clark Kerr argued, they were now "puzzled by our sustained and indeed increased interest in Polish affairs."[57]

Although Clark Kerr at this point encouraged Eden to approach Molotov over the handling of British POWs, he was skeptical of the results, among other reasons because of the similar difficulties the Americans were already experiencing in their negotiations with the Soviets over their own liberated POWs.[58] Clark Kerr agreed with his American counterpart Harriman that only a firm stand on the part of Whitehall could influence Moscow's position. Eden, although of one mind with his ambassador that the present position was unsatisfactory, preferred not to send a personal message to Molotov at this time. "Our impression here," he wrote to Clark Kerr, "is that generally speaking the case that there is ill-will has not yet been proved and that the real trouble seems to be that action at all points by Russians is far too slow and that this is due to deficient organisation." Instead, his plan was to concentrate on inducing the Russians to produce more rapid results on the basis of the Yalta agreement. Eden therefore instructed Clark Kerr to hold the Russians to their promise to permit immediate visits by contact teams to the three centers of Lwow, Volkvysk, and Bronnitz. If it turned out that there were concentrations of British subjects farther west, the ambassador was to press for visits to those places, too. Eden pointed out, however, that under the agreement Britain could not claim to visit those "who are at large" if by this was meant that British officers were to search out and collect individual POWs "in the back areas of the Soviet armies." He also suggested that contact teams be allowed to make their way to hospitals in Praga, Lublin, and elsewhere in order to verify the reports. For political reasons, Eden did not take up the ambassador's suggestion to request help from the Polish embassy in forwarding supplies and looked on the American Red Cross as a more suitable channel of distribution. "It is the duty of the Soviet government," Eden concluded, "to overcome such difficulties."[59] Clark Kerr was convinced that a great many sick POWs were left behind in hospitals in Poland and that thousands of liberated British prisoners still remained in Poland. He did not accept the continued denial by the Russians, maintaining that these men were dependent for their existence on whatever hospitality they could beg from the Poles; they were being directed by the Russians by means of posters written in several languages to go to "camps for recollection" at Praga, Lodz, Lublin, and Wrzesnia, from which they would be sent to Odessa.[60] By now Clark Kerr dismissed the idea of approaching Molotov again, quoting Harriman's words about having exhausted all arguments with Molotov. He recommended that Churchill send a "rough" personal message to Stalin.[61]

The British ambassador believed that in general the Soviets judged Britain by its readiness to stand up for its rights and interests. "Wherever and whenever we show signs of weakening," he maintained, "we may expect to be pounced upon. We must therefore not only be strong, we must look strong and, so far as possible, we should confine our quarrels with the Russians to issues on which we are prepared to stand our ground."[62] He regarded the question of British prisoners as falling within this category. Eden was convinced by Clark Kerr's arguments and furnished him with two messages, one from himself to Molotov and one from Churchill to Stalin. Clark Kerr was also told to instruct the British officers in Lublin to adopt the same line as their American colleagues about leaving that location— American liaison officers in Lublin who had been told by Soviet military authorities to leave on the expiration of their fifteen-day permits had been instructed by General John Deane, head of the U.S. Military Mission to Moscow, to stay there unless actually removed by force. By this time, however, the Lublin camp had been closed, and the members of the BMM had already left for Moscow. The Russians had been unwilling to grant them facilities to communicate with Moscow from the field or to travel elsewhere in Poland.[63]

In his note to Molotov of 21 March, Eden complained that for more than a month Britain had received no information regarding its prisoners. Moreover, he knew that only 1,847 of the 2,611 British men that the Soviet authorities said had been assembled had actually arrived at Odessa in time to embark on the ship sent to collect them. Eden also criticized the obstacles that were continually being created regarding visits by British officers and with respect to furnishing supplies to hospitals and other places where British subjects were assembled on their way to embarkation points. Britain had no idea of the total number or the names of the men concerned, their living conditions, or their needs. The only places to which visits had been permitted (namely, Volkvysk, Lublin, Lwow, and Bronnitz) were insufficient, as they were not first collection points. Eden urged Molotov to give immediate permission for visits by British officers, including medical officers, to the forward areas in Poland and elsewhere as well as to all first collection points, hospitals, and other places where London knew from reliable reports that British prisoners were collected.[64] Churchill's message to Stalin was as brief as it was direct. The prime minister referred to the message that Eden had sent Molotov and expressed great distress at the position of British POWs. There was no subject on which the British nation was more sensitive than the fate of British prisoners in German hands. Their speedy deliverance from captivity and return to their own country were essential. Churchill asked Stalin to give the matter his personal attention, "as I am sure you would wish to do your best for our men."[65]

Both Stalin and Molotov quickly and firmly rejected the criticism from London. Stalin told Churchill that he had no grounds for anxiety concerning British POWs because "they are living in better conditions than was the case with Soviet prisoners of war in English camps, when the latter in a number of cases suffered persecution and even blows." The Soviet leader also maintained that there were no longer any English prisoners left in Soviet camps, as the remainder were en route for Odessa and the voyage home.[66] For his part, Molotov firmly denied that the agreement on POWs had been unsatisfactorily carried out on the Soviet side, as Eden had asserted; "I cannot regard as justified," Molotov responded, "exaggerated claims which do not follow from the agreement."[67] Moscow's line was as consistent as it was clear: on the one hand, the Soviets insisted that British POWs were in good condition; on the other, they accused the British of improper treatment of Soviet nationals in the United Kingdom.

Both Stalin's and Molotov's responses were characterized in London as "rude messages." Sargent had no doubts about the Soviets' motives. Their determined refusal to permit a British mission to go into Poland proper derived from Moscow's suspicion that the mission would "at once under cover of dealing with prisoners of war proceed to contact Polish leaders, and in fact convert itself into the Observation Mission which we have been trying in vain to get the Russians to allow us to send in connection with our Polish negotiations." He thought that London should act in concert with the White House, since President Roosevelt had gone further than Britain and telegraphed Stalin directly. Although the president had received an equally unsatisfactory reply, Sargent maintained, it was not as rude as that sent to Whitehall. Still, as the British mission was at the time making its way to the camps at Lwow and Volkvysk, both east of the Curzon line, Sargent advocated restraint. If the mission's reports were very bad, Britain should renew its attempt to send a mission to Poland proper. Up to now, he pointed out, Stalin and Molotov had denied that any concentration points existed or that there were any POWs in hospitals in Poland west of the Curzon line.[68]

Sargent's analysis seems reasonable, since on 27 February 1945 Molotov offered both the British and the American ambassadors facilities to enable their countries' observers to go to Poland in order to obtain firsthand impression of the situation. Within a few days, however, Molotov reneged on his offer. In his memoirs, Churchill wrote, "[Molotov] had offered to allow us to send observers to Poland, and had been disconcerted by the readiness and speed with which we had accepted. When our Ambassador raised the point he made difficulties, arguing among other things, that it might affect the prestige of the Lublin Provisional Government." Churchill was sure that Molotov wanted "to stop us seeing the liquidations and deportations and all the maneuvers of setting up a totalitarian régime before elections were held and even before a new Government was installed."[69]

Moscow's change of mind in fact was influenced by the deadlock in the three powers' negotiations over the future government of Poland. When the offer was made, Molotov still thought that the British and the Americans were willing to accept the Kremlin's line. But when it learned that this was not the case, the Kremlin decided to block any visits to Poland by Western officials, including British liaison officers. As the Soviets saw it, the latter would not limit their activities just to searching for British prisoners.[70]

Although concerned about the Soviets' refusal to allow British officers into Poland, Foreign Office officials acknowledged among themselves that Britain harbored no particular complaints about the treatment itself of British POWs, as this had been slightly better even than how the Red Army treated its own soldiers. Debriefing of several liberated POWs who had been repatriated from Odessa revealed a total lack of any proper organization for the collection and evacuation of British POWs from the front. It appeared that when Soviet front-line troops first came across these British prisoners, they regarded them with suspicion but that the treatment proffered was cordial and, under the circumstances, reasonably good, even friendly. Also the trip to Odessa in railway cattle cars had been made in conditions that were considerably better than Red Army men encountered when moved by rail. In Odessa, too, the Soviet authorities had done their best to give all POWs a fair deal. Yet reports reaching London indicated that there were probably many isolated groups of released British POWs wandering around in Poland not knowing where to report.[71]

In his memoirs, POW chaplain David Wild recalled his first meeting with Soviet soldiers.

> Russian local commanders had no instructions or only very hazy notions about what to do with British POWs. Usually the stragglers were told to take their way to some collecting centre, among those mentioned being Bromberg, Hohensalze, Ciechocinek and Lublin. It became clear, however, to us at Ciechocinek that many British ex-prisoners were scattered

all over the countryside, having drifted back to their farms and girl-friends; others were going aimlessly from place to place, at increasing risk to themselves as the Russians found more time to round them up.[72]

Wild also told of his meeting with three British who told him "that under Russian instructions they had hitchhiked by truck and train several hundred kilometers to Lublin. There they had found dismal conditions and no further instructions; in despair, they had made the long journey back to Bromberg, where they knew that they had Polish friends."[73] Wild referred as well to his short stay at the collecting camp at Wrzesnia, east of Poznan: "Eventually we were told to take over the totally unfurnished ground floor of a house that had been previously occupied by Italians. It was a mass of every kind of filth and excrement, and any wooden furniture or fixtures had been ripped out, chopped up and used for firewood. . . . There were no latrines, and when I was smitten with diarrhea in the middle of the night I crawled out several times into the snow outside while an air raid was going on overhead."[74]

Meanwhile, the British learned that the Soviet authorities at Lwow had refused to extend the permits of the British contact officers beyond 5 April and had ordered them to return to Moscow. Admiral Archer instructed the officers to stay where they were, but they had been confined to their hotel and thus were unable to report on any British POWs who might be in the Lwow camp. From recovered POWs the mission learned that the Russians had been using Cracow and Czestochowa as forward collection points and that large numbers of British prisoners were hiding in Poland. Some of them had gone to Cracow but returned to previous billets when they had failed to find any British officers there. The British contact officers at Volkvysk returned to Moscow after the Soviets had instructed them in writing to leave by 5 April. Unlike the team in Lwow, the Volkvysk team received no instructions from Archer or any telegram from the BMM to stay. The Volkvysk party reported Soviet obstacles preventing the team from operating. Clark Kerr urged Molotov to allow the British officers to remain until they had completed their duties.[75]

Molotov did not even bother to respond, and on 16 April Clark Kerr once again asked him whether the Soviet government had reconsidered its decision on the Lwow and Volkvysk missions. The ambassador told his superiors that further information he had received made "it harder than ever for me to understand what the Soviet authorities can have had in mind when they ordered our officers to leave." Clark Kerr contradicted General Golubev's statement about the absence of liberated British POWs in Lwow or Volkvysk.[76] The Soviets, however, stuck to their position. First Deputy Commissar for Foreign Affairs Andrei Vyshinski wrote to Clark Kerr that there had been no British prisoners in the camps in question and that the presence of British liaison officers was neither necessary nor in the spirit of the Yalta agreement. When more British prisoners arrived, Vyshinski stated, British officers would be given facilities to visit the camps.[77]

Although greatly frustrated with the Soviets' behavior, Foreign Office officials differed over what course of action they ought to take. Walter Roberts, head of the PWD, preferred not to react, stating that not only the local situation but also the position of British POWs who had not yet been freed had to be taken into account. On the basis of the War Office's estimation, there were only 700 liberated prisoners in Russian hands still unaccounted for. Before the Russian offensive, the total number of British POWs in those areas was estimated at 68,500. According to ICRC calculations, the Germans had moved 64,400 out of those areas. Of these, the Russians had already recovered 3,400. This, therefore, accounted for 67,800 POWs, leaving a remainder of 700.

Roberts further argued that when in the early stages 2,600 had reached Odessa, this contingent was generally assumed to be only the advance guard of a much larger number. The Red Army, however, had not moved forward on a wide front during March. Therefore, "if the above estimates are sound, it looks as if the size of our problem has been over-estimated." Roberts himself thought that a few hundred more of those who had escaped through the lines before the Russian offensive and now lay hidden among the Poles should be added to the 700 figure. Still, he felt uncomfortable with the messages to the Soviets that spoke of thousands and thousands of former British prisoners waiting to be sent to Odessa. The Soviets, he argued, had not accepted this as true, and indeed the numbers passing down the lines of communication were small. The consequence, as he saw it, was that "[a]ll this has increased their suspicion that our contact officers are really political intelligence officers in disguise." Roberts believed that the POW issue should serve to foster cooperation, not breed confrontation, with the Soviets. Britain ought to be concerned not only with those POWs who were already in Russian hands but also with the large number of British prisoners who were in camps in Upper Bavaria, Saxony, and Austria that were soon to be overrun by the Red Army. He further pointed to the secretary of war's wish that the Russians hand over these POWs to Eisenhower's forces as soon as operational considerations allowed and not to continue the present arrangement of moving them eastward to Odessa. Britain could obtain the Soviets' "consent more easily if we are not in the middle of a dispute about contact officers in Poland, the Ukraine or White Russia." He therefore recommended that London not press the issue of British prisoners in Poland.[78]

Given his function, Roberts was primarily concerned with the state of the POWs and less with the overall relations with the Soviet Union. Other Foreign Office officials, however, thought differently. "If the Russians have in fact been guilty of breaches of the Yalta Agreement about prisoners of war," Geoffrey Wilson of the Northern Department of the Foreign Office stated, "I am all in favour of making a fuss about them, irrespective of what other discussions may be going on." The Russians, he continued, should expect to be held to their agreements "in exactly the same way as they always insisted on holding Britain to ours, and to ignore any breaches merely weakens our position hereafter." Patrick Dean, the assistant legal adviser, who had been on the team drafting the text for the Yalta agreement on POWs, agreed with Wilson and pointed to a telegram from Washington showing American dissatisfaction with the continued breaches of the Yalta agreement by the Soviet government. U.S. Secretary of State Stettinius was asking for as much evidence as Britain could supply to enable him to support his planned representation to the Russians. Dean, like Wilson, thought that approaching the Soviets about evacuating British prisoners westward, rather than to Odessa, should not prevent London from taking up with them the matter of breaches of the Yalta agreement.[79]

Although it had little hope of changing the Soviets' conduct, the Foreign Office instructed Clark Kerr on 20 April to issue a strong complaint over the breaches of the agreement in regard to Lwow and Volkvysk.[80] On the same day, Eden wrote to Stettinius that it was clear the Kremlin would not allow British contact teams into Poland. The Russians even denied the existence of British POWs in Poland, despite evidence of British POW concentrations in Cracow and Czestochowa. Britain's main aim now was to see to it that British POWs in Poland received medical supplies and comforts.[81] Eden's pessimistic assessment of the situation was not groundless. Several days earlier, Stalin had declined Churchill's request to allow British observers into Poland, stating that the Poles would regard such as an insult to their national dignity in light of the British government's unfriendly attitude toward the provisional government.[82] Stalin complained about Churchill's refusal to regard the Polish Provisional Government as the core of a future

Polish Government of National Unity and blamed the British prime minister for departing from the understanding reached at Yalta on this issue.[83] Stalin's message to Churchill was clear: London's attitude toward the Polish Provisional Government "precludes the possibility of an agreed decision on the Polish question."[84]

The dispute between the British and the Soviets became public when, on 30 April 1945, *Pravda* published an interview with Colonel General Filip Golikov, head of the Soviet Repatriation Committee.[85] Golikov compared a figure of more than 1.5 million Soviet citizens repatriated from areas overrun by the Red Army with the lowly figure of 35,000 Soviets repatriated out of a total of more than 150,000 liberated by the Allies. "Thousands of Soviet citizens," he claimed, "were forced to wait many months for transport to their native land." Not everywhere, he charged, were former Soviet POWs being treated as citizens of an Allied power. The Russian repatriation official then gave several examples of breaches of the Yalta agreement by the Allies: failure to report the presence of more than 1,700 Soviet citizens in three American-run camps in Britain; failure to hand over 300 Soviet citizens whose existence in Britain was known; efforts to deter Soviet citizens in Egypt from returning to the Soviet Union; failure to properly segregate Soviet POWs from Germans in Camp 307 in Egypt; and failure to expedite the return to the Soviet Union of 1,156 Soviet officers and men. Sick Russians, furthermore, were being sent to German camp hospitals. Local censorship, he asserted, had prevented the Soviet repatriation administration from discovering "these infamies" until much later.

The Soviet's own conduct, Golikov stated categorically, was entirely different. Of the 205,000 Allied and other foreign POWs and citizens liberated since the January 1945 offensive, 64,188 had already been repatriated. In particular, this included all the British and Americans, with the exception of odd individuals and small groups of sick prisoners. The repatriation of the remaining number was merely a question of transport, of which there was a great shortage. Well before the Yalta agreement, according to Golikov, the Soviet government had set up an organization for repatriation duties. The transfer of prisoners to Germany, however, had made it difficult to find and concentrate liberated prisoners; nevertheless, hundreds of officers from both field and repatriation units were working ceaselessly to overcome the obstacle. Golikov further maintained that the information provided by Allied Military Missions on numbers and whereabouts of liberated prisoners was not always accurate. As for the evacuation process, the Soviet field army collected the liberated prisoners at evacuation points and, as a rule, quickly dispatched them by railway and aircraft to repatriation assembly points and transit camps, where the soldiers among them were formed into military subunits. Internal administration was composed of officers of the same nationality as the former POWs, and internal arrangements and control were set up in accordance with military orders and the laws of their country. The Red Army provided uniforms, linen and bedding, soap, tobacco, matches, and hot food. Special arrangements for the sick and wounded had prevented the spread of infectious disease. Golikov concluded by saying that numerous liberated prisoners, soldiers, and civilians had testified to the good and even generous treatment that they had received in the camps from advanced units of the Red Army.[86]

While the Foreign Office preferred to avoid public recriminations with Golikov for fear that this would poison the atmosphere further and impede finding solutions to thorny POW questions, Whitehall recognized that they could not entirely ignore Soviet propaganda, especially as Golikov's statements had given rise to a number of parliamentary questions. On 2 May, for example, MP Thomas Henry Hewlett asked the foreign secretary "whether, in view of the excellent treatment given by the Russians to British prisoners of war whom they liberate, he can state whether special effort is made to extend similar treatment to Russian prisoners of war liberated by the British." Undersecretary of State Richard Law dispelled "misleading statements" that had appeared in the press about British officials' treatment of Soviet citizens liberated by British forces. Law told the House that many of the large numbers of Soviet citizens who had been liberated by the advancing Anglo-American armies since D-Day had been, or were at the time of their liberation, serving in the Todt and other German official criminal organizations; furthermore, a considerable number of them had fallen into Allied hands while still in German uniform. Law's tactic was first to categorize the Soviet citizens as German collaborators and then to state that the vast majority of Soviet POWs had been forced to serve the Germans against their will.

Members of Parliament were further told that 42,421 Soviet citizens had been repatriated from the United Kingdom and the Mediterranean area since October 1944; to this figure ought to be added the 14,565 liberated by U.S. forces. With the exception of one ship provided by the Americans, all the shipping and other transport for these 56,986 Soviet citizens had been provided by London, which meant there were less funds for other vital purposes. Pointing a finger at the Soviets, Law contended that the remaining Soviet citizens in western Europe could have been repatriated much earlier if the Soviet government had also provided shipping. For their part, the Soviet authorities had notified Britain of 3,854 British subjects liberated by their forces up to 21 April 1945; of these, 3,639 had passed through the camp in Odessa, which was the most advanced point to which the Soviet authorities had allowed British officers to have regular access. In this case, too, British shipping alone had been employed to bring these men home. Law concluded by giving a hint of Whitehall's dissatisfaction with the Soviets' decision to go public with their criticism.[87]

London, however, did not stop at Law's public statement, and on 3 May, Eden presented Molotov with a memorandum expressing dissatisfaction with isolated Soviet acts and criticizing the condition of British POWs in the Soviet Union. The foreign secretary wanted to see greater openness and trustfulness on the Soviet side as well as greater personal contact between the representatives of the two countries.[88] Although the Foreign Office realized that protests were largely made for the record, as they seldom obtained redress, the ministry still believed that they could serve as a counterweight to the numerous complaints emanating from the Soviet embassy in London.[89]

The end of the war did little to halt the mutual criticism. The day after Germany's surrender, Richard Law stated in reply to questions on the POW issue in the House of Commons that "His Majesty's Government's main grounds for complaint have been the absence of adequate facilities for visits by British officers to first collection points, hospitals, and other places in forward areas where it was known from reliable reports that British prisoners were collected, and the slowness with which the prisoners have been concentrated and moved to the port of embarkation. There have also been a certain number of exceptional cases where our prisoners have suffered hardships, including robbery of their personal possessions. It is these matters which have formed the subject of representations to the Soviet Government." Law also confirmed MP Captain James Alexander Lawson Duncan's statement that British officers were not allowed to see British repatriated POWs until they had reached Odessa. The undersecretary informed the House that further representations would be made to allow British officers to contact escaped British POWs.[90]

British Foreign Office criticism of their treatment of British POWs obviously served the Soviets to widen their counterattack.[91] In early June, Vyshinski categorically rejected the British accusation that the attitude of the Soviet government did not correspond with either the letter or the spirit of the Yalta agreement. The deputy commissar of Foreign Affairs maintained that the assembly and subsequent dispatch to Odessa of liberated British personnel had been executed with the highest level of speed that military operations on the Soviet-German front had allowed. Isolated cases of delay were due to the fact that some British personnel had avoided registration and had not notified the authorities appointed for this purpose. Vyshinski also forcefully denied complaints about the admission of British repatriation officers into assembly camps and billets and strongly objected to the assertion that British representatives in Odessa had not been allowed to verify the internal arrangement of the camp. British representatives, he argued, had freedom of access to the Odessa camp, knew the internal arrangement of the camp well, and were aware that British officers made up the internal administration of the camp. References to various collection points were without foundation, since at this point no other camps existed apart from Odessa. Soviet authorities had done and would do everything in their power to ensure the exact and prompt execution of their obligations, Vyshinski promised.[92]

The exchange of accusations did not prevent the British from accepting Vyshinski's proposal of 30 April to repatriate POWs and civilians overland. Instead of sending British prisoners home by the long Odessa route and Soviet prisoners by sea via Marseilles, he had suggested an overland route and that the exchange take place in Germany, whether in Torgau, where Allied armies had already linked up, or any other place.[93] Negotiations between SHAEF and Soviet delegations were conducted in mid-May 1945 and, on 22 May, resulted in the so-called Halle Agreement, which regulated the exchange of all former Soviet POWs and citizens liberated by the Allied forces and all former Western Allied POWs and citizens liberated by the Red Army.[94] When joint interests were at stake, the two countries had little difficulty in concluding agreements.

The Halle Agreement and the subsequent quick repatriation of the POWs and civilians of both countries did not, however, bring an end to mutual recriminations on the matter.[95] The Foreign Office explained to Clark Kerr that counterstatements to any Soviet assertions had to be made, "otherwise they may well be repeated on subsequent occasions with the implication that we have been unable to refute them." Most of the complaints the Soviet embassy in London was issuing about the treatment of individual liberated Soviet citizens, it was maintained, were extremely flimsy and seemed to be designed merely to irritate.[96] The formal recognition on 5 July 1945 by

London and Washington of the new Polish Provisional Government made no difference. British efforts to convince both the Soviet and Polish authorities to permit British teams to search Polish territory, as the Soviets had been able to do in France, Belgium, Holland, and Czechoslovakia, were rebuffed.

In mid-July 1945, the War Office estimated that there were about 200 former British POWs still at large in Poland. It was believed that some of the escaped POWs preferred "to lie low rather than to report to Soviet authorities."[97] Pressure in Parliament continued, and in November 1945 government officials confirmed that the Soviet authorities still refused requests for British search parties to enter the Soviet zone. By then, 105 POWs were still unaccounted for.[98] In late November, the Polish government promised to instruct local authorities to make full inquiries about any British servicemen who might have been cut off in Poland. Victor Cavendish-Bentinck, British ambassador in Poland, thought that the Polish government's refusal had been dictated by the Soviet authorities' desire "that we should not have at our disposal increased means of obtaining information regarding widespread disposal of their forces with no apparent relations to their lines of communication."[99] But by mid-December the Soviets seemed to have partially changed the course they had followed until then when they allowed British search teams as well as British correspondents and MPs to visit the Soviet zone of Germany.[100] Finally, despite ongoing recriminations—indicative of the approaching Cold War—both sides got what they wanted: the relatively rapid repatriation of, for the Russians, all Soviet nationals and, for the British, virtually all British Commonwealth POWs.

A U.S.-Soviet Package Deal

U.S. POWS COME FIRST

"My darkest days in Russia," Major General John R. Deane wrote in his memoirs, "were in the winter of 1944–45, when I was trying to arrange for the best possible care and speedy repatriation of American prisoners of war liberated by the advance of the Red Army."[1] Deane was head of the U.S. Military Mission in Moscow and as such in charge of the negotiations with the Russians over the mutual exchange of POWs. He soon discovered, as did his British counterparts, that the Soviets had decided to exploit the large numbers of Allied POWs they were expected to liberate to achieve two main objectives. One was the repatriation of all "Soviet nationals," the other recognition by the West of the Soviet-installed regime in Poland as that country's legitimate government and of the Baltic countries and eastern Poland as inseparable parts of the Soviet Union.

With U.S. ambassador Averell Harriman, Deane was one of the very first U.S. officials to register the shift in Soviet policy that before long would bring down the Iron Curtain. In an oblique effort to influence President Roosevelt to reverse his cooperative stand toward the Kremlin, Deane and Harriman, for their part, now began exploiting the POW issue, giving their reports from Moscow a clearly negative slant. Set in this context, Deane's "darkest days" may well refer to the sense of foreboding he must have felt as the early winds of the Cold War seemed to frustrate his efforts at almost every turn of the road.

Several days before D-Day, Eisenhower learned that large numbers of Russians under German command were stationed on the French coastline. In an effort to diminish whatever motivation these Soviet nationals might have to fight on the German side, Molotov was asked to publish a statement promising them amnesty or considerate treatment if they surrendered to the Allies at the first opportunity. Molotov declined to do so, responding that the number of Soviet nationals serving in the German army was insignificant and that such an appeal ran counter to Soviet political interests.

Very quickly, however, Molotov was proved wrong, as the number of Soviet nationals captured turned out to be far from "insignificant."[2]

Like the British, the Americans recognized that the Red Army would soon overrun German POW camps where most of the U.S. prisoners were held. In early August 1944, Major General Robert L. Walsh, chief of the Air Division, warned Major General N. V. Slavin, assistant chief of staff of the Red Army, that the Germans might fail to evacuate POWs and civilians because the extensive successes of the Soviets were already making it difficult for the German army to extricate its own forces. Slavin was asked to inform Soviet army commanders of the location of seven POW camps in Poland and Germany with U.S. prisoners.[3] The U.S. general suggested sending in American officers and medical personnel to take charge of the American soldiers in these camps under Soviet supervision. Stalag Luft VI at Heydekrug, for example, where 2,411 USAAF enlisted men were held, was directly in the line of the Red Army's advance in Estonia and was within approximately sixty miles of the Soviet front line.[4]

While waiting for the Soviets to reply, Eisenhower's chief of staff, Lieutenant General Walter Bedell-Smith, urged Ambassador Harriman to call on Molotov to work out a plan as far in advance as possible for the prompt return of both American and Soviet prisoners to their home countries. The United States wanted to send officers into the camps that would come under control of the Red Army in order to establish which POWs were of U.S. nationality and to take charge of them during their evacuation. Harriman further suggested that individuals or small groups claiming Soviet or American nationality who might surrender to or be captured by the military authorities of either country should be reported promptly in order to check their claim. This category might include air personnel who had landed in hostile territory, escapees from Axis POW camps, and soldiers and civilians who had been able to evade capture by the Axis forces.[5]

Meanwhile, Andrei Gromyko, Soviet ambassador in Washington, made clear that for his government the term "Soviet citizen" included not only Russian POWs but also civilians forcibly removed from Russia for labor purposes by Germany and Russians who had been fighting with the German army. The Soviet government expected all Soviet citizens, including prisoners who had been shipped to England, the United States, and Canada, to be returned to the Soviet Union at the earliest opportunity.[6] Gromyko played down the fact that Soviet citizens who had been captured in North Africa, Italy, and France had actually served with the Germans, and he blamed the Germans for forcing these people to perform various duties, whether working in kitchens or doing manual labor. He naturally preferred to ignore the fact that not only had many of these Soviet prisoners freely chosen to join the Germans but they also had actually served as combatants.

After forcefully presenting his government's stand that Soviet prisoners were victims of German aggression, the Soviet ambassador criticized the Americans for treating them as German POWs after bringing them to the United States.[7] Accordingly, he expected the U.S. authorities to issue the following instructions immediately: that liberated Soviet citizens should be regarded not as POWs but as free citizens of an Allied power; that all authorities should without delay inform the appropriate Soviet diplomatic representatives of all Soviet citizens on liberated territory and should assure the Soviets free access to these citizens; that liberated Soviet citizens should be assured normal conditions of existence; that their work assignments should be made with the knowledge and consent of Soviet representatives; that freed Soviet citizens could not be transferred from Europe to other parts of the world without the knowledge and consent of Soviet representatives; that spreading of propaganda hostile to the Soviet Union among liberated Soviet citizens should categorically be forbidden; that the recruitment of liberated Soviet citizens for the armed forces of other Allies should not take place; and that all necessary measures should be taken to facilitate the most speedy return of liberated Soviet citizens to their own country.[8]

Secretary of State Hull rejected Gromyko's claim that Soviet citizens were being reenlisted—the United States had 12 million men of its own in uniform and had no need for any additional soldiers, especially as these Russian prisoners had first been taken to Germany to do forced labor or military service. Hull further explained the difficulty in identifying people of different nationalities and determining whether they had in fact collaborated with the Germans freely or under duress. As to the rest of the Soviets' demands, the secretary of state was careful not to give Gromyko any assurances, telling him that the Soviet request would be conveyed to "the proper military authorities."[9]

Meanwhile, in early November, Washington learned of the personal assurance that Stalin had given to Eden at the Moscow Conference in October, to the effect that every effort was to be made to provide for British prisoners. Bedell-Smith, troubled that no such agreement was as yet in place with the Soviets over the care and handling of American POWs, told General Deane that although Major General A. Vasiliev of the Russian mission in London had made numerous promises to furnish information on where U.S. and

British officers were placed with Russian armies, so far these assurances had produced nothing. Having little faith in gaining the Soviets' cooperation, Bedell-Smith suggested exerting pressure, for example, by curtailing the activity of Russian officials who were on duty with SHAEF in connection with Russian POWs and displaced persons.[10] Though less concerned by the absence of information, Deane did admit that the United States had obtained no definite commitments from the Soviet Foreign Office or the Red Army General Staff concerning the treatment that U.S. POWs to be released by the Red Army would receive. He told Bedell-Smith that the USMMM was coordinating its activities with those of the British; therefore, whatever commitments had been made to the British would apply equally to the Americans. Thus, Deane did not foresee any difficulty with regard to prisoners evacuated from Poland or eastern Germany; still, he agreed that the United States should conclude definite arrangements with the Soviets in advance.[11]

When, at Bedell-Smith's urging, Deane raised the issue with the Red Army General Staff representative, the latter told him that instructions had been issued to all front commanders to give every assistance to all American POWs and to effect their prompt evacuation. When Deane pressed for a general agreement that should include blanket authority to send American officers to POW camps as quickly as possible, the Soviet official told him he preferred to act on each case as it arose and failed to accept Deane's suggestion to send representatives of the USMMM out into the field with the Red Army headquarters in order to contact released prisoners quickly. A heated debate developed when the Soviets blamed the Americans for ill-treatment Soviet POWs in France were receiving after they had been freed by American forces. Deane was particularly furious at the charge because the Soviets failed to give any details, maintaining that the matter was being studied. In his memoirs Deane later wrote, "It was an attack typical of the Russians when they fully realized the insecurity of their own position."[12] In any case, Deane did not anticipate any great trouble in regard to American POWs, as he believed that the Russians would evacuate them promptly and would meet the Americans' requests in each case. "Nevertheless," he concluded, "I shall keep pressing the matter with them until I get some satisfaction and will request our Embassy to do the same with the Foreign Office."[13]

Accordingly, in early November, George F. Kennan, U.S. chargé d'affaires, called Molotov's attention to the fact that the U.S. embassy had as yet received no response to Harriman's proposal of 30 August 1944 to lay down general principles for the prompt return of liberated POWs. As Soviet armies had already overrun the site of one POW camp known to have contained a large number of American POWs and were apparently approaching the location of another such camp near Budapest, it was clearly desirable that the Americans and the Soviets no longer delay in arriving at an understanding along the lines proposed by Ambassador Harriman.[14]

While pressing Moscow for an agreement, the State Department finally replied to Gromyko's request of 23 September that the United States issue instructions for the treatment of freed Soviet citizens. Stettinius, acting secretary of state at the time, told the Russians that U.S. policy was not to transport to the United States "claimants to Soviet citizenship" who had been captured by Allied forces in the fighting against Germany. Rather, these were turned over to the British authorities for eventual disposition. Stettinius admitted, though, that some Soviet citizens had been transported to North America because, in the unsettled conditions that prevailed in combat areas, their identity as Soviet citizens had not been established. It was, moreover, quite difficult to inform the Soviets at this time who among the approximately 300,000 POWs in detention in the United States were "claiming Soviet citizenship." Nevertheless, Washington intended to make the necessary arrangements to segregate the latter and to allow representatives of the Soviet embassy access to interview these POWs.

Stettinius further assured Gromyko that "any such personnel whose claims to Soviet citizenship are verified by the American military with your Embassy's cooperation, and whose return to Soviet control is requested by you, will be turned over to your authorities." Pending such verification, these individuals would be housed, clothed, fed, and given necessary medical care according to the same standards that applied to U.S. military personnel. Stettinius denied that propaganda hostile to the Soviet Union had been spread among its citizens and left it to the Soviet government to decide whether they had the right to receive newspapers, magazines, and other literature normally published and circulated in the United States, some of which, he added tongue in cheek, might contain material not entirely favorable to aspects of Soviet policy.[15] Significantly, throughout his message to Gromyko Stettinius carefully avoided using the term "Soviet citizens" and instead spoke of "claimants to Soviet citizenship," terminology designed to give the Americans space to maneuver with regard to Soviet demands.[16] This was in marked contrast to the British, who, as we saw, from the start had accepted the Soviet definition without reservation.

Meanwhile, a campaign in the Soviet press had begun calling for the speediest possible return to the Soviet Union of Soviet citizens in western Europe. As Kennan saw it, the Soviets feared that "such persons may become a source of trouble if they are not repatriated at first opportunity and that the prestige of the Soviet Union will suffer if it becomes generally known that some Soviet citizens are not accepting with enthusiasm offers of repatriation."[17] This campaign, of course, was not incidental, and at the end of November, Molotov wrote to Kennan that the Soviet government was interested in immediately assisting Soviet prisoners to return to their homes. This also applied to Soviet citizens who had been forcibly deported by the Germans to Germany and to countries occupied by Germany. As with the British, Molotov used the opportunity to demand again that Soviet citizens be regarded not as POWs but as free citizens of an Allied power and that they be separated from German POWs. He did not leave any doubt that Soviet treatment of American POWs depended on Washington's accepting Moscow's stand regarding Soviet citizens.[18] Deane later commented in his memoirs: "It was the old question of Russians captured in German uniforms while in the act of shooting American soldiers. We could hardly be expected to put them at the Ritz in Paris or the Mayflower in Washington—at least not until we found out that they were really our friends."[19]

Washington accepted Molotov's suggestion of discussing their respective countries' POWs and civilians together.[20] Washington's stand at the time was "that all claimants to Soviet nationality will be released to the Soviet Government irrespective of whether they wish to be so released."[21] Accordingly, approximately 1,100 Soviet nationals interned in Camp Rupert in Idaho were shipped to the Soviet Union at the end of December. Included in this group were 70 men who previously had claimed Soviet nationality but refused to return as well as 3 persons who had attempted suicide.[22] Still, Stettinius, now secretary of state, instructed Harriman not to make any connection between the return of Americans found in German POW and civilian internment camps, on the one hand, and Soviet nationals found among German POWs captured by American forces, on the other.[23]

The Russians, Secretary of War Stimson wrote in his diary on 16 January 1945, "are making some awkward demands on us. They wish to have turned over to them German prisoners that we have taken who are of Russian citizenship, and the State Department has consented to this in spite of the fact that it seems very likely that the Russians will execute them when they get home." Stimson argued that that was contrary to the traditions of sanctuary that the English peoples always had adhered to, and "besides it violated the rules of the Geneva protocol towards prisoners of war. We were responsible for these prisoners," he concluded, "and this ought not to be done. Unfortunately the step had already been taken."[24]

Harriman, however, was more realistic than both Stettinius and Stimson in assessing the Soviet position. "Great interest was manifested in the return of all categories of Soviet Nationals or persons who could be claimed as such, particularly those found among German forces captured by Allies," the ambassador told Stettinius. He also reported on a special Soviet commission that had been established to expedite repatriation and on the extreme touchiness that was being shown over the reported reluctance of many of these Soviet prisoners to return, as well as over the alleged encouragement such sentiments were given. Soviet propaganda tactics included press stories of warm receptions accorded repatriates. Such newspaper articles did not accord with reports by embassy observers, Harriman noted, but were meant to disarm the suspicions of those still abroad.[25]

In the negotiations that began in mid-January 1945, Lieutenant General Golubev, head of the Soviet POW directorate, and Major General Slavin, Red Army General Staff contact officer, presented Deane with a draft agreement that included seven articles covering their demands in regard to Soviet citizens.[26] Although the draft was nearly identical to the one that had been presented to the British, the Soviets, as we already saw, decided it was to in their advantage to conduct separate agreements.[27] The draft agreement was put on the agenda of a joint meeting of the War Department's Joint Logistics Committee and the high-level State-War-Navy Coordinating Committee, which had been established in December 1944 to deal with the increasing number of politico-military issues arising between the two Allies. Both agencies thought that a clear distinction should be preserved between former U.S. or Soviet military personnel who were liberated as POWs held by Germany and persons claiming Soviet nationality who had been captured by U.S. forces while collaborating with Germany and even wore German uniforms. The latter category, in the American view, should include "Nationals of the contracting parties present in enemy or enemy occupied territory at the beginning of hostilities and interned, Nationals of the contracting parties found by the enemy in territory occupied by him and forcibly deported therefrom, and Nationals of the contracting parties, serving in or accompanying enemy armed forces by coercion or otherwise." Introducing the term "claimants to Soviet citizenship" in the draft agreement was meant to avoid the question of whether persons originating in Latvia, Estonia, Lithuania, and eastern Poland were to be considered Soviet citizens. It also meant to circumvent the necessity of an investigation to determine the citizenship of all enemy POWs and liberated persons and to place the burden of proof on persons claiming Soviet citizenship to verify their claim. Last, but of significant weight in U.S. considerations, the "use of this phrase is intended to avoid any U.S. assumption of obligation to repatriate to U.S.S.R. any person not himself affirmatively asserting U.S.S.R. citizenship."[28]

It would appear that, unlike the British, officials in Washington failed to perceive how determined the Soviets were to have all Soviet citizens returned, including those from countries and territories annexed in 1940.[29] From the Soviet point of view, the issue at stake touched on a central aspect of Soviet policy that had both important political and propaganda implications domestically as well as internationally. The Soviets would never be able to acknowledge that Soviet nationals not only had voluntarily joined the German forces but even preferred the status of German POW in order to avoid being returned to the Soviet Union. Equally important was the principle of the return of citizens from the Baltics and eastern Poland. Repatriation of these people by the Western powers meant de facto recognition of the incorporation of the Baltic republics and Polish territory into the Soviet Union.[30]

Acting Secretary of State Joseph C. Grew told Nikolai Novikov, the Soviet chargé d'affaires, at the beginning of February that although the Geneva Convention did not specifically provide for such situations as Germany's incorporation of captured persons into German military formations, for U.S. authorities the intention of the convention was clear: POWs should be treated on the basis of the uniforms they were wearing when captured, and the detaining power should not look behind the uniform to determine ultimate questions of citizenship or nationality. There were numerous aliens in the U.S. Army, including citizens of enemy countries, and the U.S. government took the position that these persons were entitled to the full protection of the Geneva Convention. Moreover, the German government was informed that all POWs entitled to repatriation under the convention should be returned to U.S. custody, regardless of the prisoner's nationality. Grew contended further that if the Americans released from POW status persons who claimed protection under the Geneva Convention because they were captured while fighting in a German uniform as members of German formations, "the German Government might be afforded a pretext to subject to reprisal American prisoners of war in German hands." The acting secretary of state expected the Soviet government to understand that Washington could not justify vis-à-vis the American people taking any steps that might jeopardize the situation of American POWs. He made it clear that although the United States would turn over to Soviet control POWs captured in enemy uniform who were claimants to Soviet citizenship, it had a fundamental interest in protecting the status of American POWs in German hands: "We must reserve the right to retain as prisoners of war persons whose detention is deemed to be vital to the protection of American personnel in the hands of the enemy."[31]

Grew then turned to the Soviet embassy's complaints, particularly those in regard to a small number of German POWs at Camp Rupert who said they were German soldiers and officers and demanded to be treated as such under the provisions of the Geneva Convention. He explained that they had not been found as POWs held by the enemy but had been captured while in German uniform and serving Germany in German military formations against American troops. Thus, they could not be compared with American or Soviet military personnel liberated from German POW camps. There was no reason to believe that they were anything other than German military personnel, and therefore they had been classified by American military authorities as German POWs, and the appropriate German authorities had been so notified.[32]

The Soviets were not alone in opposing the American stand. British Foreign Office officials recognized that the State Department's wish to use the term "claimants to Soviet citizenship" instead of "Soviet citizens" in the draft agreement was aimed at countering the Soviet government's demand for also surrendering Balts and Poles who might be found among liberated Russians. The Foreign Office opposed such an amendment, arguing that it "would inevitably lead to prolonged discussion with [the] Soviet Government and that all chance of early conclusion of agreement will disappear."[33] As we already saw, Foreign Office officials wished to reach an agreement on British and American POWs during the upcoming conference at Yalta (4–12 February). Furthermore, the British were well aware of American fears that accepting Soviet terms might endanger non-Americans captured in American uniform. It was the British position that "[i]f this view were accepted all traitors could evade responsibility and could claim to be treated as prisoners-of-war merely by putting on [an] enemy uniform and fighting actively against their own country."[34]

This explains why we find Eden urging Stettinius to accept the British draft, which harmonized with the Soviet proposals, arguing forcefully that "[i]n present circumstances where the Soviet forces are overrunning the sites of British and United States prisoners of war camps very fast, and we know that a number of British prisoners of war (though not exactly how many) are in Soviet hands, and no doubt some United States prisoners of war also, it is really urgent to reach agreement with the Soviet Government on this draft Agreement during ARGONAUT [Yalta Conference]."[35]

Eden may have been playing here on the fact that the fate of American POWs in eastern Europe was central in the concerns of U.S. officials, particularly Generals Marshal, Eisenhower, and Deane, who supported unconditional repatriation of Soviet POWs.[36] Significantly, when Grew protested that the British draft ignored several points the U.S. counterproposals had insisted on, Stettinius wrote to him from Yalta: "The consensus here is that it should be unwise to include questions relative to the protection of the Geneva Convention and to Soviet citizens in the U.S. in an agreement which deals primarily with the exchange of prisoners liberated by the Allied Armies as they march into Germany. With respect to 'claimants,' notwithstanding the danger of German retaliation, we believe there will be serious delays in the release of our prisoners of war unless we reach prompt agreement on this question." Stettinius's retreat from his previous stand largely stemmed from the support he had found leading military commanders— including the JCS and CCS—were giving to the British-Soviet draft agreement.[37] In the end, the agreement that Major General Deane and Soviet lieutenant general A. A. Gryzlov signed on 11 February 1945 proved to be identical to the one signed between the British and the Soviets.[38]

"The Agreement," Deane noted later in his memoirs, "was a good one, but, so far as the Russians were concerned, it turned out to be just another piece of paper."[39] When writing his own memoirs, Harriman explained the motives for signing the agreement: "Our officers were thinking of the welfare of our own prisoners, some seventy-five thousand men, who without exception could not get home quickly enough." Writing almost thirty years after Yalta and well aware of subsequent criticism of the agreement, Harriman tried, on the one hand, to absolve himself of any responsibility and, on the other, to justify the policy adopted. "We had no idea that hundreds of thousands of the Soviet citizens should refuse because they had reason to suspect they should be sent to their deaths or to Beria's prison camps. That knowledge came later." Here Harriman conveniently ignored embassy accounts that, even before the signing of the agreement, spoke of the Soviets' efforts to conceal their real treatment of returnees.[40] Furthermore, as early as mid-January, Stimson reported on the terrible fate Soviet POWs awaited on their return. Similarly, when Harriman writes that "not a word in the agreement required the American and British commanders to forcibly re-patriate Soviet citizens against their will,"[41] this was literally, of course, correct. However, both parties recognized that such a possibility existed but preferred not to raise it. To put them in context, Harriman's efforts to justify the decision the administration had taken at the time came at the height of the Cold War. But in 1945 there was little or no hesitation, certainly not on the part of the then U.S. ambassador to the Soviet Union.

Although the British and the Soviets were the driving forces at Yalta behind the signing of the agreement regarding POWs, the Americans were no less eager to reach such a pact. Like the British, the Americans were determined to protect their liberated POWs in eastern Europe and to ensure their speedy return home. It seemed unlikely that the Soviets would carry out implied threats to treat former American POWs in Soviet-occupied ter-ritories as hostages, but the U.S. administration did take the possibility into account. Given the Kremlin's indifferent attitude to its citizens, not least its own POWs, the administration had reason to be apprehensive and in any case refused to take any chances, especially as it had no interest in keeping Soviet citizens. To this should be added the conciliatory and cooperative atmosphere that prevailed at the Yalta Conference, which facilitated the Americans' willingness to treat Soviet demands favorably. The question of the POWs was regarded as a minor issue—Roosevelt and Stalin never even discussed it.

For these reasons, then, in the final agreement the Americans proved willing to let go of the term "claimants to Soviet citizenship," adopting instead "Soviet citizens," and no longer insisted on defining the latter. But the Americans' attitude still differed from that of the British: the general tone of the agreement enabled the administration to hold to its position that nationals of the Baltic republics and those parts of Poland annexed to the Soviet Union could not be repatriated to the Soviet Union unless they affir-matively claimed Soviet citizenship. It also left an outlet for Soviet nationals who demanded to be recognized as German POWs.

CONTACT OFFICERS REBUFFED

Several days after the signing of the POW agreement, Lieutenant General Golubev, who was charged with implementing it on the Soviet side, told Deane that the Russians were holding about 450 Americans they had liber-ated. Deane meanwhile was satisfied with the authority the Soviets had extended to him to send contact officers to both Odessa, where the Soviets had set up their transit camp, and Lublin, where some former American prisoners were expected to be located. The Soviets "will act in good faith and . . . the agreement will be carried out," he thought. At the same time, the Soviets appeared slow both in notifying him of liberated Americans, particularly those hospitalized, and in authorizing American officers to visit liberated Americans. It was too early, he thought, to be able to assess the Soviets' treatment of U.S. and British POWs.[42]

At a meeting with the Soviet Repatriation Committee on 3 March, Deane learned that by now there were all together 1,600 American POWs under Russian control, of whom 1,200 were in Odessa. This figure would rise to perhaps somewhere between 2,000 and 3,000 by the time all prisoners had been collected. According to reports the general received from Odessa, the conditions there were "extremely satisfactory," although the evacuation from points of escape or liberation had been "pretty rugged on the individuals." The POWs had been broken up into small groups and had lived in the countryside until finally brought together by the Russians at hastily organized collection points, from where they were then evacuated by rail to Odessa. The Soviets had agreed to allow U.S. contact teams to be present at four or five points of concentration in Poland, to have supplies flown into those points, and to evacuate the sick by air to Poltava. "As soon as the plans the Soviets now have, which are the same as we have been striving for, are put into effect," a still optimistic Deane anticipated, "I think that the situation will clear up and that our ex-prisoners of war will have the best treatment possible under the condition." He spoke in glowing terms of the Soviets' goodwill: "They have done an almost miraculous job in getting all these prisoners from their present front to Odessa in such a short time."[43]

As Deane sent off this report to Washington, Secretary of War Stimson was seeing President Roosevelt with a memorandum on the collection, supply, and evacuation of American POWs and stranded American airmen based on information Deane had sent the previous day (2 March). Stimson told Roosevelt that a serious problem existed in regard to the evacuation of these men, many of whom were sick or injured, from within the Russian lines. The Soviets had rebuffed the constant efforts of Deane and Harriman to obtain authority for the use of American aircraft and crews to deliver supplies to these former prisoners or to evacuate the sick and wounded. Instead, Stimson pointed out, the Russians had indicated that they would use their own aircraft for this purpose, though they did allow two American planes with Soviet crews to operate in Poland. The secretary of war regarded this solution as unsatisfactory. Moreover, an American correspondent who had just returned from Poland had told Deane that a serious condition still existed with regard to the collection of American POWs. Food was inadequate, and many men had still not been evacuated. The president was then given the outlines of Deane's proposal to place several contact teams at various points in Poland in order to supply American POWs with supplementary clothing, food, and medical attention prior to their evacuation by rail to Odessa or, if they were sick, by air to Poltava. Stimson urged Roosevelt to send a message to Stalin requesting authority for ten American aircraft and crews to operate in Russia and Poland for the relief of American POWs.[44] When he approached the president on 3 March, it was too early for Stimson to have seen the far more favorable report Deane had sent off that very same day.[45]

Roosevelt followed Stimson's advice and thus urgently asked Stalin, on 4 March, to issue instructions authorizing ten American aircraft with American crews to operate between Poltava and places in Poland where liberated American POWs and standard airmen might be located. "I regard this request to be of the greatest importance," Roosevelt told the Soviet leader, "not only for humanitarian reasons but also by reason of the intense interest of the American public in the welfare of our ex-prisoners of war and stranded aircraft crews." Roosevelt also reminded Stalin that, as the number of Russian, British, and U.S. POWs in Germany was very large, something ought to be done very quickly.[46]

Stalin immediately replied (as he had done in the case of the British) that the difficulties the Soviet forces had to contend with to effect a speedy evacuation of American POWs were now considerably fewer, which meant that the organization the Soviet government had specially formed to deal with foreign POWs now had an adequate number of people, transport facilities, and food supplies.[47] When new groups of American POWs were found, immediate measures would be taken to help them, including evacuating them to collection points for subsequent repatriation. At present, Stalin maintained, there were no groups of American POWs in Poland or in other places liberated by the Red Army, since, with the exception of sick persons who were in hospitals, all had been sent to the collection point in Odessa. Stalin mentioned that some 1,200 American POWs had already arrived there and more were expected in the nearest future. Under the present conditions, Stalin saw "no necessity to carry on flights of American planes from Poltava to the territory of Poland on the matters of American prisoners of war." In case American planes might be needed, Soviet military authorities would apply to the U.S. military representatives in Moscow. Stalin assured

Roosevelt, though, that the Soviet Union would do everything possible to create favorable conditions for American POWs.[48]

Questioning Stalin's information, Ambassador Harriman subsequently told Roosevelt that on 8 March the Russians had claimed there were 2,100 American POWs of whom 1,350 had arrived in Odessa while the rest were en route by train—Stalin had talked about only 1,200 prisoners. According to Harriman's information, taken from liberated American prisoners, 4,000–5,000 officers and enlisted men had been freed. Harriman explained that the Kremlin's reports were from concentration points within Poland where American prisoners had been collected; however, there appeared to be hundreds of American prisoners wandering about Poland trying to locate American contact officers for protection. American prisoners, according to the ambassador, did not like the idea of going into a Russian camp. The Polish people and the Polish Red Cross were being extremely hospitable, whereas food and living conditions in Russian camps were poor. Harriman went so far as to accuse Stalin of not telling the truth. "For the past ten days, the Soviets have made the same statement to me that Stalin has made to you, namely that all prisoners are in Odessa or entrained thereto, whereas I have now positive proof that this was not true on February 26th, the date on which the statement was first made. This supports my belief that Stalin's statement to you is inaccurate."[49]

Still, the U.S. ambassador also had some good things to say about the Soviets. Contact officers in Odessa had reported that the Russians had done "a first rate job" in quickly providing a reasonably adequate camp in Odessa and that the prisoners were "reasonably well provided with food, etc." The American officers, furthermore, were allowed to communicate with the embassy daily.[50] In an interim report, Major Paul S. Hall, who headed the mission in Odessa, wrote in early March, "We are quite satisfied that the Soviet authorities here are doing everything in their power to improve the welfare of our men." Qualifying this by adding that "their criterion of a living standard is of course far below ours, and is in some cases quite unsatisfactory," he nevertheless thought that it was apparent "that American officers and men are receiving at least equal, and probably better, care than accorded by the Soviets to their own troops."[51] The morale of U.S. troops in the Odessa transit camp, Hall concluded, was high, and the men were quite satisfied with their living conditions and appreciated Soviet efforts to make them comfortable.[52]

Harriman also had no complaints about the speed with which the American prisoners had been moved from Poland by train, considering the overall shortage of transportation.[53] Still, the Soviet government was not carrying out the agreement signed at Yalta that called for contact officers to be sent immediately to points where American prisoners had been first collected and to evacuate the POWs, particularly the sick among them, in American airplanes or to send supplies to points other than Odessa, which was 1,000 miles from the point of liberation. Since the Yalta Conference, Harriman told the president, he and Deane had constantly tried to push the Soviets to carry out the agreement in full, but "we have been baffled by promises which have not been fulfilled or have been subsequently withdrawn." Even the success, after considerable delay, in getting one contact team, consisting of an officer and a doctor, to Lublin had been only partial, as it had not been permitted to move to other points, and the infrequent communication with the team had been conducted largely through the friendly intervention of the Polish embassy in Moscow. Harriman, however, drew some encouragement from the authorization that Deane had received to go to Poland.[54] Deane estimated that between 20,000 and 30,000 POWs held in Germany would be evacuated through Russia prior to the collapse of Germany.[55]

The optimism, however, of both Harriman and Deane was short lived, as on 11 March the People's Commissariat for Foreign Affairs withdrew its approval for Deane's trip on the grounds that there were no longer any former American POWs in Poland and that therefore there was no reason for his trip. In a strongly worded letter to Molotov, Harriman insisted that the Soviet government grant a "small courtesy" to the U.S. government of allowing Deane to make a survey of the situation in Poland and visit American prisoners, particularly the sick and wounded who still remained in Poland. (According to a report from the Red Cross, there were some 300 seriously wounded Americans concentrated near Sagan).[56] The trip's cancellation, Harriman wrote to Roosevelt, should be seen as part of a wider move by Soviet authorities that included the retraction of permission for the contact team to remain in Lublin and the cancellation of a plane that had been scheduled to leave on 12 March from Poltava for Lublin with a load of supplies. The team at Lublin, Harriman pointed out, had been the only means by which the United States had been able to help former American POWs in Poland, and it had been working day and night on behalf of those who had found their way to Lublin. Harriman believed that the Soviets "have been attempting to stall us off by misinformation from day to day in order to hold up the sending in of more of our contact officers until they get all of our prisoners out of Poland."[57] For his part, Deane instructed Lieutenant Colonel James Dudley Wilmeth, who headed the American mission in Lublin, to ignore the Soviet directive to remain only ten days and "not to leave unless they [the Soviets] threaten to forcibly make you."[58] In the end, the American mission managed to remain in Lublin for three weeks but had to operate under difficult conditions, the Soviet authorities constantly pressing its members to return to Moscow.[59]

When Harriman met Molotov in mid-March, the Soviet commissar claimed that Moscow had been fulfilling its obligation under the agreement but that both Red Army authorities and the Polish Provisional Government objected to the presence of American officers in Poland. Molotov gave Harriman reason to believe, however, that if the United States reached an agreement with the Polish Provisional Government, the Red Army would remove its objections.[60] Harriman was convinced that the objection came from Moscow, not from the Polish Provisional Government. The AAM had been in informal contact with the Polish embassy in Moscow, which had proved extremely cooperative in regard to American prisoners in Poland. In fact, all Polish authorities, including the Polish Red Cross, were helpful. In other words, according to Harriman, at the heart of the current obstruction lay geopolitics: the Soviet government was trying to use liberated American POWS "as a club to induce us to give increased prestige to the Provisional Polish Government by dealing with it in this connection as the Soviets are doing in other cases."[61]

Harriman believed that "[u]nless some steps can be taken to bring direct pressure on the Soviets, our liberated prisoners will continue to suffer hardships, particularly the wounded and sick."[62] This recommendation fell in line with both Harriman's and Deane's overall efforts at the time—March and April—to influence a reluctant Roosevelt to reverse his policy of cooperation with the Soviets in favor of a firm stand, including retaliatory measures.[63] They portrayed the refusal to allow U.S. contact officers into Poland as another breach of the agreement reached at Yalta and a blatant disregard of U.S. interests. Although both Harriman and Deane were naturally concerned about the welfare of former American POWS liberated by the Red Army, they were now actually taking advantage of this sensitive issue to further their objectives at a time when the overall relations between the two powers had become strained. That only a short while ago they had reported that conditions in Odessa for the freed Americans were "extremely satisfactory" and that neither had had any complaint about the speed with which the liberated POWs had been moved to Odessa also seem to highlight the shift in their geopolitical agenda.

State Department officials preferred another direct approach by Roosevelt to Stalin rather than retaliatory action because the Russians could "better us at that game" and such a step might result in trouble with Soviet authorities over other matters of greater national, military, and political importance.[64] And indeed, one of the subjects Roosevelt broached with Stalin was Russia's decision to cancel Deane's survey of American POWs in Poland. As there were a considerable number of sick and injured Americans in hospitals in Poland and also large numbers of liberated U.S. prisoners in good health who were awaiting transport from Poland to Odessa or were dispersed in small groups that had not yet made contact with Soviet authorities, the president failed to understand Stalin's reluctance to permit American officers to assist their own people in this matter, especially since the U.S. government had done everything to meet each of Stalin's requests.[65]

Stalin argued that Roosevelt's information was inaccurate, that as of 16 March 1945 there were only seventeen sick U.S. servicemen on Polish soil and that they were to be flown to Odessa within a few days. Claiming his hands were tied—"if it concerned me personally I should be ready to give way even to the detriment of my interests"—Stalin put the onus of the decision on Soviet commanders who did not want to have odd foreign officers around as they "need looking after, want all kinds of meetings and contacts, protection against possible acts of sabotage by German agents not yet ferreted out, and other things that divert the attention of the commanders and their subordinates from their direct duties." Soviet commanders bore full responsibility for the state of affairs at the front and in the immediate rear, and he did not see how he could restrict their rights to any extent. Stalin concluded with the by now familiar refrain that U.S. POWs liberated by the Red Army received better conditions than those accorded Soviet POWs in American camps, "where some of them were lodged with German war prisoners and were subjected to unfair treatment and unlawful persecutions, including beating, as has been communicated to the U.S. Government on more than one occasion."[66]

In Moscow, Harriman and Deane did not question that Stalin had been told by Red Army commanders that there were only seventeen liberated American POWs in Poland, but they continued to insist that there were a number of former American prisoners, including sick soldiers, at large in Poland. Stalin's description of the Soviet camps as being in good condition was "far from [the] truth," Harriman claimed—Soviet facilities in Odessa met the barest minimum needs, and until the arrival of American contact officers "the hardships undergone have been inexcusable." The Red Army had made no effort whatsoever to make life easier for these men until Americans started drifting into camps at Warsaw, Lodz, Lublin, and Wrzesnia that the Red Army had advertised as point of assembly. The camps were hundreds of miles from points of liberation, "and our men should have starved if it had not been for the generosity and hospitality of the Polish people." While individual Red Army headquarters had sometimes given a meal to American POWs, Harriman continued, nothing was done in other places; moreover, Red Army soldiers had taken away wristwatches, clothing, and other articles at gunpoint. Reports from liberated prisoners, he stated, showed that whereas the Americans were grateful to the Polish people and Polish Red Cross, they felt nothing but resentment for the treatment they received from the Russians.[67]

While admitting that only relatively few former American POWs were possibly still in Poland, Harriman thought that additional numbers could be liberated at any time and that there was no reason to believe that they would receive better care. He described as preposterous Stalin's claims that the Red Army command could not be bothered with a dozen American officers in Poland. In contrast to Soviet behavior, he forcefully argued, General Eisenhower gave Soviet contact officers complete freedom of movement to visit Russian citizens wherever they might be. The ambassador wanted Roosevelt to send Stalin another message and again recommended some retaliatory measures. Harriman was not afraid of reprisals, since he thought it was impossible for the Russians to do less than they were doing at the moment for American prisoners. In an effort to influence the president's decision in favor of firm measures, Harriman warned that "when the story of the treatment accorded our liberated prisoners by the Russians leaks out I cannot help but feel that there will be great and lasting resentment on the part of the American people."[68]

Roosevelt declined to send another message to Stalin,[69] and the Joint Chiefs of Staff opposed a policy of reprisal. "Retaliatory acts on our part," they argued, "should not accomplish the end desired but should increase suspicion and ill-feeling and might well provoke further Russian measures leading finally to a break in Allied unity."[70] Roosevelt may have come to realize that another message would not convince Stalin to change his stand, especially as discord and tension between the two powers were deepening, in particular over the future of Poland.[71] At the end of March 1945, Roosevelt warned Stalin that if the Polish issue was not settled fairly and speedily, "all the difficulties and dangers to Allied unity which we had so much in mind in reaching our decisions at the Crimea will face us in an even more acute form."[72] Roosevelt did not live to see how the question of Poland was solved. This came only after the end of the war when President Harry S. Truman's personal envoy, Harry Hopkins, visited Moscow between 25 May and 7 June 1945 and yielded on Washington's position.[73]

For Deane it was clear that the Soviets opposed visits by American and British contact officers to Poland because the Kremlin wanted to prevent U.S. officers from observing how Poland was being brought under the domination of the Soviet Union. "The world was to be led to believe" he wrote in his memoirs, "that the Poles were enthusiastically happy at their deliverance from the Germans, that they wanted nothing more than to embrace their Russian liberators, including their ideology."[74] If Deane's assessment is correct—and it probably is—it stands to reason that the refusal of the Soviets to allow American contact officers into Poland did not mean any deliberate discrimination against American POWs.[75] From the Soviets' point of view, the treatment they gave former American POWs was reasonably good. By the end of the war, 2,858 of them had been repatriated through Odessa.[76] Deane and Harriman themselves tended to agree, as late as mid-March, that liberated American prisoners received fair treatment. As we already saw, their criticism of the Soviets in the final weeks of the war was not groundless, but its true aim was to try to influence Roosevelt into changing his attitude of cooperation toward the Kremlin.[77] In what turned out to be his last message to Churchill, who had asked him for advice on a statement he was to make in the House of Commons, it was clear that Roosevelt was not to be moved: "I should minimize the general Soviet problem as much as possible because these problems, in one form or another, seem to arise every day and most of them straighten out as in the case of the Bern incident."[78]

FINAL REPATRIATION

Other differences the Americans and Soviets had preferred to push aside at Yalta while discussing the agreement inevitably came to the fore not long after it was signed. Not surprisingly, they centered around the category of "all Soviet citizens liberated." As the commanding general of U.S. Armed Forces in the Mediterranean Theater of Operations, Lieutenant General Joseph T. McNarney, put it to the JCS: Who fell within this category? What was the status of liberated persons who were nationals of Latvia, Estonia, Lithuania, and Poland east of the 1939 line of demarcation? And what standing did persons have who claimed to be citizens of countries other than the Soviet Union and whose claim to citizenship had already been accepted by representatives of those countries?

The JCS, following consultation with the secretaries of state, war, and navy, construed the Yalta agreement as requiring the United States to perform three acts: (1) to return to the Soviet Union all Soviet military personnel who had been held as POWs by the Germans and been liberated from German POW camps; (2) to return to the Soviet Union all liberated civilians not physically within the territorial borders of the United States who were Soviet citizens; and (3) to return to the Soviet Union Soviet citizens who had been captured in German uniform so long as they did not demand to be retained as German POWs and thus would come under the Geneva Convention. Latvians, Estonians, Lithuanians, and Poles whose homes were east of the 1939 line of demarcation could not, therefore, be repatriated to the Soviet Union unless they affirmatively claimed to be Soviet citizens. This latter rule was based on the reasoning that Washington had not formally recognized any territorial changes brought about by the war in Europe.[79]

Following JCS instructions, Eisenhower ordered that the following people would not be returned to the Soviet Union: "(1) Those who state that they do not desire to return to Russia but wish to remain in the status of prisoner of war. (2) Recognized war criminals or suspects; and (3) Citizens of Estonia, Latvia and Lithuania."[80]

U.S. policy was put to the test in the case of 118 German POWs who claimed to be German soldiers whereas representatives of the Soviet embassy insisted they were Soviet citizens. Discussions about this group had begun before the signing of the agreement at Yalta and continued after the war had ended. The retention of these POWs under the Geneva Convention of 1929, Grew told Ambassador Gromyko toward the end of March 1945, had nothing to do with questions of their citizenship or nationality; it was determined solely by their demand to be treated as German POWs under the Geneva Convention. As he reiterated, the convention held that POWs were entitled to be treated on the basis of the uniform they were wearing at the time of their capture and that the detaining power should not look behind the uniform to determine questions of citizenship or nationality without a POW's consent. Grew explained that his government was anxious not to give the German government a pretext to retaliate against American POWs still in German hands, which was likely to happen if the U.S. authorities rejected the demand of POWs to be treated as German POWs when captured in a

German uniform and part of German military formations. In an effort to conciliate the Soviets, Grew gave Gromyko reason to believe that this policy was only temporary and that the disposition of such prisoners "will be taken up again between the two Governments when organized resistance in Germany shall have ceased."[81]

Moscow rejected Grew's arguments. Gromyko denied out of hand the possibility that Soviet citizens had joined the Germans voluntarily. According to the ambassador, the Germans, in violation of universally accepted rules of international law, frequently employed threats and repressions to compel Soviet POWs and Soviet citizens; that is, the latter had been forcefully deported to Germany to enter special military units organized by the Germans. As these unlawful activities were juridically invalid, "Soviet citizens falling into the hands of Allied armies, even though they be dressed in German military uniforms, cannot be counted as military personnel of the German army, but must be considered as ordinary liberated Soviet prisoners of war or civilians deported to Germany."[82] Neither did Gromyko accept the analogy Grew had made between Soviet citizens and foreign citizens serving in the American armed forces for whom the Americans claimed full protection under the Geneva Convention, including repatriation to the United States regardless of nationality. The Soviet government insisted that all Soviet citizens who had been and would be liberated by U.S. armies in the course of military operations against Germany ought to be returned to the Soviet Union.[83]

While the debate over the interpretation of the Yalta agreement continued, mutual recriminations were raised about how each side was treating its freed POWs.[84] This reached a new stage when, at the end of April, the Soviets decided to go public with their complaints in an attempt to influence public opinion in the West and increase pressure on the administration.[85] The State Department quickly refuted the Soviet charges and denied the "unfounded allegations" that the American government had not lived up to the Yalta agreement.[86] This, however, did not prevent them from discussing the possibility of exchanging POWs over land. A few days before the end of the war, Andrei Vyshinski, the Soviet deputy commissar for foreign affairs, suggested that they effect this exchange not via Odessa and Marseilles but through the line of demarcation in Germany. Kennan, suspicious of Soviet intentions, pointed out the possibility that the Soviets "will construe our acceptance of this proposal in such a way that we will be obliged to surrender all Soviet nationals we find, irrespective of status, before we have an opportunity to screen out those who may be found fighting with the German armed forces."[87]

The Supreme Headquarters of the Allied Expeditionary Force, however, was eager to reach such an agreement because it was receiving information indicating that thousands of U.S. and British POWs in camps in rear Russian lines were being held in close confinement under unsatisfactory conditions. It wanted the Soviets' immediate concurrence on the initiation of the evacuation by air of these POWs, numbering some 40,000 in all, and on the establishment of a joint SHAEF-Soviet committee that would work out the day-to-day details of the overland exchange. Eisenhower believed that if the Soviets had cooperated earlier by permitting the landing of planes at nearby airfields, as specifically authorized by Article 4 of the Yalta agreement, the POWs could have been evacuated by air before the final surrender of German forces.[88]

Delegations from both sides met in mid-May 1945 to develop a plan for the immediate implementation of an overland exchange of Allied and Soviet POWs and displaced persons. The Soviet delegation, headed by Lieutenant General Golubev, included four major generals and some forty officers, while Major General Ray W. Barker, SHAEF G-1, who headed SHAEF's delegation, was assisted by Brigadier General Stanley R. Mickelsen, chief of displaced persons affairs for Eisenhower, and a dozen British and American officers.[89] It took six days of conversations to reach an agreement. The Soviets' draft went into meticulous detail as to who was to be exchanged, binding the signatories to deliver "without exception" and "up to the last individual" and directing the two supreme headquarters to "unswervingly" carry out this contract. Representatives of SHAEF then argued that such language was inappropriate for a military staff plan drawn up by allies and that they were not authorized to touch on matters being dealt with on a governmental level; they were there to work out a problem in transportation, sanitation, and accommodations. The SHAEF delegation succeeded in avoiding discussion on contentious matters, such as the definition of the term "Soviet citizen" as used in the Yalta agreement and the problem of Soviet citizens captured in German uniform.

For their part, the members of the Soviet delegation remained adamant in refusing permission for Allied aircraft to enter Soviet-occupied German territory to pick up U.S. and British personnel, even though these planes would also deliver Soviet citizens. They gave as reasons the lack of appropriate landing facilities and similar excuses. The Red Army delegation also

American POWs at Stalag III A (Luckenwalde), liberated by
the Russians, washing clothes in the only available water trough.
(Courtesy National Archives, College Park, Md.)

rejected the idea of establishing a standing working committee to be set up near the demarcation line, such as at Leipzig or Halle, and charged with handling the day-to-day details of the exchange. It also would not agree to the establishment of additional transfer points on the Soviet side, south of Leipzig, and in Austria even though the points it did offer only partially corresponded to transportation facilities on the Allied side.[90]

According to the plan Major General Barker and Lieutenant General Golubev signed on 22 May 1945—the so-called Halle Agreement—all former POWs and citizens of the Soviet Union liberated by the Allied forces and all former POWs and citizens of Allied nations liberated by the Red Army were to be delivered through the army lines to the corresponding army command of each side. The exchange was to begin twenty-four hours after the signing of the agreement. Seven exchange points were to be set up in the territory of the Red Army and three points in the territory of the Allied forces. As it specified the transfer of approximately 20,000 to 50,000 individuals per day, the plan also dealt with the question of transportation, personal property, documentation, rations for the repatriables, priorities in movement, and the respective commands' responsibility.[91]

Following the signing of the Halle Agreement, the Soviets quickly began returning U.S. and British POWs. "The next to the last day of the meeting," Robert Murphy, political adviser for Germany, wrote to Stettinius, "some 2500 U.S. and UK POWs were deposited on the demarcation line near Magdeburg having just been brought from the camp at Luckenwalde now reported empty. It is understood that the several thousand U.S. and UK personnel at Riesa whose proximity to the scene of conversations made them appear almost in the character of hostages were moved yesterday."[92] By 28 May 1945, that is, in less than a week, all of the 28,662 liberated American prisoners reported to be held by the Soviets had been returned. General Golikov, head of Soviet Repatriation Committee, assured Deane that every effort would be made to locate individual Americans who might still be stranded somewhere in Soviet-occupied territory; when located, they would be evacuated by any route requested.[93]

The Halle Agreement was an important step in furthering the mutual repatriation of Allied POWs and citizens. Although not everyone in the administration felt comfortable with the forced repatriation of certain categories of Soviet nationals, considerations of realpolitik dominated. Not the least among them was the wish "to avoid giving Soviet authorities any pretext for delaying return of American POWs of [the] Japanese now in Soviet occupied zone, particularly in Manchuria."[94] The question of involuntary repatriation, however, became more complicated not only because American troops and their commanders objected to using force and leading officials in Washington had doubts about whether it was the right thing to do but also because the press began to report this reluctance and to editorialize that the Yalta agreement should perhaps be revised or even abrogated.[95]

At first the administration had no reservations about handing over to the Russians even unwilling Soviet citizens. In June 1945, for example, the Combined Chiefs of Staff authorized SACMED field marshal Alexander to transfer to the Soviet authorities approximately 50,000 Cossacks who had been serving with the German armed forces at the time of their capture.[96] But the pressure on Washington had a cumulative effect, especially as public opposition to forced repatriation increased and there were no American soldiers in territories under Soviet control. Finally, on 21 December 1945, the commanding general of U.S. forces in the European Theater and the commander in chief of U.S. forces of occupation in Austria were instructed not to compel the involuntary repatriation of persons who had been citizens of and actually had resided within the Soviet Union on 1 September 1939 but who did not fall into any of the following classes: those captured in German uniform; those who had been members of the Soviet armed forces on or after 22 June 1941 and who had not subsequently been discharged; and those who had been charged by the Soviet Union with having voluntarily rendered "aid and comfort to the enemy."[97] By the time these instructions were given, more than 2 million Soviet citizens had already been repatriated from western Germany. This left only approximately 20,000 Soviet citizens in the U.S. zone in Germany.[98] Moscow had attained its goal, but so had Washington: it achieved the quick repatriation of U.S. POWs liberated by the Red Army—all together approximately one-third of all U.S. POWs—and at the same time succeeded in ridding itself of the responsibility for millions of unwanted Soviet citizens in western parts of Germany.

CONCLUSION

Barely one month into the war British intelligence had warned: "It appears very probable that the Germans will fight this war on no rules whatsoever, and that our conceptions of the treatment of prisoners of war will have to be entirely revised. It is even possible that certain Prisoners of War camps in Germany will be in the hands of the Gestapo, in which case no human feelings on the part of the camp staff are to be expected and discipline will be enforced by sheer brutality."[1] With hindsight the assessment appears realistic enough—it certainly proved true for the 3.25 million Soviet POWs who perished in German captivity. And it is undeniable that the war was fought on very different rules than any previous war. Both World War I and World War II were total wars in which millions of troops were wiped out on the battlefield. What made World War II different was the indiscriminate death it brought to countless masses of ordinary civilians. But the truly unprecedented horror of World War II lies, of course, in the way the Nazis harnessed their racist ideology to modern technology and so achieved the systematic murder of millions of innocent human beings, notably Jews.

In this book I have sought to analyze how it could happen that almost all the 300,000 British and American troops who in the course of World War II fell into German hands survived captivity in Nazi POW camps and were repatriated almost as soon as the war had ended. My point of departure and main interest thereby has been to trace and assess the policies and actions the British and American governments took—but also failed to take—on behalf of their POWs in Germany.

In the racial ideology of the Nazis, both the British and the American peoples were, of course, inferior to the Aryan German Volk but as Anglo-Saxons nevertheless ranked high in the hierarchy of races. Already in *Mein Kampf* Hitler had written: "The Germanic inhabitant of the American continent, who has remained racially pure and unmixed, rose to be the master of the continent."[2] It was true that both Western countries and Germany were now pitted against each other as bitter enemies, but the Nazis' *Vernichtungskrieg* (war of annihilation) was directed against the Soviet Union, not the West. This was part of the reason why, where British and U.S. prisoners of war were concerned, Berlin adhered throughout the war to the 1929 Geneva Convention on the treatment of POWs. The contrast with the Soviet troops the Nazis captured could not be starker: these were *Untermenschen* (subhumans) who did not deserve to live in the first place. Moreover, fair treatment of Western POWs meant the Germans could count on reciprocity by Britain and the United States vis-à-vis their own troops imprisoned in the West.

Reciprocity first emerged as a main principle between the two sides during the shackling crisis. This crisis started out, in the fall of 1942, as an attempt by Berlin to force London to put a halt to British commando raids on German positions—German troops abducted in this way for intelligence purposes had their hands tied behind their back. Because London refused to give in, 4,000 POWs, most of them Canadians, spent more than a year in manacles. Remarkably, whenever the War Cabinet debated what steps to take during the crisis—at one point it partially relented because of domestic pressure and opposition by the Dominion governments—its members never broached the overall POW problem. What is more, it is doubtful that the hardship their policy inevitably entailed for the POWs themselves ever played much of a role. This was, of course, partly because even in captivity these men remained soldiers and thus were duty-bound to fight and die for their country. But, no less significant, there was also the recognition that more than three years into the war—and in contrast to the extreme situation in the Far East—no immediate threat existed to the lives and health of British Commonwealth and U.S. troops held in German POW camps. To a great extent, this was what mattered most to policy makers in London and Washington. The assessment, which surfaced soon after Dunkirk, would form the basis for their decisions regarding the POWs almost unvaryingly until D-Day. At the same time, the attitude did little to assuage the anxieties of the families and friends of POWs in German camps; nor did it satisfy MPs who regularly took the government to task for failing in its duties. Public criticism of this kind became a thorn in the side of Whitehall especially toward the end of the war.

It was the Germans who first suggested—even before any soldier had been captured by either side—that a mechanism be put in place to facilitate exchanging seriously injured and sick POWs. This may have been no more than a signal to the British and the Americans, then the protecting power, that they intended to adhere to the Geneva Convention, since they then failed to follow up their gesture—the initial disparity in numbers and the shackling crisis being part of the reason—until the summer of 1943 when, with their defeat in northern Africa, large numbers of Germans fell into Western hands. How much weight Berlin attached to the success of the endeavor becomes clear when one realizes that both the exchanges themselves and the negotiations that led up to them took place at a time when London and Washington were carrying out devastating bombing raids on German cities: at no point did Berlin condition the exchanges by demanding a halt to these campaigns. In other words, whenever they wanted to secure what they saw as a major goal, the Germans were able to demonstrate a persistently pragmatic attitude. All together, Berlin retrieved about 13,000 of its troops.

For Whitehall, the return between October 1943 and January 1945 of more than 10,000 seriously wounded and sick POWs—in addition to the human aspect involved—was a welcome political achievement. It temporarily strengthened the government's hand vis-à-vis the criticism it was subjected to at home and helped deflect attention away from the fact that efforts to bring back long-term POWs were being frustrated.

Whereas Britain and the United States had presented a united front on the exchange of seriously wounded and sick POWs, differences began to emerge between them over the question of the mutual repatriation of long-term prisoners. What weighed strongly for the Americans was the crucial fact that until D-Day only a relatively small number of U.S. troops were in German captivity. By August 1944, for example, the Germans held about 160,000 British Commonwealth POWs but only 28,000 Americans. This meant that Washington accepted as reasonable the fact that in the four exchanges of seriously wounded and sick POWs the Germans had repatriated approximately 800 American troops. It also helped that there was effectively no domestic public pressure on the administration.

Obviously, long-term prisoners were prey to increased suffering during the final year of the war. As more and more troops fell captive, camps became hugely overcrowded, with the result that thousands of POWs were now sleeping on bare floors, were no longer housed in barracks but in tents, were deprived of heating facilities, and were given German rations that kept shrinking. More ominous, in the fall of 1944 authority in the POW camps was transferred to the SS and the Gestapo, signaling a radicalization of the entire command structure. One of Himmler's first actions was to prohibit the accumulation of any food reserves. As the winter months that followed proved exceptionally harsh, cold temperatures and undernourishment combined to further undermine the health and strength of many POWs.

In London, the government was well aware of the lack of priority it had given to the issue—first initiatives to seek an agreement with Berlin on mutual exchanges of long-term POWs had come as late as four years after Dunkirk. Progress was further hindered when Berlin failed to respond for almost a year. The Germans then sought the return of 25,000 prisoners, which the British immediately accepted. Given the worsening situation in Germany and the near collapse of its infrastructure, Whitehall acted out of concern for the growing distress long-term POWs were suffering but also, again, with an eye toward the public at home.

In Washington, very different considerations were at play. The German offensive in the Ardennes, in mid-December 1944, had cost the Americans large numbers of casualties. This strengthened U.S. secretary of state Stimson's opposition to any exchange of able-bodied POWs, as he claimed they could help fortify Nazi combat forces. In the end, Whitehall proved unable to effectuate the repatriation during the war of any number of long-term POWs held in German captivity.

In the final assault on Nazi Germany, the devastating Western air raids on its cities were intended to demoralize ordinary German civilians. But they also raised the specter of revenge killings, of guards turning against defenseless POWs, especially after the ss and the Gestapo had been put in charge of the camps. Growing concern about reprisal acts had already emerged in London and Washington in the fall of 1943 following their initial bombardments of German cities. Reports were coming in about the lynching of air force crews who had parachuted out of their downed planes. The murder by the Gestapo of fifty RAF officers who had escaped from Stalag Luft III (Sagan) in March 1944 was another indication of the real dangers threatening Western POWs. In October 1944, the German troops were ordered by the headquarters of the Führer himself to execute on the spot any Allied commando mission that fell into their hands even if the latter had surrendered. Seventy U.S. soldiers were murdered in this way at Malmédy, Belgium, on 17 December 1944.

Most of the approximately 300,000 British Commonwealth and American POWs were held in remote camps in the east. This was done on purpose: it made it almost impossible for POWs who had escaped to rejoin their own forces. Although the outcome of the war was by now a foregone conclusion, it was as yet impossible to predict—given the setbacks the Allies had suffered in December—when the war itself would be brought to an end. The intervening weeks or perhaps months, the Allies knew, would be crucial for the safety of the POWs in these camps, and different possibilities as to how to safeguard their lives were contemplated: dropping arms into POW camps so that prisoners could defend themselves against revenge killings or even parachuting troops behind enemy lines to shield prisoners from such attacks. The first option was dismissed as actually endangering the prisoners' lives, the second ruled out as militarily not feasible—prisoners were widely dispersed over enormous distances in thousands of work camps sometimes holding no more than a few dozen POWs. In both London and Washington, the overriding consensus, military as well as political, came out in favor of the decision not to divert troops but to press on with the total defeat of Germany.

What the Allies could not have known was that, threatened by the hugely successful Soviet offensive in January 1945, the Germans had begun evacuating POW camps in the east by marching large convoys of thousands of prisoners to locations in Germany proper. In the heart of winter, troops were forced to walk on foot under the most grueling circumstances, over huge distances and with little or no provisions made for shelter, food, or drink on the way. The overwhelming majority nevertheless survived the ordeal.

As these marches were under way, not only did the Allies keep up their bombing raids on German towns, but the Nazis themselves knew they had lost the war and that their Third Reich was about to collapse. What, then, held them back from retaliating against the British and American troops they were holding captive?

Shortly before he committed suicide, Hitler is alleged to have told his servants that he hoped for them they would succeed in falling into the hands of the Americans and British and not the Russians.[3] There was obvious panic toward the end throughout the entire Nazi hierarchy at the possibility of capture by the Soviets, prompting some—notably Himmler—to try to enter into some form of peace negotiations with the Western powers: a last-minute revenge killing of British and U.S. POWs would not have served the purpose. This may have been one final instance of Nazi "pragmatism." But it could also have been the Nazis' racist ideology holding out even as the Reich itself was crumbling before their very eyes. At the same time they were evacuating POW camps, the Nazis began emptying concentration camps and moving their inmates away from the east and the rapidly advancing Soviet forces. There are harrowing eyewitness accounts of how the paths of such columns would sometimes cross or even how for a while they marched alongside each other. But more than one-third of the approximately 750,000 concentration camp inmates never made it: they either froze or starved to death or were killed outright by their guards.

The forced marches of POWs back into Germany so close to the end caught London and Washington by surprise. The immediate reaction in both capitals was that it would be better for the POWs to stay put in the camps, whatever the risks, and wait for them to be liberated by the Red Army. But for this to happen not only did they need to persuade the Germans—who agreed to halt the marches on 1 May 1945!—but the Russians, too, would have to be convinced: Moscow feared Berlin might take advantage of the situation by positioning Allied POWs at strategic points and thus hinder the advance of the Red Army while covering its own withdrawal.

The Soviets now began to play a major role. Keenly aware that its Western allies were eager to see the POWs whom the Red Army was liberating repatriated as swiftly as possible, the Kremlin exacted a price: the repatriation of all "Soviet nationals," including citizens of the Baltic states and eastern Poland. This, in effect, meant the de-facto recognition by London and Washington of the annexation by the Soviet Union of these regions, but it also required that they ignore the horrible fate they knew would await all returnees. There were only a few qualms about this in Washington and even fewer in London: besides concern for the safety of their liberated POWs, the businesslike character of the negotiations betrayed an eagerness to silence the anticipated criticism at home over the way the government had been handling the POW issue and to be rid of more than 2 million Soviet POWs and civilians. But Moscow wanted more: recognition of the transitional government the Soviets had meanwhile installed in Poland. Here it held out as bait permission for the Western Allies to send contact officers into areas liberated by the Red Army, Poland foremost among them. Given the geopolitical implications it involved, the bargain was turned down. As Churchill was to write in his memoirs: "Poland had indeed been the most urgent reason for the Yalta Conference, and was to prove the first of the great causes which led to the breakdown of the Grand Alliance."[4] At the same time, the negotiations left no doubt in Moscow as to the concern London and Washington attached to the well-being of their POWs, and this clearly had an impact on the way the Red Army treated them. Despite the aggressive nature of the meetings that led up to it, the Halle Agreement, signed on 22 May, guaranteed the swift repatriation of all POWs on both sides.

David Wild voiced the sentiments of many when, on his return home after the war, he described the five years he had spent in German captivity as "useless incarceration."[5] Private Less Allan, also captured at Dunkirk, wrote many years later that people felt "we were lucky to have been prisoners as so many other fellows had been killed."[6] Policy makers in London and Washington appear to have approached the POW issue along much the same lines. They never actually neglected their men in German hands but found no reason either to give preference to their plight. That the overwhelming majority of British Commonwealth and U.S. prisoners would survive captivity in Nazi POW camps, however, was ultimately far from self-evident, especially after D-Day. London and Washington knew of the dangers but, when they set their priorities during the final months of the war, decided to act on the assumption that the SS and the Gestapo would refrain from murdering Western POWs. It was a calculated risk.

NOTES

INTRODUCTION

1 Wild, *Prisoner of Hope*, 269. Wild was a chaplain with the British army when he fell prisoner to the Germans at Dunkirk in May 1940. Allowed to exercise his ministry as chaplain during his captivity, he was freed in January 1945 and arrived back in England in April 1945, after which he started "scribbl[ing] down into old notebooks all that I could remember about five years as prisoner" (11).

2 Ibid., 271.

3 PRO, FO916/1183, C. E. King, SHAEF, Political Office, British, to PWD, 30 May 1945; statistics of U.S. POWs, see below, chap. 3. On the difficulties involved in arriving at accurate numbers, see Nichol and Rennell, *The Last Escape*, app. 4; Vourkoutiotis, *Prisoners of War and the German High Command*, 5–6.

4 Churchill, *Their Finest Hour, The Grand Alliance, The Hinge of the Fate, Closing the Ring,* and *Triumph and Tragedy*; Burns, *Roosevelt*; Sherwood, *Roosevelt and Hopkins*; Stimson and McGeorge, *On Active Service in Peace and War*; Hull, *The Memoirs of Cordell Hull*; Eden, *The Eden Memoirs*; Eisenhower, *Crusade in Europe*; Montgomery, *The Memoirs of Field-Marshal the Viscount Montgomery of Alamein*; North, *The Alexander Memoirs*; Arnold, *Global Mission*; *The Memoirs of General the Lord Ismay*.

5 PRO, WO208/3242, message from the prime minister to the prisoners of war, 3 August 1941.

6 See, e.g., Moore and Fedorowich, *Prisoners of War*, 8; Mackenzie, "Prisoners of War and Civilian Internees," 302–3, 308.

7 On German treatment of Soviet POWs, see Streim, *Die Behandlung sowjetischer Kriegsgefangener*; Streit, *Keine Kameraden*; Bartov, *The Eastern Front*, 106–41; Werth, *Russia at War*, pt. 6, chap. 10; Schulte, *The German Army*, chap. 8; Förster, "The German Army," 15–29; Fried, "The Fate of Soviet POWs," 203–25; Junod, *Warrior without Weapons*, 202–7; Müller, "Die Behandlung sowjetischer kriegsgefangener," 283–302.

8 For a study on German policy toward British and American POWs based on German archival sources, see Vourkoutiotis, *Prisoners of War and the German High Command*.

9 *Prisoners of War Bulletin* (published by the American National Red Cross for the relatives of American prisoners of war and civilian internees) 2 (November 1944).

10 NACP, RG 59, GRDS, Decimal File, 1945–49, "American Prisoners of War in Germany," prepared by Military Intelligence Service, War Department, 1 November 1945.

CHAPTER ONE

1 Umbreit, "The Battle of Hegemony in Western Europe," 278–304; Gilbert, *The Second World War*, 75–83; Atkin, *Pillar of Fire*.

2 Ray, *The Night Blitz*; Maier, "The Battle of Britain," 2:374–407.

3 PRO, FO369/2562, American embassy to London, nos. 1892, 1883, 2 February 1940; each report covered seventeen aspects of camp life: General Description (Location, Buildings, Grounds, Security Measures, Air Raid Chambers); Capacity and Personnel; Interior Arrangements (Quarters, Bedding, Heat, Light); Bathing

and Washing Facilities; Toilet Facilities; Food and Cooking; Medical Attention and Sickness; Clothing; Laundry; Money and Pay; Canteen; Religious Activity; Recreation and Exercise; Mail; Welfare Work; Complaints; and General Impressions. Three British officers who had succeeded in escaping from POW camps before the Dunkirk evacuation confirmed that British POWs in German captivity were generally treated well. PRO, AIR14/461, "Lessons Learned from Escapers of British Personnel after Capture during Recent Operations (Open Warfare)," 14 June 1940.

4 "Department" refers to the War Office's Directorate of Prisoners of War (DPW).

5 Satow and Sée, *The Work of the Prisoners of War Department*, 5. See also PRO, FO370/1806, for correspondence between FO and WO officials regarding this volume.

6 Rolf, *Prisoners of the Reich*, 11–14.

7 Of the approximately 37,000 British POWs held by the Germans after the evacuation of Dunkirk, 36,077 were army (including 1,341 officers), 363 Royal Navy (50 officers), 351 Royal Air Force (182 officers), and 396 merchant navy (74 officers). PRO, FO916/1173, "Prisoners of War as at 1 July 1940."

8 PRO, KV2/172, The Kriegsgefangenenwesen, May 1945; Durand, *Stalag Luft III*, 132–35, 147–52; Hasselbring, "American Prisoners of War," 103–5, 122–23, 199–205; Foy, *For You the War Is Over*, 12, 17–19; Vourkoutiotis, *Prisoners of War and the German High Command*, 29–31.

9 PRO, FO916/2775, report on visit to Stalag XX A, 31 July 1940.

10 See also Vourkoutiotis, *Prisoners of War and the German High Command*, 65–67.

11 PRO, FO916/2775, report on visit to Stalag XX A, 31 July 1940.

12 Quoted in Rolf, *Prisoners of the Reich*, 31.

13 Article 43 of the Geneva Convention ruled that in every place where there were POWs, they should be allowed to appoint "agents entrusted with representing them directly with military authorities and Protecting Powers." The agents "shall be entrusted with the reception and distribution of collective shipments. Likewise, in case the prisoners should decide to organize a mutual assistance system among themselves, this organization would be in the sphere of the agents." In camps of officers and persons of equivalent status, the article continued, "the senior officer prisoner of the highest rank shall be recognized as intermediary between the camp authorities and the officers and persons of equivalent status who are prisoners." Friedman, *The Law of War*, 1:504.

14 PRO, FO916/2775, report on visit to Oflag VII C, 19 June 1940.

15 Ibid. The convention's Article 11 reads as follows: "The food ration of prisoners of war shall be equal in quantity and quality to that of troops at base camps. Furthermore, prisoners shall receive facilities for preparing, themselves, additional food which they might have. A sufficiency of potable water shall be furnished them." Friedman, *The Law of War*, 1:496.

16 PRO, FO916/2775, report on visit to Oflag VII C, 19 June 1940.

17 Each prisoner received a daily ration of 1,000 grams of potatoes, 50 grams of meat, 50 grams of jam or cheese, 10 grams of butter and sugar. They also received 100 grams of fish weekly and fresh vegetables.

18 PRO, FO916/2775, report on visit to OFLAG VII C/H in September 1940.

19 Ibid., American embassy, London, to the British foreign secretary, 7 October 1940.

20 PRO, PREM4/98/1, letter from Mrs. C. Tennant, 20 November 1940; see also Wild, *Prisoners of Hope*, 17–19.

21 PRO, FO916/2577, Switzerland to FO, no. 225, 18 October 1940; see also ibid., report on visit to Stalag XX B, 2–3 August 1940; PRO, FO916/2775, report on visit to Stalag VIII B, 13 August 1940, and report on visit to Stalag Luft, 22 October 1940. About the YMCA, see Shedd et al., *History of the World's Alliance of Young Men's Christian Associations*.

22 PRO, FO916/2576, the American chargé d'affaires to the British foreign secretary, 18 November 1940.

23 By the autumn of 1941, the DPW consisted of three official branches and three unofficial ones. Of the official branches, PW1 dealt with the administration of enemy POW camps and the provision of guards for civilian internee camps; PW2 dealt with the interpretation of conventions and the policy of treatment of enemy POWs; PW3 was in charge of the welfare of British POWs in enemy hands. Unofficial branches included PW4, mainly for correspondence and censorship; PW5, for security and inspection of POW camps holding enemy POWs; and PW6, which dealt with movements of enemy POWs. Gepp reorganized the DPW so that PW1 administered all aspects of enemy POWs and PW2 was responsible for the welfare of British POWs, policy toward enemy prisoners, and all questions of reciprocity. As the war progressed, another three branches were added. In March 1945, the directorate consisted of thirty-six military officers, nine junior civil assistants, and seventy-eight clerks. PRO, WO366/26, Colonel H. J. Phillimore, "The Second World War, 1939–1945, Army: Prisoners of War," WO, 1949, 9–11.

24 Satow and Sée, *The Work of the Prisoners of War Department*, 5.

25 See, e.g., the correspondence between Lord Vansittart, former permanent undersecretary in the Foreign Office, who had served for some time as the head of the PWD during World War I, and the Foreign Office. PRO, FO916/562, Vansittart to David Scott, FO, 1 April 1943, and Scott to Vansittart, 14 April 1943; see also PRO, FO916/276, memorandum, "Work of the Prisoners and Aliens Department of the Foreign Office and the Prisoners of War Department," 17 April 1919. Hately-Broad, "Prisoners of War Families," 257.

26 See, e.g., PRO, FO916/264, Richard K. Law, FO, to E. D. Sandys, WO, 15 July 1942, and Sandys to Law, 16 July 1942.

27 Viscount Cranborne, secretary of state for Dominions affairs, announced its formation in the House of Lords on 30 April 1941. In practice, however, the committee's work was more often exercised by two subcommittees it had appointed under the chairmanship of Richard Law, the financial secretary of the War Office. Sub-Committee A's terms of reference read as follows: "To consider such questions affecting policy and general administration of prisoners of war as concerned more than one Government within the Empire with a view to avoiding undesirable differences of treatment." Sub-Committee B's terms of reference were "[t]o consider financial questions arising in the administration of prisoners of war which concerned more than one Department in the United Kingdom or more

than one Government in the Empire." *Hansard, House of Commons*, vol. 374, cols. 1223–24, 14 October 1941; PRO, WO163/583, minutes of the meeting of the Inter-governmental Committee of Prisoners of War, Sub-Committee A, 26 June 1941; PRO, WO163/582, minutes of the first meeting of the Imperial Prisoners of War Committee, 5 November 1941; Phillimore, "The Second World War," 9–13, 23–26; Satow and Sée, *The Work of the Prisoners of War Department*, 5–7, 166–67; Moore and Fedorowich, *The British Empire*, 16–17; Rolf, "'Blind Bureaucracy,'" 48–51, 54–55; Mason, *Prisoners of War*, 10–11, 43–44. See also Hately-Broad, "Prisoners of War Families," 16–19, 152–55. About the Canadian administration of POW issues, see Vance, *Objects of Concern*, 107–12, 121–25, 181, 247–48.

28 *Hansard, House of Commons*, vol. 352, cols. 890–91, 18 October 1939, and cols. 1378–79, 25 October 1940.

29 Ibid., vol. 355, cols. 437–38, 5 December 1939, and cols. 1311–12, 14 December 1939; and vol. 358, cols. 984–85, 12 March 1940. On the BRCS, see Cambray and Briggs, *Red Cross*.

30 Phillimore, "The Second World War," 50–52; Hately-Broad, "Prisoners of War Families," 196–98; Rolf, *Prisoners of the Reich*, 84.

31 Rolf, "'Blind Bureaucracy,'" 48–52; Phillimore, "The Second World War," 53.

32 Cambray and Briggs, *Red Cross*, 138–45; *Red Cross & St. John War Organisation 1939–1947*, 112–26; Phillimore, "The Second World War," 98–99.

33 Cambray and Briggs, *Red Cross*, 150–51.

34 *Hansard, House of Commons*, vol. 360, cols. 1186–87, 5 November 1940. Major General Knox had served as military attaché at the British embassy in Petrograd and liaison officer with respect to the Russian army (1911–18). On the activities of the International Red Cross, see *Report of the International Committee of the Red Cross*, vol. 2, pt. 3, chaps. 1–7; Durand, *History of the International Committee of the Red Cross*, 447–70.

35 Phillimore, "The Second World War," 51–52.

36 PRO, PREM4/98/1, memorandum for the prime minister, 21 December 1940. In August 1942, A. H. S. Coombe-Tennant succeeded in escaping from Oflag VI B and reached Spain. Levine, *Captivity, Flight, and Survival in World War II*, 100–102.

37 PRO, PREM4/98/1, letter from Mrs. C. Tennant, 20 November 1940; Rolf, "'Blind Bureaucracy,'" 50–54. About the complicated relations between POWs' kin and the government, see Hately-Broad, "Prisoners of War Families," 206–9; Phillimore, "The Second World War," 53–55.

38 PRO, PREM4/98/1, "British Prisoners of War," 29 November 1940; see also ibid., notes of a meeting held in the secretary of state's room, 28 November 1940.

39 Ibid., letter from Mrs. C. Tennant, 3 December 1940.

40 Ibid., letter from Mrs. C. Tennant, 12 December 1940.

41 Ibid., letter from Mrs. C. Tennant, 4 January 1941.

42 PRO, FO916/2577, minute, 3 January 1941.

43 The average number of parcels packed during the first weeks of 1941 was 53,000 weekly. Cambray and Briggs, *Red Cross*, 151–52.

44 *Hansard, House of Commons*, vol. 368, cols. 1–6, 21 January 1941; see also cols. 324–26, 23 January 1941.

45 Ibid., and cols. 426–28, 28 January 1941; see also PRO, FO916/38, report on visit to Oflag VII C/H, December 1941; Rolf, "'Blind Bureaucracy,'" 50–54.

46 PRO, FO916/2577, the American chargé d'affaires, London, to Eden, 16 December 1940. The daily quantities of food per man in this camp included one-half liter of coffee, 321 grams of bread, 55 grams of meat, 1,500 grams of potatoes, 47 grams of cheese, 35 grams of fat, 10 grams of grain, 7 grams of beans, vegetables when available, sugar as required, and dried fruit occasionally on Sundays.

47 PRO, FO916/45, the American chargé d'affaires, London, to Eden, 2 January 1941.

48 PRO, FO916/46, note verbale, 27 January 1941; see also PRO, FO916/2577, the American chargé d'affaires, London, to Eden, 19 February 1941. Article 12 of the Geneva Convention states: "Clothing, linen and footwear shall be furnished prisoners of war by the detaining Power. Replacement and repairing of these effects must be assured regularly. In addition, laborers must receive work clothes whenever the nature of the work requires it." Friedman, *The Law of War*, 1:496.

49 PRO, FO916/45, Churchill to Herschel Johnson, no. K.W.2/20, 22 February 1941.

50 Ibid. On the treatment of German POWs by Britain, see Moore, "Axis Prisoners in Britain," 19–46; Moore, "Turning Liabilities into Assets," 117–25, 133–36.

51 Speed, *Prisoners, Diplomats, and the Great War*, 32–33; see also Vourkoutiotis, *Prisoners of War and the German High Command*, 28–29.

52 *Hansard, House of Commons*, vol. 368, cols. 777–79, 5 February 1941.

53 Ibid., vol. 369, col. 14, 18 February 1941.

54 About the organization activities during World War I, see Jackson, *The Prisoners*, 62–69.

55 Favez, *The Red Cross and the Holocaust*, 4–5, 14–15, 45–52; Mason, *Prisoners of War*, 8–11, 42–43, 146–48; Hately-Broad, "Prisoners of War Families," 190–95; see also Vourkoutiotis, *Prisoners of War and the German High Command*, 137–40.

56 *Hansard, House of Commons*, vol. 369, cols. 745–50, 4 March 1941. Law told the MPs that a daily "Menu of Food" issued to British POWs in Germany consisted of the following: (morning) 7 grams of coffee, 15 grams sugar, 24 grams honey; midday: 70 grams beef, 350 grams fresh beetroot, 1,000 grams potatoes, 10 grams flour, 15 grams salt; (evening) 7 grams coffee, 15 grams sugar, 300 grams bread, and 25 grams fat.

57 PRO, PREM4/98/1, memorandum for the prime minister, 13 March 1941.

58 Ibid.; see also PRO, FO916/32, Samuel Hoare to Eden, 24 February 1941.

59 PRO, FO916/112, S. J. Warner to Francis Fremantle, House of Commons, 6 May 1941; see also ibid., Churchill to Kelly, no. 30, 7 April 1941.

60 *Hansard, House of Commons*, vol. 373, cols. 2133–34, 7 August 1941.

61 Speed, *Prisoners, Diplomats, and the Great War*, 31, 73.

62 PRO, FO916/45, American embassy, Berlin, to American embassy, London, 15 November 1941; see also *Hansard, House of Commons*, vol. 376, cols. 171–72, 18 November 1941.

63 PRO, AIR2/6366, American embassy, London, to Eden, 13 October 1941.

64 See also Rolf, *Prisoners of the Reich*, 11–15.

65 Speed, *Prisoners, Diplomats, and the Great War*, 67–68, 73–74; Jackson, *The Prisoners*, 31, 110–11.

66 PRO, AIR2/6366, American embassy, London, to Eden, 13 October 1941.

67 Reports on different Lazarette, see PRO, FO916/30, report on Reserve Lazarett Schemeckwitz, 5 May 1941; PRO, AIR2/6366, report on Reserve Lazarett Obermassfield, 30 May 1941.

68 The hot meal, one liter of stew served at midday, contained an average of 50 grams on the two meatless days and came with 250 to 750 grams of potatoes, depending on how many other vegetables were available, seasoned with salt and pepper; "I have often eaten it," Dr. Murray wrote, "and always found it palatable." The stew was cooked in large steam pressure kettles and served up in a "clean and expeditious" manner so that it could be eaten while still hot. As their evening meal, the POWs received 300–375 grams of army bread, 125 grams of marmalade, 30 grams of artificial honey, 40 grams of sausage or cheese, 30 grams of margarine, 16 grams of sugar, and 2 grams of substitute tea. Breakfast included 9 grams of substitute coffee and 16 grams of sugar. PRO, AIR2/6366, American embassy, London, to Eden, 13 October 1941.

69 Ibid.; see also Vourkoutiotis, *Prisoners of War and the German High Command*, 61–63.

70 See also Dr. Murray's report on conditions in Stalag XX A (Thorn Podgorz), where approximately 12,000 British prisoners were being held in the camp itself, its dependent work camps, and its Reserve Lazarett 2. PRO, FO916/25, Eden to John G. Winant, no. K.W.2/4, 19 May 1941, and Eden to Winant, no. K.W.2/4, 24 May 1941.

71 In mid-September Stalag XX A held 8,790 British prisoners. PRO, FO916/26, report on visit to Stalag XX A, 17 September 1941. On conditions in Stalag XVIII A (Wolfsberg, Austria), see PRO, FO916/24, report on visit to Stalag XVIII A and dependent work camps, 26 August 1941; see also Williams, *Arbeitskommando*, chap. 2.

72 Dr. Descoeudres of the Red Cross visited the camp in October 1941. In concluding his report, he stated that Stalag XVIII D "is absolutely inadequate for its purpose. Everything is in disorder and very badly organised. The sanitary conditions are deplorable. The camp is a real danger to the health of the prisoners, and it is to be hoped that very serious measures will be taken before the winter to improve the present conditions in this Stalag." PRO, WO222/1361, report on Stalag XVIII D, 23 October 1941; PRO, FO916/25, report on Stalag XVIII D, 30 October 1941.

73 PRO, FO916/33, American embassy, Berlin, to American embassy, London, 19 September 1941.

74 The main relatives organization that operated on a national level, however, was the *Prisoners of War Relative Association*. On the activities of the two organizations, see Hately-Broad, "Prisoners of War Families," 19–21, 191–92, 202–18.

75 On the work in the mines, see below, chap. 2.

76 PRO, INF1/271, Newsletter No. 2, 19 May 1941; see also PRO, FO916/22, American embassy, London, to the foreign secretary, 7 and 21 March 1941; Rolf, "The Education of British Prisoners of War," 257–65.

77 *Hansard, House of Commons*, vol. 373, cols. 1799–80, 5 August 1941.

78 PRO, FO916/22, the American ambassador, London, to the British foreign secre-

tary, 29 October 1941; Mason, *Prisoners of War*, 88–90. On the process of ICRC inspection of the camps, see Durand, *History of the International Committee of the Red Cross*, 441–61.

79 R. P. Evans, no. 90/18/1, p. 33, Unpublished Memoirs, Department of Documents, Imperial War Museum, London.

80 Ibid., 34.

81 Ibid.

82 Ibid., 38. See also Moorehead, *Dunant's Dream*, 384–85.

83 PRO, FO916/244, memorandum, 19 March 1942.

84 Ibid.

85 Ibid., DPW to FO (PWD), 24 April 1942.

86 Hasselbring, "American Prisoners of War," 158–59.

87 PRO, FO916/244, report on visit to Stalag VIII B, 5 May 1942; see also *The Prisoners of War*, May 1942.

88 PRO, FO916/244, minute, 21 July 1942; see also ibid., WO (DPW) to FO (PWD), 30 April 1942.

89 *Hansard, House of Commons*, vol. 379, cols. 342–43, 16 April 1942.

90 Ibid.

91 Ibid., vol. 382, cols. 1274–91, 6 August 1942; see also ibid., vol. 380, cols. 23–24, 19 May 1942; cols. 502–4, 2 June 1942; and cols. 1367–68, 16 June 1942; and vol. 381, cols. 20–21, 30 June 1942. In April 1942, 263,700 standard Red Cross food parcels and food in bulk equivalent to more than 90,000 parcels had been dispatched from Geneva; in May, the figure went up to 360,000 and in June jumped to 550,000 parcels.

92 Phillimore, "The Second World War," 51.

93 PRO, FO916/245, report on visit to Stalag VIII B, 5 September 1942.

94 Ibid., Bern to FO, no. 4762, 22 December 1942; ibid., minute, 3 February 1943.

95 PRO, FO916/241, report on visit to Stalag XX B, 1 May 1942.

96 Ibid., FO to Bern, no. 1808, 3 July 1942; see also ibid., Bern to FO, no. 2294, 29 June 1942.

97 Ibid., Bern to FO, no. 3934, 5 November 1942; see also below, chap. 2, and Vourkoutiotis, *Prisoners of War and the German High Command*, 75–87.

98 PRO, FO916/60, minute by Roberts, 15 August 1941.

99 Phillimore, "The Second World War," 39–44; Rolf, "'Blind Bureaucracy,'" 55–56.

100 PRO, FO916/251, Number of British P/W in Germany at 30 June 1942, IRCC telegram of 17 July 1942; for different data, see *Hansard, House of Commons*, vol. 383, cols. 63–64, 8 September 1942.

CHAPTER TWO

1 Gilbert, *The Second World War*, 353–54; Dancocks, *In Enemy Hands*, chap. 2.

2 PRO, WO32/10719, brief for the chief of the Imperial General Staff, German Threat of Reprisals on British POWs, 8 October 1942.

3 Ibid.; PRO, CAB65/28, conclusions of 136th War Cabinet meeting, 8 October 1942. Article 2 of the Geneva Convention stated that prisoners should at all times

be humanely treated and protected, "particularly against acts of violence and from insults and from public curiosity." Friedman, *The Law of War*, 1:494.

4 PRO, CAB66/30, note by the secretary of the War Cabinet, 10 October 1942.

5 PRO, PREM3/363/2, official statements by His Majesty's Government on shackling of POWs, 10 December 1942. See also Mackenzie, "The Shackling Crisis," 78–98; *Trials of War Criminals before the Nuremberg Military Tribunals*, 11:128.

6 PRO, WO32/10719, DO to the Dominions governments, no. 408, 10 October 1942.

7 PRO, PREM3/363/2, official statements by His Majesty's Government on shackling of POWs, 10 December 1942.

8 PRO, WO32/10719, total German POWs as of 15 November 1942.

9 MacKenzie, "The Shackling Crisis," 88; Moore and Fedorowich, *The British Empire*, 19–23.

10 PRO, CAB65/28, conclusions of 136th War Cabinet meeting, 8 October 1942. About captured Italian servicemen, see Fedorowich and Moore, "Co-Belligerency and Prisoners of War," 28–29.

11 PRO, CAB65/28, conclusions of 137th War Cabinet meeting, 9 October 1942; PRO, CAB66/29, DO to Dominion governments, no. 408, 10 October 1942; PRO, WO32/10719, statement of the British government, 8 October 1942.

12 PRO, WO32/10719, Canada (government) to Dominions Office, no. 214, 9 October 1942; PRO, PREM3/363/2, Vincent Massey, Canadian high commissioner in London, to Clement Attlee, 10 October 1942; see also Vance, "Men in Manacles," 483–504.

13 PRO, WO32/10719, Canada to Dominions Office, no. 216, 10 October 1942, and Canada to Dominions Office, no. 214, 9 October 1942. The Canadian government came up with five possibilities for the German move: (a) an effort to compel the two sides to reach an agreement to refrain in all circumstances from tying prisoners up immediately after capture; (b) an attempt to make commando raids less effective; (c) part of a policy of general terrorism; (d) a means of distracting attention within Germany from the Russian campaign; or (e) an outright act of vengeance for an alleged insult to "the master race." Ibid., WO32/10719, Canada to Dominions Office, no. 216, 10 October 1942; PRO, PREM3/363/2, Canada to Dominions Office, no. 217, 11 October 1942.

14 PRO, WO32/10719, Australia to Dominions Office, no. 456, 11 October 1942. See also Waters, "Australia, the British Empire and the Second World War," 93–107.

15 PRO, WO32/10719, F. J. du Toit (in the absence of the high commissioner for Union of South Africa) to Attlee, 12 October 1942; PRO, CAB65/28, conclusions of 137th War Cabinet meeting, 9 October 1942; see also Vance, "The Trouble with the Allies," 69–85; Dancocks, *In Enemy Hands*; Mason, *Prisoners of War*, 238–39.

16 PRO, PREM3/363/2, Churchill to Attlee, 11 October 1942.

17 Ibid., conclusions of 139th War Cabinet meeting, 12 October 1942, and FO to Bern, no. 2799, 12 October 1942.

18 *Hansard, House of Commons*, vol. 383, cols. 1502–3, 13 October 1942.

19 PRO, PREM4/98/2, William Canterbury to Churchill, 12 October 1942; see also Rolf, "'Blind Bureaucracy,'" 56–60. On POWs' relative organizations, see Hately-Broad, "Prisoners of War Families," 202–18.

20 PRO, CAB65/28, conclusions of 141st War Cabinet meeting, 14 October 1942.

21 PRO, WO32/10719, memorandum for the secretary of state for war, 17 October 1942; PRO, PREM3/363/2, minute, 15 October 1942.

22 Lord Russell of Liverpool, *The Scourge of the Swastika*, 26–30; see below, chap. 6.

23 On German treatment of Soviet POWs, see above, preface, note 7.

24 PRO, PREM3/363/2, conclusions of 144th War Cabinet meeting, 22 October 1942; PRO, WO163/584, meeting of Sub-Committee A of Imperial Prisoners of War Committee, 24 October 1942.

25 PRO, WO32/10719, Canada to Dominions Office, nos. 239, 240, 3 November 1942.

26 Vance, *Objects of Concern*, 134–38.

27 PRO, FO916/273, minute, 7 November 1942; see also PRO, FO916/272, minute by Roberts, 5 November 1942.

28 PRO, WO32/10719, Dominions Office to Dominions governments, no. 453, 11 November 1942; ibid., extract from conclusions of 151st War Cabinet meeting, 9 November 1942.

29 Ibid., minute for the secretary of state for war, 4 November 1942, and PWD to G. Ignatieff, Canada House, 21 November 1942.

30 The Second World War Diary of Major E. Booth, February 1940–10 May 1945, Unpublished Memoirs, Department of Documents, Imperial War Museum, London.

31 PRO, WO193/355, Bern to FO, no. 4323, 28 November 1942.

32 Ibid.; PRO, WO32/10719, memorandum, 24 November 1942. On German POWs in Britain, see Sullivan, *Thresholds of Peace*.

33 PRO, CAB122/232, Eden to Lord Halifax, no. 215, 28 November 1942.

34 PRO, FO916/273, minute by Roberts, 30 November 1942.

35 PRO, WO193/355, extract from the War Cabinet minutes of the 162nd meeting, 30 November 1942.

36 *Hansard, House of Commons*, vol. 385, cols. 889–90, 26 November 1942, and cols. 988–89, 1 December 1942.

37 PRO, PREM3/363/2, the Canadian high commissioner in London to Dominions Office, 2 December 1942, and minute for Churchill, 2 December 1942.

38 PRO, CAB65/28, conclusions of 164th War Cabinet meeting, 3 December 1942.

39 PRO, WO32/10719, FO to Bern, no. 3465, 3 December 1942.

40 PRO, FO916/273, Bern to FO, no. 4469, 7 December 1942; PRO, WO32/10719, FO to Bern, no. 3465, 3 December 1942.

41 PRO, WO32/10719, extract from conclusions of 165th War Cabinet meeting, 7 December 1942.

42 PRO, PREM3/363/2, official statement by His Majesty's Government on shackling of POWs, 10 December 1942; PRO, WO32/10719, extract from conclusions of 165th War Cabinet meeting, 7 December 1942, and Canada to Dominions Office, no. 264, 10 December 1942.

43 PRO, FO916/274, Bern to FO, nos. 4581, 4583, 13 December 1942.

44 PRO, WO32/10719, extract from conclusions of first War Cabinet meeting, 4 January 1943; PRO, CAB65/33, conclusions of eighteenth War Cabinet meeting, 27 January 1943; PRO, PREM3/363/2, Bern to FO, nos. 4657, 4658, 17 December 1942; PRO, CAB65/28, conclusions of 168th War Cabinet meeting, 14 December 1942.

45 PRO, WO32/10719, FO to Bern, no. 572, 10 February 1943. The British denied that there was any ground to Berlin's assertion that they had established a difference in the way they treated POWs, that is, between soldiers caught on the battlefield and prisoners brought to enemy territory. Article 1 of the Geneva Convention, they pointed out, specified that a combatant was deemed to be a POW—and therefore entitled to the protection accorded by the relevant provisions of the convention—as soon as he had been captured by the enemy. In other words, there was no disagreement between the two governments on this point. On the phrasing of Article 1, see Friedman, *The Law of War*, 1:49–50; PRO, WO32/10719, FO to Bern, no. 572, 10 February 1943; see also *Hansard, House of Commons*, vol. 386, cols. 352–53, 26 January 1943, and cols. 742–43, 2 February 1943.

46 PRO, WO32/10719, German legation, Bern, to the Swiss government, 11 March 1943; PRO, CAB65/33, conclusions of forty-fourth War Cabinet meeting, 22 March 1943.

47 PRO, WO32/10719, Bern to FO, no. 1507, 29 March 1943.

48 Ibid., Bern to FO, no. 1355, 19 March 1943; see also report on Oflag III C (Lübben), ibid., Bern to FO, no. 1346, 19 March 1943; PRO, WO193/355, Bern to FO, no. 2024, 22 April 1943. On Stalag 383, see also McKibbin, *Barbed Wire*. Report on Stalag VIII B, see PRO, WO32/10719, Bern to FO, no. 1871, 16 April 1943; PRO, WO193/355, Bern to FO, no. 2024, 22 April 1943; see also PRO, FO916/274, Bern to FO, no. 4779, 23 December 1942.

49 On report of a representative of the Swiss legation in Berlin who visited Oflag VII B, see PRO, WO193/355, Bern to FO, no. 2237, 6 May 1943.

50 The Second World War Diary of Major E. Booth, February 1940–10 May 1945.

51 Ibid.

52 *Hansard, House of Commons*, vol. 388, cols. 1657–59, 21 April 1943; see also PRO, PREM3/363/2, memorandum by Eden, "Shackling of Prisoners of War," W.P. (43) 158, 16 April 1943, and extract from fifty-sixth War Cabinet meeting, 19 April 1942.

53 PRO, WO32/10719, Dominions Office to Dominion governments, no. 279, 10 May 1943, and Bern to FO, no. 2335, 11 May 1943.

54 The Second World War Diary of Major E. Booth, February 1940–10 May 1945.

55 PRO, FO916/531, a meeting at the Foreign Office, PWD, 28 May 1943; PRO, WO193/355, FO to Bern, no. 1910, 17 May 1943.

56 Lochner, *The Goebbels Diaries*, 382.

57 *Hansard, House of Commons*, vol. 389, col. 921, 18 May 1943; see also Moore and Fedorowich, *The British Empire*, chap. 3.

58 PRO, WO193/355, Bern to FO, no. 3081, 25 June 1943. About Ribbentrop activities during the war, see Weitz, *Joachim Von Ribbentrop*.

59 PRO, CAB66/39, note by the prime minister, W.P. (43) 348, 30 July 1943.

60 PRO, WO32/10719, brief for the secretary of state for war on shackling of POWs, 2 August 1943.

61 Ibid.

62 PRO, PREM3/363/2, extract from conclusions of 109th War Cabinet meeting, 2 August 1943.

63 They were distributed among five camps: Oflag VII B—321 officers and 60 NCOs; Stalag 383—1,853 NCOs; Stalag VIII B—1,853 privates; Stalag IX C—289 privates; Marlag Milag Nord—27 privates. PRO, WO32/10719, Bern to FO, no. 4379, 14 September 1943.

64 Ibid.

65 PRO, WO193/355, Bern to FO, no. 3783, 6 August 1943. On Pilet-Golaz, see Wylie, "Pilet-Golaz," 158–70.

66 PRO, WO193/355, Bern to FO, no. 3894, 16 August 1943.

67 See below, chap. 3.

68 PRO, WO193/355, Bern to FO, no. 5621, 23 November 1943; see also PRO, WO32/10719, Bern to FO, no. 6100, 20 December 1943, and Bern to FO, no. 6220, 24 December 1943.

69 PRO, WO32/10719, Ministry of Information, Enemy and Allied POWs, 6 December 1943; PRO, WO193/355, FO to Bern, no. 4464, 16 December 1943; PRO, PREM3/363/2, Dominions Office to Newfoundland, Southern Rhodesia, no. 729, 20 December 1943.

70 About Whitehall and the involving of the Dominions in handling the POW issue, see PRO, FO916/562, Vansittart to David Scott, FO, 1 April 1943, and Scott to Vansittart, 14 April 1943.

71 Of the officially listed United Kingdom prisoners, 2,130 were officers and 49,761 men of other ranks in the army; 1,105 were officers and 3,308 men of other ranks in the air force; and 274 were officers and 2,217 men of other ranks in the navy, totaling 3,509 United Kingdom officers and 55,286 men of other ranks held by the Germans. PRO, FO916/555, monthly report by the Central Statistical Office of imperial POWs and internees, 30 September 1943; NACP, RG 389, ROPMG, American Prisoners of War Information Bureau, Records Branch, General Subject File, 1942–46, Camp Reports: Germany, Stalag (Enlisted Men), Stalag 4B to Stalag 7A, file Stalag 2A, Harrison to the secretary of state, 1 October 1943; PRO, WO224/223, report of the numbers of British and American POWs and internees at POW and internee camps, June 1943. About British POWs in Italy, see Mason, *Prisoners of War*, 110–26, 139, 154, 233.

72 Satow and Sée, *The Work of the Prisoners of War Department*, 30–31; Kimball, *Churchill and Roosevelt*, 2:352.

73 This Stalag continued to hold the largest number of British POWs. In Stalag XX B there were 1,100 British in the base camp and 9,070 in work detachments. Only 13 were not English. A large number of British POWs, 7,325, were also in Stalag XVIII A, while in Stalag XX A, 1,292 were in the base camp, 4,057 in work detachments, 162 in the hospital, and 193 in prison. In Stalag 383, 4,116 were in the base camp and 11 in the hospital. In Stalag IX C 398 British were in the base camp, 319 in the hospital, and 2,099 in work detachments. In Stalag Luft III, 1,888 were in camps (216 Canadians, 98 Australians, 112 New Zealanders, 67 South Africans, and 510 Americans). PRO, FO916/555, report from the prisoner of war and internment camps of the number of British and American POWs and internees, July 1943.

74 NACP, RG 389, ROPMG, American POW Information Bureau, Records Branch,

General Subject File, 1942–46, Camp Reports: Germany, Stalag (Enlisted Men), file Stalag VIII B Teschen, report on Camp Stalag VIII B, 15 November 1943.

75 Ibid. On POW camps in Italy, see Barber, *Prisoner of War*, chap. 8; Mason, *Prisoners of War*, 291–317.

76 See below, chap. 4.

77 PRO, FO916/887, Summary of Reports of Repatriated Prisoners of War on Condition in Camps in Germany, February 1944.

78 Ibid., report on Stalag 383 Hohenfels, Bavaria, where 3,015 of 4,696 prisoners were English, stated that apart from the heating problem and the dampness connected with the winter, the general conditions were bearable. The Swiss inspector stated that despite unsatisfactory quarters, the prisoners refused to be transferred elsewhere, as they highly appreciated the freedom the commandant was allowing them in the running of their internal affairs. PRO, FO916/835, report on Stalag 383 Hohenfels, 24 February 1944; see also PRO, FO916/835, report on Stalag 383 Hohenfels, 8 June 1944; *The Prisoners of War*, March 1944. A Swiss inspector who at the beginning of May 1944 visited Stalag Luft VI, where 3,000 English and 2,214 American prisoners were held, reported that an excellent atmosphere prevailed in the camp and that the understanding between camp authorities and the prisoners was very good. The main problem was that the camp was overcrowded and the number of prisoners was to increase from about 6,000 to 9,000. PRO, FO916/842, report on Stalag Luft VI, 3 May 1944. Favorable reports were also received on the situation in a few Lazarette; for instance, a report on Reserve Lazarett Elsterhorst (Stalag IV A), where 408 patients were hospitalized, was highly positive. Among the patients 365 were tuberculars. The Lazarett "produced an excellent impression, both from the point of view of installations and facilities for various treatments and from the point of view of the general atmosphere and the quality of supervision." PRO, WO219/838, report on Reserve Lazarett Elsterhorst (Stalag IV A), 15 April 1944. See also NACP, RG 389, ROPMG, American POW Information Bureau, Records Branch, General Subject File, 1942–46, Camp Reports: Germany, Stalag (Enlisted Men), file Stalag VIII C Sagan, report on Stalag VIII C Camp Hospital, 23 May 1944.

79 At the beginning of May 1944, the number of United Kingdom POWs officially listed as being in German hands amounted to 85,712. With the addition of 3,120 Canadians, 5,581 Australians, 6,537 New Zealanders, 6,482 South Africans, 8,323 Indian army troops, and 3,034 colonial forces, the total figure was 118,798. All together, the number of British Commonwealth POWs believed to be under German control in Europe was 152,850, of whom 105,033 were from the United Kingdom. PRO, PREM3/364/17, memorandum for the prime minister, 7 May 1944.

80 NACP, RG 407, Army-AG, Classified Decimal File, 1943–45, file 383.6, Repatriation of Able-bodied Prisoners, Harrison to Hull, no. 2108, 5 April 1944. A report on the general situation in Stalag Luft III at the time pointed out that thirty-seven officers in the East Compound were sleeping on the floor owing to lack of beds, that the roof in the North Compound leaked, that there were no bathing facilities in South

Compound, and that in the East Compound toilet drainage were unsatisfactory. More distressing were further cases of shooting inside the compound. Sentries were allowed to shoot without warning when prisoners were seen outside barracks at night or away from certain paths between 8 P.M. and lights out or during air raid alarm. The general feeling in the camp was bad. PRO, FO916/881, Bern to FO, no. 2313, 24 May 1944. Swiss inspectors who visited the camp two months later reported that enough beds had been supplied so that none of the prisoners had to sleep on the floor any longer. Relations between the British POWs and the Germans continued to be very strained, and the general feeling of insecurity felt by the POWs still prevailed. Nevertheless, the prisoners had no serious complaints against the new German camp staff; the new commander was strict but fair, and the prisoners knew "where they stand." PRO, FO916/840, report on Stalag Luft III, 17 July 1944. In a letter sent in June 1944 and published in *The Prisoners of War* in October 1944, an anonymous POW wrote, "I am out in the open from 7 a.m. until dusk, and it will please you to know that I am in perfect health. Food remains good and I am still putting on weight." He also reported that camp entertainment continued to be good: "To-night I have been to a seaside show, and it was not until I came out that I realised I was a P.O.W."

81 PRO, WO32/10757, report on the mental health of POWs by the senior British medical officer, Stalag Luft III, 17 February 1944. See also Lunden, "Captivity Psychoses among Prisoners of War," 721–33; Durand, *Stalag Luft III*, 178–79, 213–14.

82 PRO, WO32/10757, memorandum for the permanent undersecretary of state for war, 16 August 1944.

83 Quoted in Mason, *Prisoners of War*, 494, 526–28.

84 Vietor, *Time Out*, 56–60.

85 PRO, AIR40/2361, summary of mail from RAF prisoners of war (period covered: June 1944), 26 July 1944.

86 Ibid.

87 Ibid.

88 Ibid.

89 Ibid., report on morale of RAF prisoners of war in Germany, 24 March 1945.

90 Quoted in Carlson, *We Were Each Other's Prisoners*, 83.

91 PRO, ADM116/5353, Dean to the undersecretary of state, WO, 17 August 1944; PRO, FO916/1173, minute, 6 January 1945; PRO, AIR20/2361, report on morale of RAF prisoners of war in Germany, 24 March 1945.

92 See below, chap. 5.

93 Rolf, *Prisoners of the Reich*, 62, chap. 10; Mason, *Prisoners of War*, 494, 526–33. See also Sutker and Allain, "Psychological Assessment of Aviators Captured in World War II," 66–68; Sutker, Allain, and Johnson, "Long-Term Cognitive and Emotional Sequelae to World War II Prisoners-of-War Confinement," 3–10; Engdahl, Page, and Miller, "Age, Education, Maltreatment, and Social Support," 63–67; Polivy, Zeitlin, Herman, and Beal, "Food Restriction and Binge Eating," 409–11; Nichol and Rennell, *The Last Escape*, chap. 15.

94 Williams, *Arbeitskommando*, 7–8. See also Beaumont, "Rank, Privilege and Pris-

oners of War," 74–78. About the economic advantages of POWs, see Davis, "Prisoners of War in Twentieth-Century War Economies," 623–34.

95 Friedman, *The Law of War*, 1:500–501.

96 Wild, *Prisoner of Hope*, 103.

97 Ibid., 134.

98 NACP, RG 389, ROPMG, American POW Information Bureau, Records Branch, General Subject File, 1942–46, Camp Reports: Germany, Stalag (Enlisted Men), file Stalag VIII Teschen, reports on work camps of Stalag VIII B, 30 June 1943; See also Mason, *Prisoners of War*, 242–48; Vourkoutiotis, *Prisoners of War and the German High Command*, 109–33, 198–200.

99 NACP, RG 389, ROPMG, American POW Information Bureau, Records Branch, General Subject File, 1942–46, Camp Reports: Germany, Stalag (Enlisted Men), file Stalag VIII Teschen, reports on work camps of Stalag VIII B, 30 June 1943.

100 Ibid. See also Barber, *Prisoner of War*, chap. 3; *Trials of War Criminals before the Nuremberg Military Tribunals*, 603–25.

101 PRO, FO916/520, memorandum to the Swiss legation at Berlin, 20 July 1943. See also Rolf, *Prisoners of the Reich*, 63–67; Barker, *Behind Barbed Wire*, 99–100.

102 NACP, RG 389, ROPMG, American POW Information Bureau, Records Branch, General Subject File, 1942–46, Camp Reports: Germany, Stalag (Enlisted Men), file Stalag VIII B, Teschen, report on Stalag VIII B, 2 August 1943.

103 By December 1943, because of the overcrowding at Lamsdorf, the Germans formed two new base camps, Stalag VIII B at Teschen and Stalag VIII C, while the original camp at Lamsdorf was renamed Stalag 344. Mason, *Prisoners of War*, 198.

104 PRO, FO916/520, Bern to FO, no. 6043, 16 December 1943.

105 A. Scales, no. 83/48/1, Unpublished Memoirs, Department of Documents, Imperial War Museum, London; Elvet Williams, who was captured on Crete in May 1941, also mentions working during the terrible cold winter, when "the temperature never rose above twenty degrees of frost Centigrade." Williams, *Arbeitskommando*, 86.

106 PRO, FO916/844, British legation, Bern, to FO, 14 December 1943; PRO, FO916/520, Bern to FO, no. 6043, 16 December 1943; see also Mason, *Prisoners of War*, 374–76.

107 PRO, FO916/844, WO to the undersecretary of state, FO, 14 December 1943. The Army Council consisted of the secretary of state for war, the parliamentary undersecretary, the chief of the Imperial General Staff, the adjutant general, the quartermaster general, the vice chief of the Imperial General Staff, the deputy chief of the Imperial General Staff, the financial secretary, and the permanent undersecretary. Cantwell, *The Second World War*, 180–81.

108 PRO, FO916/520, memorandum to the Swiss government from the British government, 24 December 1943.

109 *Hansard, House of Commons*, vol. 399, col. 1911, 10 May 1944.

110 PRO, WO224/223, notice from Bern, 7 September 1944; PRO, FO916/844, DPW to PWD, no. 507, 8 September 1944; see also *Trials of War Criminals before the Nuernberg Military Tribunals*, vol. 13, pt. 11.

111 PRO, FO916/844, memorandum by the German FO, 30 September 1944.

112 Kershaw, *Hitler*, 707–8.

113 PRO, FO916/844, PWD to the British legation, Bern, 18 December 1944.

114 PRO, FO916/899, meetings with representatives of the Swiss government, 25 November 1944.

115 PRO, FO916/1159, memorandum, 6 April 1945.

116 PRO, WO193/345, circular letter 288/44 on reorganization of the control of prisoners of war by Martin Bormann, 30 September 1945; see also below, chap. 6.

117 What was at play here for the British was, of course, also the question of casualties among Commonwealth POWs as result of Allied air raids—between May and August 1944, eighty-five POWs had been killed and thirty-nine wounded in Germany alone, most of them in Stalags IV C (Wistritz bei Teplitz) and VIII B (Teschen). PRO, FO916/899, meetings with representatives of the Swiss government, 25 November 1944; on Allied air raids on POWs, see ibid., WO to A. J. Gardener, FO, 14 October 1944; see also ibid., Bern to FO, no. 4890, 23 October 1944, and PWD to the British legation, Bern, 15 November 1944, and M. M. Low to H. J. Phillimore, WO, 24 November 1944.

118 PRO, FO916/821, Bern to FO, no. 4860, 20 October 1944, and Bern to FO, no. 4940, 27 October 1944.

119 *Hansard, House of Commons*, vol. 406, cols. 2352–58, 17 November 1944; See also PRO, CO980/207, British Prisoners of War Relatives Association to Lieutenant Colonel J. C. Cole, CO, 4 October 1944.

120 This issue is extensively dealt with below; see chap. 5.

121 *Hansard, House of Commons*, vol. 406, cols. 2364, 17 November 1944. On dissatisfaction among the kin of prisoners of war regarding the government treatment of POWs' families, see Hately-Broad, "Prisoner of War Families," 206–9.

122 *Hansard, House of Commons*, vol. 406, cols. 2368–70, 17 November 1944; see also Phillimore, "The Second World War," 19–21.

123 *Hansard, House of Commons*, vol. 408, cols. 1391–94, 28 February 1945.

124 Ibid., emphasis added; PRO, WO163/588, statement by James Grigg on POWs in Germany, 28 February 1945; see also the *Times*, 1 March 1945; PRO, FO916/1180, FO to Bern, no. 436, 1 March 1945. On an interdepartmental meeting about possible solutions for getting help to British and American POWs in German hands, see PRO, CAB122/694, memorandum by the WO, COS (45) 126 (o), 23 February 1945.

125 PRO, FO916/1183, C. E. King to PWD, 30 May 1945.

126 PRO, CAB122/694, memorandum from the chairman, PWD, to Sir Ernest Burdon, 2 February 1945.

127 On the marches, see below, chap. 6.

128 PRO, FO916/1182, Wasmer to A. R. Armstrong, acting British consulate, Geneva, 12 March 1945, emphasis in original; see also *Hansard, House of Commons*, vol. 408, cols. 2391–93, 9 March 1945; PRO, FO916/1181, W. St. C. Roberts, FO, to Victor Mallet, Stockholm, 14 March 1945; Favez, *The Red Cross and the Holocaust*, 258–59.

129 PRO, FO916/1181, PWD, to the British embassy, Paris, 16 March 1945.

130 Vietor, *Time Out*, 128. On the failure to supply food to concentration camps, see Zweig, "Feeding the Camps," 825–51.

131 See below, pts. II, III, and IV.

CHAPTER THREE

1 Rosenman, *The Public Papers and Addresses of Franklin D. Roosevelt*, 532.

2 *Appendix to the Congressional Record*, 78th Cong., 2nd sess., vol. 90, pt. 2, A281, Hull to Congressman Emanuel Celler, 18 January 1944.

3 Speed, *Prisoners, Diplomats, and the Great War*, 8, 19–30, 43–59; Jackson, *The Prisoners*, 113.

4 According to War Department figures of November 1945, Germany held a total of 92,965 American POWs, of whom 32,730 belonged to the air force and 60,235 to the ground forces. Approximately 10 percent of the latter were officers, while almost 50 percent of the air force POWs were officers. NACP, RG 59, GRDS, 740.00114A EW/11-145, American Prisoners of War in Germany, prepared by Military Intelligence Service, War Department, 1 November 1945. Army figures give the number of 96,048; of these, 94,320 had been recovered alive, and 1,368 were listed as having died in captivity. By January 1946, 360 American men still remained unaccounted for. NACP, RG 160 (Army Service Forces), Office of the Commanding General Control Division, Administrative Management Branch, Historical File, 1941–46, the Army Service Forces in World War II, Colonel John D. Millett, 3 January 1945. In March 1945 SHAEF put the total number of American POWs held by the Germans at 76,854. NACP, RG 165, RWDGSS, OCOS, Security-Classified General Correspondence, 1942–47, file 383.6, sec. 3, cases 81–135, Strengths of POW Camps in Germany as Known to PWX-Division, SHAEF, at 15 March 1945. See also Foy, *For You the War Is Over*, 12–13; Hasselbring, "American Prisoners of War," 283, 285; Bird, *American POWs of World War II*, 141.

5 NACP, RG 389, ROPMG, American POW Information Bureau, Records Branch, General Subject File, 1942–46, Camp Reports: Germany, Stalag (Enlisted Men), file Stalag 8B Teschen, report on Stalag VIII B, 5 September 1942; see also NACP, RG 59, 740.00114 A EW 1939, report on Marlag, 22 November 1942; NACP, RG 389, ROPMG, American POW Information Bureau, Records Branch, General Subject File, 1942–46, Camp Reports: Germany, Ilag to Oflag (5A–13B), file Dulag Luft, Frankfort, report on Air Dulag, 15 November 1943; NACP, RG 389, ROPMG, American POW Information Bureau, Records Branch, General Subject File, 1942–46, Camp Reports: Germany, Stalag (Enlisted Men), Stalag IV B to Stalag VII A, file Stalag VIII C Sagan, George Tait, first secretary of the American legation, Bern, to Hull, no. 6751, 1 December 1943.

6 NACP, RG 389, ROPMG, American POW Information Bureau, Records Branch, General Subject File, 1942–46, Camp Reports: Germany, Stalag L. I to Stalag L. IV, file Stalag Luft III, report on Stalag Luft III, 9 December 1942.

7 Ibid.; Hermann Göring, who had himself been an air force pilot in World War I and now was the commander in chief of the Luftwaffe, was probably responsible for the better treatment given air force men. Durand, *Stalag Luft III*, 133–34.

8 Regarding captured British air force personnel, see, e.g., PRO, FO369/2562, the

American chargé d'affaires to the British secretary of state, no. 1892, 5 February 1940.

9 Prisoners were asked to provide the following information: (a) name, surname, service number, rank, trade and service; (b) date and place of birth; (c) profession; (d) religion; (e) whether married or single, number of children; (f) home address, address of next of kin; (g) pay during the war; (h) when, where, and by whom shot down; (i) where and by whom taken prisoner; (j) squadron, group, command, station, and station number; (k) letters and number of aircraft, type of aircraft; (l) state of health, whether wounded or not; (m) mames, surnames, numbers of crew, whether crew wounded, killed, or taken prisoner. PRO, WO208/3269, Camp History of Dulag Luft (Oberursel) Air Force Personnel, December 1939–June 1941.

10 Ibid.; see also Winograd, "Double Jeopardy," 10–12.

11 NACP, RG 59, GRDS, 740.00114A EW/11-145, American Prisoners of War in Germany, prepared by Military Intelligence Service, War Department, 1 November 1945; Durand, *Stalag Luft III*, chap. 3; Foy, *For You the War Is Over*, chap. 3; Hasselbring, "American Prisoners of War," chap. 2; Mason, *Prisoners of War*, 3–5, 23–29, 139–43; Rolf, *Prisoners of the Reich*, 21–25.

12 PRO, AIR40/281, German Interrogation Methods, 5 February 1945; Hasselbring, "American Prisoners of War," 73–80; Foy, *For You the War Is Over*, 56–58; Durand, *Stalag Luft III*, 62; Barker, *Behind Barbed Wire*, 61–64; Toliver, *The Interrogator*. About interrogation of Axis POWs, see Fedorowich, "Axis Prisoners of War," 156–78; Moore and Fedorowich, *The British Empire*, 92–106.

13 NACP, RG 59, GRDS, 740.00114A EW/11-145, American Prisoners of War in Germany, prepared by Military Intelligence Service, War Department, 1 November 1945.

14 Ibid.

15 PRO, WO224/223, report of the numbers of British and American POWs and internees at POW and internee camps, June 1943.

16 NACP, RG 389, ROPMG, American POW Information Bureau, Records Branch, General Subject File, 1942–46, Camp Reports: Germany, Stalag III B to Stalag IV B, file Stalag III B (Fürstenburg), report on Stalag III B, 22 May 1943.

17 Weekly quantities were as follows: bread, 2,250 grams; margarine, 225 grams; meat, 286 grams; marmalade, 175 grams; potatoes, 5,250 grams; cheese, 50 grams; vegetables, 2,400 grams; sugar, 175 grams; salt, 240 grams.

18 Friedman, *The Law of War*, vol. 1, chap. 7, art. 23, 499, and chap. 5, art. 34, 501–2.

19 NACP, RG 389, ROPMG, American POW Information Bureau, Records Branch, General Subject File, 1942–46, Camp Reports: Germany, Stalag III B to Stalag IV B, file Stalag III B (Fürstenburg), report on Stalag III B, 22 May 1943.

20 Ibid., American Interest–Germany report no. 2 on prisoners of war camp at Stalag III B and associated work camp and hospital, 28 September 1943; see also ibid., report on Stalag III B, 12 May 1943.

21 Ibid., Work Camp Trattendorf, USA No. 1, 29 September 1943; see also ibid., Labor Detachment No. 1, 20 July 1944, and Work Detachment under the Jurisdiction of Stalag III B, 18 November 1944.

22 NACP, RG 389, ROPMG, American POW Information Bureau, Records Branch, General Subject File, 1942–46, Camp Reports: Germany, Stalag I A to Stalag III B, file Stalag III B (Fürstenberg), report on Stalag III B (American Camp), 29 February 1944.

23 Ibid.; see also NACP, RG 59, GRDS, 740.00114A EW/11-145, American Prisoners of War in Germany, prepared by Military Intelligence Service, War Department, 1 November 1945. On relations between POWs and camp authorities and the question of discipline, see Durand, *Stalag Luft III*, 192–203; Foy, *For You the War Is Over*, 120–25.

24 NACP, RG 389, ROPMG, American POW Information Bureau, Records Branch, General Subject File, 1942–46, Camp Reports: Germany, Stalag (Enlisted Men), Stalag I A to III B, file Stalag III B (Fürstenburg), Work Camp Trattendorf, USA No. 1, 18 May 1944.

25 Ibid., report on Stalag III B (Fürstenburg), 20 May 1944.

26 Ibid., report on Stalag III B (Fürstenburg), 29 July 1944. About the bartering system, see Foy, *For You the War Is Over*, 103–6.

27 NACP, RG 389, ROPMG, American POW Information Bureau, Records Branch, General Subject File, 1942–46, Camp Reports: Germany, Stalag (Enlisted Men), Stalag I A to III B, file Stalag III B (Fürstenburg), Labor Detachment No. 1, 20 July 1944.

28 Ibid., Decimal File, 1942–45, 387.7 to 704, file 250.1, American P/W, Sergeant Harry J. Curry, spokesman, to the Swiss legation, Berlin, 3 September 1944.

29 Ibid.

30 Quoted in Carlson, *We Were Each Other's Prisoners*, 92.

31 Ibid.

32 NACP, RG 389, ROPMG, American POW Information Bureau, Records Branch, Decimal File, 1942–45, 387.7 to 704, file 250.1, American P/W, Sergeant Harry J. Curry, spokesman, to the Swiss legation, Berlin, 4 September 1944.

33 Ibid., Stettinius to Bern, no. 55, 4 January 1945.

34 Satow and Sée, *The Work of the Prisoners of War Department*, 71–72.

35 NACP, RG 389, ROPMG, American POW Information Bureau, Records Branch, General Subject File, 1942–46, Camp Reports: Germany, Stalag (Enlisted Men), Stalag I A to III B, file Stalag II B, Hammerstein, report on Stalag II B (American Camp), 1 March 1944.

36 Ibid.

37 Ibid.

38 In Stalag Luft III (Sagan), for example, prisoners could even receive academic credit for courses. Durand, *Stalag Luft III*, 224–27; see also Foy, *For You the War Is Over*, chap. 7. On entertainment in Stalag II B, see also a report by Christian Christiansen, a Danish representative who visited the camp in April 1944 and reported to War Prisoners Aid of the YMCA. *Prisoners of War Bulletin* 2 (November 1944); Shavit, "'The Great Morale Factor,'" 113–34.

39 NACP, RG 389, ROPMG, American POW Information Bureau, Records Branch, General Subject File, 1942–46, Camp Reports: Germany, Stalag (Enlisted Men), Stalag I A to III B, file Stalag II B, Hammerstein, report on Stalag II B (American

Camp), 1 March 1944; see also a letter sent by one of the American POWs who worked in a farm in Germany and published in *Prisoners of War Bulletin* 2 (November 1944). For a more critical report on conditions at labor detachments that were dependent on Stalag II B, see NACP, RG 389, ROPMG, American POW Information Bureau, Records Branch, General Subject File, 1942–46, Camp Reports: Germany, Stalag (Enlisted Men), Stalag I A to III B, file Stalag II B, Hammerstein, Harrison to Hull, no. 3140, 17 May 1944.

40 See below, chap. 4.

41 NACP, RG 59, GRDS, Records of the Special War Problems Division Policy Books, 1939–45 (Lot File No. 58D8), file Stalag VIIA May–December 1944, information concerning conditions at Stalag II B, obtained in interviews with American prisoners of war from that camp who were repatriated on the *Gripsholm* in May 1944, 15 June 1944.

42 Ibid.

43 Ibid.; see also Spiller, *Prisoners of Nazis*, 38; Vourkoutiotis, *Prisoners of War and the German High Command*, 101–5.

44 See, e.g., Cowdrey, "Die medizinische Versorgung von amerikanischen Kriegsgefangenen im Zweiten Weltkrieg," 165–73; Stelzl, "Im Gewahrsam des 'Dritten Reiches,'" 147–52.

45 NACP, RG 389, ROPMG, American POW Information Bureau, Records Branch, General Subject File, 1942–46, Camp Reports: Germany, Stalag XIII B to Stalag 398, file Stalag XVII B Gneixendorf, Hull to Bern, no. 1522, 2 May 1944. Stelzl, "Im Gewahrsam des 'Dritten Reiches,'" 133–52. See also NACP, RG 389, ROPMG, American POW Information Bureau, Records Branch, General Subject File, 1942–46, Camp Reports: Germany, Stalag (Enlisted Men), Stalag I A to III B, file Stalag II B, Hammerstein, Report on Stalag II B, 23 August 1944. In a critical report on Stalag II B written after the war, the War Department's Military Intelligence Service was to conclude: "Treatment was worse at Stalag 2B than at any other camp in Germany established for American PW before the Battle of the Bulge. Harshness at the base Stalag degenerated into brutality and outright murder of some at the Arbeitskommandos. Beatings of Americans by their German overseers were too numerous to list, but records show that 10 Americans in work detachments were shot to death by captors." NACP, RG 59, GRDS, 740.00114A EW/11-145, American Prisoners of War in Germany, prepared by Military Intelligence Service, War Department, 1 November 1945. For reports on conditions at Stalag XVII B (Gneixendorf, Austria), see NACP, RG 389, ROPMG, American POW Information Bureau, Records Branch, General Subject File, 1942–46, Camp Reports: Germany, Stalag XIII B to Stalag 398, file Stalag XVII B Gneixendorf, reports on XVII B, Gneixendorf, 7 December 1943, 15 March 1944, 31 May 1944, 24 October 1944, 14 December 1944, and 19 January 1945.

46 See, e.g., *Congressional Record*, House, 79th Cong., 1st sess., vol. 91, 4 February 1945, 980–81; *Appendix to Congressional Record*, 79th Cong., 1st sess., vol. 91, pt. 10, A882, 26 February 1945, and vol. 91, pt. 10, A1021–24, 5 March 1945, and vol. 91, pt. 11, A1707, 12 April 1945. On German POWs held in the United States, see NACP, RG 107, Office of the Secretary of War, Office of the Undersecretary of

War, Administrative Office, Decimal File, March 1943–November 1945, file 383.6 (POWs), 16 March 1943 to 31 December 1944, Report No. 1992, Committee on Military Affairs, House of Representatives, 78th Cong., 2nd sess. (Pursuant to H. Res. 30); Lewis and Mewha, *History of Prisoner of War Utilization*, chaps. 9–11; Krammer, "American Treatment of German Generals," 27–46; Krammer, *Nazi Prisoners of War in America*; Robin, *The Barbed-Wire College*; Bischof, "Einige Thesen zu einer Mentalitätsgeschichte deutscher Kriegsgefangenschaft in amerikanischem Gewahrsam," 175–212.

47 NACP, RG 389, ROPMG, American POW Information Bureau, Records Branch, General Subject File, 1942–46, Camp Reports: Germany, Stalag (Enlisted Men), Stalag I A to III B, file Stalag II B, Hammerstein, Hull to Bern, no. 1836, 27 May 1944.

48 See, e.g., *Appendix to the Congressional Record*, 78th Cong., 2nd sess., vol. 90, pt. 9, A2167, Hull to Arthur Klein, 4 May 1944, and A281, Hull to Emanuel Celler, 18 January 1944.

49 NACP, RG 107, Office of the Secretary of War, Administrative Office, file 383.6, American, B. M. Bryan, brigadier general, assistant provost marshal general, to Vincent A. Carroll, 6 December 1944.

50 In contrast, during World War I, Washington threatened the Germans with retaliation and so forced them to respond favorably to improve conditions. Speed, *Prisoners, Diplomats, and the Great War*, 45–47.

51 The daily food ration issue per man amounted to 346 grams of bread, 21 grams of margarine, 14 grams of sausage, 9 grams of cheese, 25 grams of jam, 85 grams of cabbage, 28 grams of barley, 20 grams of meat, 10 grams of fat, 25 grams of sugar, 170 grams of swedes (turnips), 400 grams of potatoes.

52 NACP, RG 389, ROPMG, American POW Information Bureau, Records Branch, General Subject File, 1942–46, Camp Reports: Germany, Stalag L. I to Stalag L. IV, file Stalag Luft I, Barth and Lazarett, report on Kriegsgefangenenlager No. 1 der Luftwaffe, Barth (Pommern), 4 May 1944; see also Vourkoutiotis, *Prisoners of War and the German High Command*, 55–58.

53 Vietor, *Time Out*, 117–20; see also the memoirs of Second Lieutenant Carl W. Remy, in Spiller, *Prisoners of Nazis*, 114–16; McKibbin, *Barbed Wire*, 31–41.

54 Vietor, *Time Out*, 142–44; see also Durand, *Stalag Luft III*, 237–40; Foy, *For You the War Is Over*, 84–86. Mail was a sensitive issue in all camps. The average time of delivery of a letter from Stalag Luft I camp was twelve to thirteen weeks from England, nineteen weeks from the United States, Canada, and New Zealand, and twenty-four weeks from Australia. All incoming mail was censored by the central office for air force personnel at Sagan, thus causing an additional delay of about three weeks. As a result, several prisoners who had been in captivity for more than half a year had still not received word from their families. The censoring of outgoing mail also caused great delays; in some cases, no letter had been received by relatives in five months. NACP, RG 389, ROPMG, American POW Information Bureau, Records Branch, General Subject File, 1942–46, Camp Reports: Germany, Stalag L. I to Stalag L. IV, file Stalag Luft I, Barth and Lazarett, report on Kriegsgefangenenlager No.1 der Luftwaffe, Barth (Pommern), 4 May 1944.

55 See below, chap. 6. On escapes from Stalag Luft I, see Crawley, *Escape from Germany*, chap. 14.

56 NACP, RG 389, ROPMG, American POW Information Bureau, Records Branch, General Subject File, 1942–46, Camp Reports: Germany, Stalag L. I to Stalag L. IV, file Stalag Luft I, Barth and Lazarett, report on Kriegsgefangenenlager No.1 der Luftwaffe, Barth (Pommern), 4 May 1944; see also *The Prisoners of War*, May 1944.

57 PRO, FO916/1148, report on Stalag Luft I, 14 December 1944.

58 Vietor, *Time Out*, chap. 7; On the relations between the POWs and camp authorities at Stalag Luft III, see Durand, *Stalag Luft III*, 195–203.

59 NACP, RG 59, GRDS, 740.00114EW/4-3045, U.S. Congress, House, *Report of Proceedings, Hearing held before Special Committee of the Committee on Military Affairs, Treatment of Prisoners of War*, 535–36, 541–42, 549–50; Hasselbring, "American Prisoners of War," 114–17; Durand, *Stalag Luft III*, 161–64.

60 Henry L. Stimson Diaries, Yale University Library, New Haven, Connecticut, reel 9, 8 January 1945, 25.

61 PRO, PREM3/364/11, report by vice chiefs of staff, W.P. (44) 512, 9 September 1944.

62 NACP, RG 59, GRDS, 740.00114 EW/9-3044, Hull to the American embassy, London, no. 7970, 30 September 1944.

63 U.S. Congresss, House, *Hearing Held before Special Committee of the Committee on Military Affairs, Treatment of Prisoners of War*, 551.

64 NACP, RG 331, AOOH, SSAGD, Executive Section, Decimal File, 1944, 383.6 to 383.6-19, file 383.6-9#2, Strengths of Prisoner of War Camps in Germany as Known to PWX-SHAEF at 1 December 1944.

65 NACP, RG 389, ROPMG, American POW Information Bureau, Records Branch, Decimal File, 1942–45, 387.7 to 704, file 250.1, American P/W, Stettinius to Bern, no. 93, 5 January 1945.

66 Ibid., Stettinius to Bern, no. 76, 5 January 1945.

67 Vietor, *Time Out*, 126–28; see also Foy, *For You the War Is Over*, 73–76.

68 Quoted in Carlson, *We Were Each Other's Prisoners*, 78.

69 NACP, RG 407, Army-AG, Classified Decimal File, 1943–45, file 383.6 (13 January 1945), Drake to McCloy, 10 January 1945. On the complicated relations between Switzerland and the Anglo-Saxon powers, see Wylie, "Switzerland," 331–54; Wylie, "Pilet-Golaz," 166–67; Wylie, "'Keeping the Swiss Sweet,'" 442–67; Herren, "'Neither This Way nor Any Other,'" 175–88; Kochavi, *Prelude to Nuremberg*, 181–85; Hull, *The Memoirs of Cordell Hull*, 2:1349–51. About American POWs in Switzerland, see Prince, *Shot from the Sky*.

70 See also NACP, RG 107, Office of the Secretary of War, Assistant Secretary of War, Formerly Security-Classified Correspondence of John J. McCloy, 1941–45, file ASW 383.6, American POWs, Joseph C. Grew, acting secretary of state, to Stimson, 27 January 1945; Stimson Diaries, reel 9, 8 January 1945, 24–26.

71 NACP, RG 389, Provost Marshal General, American POW Information Bureau, Records Branch, Decimal File, 1942–45, file 383.6, American P/W #5, Vincent A. Carroll, judge, to Stimson, 30 November 1944; NACP, RG 107, Office of the Secre-

tary of War, Administrative Office, file 383.6, American, B. M. Bryan, brigadier general, assistant provost marshal general to Carroll, 6 December 1944.

72 NACP, RG 59, GRDS, 740.00114 A E.W./1-1045, memorandum for the secretary of state, 15 January 1945.

73 Ibid. See also Vourkoutiotis, *Prisoners of War and the German High Command*, chap. 6; Hasselbring, "American Prisoners of War," 117–22; Favez, *The Red Cross and the Holocaust*, 274.

74 Stimson Diaries, reel 9, 16 January 1945, 48.

75 NACP, RG 107, Office of the Secretary of War, Assistant Secretary of War, Formerly-Security Classified Correspondence of John J. McCloy, 1941–45, file ASW 383.6, American POWs, memorandum for Stimson, 22 February 1945. Countering prisoners' criticism of the protecting power for failing to improve conditions at Stalag Luft I, Swiss inspector Braun maintained that the efforts the protecting power was making "cannot always be judged by the results of the undertakings." NACP, RG 389, ROPMG, American POW Information Bureau, Records Branch, General Subject File, 1942–46, Camp Reports: Germany, Stalag L. I to Stalag L. IV, file Stalag Luft I, Barth and Lazarett, report on Kriegsgefangenenlager No.1 der Luftwaffe, Barth (Pommern), 4 May 1944.

76 NACP, RG 389, ROPMG, American POW Information Bureau, Records Branch, General Subject File, 1942–46, Camp Reports: Germany, Stalag L. I to Stalag L. IV, file Stalag Luft I, Barth and Lazarett, report on Kriegsgefangenenlager No.1 der Luftwaffe, Barth (Pommern), 4 May 1944, memorandum for the assistant secretary of war, 25 February 1945.

77 Quoted in Carlson, *We Were Each Other's Prisoners*, 111; for a different viewpoint, see, e.g., Vietor, *Time Out*, and Kalway's memoirs quoted in Carlson, *We Were Each Other's Prisoners* .

78 NACP, RG 107, Office of the Secretary of War, Administrative Assistant, file 383.6, American POWs, Stimson to Vinson, 14 March 1945.

79 According to SHAEF statistics, on 1 December 1944 there were 839 American POWs in Oflag 64. See NACP, RG 331, AOOH, SSAGD, Executive Section, Decimal File, 1944, 383.6 to 383.6-19, file 383.6-9#2, Strengths of Prisoner of War Camps in Germany as Known to PWX-SHAEF at 1 December 1944.

80 NACP, RG 107, Office of the Secretary of War, Administrative Assistant, file 383.6, American POWs, Stimson to Vinson, 14 March 1945. On conditions in Oflag 64, see also NACP, RG 59, GRDS, 740.00114A EW/11-145, American Prisoners of War in Germany, prepared by Military Intelligence Service, War Department, 1 November 1945.

81 Satow and M. J. Sée, *The Work of the Prisoners of War Department*, 72–73, 77.

82 NACP, RG 59, GRDS, 740.00114EW/11-1144, Gilbert Redfern, editor, *Prisoners of War Bulletin*, to Eldred D. Kuppinger, assistant chief, Special Division, Department of State, 11 November 1944; ibid., 740.00114EW/12-844, Redfern to Kuppinger, 8 December 1944.

83 *Prisoners of War Bulletin* 2 (November 1944): 9.

84 Ibid., 10.

85 Stimson Diaries, reel 9, 19 April 1945, 55.

86 See below, chap. 7.

87 PRO, FO916/1179, Halifax to FO, no. 1273, 24 February 1945.

88 U.S. Congress, House, *Hearing Held before Special Committee of the Committee on Military Affairs, Treatment of Prisoners of War*, 543–44.

89 Ibid., 550.

90 Carlson, *We Were Each Other's Prisoners*, xvii–xviii. See also below, chap. 7.

91 NACP, RG 389, ROPMG, American POW Information Bureau, Records Branch, General Subject File, 1942–46, Camp Reports: Germany, Stalag IV B to Stalag VII A, file Stalag VII A, Moosburg, report on Stalag VII A, 27 January 1945.

92 Ibid., report on Stalag VII A, 14 February 1945. For reports on conditions in different camps, see NACP, RG 389, ROPMG, American POW Information Bureau, Records Branch, Decimal File, 1942–46, Camp Reports: Germany, Stalag (Enlisted Men), Stalag IV B to Stalag VII A, file Stalag II, Neubrandenburg, report on visit to Stalag II, Neubrandenburg, between 19 and 23 February 1945, and Camp Reports: Germany, Stalag L. I to Stalag L. IV, file Stalag Luft III, Sagan, report on Stalag Luft III now at Nuremberg-Angwasser, 13 March 1945; NACP, RG 389, ROPMG, American POW Information Bureau, Records Branch, General Subject File, 1942–46, Camp Reports: Germany, Stalag VIII A to XIII B, file Stalag IX B, Bad Orb, report on Stalag IX B, Bad Orb, 24 January 1945, and Camp Reports: Dulag Luft to Ilag, report on Stalag IX B—Bad Orb, 23 March 1945, and Camp Reports: Germany, Stalag IV B to Stalag VII A, file Stalag IV B Muhlberg, report on Stalag IV B Muhlberg, 8 February 1945.

93 PRO, FO916/1148, report on Stalag Luft I, 22 February 1945.

94 Stalag III A held 418 U.S. officers and 43 U.S. orderlies who had been evacuated from Oflag 64 (Alt-Burgund) as well as 1,220 British officers and 137 British orderlies from Luft III (Sagan). Compound 1 housed 3,900 U.S. NCOs who had been brought in from Stalag III B (Fürstenberg); Compound 2, 1,516 British NCOs from Luft VII (Bankau) and 30 British NCOs from Stalag 344 (Lamsdorf). See also PRO, TS26/349, Special Report on Conditions during the Forced March of American and British POWs from their Former Camps to Stalag Luft III A, Luckenwalde, 8 March 1945.

95 NACP, RG 389, ROPMG, American POW Information Bureau, Records Branch, Decimal File, 1942–46, Camp Reports: Germany, Stalag (Enlisted Men), Stalag I A to III B, file Stalag III A, Luckenwalde, report on Stalag III A, Luckenwalde, 16 February 1945.

96 Quoted in Carlson, *We Were Each Other's Prisoners*, 94.

97 Weekly rations per man supplied by the Germans were as follows: bread, 1,400 grams; artificial margarine, 218 grams; honey, 175 grams; cheese, 62.5 grams; sugar, 175 grams; fresh meat, 200 grams; oatmeal or soup powder, 350 grams; potatoes, 2.8 grams; dried turnips, 2,400 grams; vegetables, 30 grams; and salt, 140 grams.

98 NACP, RG 389, ROPMG, American POW Information Bureau, Records Branch, Decimal File, 1942–46, Camp Reports: Germany, Stalag (Enlisted Men), Stalag I A to III B, file Stalag III A, Luckenwalde, report on Stalag III A, Luckenwalde,

16 February 1945; see also NACP, RG 165, RWDGSS, OCOS, Security-Classified
General Correspondence, 1942–47, file 383.6, sec. 3, cases 81–135, Strengths of
POW Camps in Germany as Known to PWX-Division, SHAEF, at 15 March 1945.

99 Quoted in Carlson, *We Were Each Other's Prisoners*, 94.

100 Ibid., 11. See also Ambrose, *Citizen Soldiers*, 357–61.

101 *Congressional Record*, House, 78th Cong., 2nd sess., vol. 90, pt. 2, 29 February
1944, 2125, and pt. 6, 7771–72, 14 September 1944, and 8039, 20 September 1944,
and vol. 91, pt. 1, 553, 29 January 1945; *Congressional Record*, Senate, 78th
Cong., 2nd sess., vol. 90, pt. 5, 14 August 1944, 6929.

102 NACP, RG 107, Office of the Secretary of War, Administrative Assistance, file
383.6, American, Stimson to May, 4 January 1944, Stimson to Thomas E. Martin,
House of Representatives, 17 March 1944, and Stimson to Hull, 19 January 1944.

103 Carlson, *We Were Each Other's Prisoners*, xvi n. 5. Carlson adds: "Finally, in 1985,
Congress created the Prisoner of War Medal and subsequently many states have
issued free license plates with 'POW' inscribed on them." Nichol and Rennell,
The Last Escape, 396–97.

CHAPTER FOUR

1 PRO, AIR2/4667, N. B. Ronald, FO, to the undersecretary of state, WO, 1
November 1939. The Geneva Convention (art. 68) stated: "Belligerents are
bound to send back to their own country, regardless of rank or number, seriously sick and seriously injured prisoners of war, after having brought them to
a condition where they can be transported. Agreements between belligerents
shall accordingly settle as soon as possible the cases of invalidity or of sickness,
entailing direct repatriation, as well as the cases entailing possible hospitalization in a neutral country." Friedman, *The Law of War*, 1:509.

The medical categories and disabilities that justified repatriation were as
follows: (a) shell splinters in the brain or lungs even if there was no local or
general reaction at the time of examination; (b) all cases of nonactively produc-
tive tuberculosis of the lungs; (c) chronic neuritis lasting more than one year
and not responding to treatment; (d) blindness of one eye even if vision in the
other is normal; (e) all cases of diminution of visual acuteness in which it was
impossible to restore vision to an acuteness of one-third in at least one eye; (f)
all cases of psychasthenia, especially barbed-wire psychosis; (g) anyone who
had undergone gastric operations; (h) chronic gastritis, having lasted for more
than one year of captivity; (i) nephrectomy for tuberculosis of the kidney even if
urine showed nothing abnormal at the time of the examination; (j) all cases of
chronic nephritis when only some traces of albumen could be demonstrated but
the disease had existed for more than a year; (k) all cases of amoeba and
bacillus dysentery that had lasted for more than a year and was not responding
to treatment; (l) all cases of vegetative neurosis that could not stand further
captivity; (m) shortening of a leg by more than five centimeters; (n) exudative
pleurisy that had begun during captivity; (o) chronic bronchitis when failure of
all treatment could be proved and the disease had lasted for one year in cap-

tivity; (p) cases in which the paralysis of only one nerve was such as to considerably incapacitate the prisoner. PRO, FO916/826, Bern to FO, no. 2377, 26 May 1944; ibid., Hugo Rast to the undersecretary of state, WO, 4 June 1944.

2 PRO, AIR2/4667, the American chargé d'affaires in London to the British FO, 23 December 1939. The establishment of mixed medical commissions was set down in Article 69 of the Geneva Convention: "Upon the outbreak of hostilities, belligerents shall come to an agreement to name mixed medical commissions. These commissions shall be composed of three members, two of them belonging to a neutral country and one appointed by the detaining power; one of the physicians of the neutral country shall preside. These mixed medical commissions shall proceed to the examination of sick or wounded prisoners and shall make all due decisions regarding them. Decisions of these communications shall be by majority and carried with the least possible delay." Friedman, *The Law of War*, 1:510; Satow and Sée, *The Work of the Prisoners of War Department*, 59–61.

3 PRO, AIR2/4667, FO to the secretary of the Admiralty, 9 August 1940.

4 Speed, *Prisoners, Diplomats, and the Great War*, 33–34.

5 PRO, AIR2/4667, George R. Warner to the secretary of the Admiralty, 9 August 1940, and Ronald to Herschel V. Johnson, 5 January 1940.

6 Ibid., note of a meeting on "Exchange and Release on Parole of Internees and Prisoners of War," 22 March 1940, and the secretary of the Admiralty to the undersecretary of state, AIR, 15 October 1940.

7 Ibid., FO to the secretary of the Admiralty, 19 October 1940.

8 Ibid., FO to Geneva, no. 159, 4 November 1940.

9 *Hansard, House of Commons*, vol. 368, col. 76, 21 January 1941.

10 PRO, AIR2/4667, Translation, Berlin, 31 January 1941.

11 *Hansard, House of Commons*, vol. 365, col. 1213, 5 November 1940. See also James, *The Battle of Britain*; Foreman, *Battle of Britain*.

12 PRO, AIR2/4667, FO to the U.S. chargé d'affaires, 26 February 1941.

13 On POWs in Canada, see above, chap. 2.

14 PRO, FO916/47, W. Roberts to Major General Alan Hunter, 18 April 1941; Roberts to T. Achilles, American embassy in London, 24 May 1941; and the American chargé d'affaires to FO, 10 June 1941; PRO, FO916/112, Churchill to Mr. Kelly (Bern), 7 April 1941.

15 PRO, FO916/47, Roberts to Victor A. L. Mallet, 24 May 1941.

16 Ibid., minute by Roberts, 16 June 1941.

17 Ibid., the American chargé d'affaires to the British foreign secretary, 10 June 1941.

18 On Irish policy during the war, see Canning, *British Policy towards Ireland*, 3–238; Dwyer, *De Valera*, chaps. 19–22; Kochavi, "Britain, the United States and Irish Neutrality," 93–115; O'Halpin, "Irish Neutrality in the Second World War," 283–303.

19 PRO, FO916/47, minute by Roberts, 16 June 1941, and Dominions Office to the undersecretary of state, 24 July 1941; on the Royal Air Force stand, see PRO, AIR2/4667, minute, 16 July 1941.

20 PRO, AIR2/4667, British FO to the Swiss legation, 10 July 1941.

21 PRO, FO916/47, aide-mémoire by the British legation in Stockholm, 4 July 1941; FO to Stockholm, no. 424, 28 June 1941; Roberts to Mallet, the British minister in Stockholm, 16 July 1941; and W. H. Montagu-Pollock, the British chargé d'affaires in Stockholm, to Per Albin Hansson, acting minister for Swedish Foreign Affairs, 29 July 1941. On Sweden's policy during the war, see Carlgren, *Swedish Foreign Policy during the Second World War*; Kochavi, "Britain's Attitude towards the Swedish Position on War Criminals," 291–306.

22 PRO, FO916/48, Stockholm to FO, no. 502, 7 August 1941, and Roberts to Colonel N. Coates, WO, 25 August 1941.

23 PRO, FO916/48, note by the secretary, War Cabinet, Joint Intelligence Committee, JIC (41) 354, 5 September 1941.

24 Ibid., and the American ambassador to the British foreign secretary, no. 3375, 9 September 1941; PRO, AIR2/4667, extract from note from the Swiss legation to FO, 1 September 1941; PRO, FO916/48, FO to His Majesty's representatives at Madrid, Stockholm, and Bern, 6 September 1941.

25 PRO, FO916/48, FO to His Majesty's representatives at Madrid, Stockholm, and Bern, 6 September 1941, and the American ambassador to the British foreign secretary, nos. 3599, 3600, 25 September 1941.

26 PRO, FO916/48, the American ambassador to the British foreign secretary, nos. 3599, 3600, 25 September 1941, and American embassy to the foreign secretary, 22 September 1941.

27 PRO, AIR2/4667, the American ambassador to the British foreign secretary, 26 September 1941.

28 PRO, FO916/48, the British foreign secretary to the American ambassador, 27, 29 September 1941.

29 Ibid.

30 Ibid., the American ambassador to the foreign secretary, no. 3780, 3 October 1941.

31 PRO, FO916/49, minutes, 2 October 1941, and the British foreign secretary to the American ambassador, no. 2/33A, 4 October 1941.

32 PRO, FO916/48, Robert Coe, American embassy, to Roberts, FO, 4 October 1941, and the American ambassador to the British foreign secretary, 6 October 1941.

33 Ibid., broadcast from Berlin and Bremen, 6 October 1941.

34 Ibid., the American ambassador to the British foreign secretary, 6 October 1941.

35 *Hansard, House of Commons*, vol. 374, cols. 849–51, 7 October 1941.

36 PRO, FO916/48, the American ambassador to the British foreign secretary, no. 3887, 8 October 1941; see also a statement issued by the official German news agency, the *Times*, 8 October 1941.

37 Phillimore, "The Second World War," 113; Satow and Sée, *The Work of the Prisoners of War Department*, 50–51.

38 PRO, FO916/48, Herschel V. Johnson, counselor at American embassy, London, to Eden, 9 October 1941.

39 Ibid., minutes by Roberts, 10 October 1941.

40 Ibid., minute, 10 October 1941; Eden to the American ambassador, 14 October

1941; and Dominions Office to the governments of Canada, Australia, New Zealand, and Union of South Africa, no. 633, 20 October 1941. For Margesson, *Hansard, House of Commons*, vol. 374, cols. 1225–26, 14 October 1941.

41 PRO, FO916/48, Bern to FO, no. 2253, 11 October 1941; minute by Roberts, 13 October 1941; and FO to Bern, no. 1439, 14 October 1941; Phillimore, "The Second World War," 111–13.

42 PRO, AIR2/4668, Harold Shantz, first secretary of the American embassy in Britain, to Eden, 24 November 1941.

43 Clark, *Barbarossa*, chaps. 8–9; Overy, *Russia's War*, chap. 4; Bartov, *Hitler's Army*, 29–44.

44 PRO, FO916/48, minute by Roberts, 25 November 1941.

45 PRO, AIR2/4668, FO to Bern, no. 58, 8 January 1942.

46 Ibid., FO to Bern, no. 299, 6 February 1942.

47 PRO, FO916/399, FO to Bern, no. 6, 1 January 1942; Bern to FO, no. 56, 8 January 1942; FO to Bern, no. 282, 4 February 1942; FO to Bern, no. 439, 18 February 1942; FO to Bern, no. 624, 9 March 1942; and Bern to FO, no. 997, 23 March 1942; PRO, FO916/400, FO to Minister of State's Office, Cairo, no. 570, 1 April 1942, and minute, Roberts, 8 April 1942. About the exchange of Italian POWs, see Phillimore, "The Second World War," 114–15; Fedorowich, "Propaganda and Political Warfare," 119–20; Sponza, "Italian Prisoners of War in Great Britain," 205–26; Moore and Fedorowich, *The British Empire*, 205–6.

48 PRO, WO163/591, Bern to FO, nos. 2104, 2105, 15 June 1942.

49 About the Repatriation Committee, see Satow and Sée, *The Work of the Prisoners of War Department*, 47–48; Phillimore, "The Second World War," 24–26; Mason, *Prisoners of War*, 261–62.

50 PRO, FO916/262, minutes by Roberts, 23, 27 June 1942, and by P. Dean, 25 June 1942.

51 PRO, FO916/530, memorandum, "Repatriation Negotiations with the German Government," 15 April 1943; PRO, FO916/262, note for the secretary of state on the negotiations for the repatriation of sick and wounded and civilians from Germany, 14 July 1942, and minute by Roberts, 14 August 1942.

52 PRO, WO193/346, Bern to FO, no. 2912, 14 August 1942; PRO, FO916/530, memorandum by the secretary of state for foreign affairs, W.P. (43) 166, 16 April 1943.

53 See above, chap. 2.

54 Altogether 9,114 Italians and 1,916 British Commonwealth prisoners were exchanged. Phillimore, "The Second World War," 114; Satow and Sée, *The Work of the Prisoners of War Department*, 51–54; Moore and Fedorowich, *The British Empire*, 206; Fedorowich and Moore, "Co-Belligerency and Prisoners of War," 74.

55 PRO, FO916/530, Bern to Eden, no. 1506, 29 March 1943; PRO, AIR2/4669, Bern to FO, no. 1547, 31 March 1943; PRO, WO32/10742, DPW, Repatriation Committee No. 1, 20 April 1943.

56 Clark, *Barbarossa*, chap. 13; Overy, *Russia's War*, chap. 6; Bartov. *Hitler's Army*, 44–51.

57 PRO, FO916/530, memorandum by the secretary of state for foreign affairs, W.P. (43) 166, 16 April 1943. See also Moore and Fedorowich, *The British Empire*, 18–19.

58 PRO, FO916/530, memorandum by the secretary of state for foreign affairs, W.P. (43) 166, 16 April 1943.

59 PRO, CAB65/34, conclusions of fifty-sixth War Cabinet meeting, 19 April 1943; *Hansard, House of Commons*, vol. 387, cols. 1336–37, 17 March 1943.

60 Parker, *Struggle for Survival*, 181; Jackson, *The North African Campaign*. On British and Americans casualties, see Ellis, *World War II*, 255.

61 NACP, RG 165, Records of the War Department, sec. 3, cases 81–116, file 383.6, Legation of Switzerland to the State Department, 17 May 1943; *FRUS*, 1943, 1:50, the Swiss chargé to the secretary of state, 27 May 1943.

62 NACP, RG 165, RWDGSS, ODPO, Top Secret "American-British-Canadian," ABC 383.6 (16 June 1943), memorandum of the Swiss legation, Washington, D.C., 18 May 1943.

63 PRO, WO193/346, FO to Washington, no. 3436, 22 May 1943; PRO, CAB122/233, British embassy, Washington, D.C., to the secretary of state, no. 371, 31 May 1943; PRO, FO916/531, minute by Roberts, 19 May 1943, and minutes of an informal meeting of the DPW, 20 May 1943.

64 PRO, FO916/532, Eden to Winant, 6 June 1943.

65 PRO, CAB122/234, Eden to Halifax, no. 3829, 9 June 1943.

66 NACP, RG 407, Army-AG, Classified Decimal File, 1943–45, file 383.6, Repatriation of Sick and Wounded POWs, Hull to Stimson, 21 May 1943, and memorandum for the assistant chief of staff, G-1, 29 May 1943; PRO, FO916/532, Washington to FO, no. 2830, 19 June 1943. On the agreement between the United States and Germany concerning repatriation of POWs, see Levie, *Documents on Prisoners of War*, doc. no. 54.

67 NACP, RG 165, Records of the War Department, sec. 3, cases 81–116, file 383.6, memorandum for the assistant chief of staff, G-1, 1 June 1943.

68 NACP, RG 407, Army-AG, Classified Decimal File, 1943–45, file 383.6, Repatriation of Sick and Wounded POWs, Stimson to Hull, 21 June 1943; NACP, RG 165, WRDGSS, ODPO, Top Secret "American-British-Canadian," ABC 383.6 (16 June 1943), note by the secretaries, JCS, J.C.S. 370, 19 June 1943, enclosure "c," Thomas T. Handy to Deane, 18 June 1943; PRO, FO916/531, the Department of State to the British embassy at Washington, 24 June 1943; PRO, WO193/346, Washington to FO, no. 2911, 25 June 1943.

69 PRO, FO916/531, FO to Washington, no. 4754, 19 July 1943.

70 *FRUS*, 1943, 1:56–59, Halifax to the secretary of state, 10 July 1943.

71 Ibid.; PRO, WO193/346, FO to Washington, no. 4377, 3 July 1943; see also PRO, FO916/531, the secretary of state to the government of India, 2 July 1943.

72 PRO, FO916/531, FO to Washington, no. 4378, 3 July 1943.

73 Ibid., FO to Washington, no. 4923, 26 July 1943.

74 NACP, RG 218, Records of the JCS, file CCS 383.6 (28 May 1943), sec. 1, JCS ninety-eighth meeting, 27 July 1943. On the JCS during the war, see Stoler, *Allies and Adversaries*.

75 NACP, RG 218, Records of the JCS, file CCS 383.6 (28 May 1943), sec. 1, note by the secretary, JCS, J.C.S. 370/2, 25 July 1943, Leahy to Hull, 27 July 1943.

76 PRO, FO916/534, Halifax to FO, no. 3461, 30 July 1943.

77 Ibid., minute by Roberts, 31 July 1943.

78 *FRUS*, 1943, 1:62–63, memorandum of conversation, 1 August 1943; PRO, FO916/
534, Washington to FO, no. 3543, 4 August 1943, and Washington to FO, no. 3565,
6 August 1943; NACP, RG 218, Records of the JCS, file CCS 383.6 (28 May 1943),
sec. 1, General Deane to the secretary of state, 2 August 1943.

79 PRO, FO916/534, FO to Washington, no. 424, 9 August 1943.

80 Ibid.

81 NACP, RG 218, Records of the JCS, file CCS 383.6 (28 May 1943), sec. 1, State
Department to the minister of Switzerland in charge of German interests in the
United States, 2 August 1943; PRO, FO916/534, Washington to FO, no. 3567,
6 August 1943.

82 PRO, FO916/535, Washington to FO, nos. 4122, 4123, 14 September 1943.

83 *FRUS*, 1943, 1:72–73, Hull to the Swiss minister, 17 September 1943.

84 PRO, FO916/535, FO to Stockholm, no. 548, 18 September 1943; PRO, FO916/537,
minute by Roberts, 29 September 1943.

85 PRO, FO916/536, FO to the minister of state, Cairo, no. 3042, 30 September 1943.

86 PRO, FO916/538, Stockholm to FO, no. 837, 12 October 1943; PRO, FO916/539,
WO to commander in chief, Middle East, 14 October 1943. On different num-
bers, see PRO, FO916/537, translation of German text in Swiss legation, note
III.C.1.B.NA/1133, 8 October 1943, and FO to Stockholm, no. 608, 8 October 1943;
PRO, FO916/539, extract from conclusions of War Cabinet meeting, 18 October
1943.

87 NACP, RG 59, GRDS, Records of the Special War Problems Division Policy Books,
1939–45 (Lot File No. 58 D 8), file Repatriation of Sick and Wounded, September
1, 1943, memorandum of conversation, 9 October 1943.

88 PRO, FO916/539, DPW, minutes of the fourteenth meeting of the CRC, 20 October 1943; on the exchange at Gothenburg, see PRO, FO916/540, report on the
exchange of seriously sick and seriously wounded POWs at Gothenburg, 23 October 1943, and Mallet to Eden, 28 October 1943.

89 PRO, PREM3/364, memorandum for the prime minister, 23 February 1944;
NACP, RG 165, RWDGSS, ODPO, General Records—Correspondence, Security-
Classified General Correspondence, 1942–45, OPD 383.6, sec. 7, cases 226–50,
Halifax to FO, no. 897, 22 February 1944; *Hansard, House of Commons*, vol. 392,
cols. 1217–19, 19 October 1943. On the exchange in Barcelona, see PRO, FO916/
540, notes on the exchange of POWs at Barcelona on 27 October 1943 by Bryan
Wallace, and David Francis, British consulate general, Barcelona, to Sir Samuel
Hoare, 3 November 1943. See also Bernadotte, *Instead of Arms*, 36–39; Vance,
Objects of Concern, 164–69.

90 *Hansard, House of Commons*, vol. 392, cols. 1218–20, 19 October 1943.

91 See below, chap. 6.

92 Gelber, *Jewish Palestinian Volunteering*, 159–60, 164–67, 176–78, 184–85, 19–98.

93 PRO, FO916/244, report on Stalag VIII B, 5 May 1942; *Appendix to the Congressional Record*, 78th Cong., 2nd sess., vol. 91, pt. 3, A2167, Hull to Congressman
Arthur Klein, 14 April 1944; *Congressional Record*, Senate, vol. 91, pt. 3, col. 3470,
18 April 1945; Durand, *Stalag Luft III*, 209; Foy, *For You the War Is Over*, 128–31;

MacKenzie, "The Treatment of Prisoners of War in World War II," 497; Bird, *American POWs of World War II*, 87–96, 97–105; Winograd, "Double Jeopardy," 3–17; see also Vourkoutiotis, *Prisoners of War and the German High Command*, 189–91.

94 PRO, AIR2/4671, FO to Swiss Legation, 10 December 1943.

95 Ibid.; see also PRO, WO163/59, DPW, paper for consideration by the Repatriation Committee, 27 November 1943; PRO, AIR2/4670, Swiss legation to the British FO, 29 October 1943.

96 NACP, RG 107, Office of the Secretary of War, Administrative Assistant to the Secretary of War, Coordination and Records, file 383.6, German, Stimson to Hull, 22 November 1943.

97 NACP, RG 389, ROPMG, American POW Information Bureau Records Branch, Decimal File, 1942–45, 000.3 to 240, file 014.35, American P/W, memorandum for General White, 10 November 1943.

98 NACP, RG 107, Office of the Secretary of War, Administrative Assistant to the Secretary of War, file 383.6, POW (June 1944–December 1944), Stimson to Hull, 17 December 1944, and Stimson to Hull, 26 November 1944.

99 PRO, FO916/852, Halifax to FO, no. 78, 6 January 1944, and Washington to FO, no. 362, 23 January 1944. About POWs of World War I, see Speed III, *POWs, Diplomats, and the Great War*, 37–41, 51–58; on the concern for the safety of the POWs, see below, chap. 6.

100 PRO, FO916/852, FO to Washington, no. 787, 28 January 1944, and FO to Washington, no. 424, 17 January 1944, and minute by Roberts, 14 January 1944. See also Woodward, *British Foreign Policy in the Second World War*, 5:356–64, and below, chap. 9, the Bern incident.

101 NACP, RG 107, Office of the Secretary of War, Administrative Assistant to the Secretary of War, Coordination and Records, file 383.6, German, Stimson to Hull, 10 February 1944.

102 PRO, FO916/853, Washington to FO, no. 592, 5 February 1944.

103 Ibid., FO to Washington, no. 1143, 9 February 1944.

104 *FRUS*, 1944, 3:790–91, Hull to Harrison, the minister in Switzerland, 5 February 1944.

105 Ibid., 793–94, Stettinius to Harrison, 10 February 1944.

106 NACP, RG 18, Army Air Process, Central Decimal Files, October 1942–May 1944, 382 Declaration of War to 384.4 Restricted zones August 1943–June 1944, file 383.6, Major General J. A. Ulio, the Adjutant General to the Commanding Generals, 4 March 1944; PRO, FO916/795, Lisbon to FO, no. 375, 3 March 1944.

107 NACP, RG 165, RWDGSS, ODPO, General Records—Correspondence, Security-Classified General Correspondence, 1942–45, OPD 383.6, sec. 7, cases 226–50, FO to the Swiss legation, 23 February 1944; NACP, RG 107, Office of the Secretary of War, Administrative Assistant to the Secretary of War, Coordination and Records, file 383.6, American (January 1944), Stimson to Hull, 10 February 1944.

108 NACP, RG 165, RWDGSS, ODPO, General Records—Correspondence, Security-Classified General Correspondence, 1942–45, OPD, sec. 7, cases 226–50, Bern to

FO, no. 1398, 31 March 1944; NACP, RG 218, Records of the JCS, file CCS 383.6 (28 May 1943), sec. 1, ETOUSA to War Department, no. 21609, 2 April 1944. See also PRO, FO916/853, Norton to FO, no. 751, 19 February 1944.

109 PRO, CAB122/664, Eden to Halifax, nos. 3005, 3006, 8 April 1944; NACP, RG 331, AOOH, SHAEF, Office of the Chiefs of Staff, Secretary, General Staff, Decimal File, May 1943–August 1945, file 383.6/1, vol. 2, Marshall to Eisenhower, no. 18098, 3 April 1944; NACP, RG 165, WDGS, ODPO, General Records—Correspondence, OPD 383.6, sec. 4-C, case 165 only, Halifax to FO, no. 1712, 5 April 1944. On the importance Eden attached to exchanging POWs, see Bernadotte, *Instead of Arms*, 62.

110 NACP, RG 165 RWDGSS, ODPO, General Records—Correspondence, OPD 383.6, sec. 4-B, case 165 only, Washington to FO, no. 1712, 5 April 1944; PRO, CAB122/664, Eden to Halifax, no. 3006, 8 April 1944; NACP, RG 331, AOOH, SHAEF, Office of the Chiefs of Staff, Secretary, General Staff, Decimal File, May 1943–August 1945, file 383.6/1, vol. 2, Marshall to Eisenhower, no. 18098, 3 April 1944.

111 MR 300, Marshall to Eisenhower, 11 April 1944.

112 NACP, RG 218, Records of the JCS, file CCS 383.6 (28 May 1943), sec. 1, ETOUSA to War Department, no. 22994, 12 April 1944; NACP, RG 165, RWDGSS, OPDO, General Records—Correspondence, OPD 383.6, sec. 4-B, case 165 only, British FO to the Swiss legation, 13 April 1944; *FRUS*, 1944, 3:797–98, Hull to Harrison, 13 April 1944.

113 NACP, RG 165, RWDGSS, ODPO, General Record—Correspondence, OPD 383.6, sec. 4-C, case 165 only, Bern to FO, no. 1831, 29 April 1944; NACP, RG 218, Records of the JCS, file CCS 383.6 (28 May 1943), sec. 1, ETOUSA, London, to War Department, no. 25153, 27 April 1944.

114 PRO, FO916/856, Norton to FO, no. 1791, 27 April 1944.

115 NACP, RG 165, RWDGSS, ODPO, General Records—Correspondence, OPD 383.6, sec. 4-B, case 165 only, FO to Bern, no. 1322, 30 April 1944.

116 PRO, CAB122/664, Eden to Halifax, no. 3843, 3 May 1944.

117 Ibid., Eden to Halifax, no. 3824, 2 May 1944.

118 NACP, RG 165, RWDGSS, ODPO, General Records—Correspondence, OPD 383.6, sec. 4-C, case 165 only, Washington to FO, no. 2506, 12 May 1944.

119 Ibid.; PRO, WO193/346, Washington to FO, no. 2505, 12 May 1944.

120 NACP, RG 218, Records of the JCS, file CCS 383.6 (28 May 1943), sec. 2, memorandum for the JCS, 14 May 1944; PRO, WO193/346, minute, 13 May 1944.

121 PRO, CAB122/664, Chiefs of Staff Committee, C.O.S. (44) 382 (o), note by the WO, 1 May 1944, and Annex II; NACP, RG 218, Records of the JCS, file CCS 383.6 (28 May 1943), sec. 1, ETOUSA, London, to War Department, no. E 25551, 29 April 1944.

122 Code name for the Allied cross-Channel invasion of France in spring 1944. PRO, CAB122/664, Chiefs of Staff to Eisenhower and Wilson, no. 2335, 3 May 1944; NACP, RG 218, Records of the JCS, file CCS 383.6 (28 May 1943), sec. 1, memorandum by the representatives of the British Chiefs of Staff, CCS, C.C.S. 564, 3 May 1944.

123 NACP, RG 218, Records of the JCS, file CCS 383.6 (28 May 1943), sec. 2, WO to

SHAEF, no. 94512, 14 May 1944; MR 300, ETOUSA, London, to War Department, no. 27641, 13 May 1944.

124 PRO, WO32/1136, Gepp to the general officer commander in chief, Northern Ireland, 20 May 1944; PRO, WO32/11136, results of a meeting held by the minister of home affairs for Northern Ireland, 22 May 1944, and minutes of a meeting of the DPW, 24 May 1944; PRO, FO916/826, Halifax to FO, no. 3096, 9 June 1944; PRO, FO916/860, DPW, CRC, 26 June 1944; *FRUS*, 1944, 3:799, Hull to the American ambassador in Spain, 13 May 1944; NACP, RG 59, GRDS, Special War Problems Division Policy Books, 1939–45 [lot file no. 58D8], file May 17, 1944 Exchange, memorandum on exchange of German and British POWs and members of the protected personnel, which took place in Barcelona on May 17, 1944; NACP, RG 407, Army-AG, Classified Decimal File, 1943–45, file AG 383.6 (16 May 1944), Repatriation of Sick and Wounded American POWs from Germany, file 383.6 (13 January 1945), Brigadier General Robert H. Dunlop, acting adjutant general, to the commanding generals, 18 May 1944; Phillimore, "The Second World War," 116.

125 PRO, CAB122/665, Halifax to FO, no. 3096, 9 June 1944.

126 NACP, RG 218, Records of the JCS, file CCS 383.6 (28 May 1943), sec. 2, Eisenhower to Personnel Division, G-1 General Staff, 5 July 1994; PRO, FO916/ 861, Eisenhower to AGWAR, no. 36305, 5 July 1944; PRO, FO916/826, Bern to FO, no. 2377, 26 May 1944.

127 *FRUS*, 1944, 3:802–3, Hull to Harrison, 11 July 1944; NACP, RG 218, Records of the JCS, file CCS 383.6 (28 May 1943), sec. 2, Personnel Division, G-1, to commanding general, ETOUSA, London, no. 62323, 8 July 1944.

128 NACP, RG 331, AOOH, SHAEF, Office of the Chiefs of Staff, Secretary, General Staff, Decimal File, 1943–August 1945, file 383.6/5, vol. 2, Marshall to ETOUSA, no. 62323, 8 July 1944.

129 PRO, WO32/11135, FO to Washington, no. 6233, 10 July 1944; PRO, CAB122/ 665, ETOUSA, London, to War Department, no. 37192, 10 July 1944.

130 PRO, FO916/861, FO to Bern, no. 2262, 11 July 1944.

131 PRO, WO32/11135, minute, 7 July 1944.

132 NACP, RG 331, AOOH, SHAEF, Office of the Chiefs of Staff, Secretary, General Staff, Decimal File, 1943–August 1945, file 383.6/5, vol. 2, Marshall to ETOUSA, no. 37192, 18 July 1944.

133 PRO, WO32/11140, WO to Allied Forces Headquarters, Algiers, no. 60335, 15 July 1944.

134 NACP, RG 407, Army-AG, Classified Decimal File, 1943–45, file 383.6, Repatriation of Sick and Wounded POWs, statement of Major W. E. Tucker, 7 December 1943.

135 PRO, CAB122/665, Halifax to FO, no. 3097, 9 June 1944.

136 PRO, FO916/826, extract of notes on conversation between Gepp and Swiss representatives, 12 October 1944. See also *Report of the International Committee of the Red Cross*, 3:296–97; Phillimore, "The Second World War," 61–63.

137 PRO, CAB122/665, Cambell to Eden, no. 3994, 24 July 1944; PRO, FO916/861, Norton to FO, no. 3412, 21 July 1944.

138 PRO, WO32/11140, Campbell to FO, no. 3995, 24 July 1944; PRO, FO916/861, Campbell to FO, no. 4018, 25 July 1944.

139 *FRUS*, 1944, 3:804–6, Stettinius to Harrison, 4 August 1944; PRO, FO916/862, Campbell to FO, no. 4147, 2 August 1944.

140 PRO, FO916/862, FO to Bern, no. 2536, 3 August 1944; PRO, FO916/861, FO to Bern, no. 2486, 29 July 1944.

141 *FRUS*, 1944, 3:806–7, Harrison to Hull, 13 August 1944.

142 Ibid., 807–8, Harrison to Hull, 23 August 1944.

143 Ibid., 808–9, Hull to Harrison, 24 August 1944.

144 NACP, RG 218, Records of the JCS, file CCS 383.6 (28 May 1943), sec. 2, ETOUSA, London, to War Department, no. 44488, 22 August 1944; PRO, WO32/11135, FO to Bern, no. 2743, 22 August 1944.

145 NACP, RG 218, Records of the JCS, file CCS 383.6 (28 May 1943), sec. 2, Marshall to Eisenhower for CRC, no. 85487, 23 August 1944.

146 PRO, FO916/864, Norton to FO, no. 3976, 24 August 1944.

147 Ibid.; PRO, WO32/11135, Norton to FO, no. 3950, 23 August 1944.

148 PRO, WO163/593, DPW, CRC, 26 August 1944, minutes of the thirty-third meeting, 25 August 1944; PRO, WO32/11132, FO to Bern, no. 2791, 25 August 1944; PRO, FO916/863, WO to Roberts, 23 August 1944; see also WO32/11140, DPW, German Repatriation Instructions No. 1, 23 August 1944.

149 PRO, WO32/11135, Norton to FO, no. 4081, 29 August 1944.

150 Weinberg, *A World at Arms*, 750–51.

151 PRO, WO32/11135, FO to Bern, no. 2844, 30 August 1944.

152 Ibid.

153 Ibid., Bern to FO, no. 4119, 30 August 1944.

154 Ibid., FO to Washington, no. 7755, 31 August 1944.

155 PRO, FO916/865, Carlos J. Warnet to Lieutenant Colonel R. E. A. Elwes, WO, 4 September 1944.

156 *FRUS*, 1944, 3:810, Hull to Harrison, 4 September 1944.

157 PRO, FO916/866, DPW, German Repatriation Instruction No. 2, 7 September 1944.

158 PRO, WO32/11135, minute for the secretary of state, 30 September 1944; PRO, FO916/867, report on the Gothenburg exchange, 19 September 1944, and Department of State, statement for the press, 26 September 1944; PRO, FO916/866, DPW, German Repatriation Instruction No. 2, 7 September 1944; NACP, RG 407, Army-AG, Classified Decimal File, 1943–45, file AG 383.6 (16 May 1944), Repatriation of Sick and Wounded American POWs from Germany, file 383.6 (13 January 1945), Ulio to Commanding Generals, 24 August 1944.

159 PRO, WO32/11138, R. E. A. Elwes, WO, to Roberts, 11 October 1944, and DPW, CRC, 21 October 1944; on the fighting at Arnhem, see Ryan, *A Bridge Too Far*; Middlebrook, *Arnhem, 1944*.

160 PRO, WO32/11138, FO to Bern, no. 3353, 12 October 1944.

161 PRO, FO916/867, Halifax to FO, no. 5615, 16 October 1944.

162 Ibid., Halifax to FO, no. 5802, 25 October 1944.

163 Ibid., minute by Roberts, 27 October 1944.

164 NACP, RG 165, RWDGSS, ODPO, General Records—Correspondence, Security-Classified General Correspondence, 1942–45, OPD 383.6, sec. 8-A, case 263 only, subnumber 1-37, Gousev to Eden, no. 1358, 21 September 1944.

165 Ibid., FO to Washington, no. 9907, 19 November 1944.

166 PRO, WO32/11138, Roberts to D. Mackillop, British legation, Bern, 9 December 1944.

167 PRO, WO163/593, DPW, CRC, 27 November 1944; PRO, WO32/11138, FO to Washington, no. 10105, 27 November 1944.

168 NACP, RG 331, AOOH, SHAEF, General Staff, G-4 Division, Executive Section, Decimal File, 1945, file 383.6, POWs, Marshall to Eisenhower, no. 86559, 4 January 1945.

169 Ibid.; PRO, WO32/11138, American embassy, London, to Elwes, WO, 5 December 1944.

170 PRO, WO32/11138, American embassy to Phillimore, 2 January 1945.

171 NACP, RG 331, Allied Operational and Occupation Headquarters, World War II, SHAEF, Special Staff Adjutant General's Division, Executive Section, Decimal File, 1945, 383.6-1 to 383.6-3, file 383.6-2 #2, Marshall to McNarney, no. 23412, 29 January 1945, and Marshall to McNarney, no. 91796, 26 January 1945.

172 On the war in the Ardennes, see *Report by the Supreme Commander to the Combined Chiefs of Staff*, 92–98; Baldwin, *Battles Lost and Won*, 315–67; Murray and Millett, *A War to Be Won*, 463–71; Dupuy, Bongard, and Anderson, *Hitler's Last Gamble*.

173 NACP, RG 165, RWDGSS, OCOS, Security-Classified General Correspondence, 1942–47, file 383.6, sec. 6, 271–350, telegram to American legation, Bern, 10 February 1945, and memorandum by Major General S. G. Henry, assistant chief of staff, G-1, "Repatriation of Surplus German Enlisted Protected Personnel," 6 March 1945; NACP, RG 331, AOOH, SHAEF, General Staff, G-1 Division Administrative Section, Decimal File, 1944–45, file 383.6/10, Repatriation of POWs, Marshall to Eisenhower, no. 21682, 16 January 1945.

174 NACP, RG 218, Records of the JCS, file CCS 383.6 (28 May 1943), sec. 2, Personnel Division, G-1, to Commanding General Allied Force Headquarters, Caserta, Italy, no. 71025, 30 November 1944; *FRUS*, 1944, 3:815–16, Stettinius to J. Klahr Huddle, the chargé in Switzerland, 5 December 1944; see also NACP, RG 333, file 383.6/5, vol. 2, Marshall to Eisenhower, no. 59301, 8 November 1944; NACP, RG 331, AOOH, SHAEF, Office of the Chiefs of Staff, Secretary, General Staff, Decimal File, 1943–August 1945, file 383.6/5, vol. 2, Marshall to Eisenhower, no. 66834, 22 November 1944.

175 PRO, WO32/11138, FO to Bern, no. 3733, 5 December 1944.

176 NACP, RG 218, Records of the JCS, file CCS 383.6 (28 May 1943), sec. 2, Marshall to Eisenhower, no. 79521, 19 December 1944, and United Kingdom Base Section, London, to War Department, no. 18888, 21 December 1944, and Personnel Division, G-1, to Headquarters Communications Zone, ETO, Paris, no. 77770, 15 December 1944; NACP, RG 331, AOOH, SHAEF, Office of the Chiefs of Staff, Secretary, General Staff, Decimal File, 1943–August 1945, file 383.6/5, vol. 2, AGWAR to Eisenhower, no. 896069, 9 January 1945.

177 *FRUS*, 1944, 3:818, Huddle to Hull, 21 December 1944; PRO, ADM116/5200, FO to Bern, no. 3869, 27 December 1944; PRO, CAB122/666, Eden to Halifax, no. 10763, 22 December 1944.

178 NACP, RG 331, AOOH, SHAEF, General Staff, G-1 Division Administrative Section, Decimal File, 1944–45, file 383.6/10, Repatriation of POWs, memorandum to Brigadier R. H. S. Venables and Colonel E. F. Straub, 8 February 1945, and SHAEF, Special Staff Adjutant General's Division, Executive Section, Decimal File, 1945, 383.6-1 to 383.6-2#2, CRC to Personnel Division G-1, no. 25178, 9 February 1945; NACP, RG 165, RWDGSS, ODPO, General Records—Correspondence, Security-Classified General Correspondence, 1942–45, OPD 383.6, sec. 4-F, case 165 only, summary of action taken in matters relating to POWs in January 1945. On the negotiations between the Americans and the British on the one hand and the Germans that preceded the exchange, see *FRUS*, 1944, 3:821–22, Stettinius to Huddle, 26 December 1944; PRO, WO32/11138, American embassy to Lieutenant Colonel H. J. Phillimore, WO, 29 December 1944; NACP, RG 218, Records of the JCS, file CCS 383.6 (28 May 1943), sec. 2, Marshall to commanding general, United Kingdom Base Section, London, no. 81584, 23 December 1944, and WO to SHAEF, no. 56213, 1 January 1945; *FRUS*, 1944, 3:823, Huddle to Hull, 29 December 1944; and 822–23, Huddle to Hull, 30 December 1944; PRO, WO32/11138, Bern to FO, no. 5371, 29 December 1944, Bern to FO, no. 79, 12 January 1945, and Bern to FO, no. 122, 17 January 1945; PRO, ADM116/5200, FO to Bern, no. 136, 17 January 1945; PRO, WO32/11138, FO to Bern, no. 153, 19 January 1945, Bern to FO, no. 175, 23 January 1945, and FO to Bern, no. 253, 19 January 1945; PRO, ADM116/5200, FO to Bern, no. 196, 25 January 1945; PRO, WO32/11695, FO to Bern, no. 512, 12 March 1945.

179 At an open meeting of next of kin of POWs held in Philadelphia in November 1944, for example, the American government was accused of failing to repatriate wounded POWs: "Whereas no exchange of Protected Personnel has as yet been effected and less than 500 of the seriously wounded and injured American soldiers have so far been repatriated since the beginning of the war, a number by far inferior to prisoners of other Allied powers has so far exchanged." NACP, RG 389, Provost Marshal General, American POW Information Bureau Records Branch, Decimal File, 1942–45, file 383.6, American P/W #5, Judge Vincent A. Carroll to Stimson, 30 November 1944. In response, the State and War departments assured a representative of the families that negotiations for such exchange would continue "as long as the conflict continues." NACP, RG 107, Office of the Secretary of War, Office Administrative, file 383.6, American, B. M. Bryan, brigadier general, assistant provost marshal general, to Carroll, 6 December 1944.

180 NACP, RG 331, AOOH, SHAEF, General Staff, G-4 Division, Executive Section, Decimal File, 1945, file 383.6, POWs, Marshall to Eisenhower, no. 42257, 23 February 1945; NACP, RG 338, Records of U.S. Army Commands, 1942–, ETOUSA, Adjutant General's Section Administration Branch, General Correspondence [1944–45], 383.116–383.6, file Exchange of Sick and Wounded POWs, Lieutenant Colonel W. L. Hays (signed Eisenhower) to AGWAR to Personnel Division for

G-1, no. 27614, 27 February 1945, and file 383.6/10, Repatriation of POWs, Marshall to CRC, no. 47572, 4 March 1945; PRO, WO32/11695, minute by Gepp, 28 February 1945, and DPW, CRC, 2 March 1945.

181 PRO, WO32/11695, FO to Bern, no. 465, 12 March 1945, and FO to Bern, no. 465, 6 March 1945; NACP, RG 331, AOOH, SHAEF, General Staff, G-4 Division, Executive Section, Decimal File, 1944–45, file 383.6/10, Repatriation of POWs, Eisenhower to AGWAR for Personnel Division G-1, no. 29278, 10 March 1945.

182 NACP, RG 331, AOOH, SHAEF, General Staff, G-4 Division, Executive Section, Decimal File, 1944–45, file 383.6/10, Repatriation of POWs, Marshall to Hayes, no. 47573, 4 March 1945; PRO, WO32/11695, American embassy to Lieutenant Colonel Elwes, 13 March 1945, and DPW, CRC, 8 March 1945; on the march of POWs westward, see below, chap. 7.

183 See below, chap. 6.

184 PRO, WO32/11695, Bern to FO, no. 592, 24 March 1945; NACP, RG 338, Records of U.S. Army Commands, 1942–, ETOUSA, Adjutant General's Section Administration Branch, General Correspondence [1944–45], 383.116–383.6, Exchange of Sick and Wounded POWs, Marshall to CRC, no. 61069, 30 March 1945.

185 PRO, WO32/11695, DPW, CRC, 29 March 1945.

186 NACP, RG 331, AOOH, SHAEF, General Staff, G-4 Division, Executive Section, Decimal File, 1944–45, file 383.6/10, Repatriation of POWs, Hays to SHAEF, no. 32749, 6 April 1945.

187 NACP, RG 338, Records of U.S. Army Commands, 1942–, ETOUSA, Adjutant General's Section Administration Branch, General Correspondence [1944–45], 383.116–383.6, Exchange of Sick and Wounded POWs, SHAEF to Hays, CRC, no. 84937, 13 April 1945.

188 Rolf, *Prisoners of the Reich*, 134–35.

CHAPTER FIVE

1 PRO, ADM116/5353, Burckhardt to undersecretary of state for foreign affairs, 13 October 1942.

2 Cf. 1929 Geneva Convention, art. 72: "Throughout the duration of hostilities and for human considerations, belligerents may conclude agreements with a view to the direct repatriation or hospitalization in a neutral country of able-bodied prisoners of war who have undergone a long period of captivity." Friedman, *The Law of War*, 1:510.

3 PRO, ADM116/5353, FO to the ICRC, May 1943.

4 Ibid., B. Dyer, English Lieutenant Commander R.N.R. ex H.M.S. *Rawalpindi*, to the British government, 3 May 1943; on the armed merchant cruiser *Rawalpindi*, see Vat, *The Atlantic Campaign*, 92.

5 Huber incorrectly dates the agreement as occurring in March 1918. PRO, FO916/568, notice of meeting, DPW, 25 November 1943. On the repatriation during World War I, see Speed, *Prisoners, Diplomats, and the Great War*, chap. 11.

6 Vance, *Objects of Concern*, 60–74; Speed, *Prisoners, Diplomats, and the Great War*, 33–42; Jackson, *The Prisoners*, 68–75.

7 The Germans treated all seamen who fell into their hands as POWs, though

they were not in general compelled to work. Phillimore, "The Second World War," 71–72.

8 PRO, ADM116/5353, Alexander to Lord Leathers, 30 September 1943. See also Hinsley et al., *British Intelligence in the Second World War*, vol. 3, pt. 1, chap. 35.

9 PRO, ADM116/5353, Alexander to Lord Leathers, 30 September 1943, and minutes, 16, 26, 29 September 1943. About captured British seamen, see Vance, "The Politics of Camp Life," 112–17. On the Battle of the Atlantic, see Weinberg, *A World at Arms*, chap. 7; Murray and Millet, *A War to Be Won*, chap. 10; Vat, *The Atlantic Campaign*, chap. 8; Morison, *The Battle of the Atlantic*; Overy, *Why the Allies Won*, chap. 2.

10 PRO, FO916/568, notice of meeting, DPW, 25 November 1943.

11 PRO, ADM116/5353, minute, 3 December 1943; Friedman, *The Law of War*, 1:511.

12 PRO, ADM116/5353, Dean to undersecretary of state, WO, 17 August 1944.

13 *Hansard, House of Commons*, vol. 396, cols. 46–47, 18 January 1944.

14 Ibid., vol. 397, col. 809, 23 February 1944.

15 NACP, RG 407, Army-AG, Classified Decimal File, 1943–45, file 383.6, Repatriation of Able-bodied Prisoners, DPW, IPWC, Sub-committee A, 8 March 1944; PRO, WO163/587, minutes of Sub-committee A, IPWC, 13 March 1944. Satow and Sée, *The Work of the Prisoners of War Department*, 61–63. About the Dieppe disaster, see above, chap. 2.

16 PRO, ADM116/5353, FO to Bern, no. 901, 16 March 1944.

17 Ibid., Bern to FO, no. 2379, 29 May 1944; FO to Bern, no. 2313, 15 July 1944; FO to Bern, no. 3100, 18 September 1944; and Bern to FO, no. 4661, 30 September 1944.

18 NACP, RG 407, Army-AG, Classified Decimal File, 1943–45, file 383.6, Repatriation of Able-bodied Prisoners, Harrison to Hull, no. 2108, 5 April 1944. See also above, chap. 2.

19 NACP, RG 407, Army-AG, Classified Decimal File, 1943–45, file 383.6, Repatriation of Able-bodied Prisoners, Harrison to Hull, no. 2108, 5 April 1944.

20 NACP, RG 165, RWDGSS, OCOS, Security-Classified General Correspondence, 1942–47, file 383.6, sec. 3, cases 81–135, Stimson to Hull, 17 April 1944.

21 NACP, RG 407, Army-AG, Classified Decimal File, 1943–45, file 383.6, Repatriation of Able-bodied Prisoners, Hull to American legation, Bern, no. 2145, 23 June 1944.

22 *Hansard, House of Commons*, vol. 399, col. 1295, 3 May 1944; see also ibid., vol. 401, cols. 168–69, 21 June 1944.

23 Ibid., vol. 404, col. 1356, 8 November 1944; see also ibid., vol. 403, cols. 1774–75, 11 October 1944; PRO, ADM116/5353, Roberts to J. C. Mossop, Military Branch, Admiralty, 8 November 1944.

24 PRO, ADM116/5353, Bern to FO, no. 4900, 23 October 1944.

25 PRO, WO163/588, WO memorandum on repatriation of POWs who have been a long time in captivity, 10 January 1945.

26 See above, chap. 4.

27 PRO, FO916/1173, minute, 6 January 1945.

28 Ibid.

29 *Hansard, House of Commons*, vol. 406, cols. 2363 and 2362, 17 November 1944.

30 PRO, AIR20/2361, summary of mail from RAF prisoners of war (period of examination, September 1944).

31 Ibid., report on morale of RAF prisoners of war in Germany, 24 March 1945.

32 Ibid.

33 PRO, PREM3/364/8, memorandum by the secretary of state for foreign affairs and the secretary of state for war, W.P. (45) 33, 15 January 1945.

34 Ibid., extract from conclusions of War Cabinet meeting, 22 January 1945.

35 See below, chap. 8.

36 PRO, FO916/1173, C. Waldock to Roberts, 24 January 1945; on French treatment of German POWs, see Moore, "Unruly Allies," 180–98.

37 Vat, *The Atlantic Campaign*, chap. 9; Weinberg, *A World at Arms*, 771–73; Hinsley et al., *British Intelligence in the Second World War*, vol. 3, pt. 2, chap. 59.

38 PRO, FO916/1173, FO to Bern, no. 339, 17 February 1945.

39 Ibid., Federal Political Department to British legation, Bern, 1 March 1945.

40 *Report by the Supreme Commander to the Combined Chiefs of Staff*, 96; Baldwin, *Battles Lost and Won*, 350; Weinberg, *A World at Arms*, chaps. 14–15; Murry and Millett, *A War to Be Won*, 446–77; Gilbert, *The Second World War*, chap. 43; Sydnor, *Soldiers of Destruction*, 303–8. On monthly totals of German POWs after D-Day, see Sorge, *The Other Price of Hitler's War*, 64.

41 See below, chap. 7.

42 PRO, FO916/1180, Bern to FO, nos. 350, 351, 27 February 1945; PRO, WO193/348, Bern to FO, no. 372, 1 March 1945; PRO, FO916/1173, memorandum, "Exchange of Able-bodied Long-term Prisoners of War," 26 February 1945. On the air war against Germany, see *The Strategic Air War against Germany*; Messenger, *"Bomber" Harris and the Strategic Bombing Offensive*; Richards, *The Hardest Victory*. See also below, chap. 6.

43 PRO, FO916/1173, FO to Bern, no. 441, 2 March 1945.

44 Ibid., minute by Roberts, 2 March 1945.

45 Ibid., FO to Bern, no. 440, 2 March 1945.

46 Ibid., Bern to FO, no. 396, 3 March 1945.

47 Ibid., FO to Bern, no. 479, 7 March 1945.

48 See below, chap. 6.

49 PRO, FO916/1174, paper for meeting of the DPW to be held on 6 March 1945 and minutes of that meeting.

50 NACP, RG 165, RWDGSS, ODPO, Top Secret "American-British-Canadian," ABC 383.6 (16 June 1943), sec. 1-C, memorandum by the Chiefs of Staff, U.S. Army, J.C.S. 1284, 9 March 1945; PRO, FO916/1174, JSM to COS, JSM 593, 12 March 1945; NACP, RG 218, Records of the JCS, file CCS 383.6 (9 March 1945), Winant to Hull, 26 February 1945; PRO, CAB122/690, FO to Halifax, no. 2065, 4 March 1945. About the CAC, see Coakley and Leighton, *Global Logistics and Strategy*, 94–95.

51 PRO, CAB122/690, COS to JSM, 14 March 1945; PRO, ADM116/5353, minutes of the sixty-eighth meeting of the COS, 14 March 1945; PRO, FO916/1174, minute by Roberts, 15 March 1945.

52 NACP, RG 218, Records of the JCS, file CCS 383.6 (9 March 1945), note by the secretaries, CAC, C.AD.C 89/1, 19 March 1945.

53 Murray and Millett, *A War to Be Won*, 463–71.

54 PRO, FO916/1175, minutes of CAC thirty-sixth meeting, 20 March 1945.

55 See above, chap. 4.

56 PRO, CAB122/690, note by the secretary, JSM in Washington, M.M.(S) (45) 18, 21 March 1945.

57 On the functions of the JLC, see Coakley and Leighton, *Global Logistics and Strategy*, 95–98.

58 NACP, RG 165, RWDGSS, ODPO, Top Secret "American-British-Canadian," ABC 383.6 (16 June 1943), sec. 1-C, note by the secretaries, JCS, J.C.S. 1284/1, 21 March 1945, report by the JLC.

59 NACP, RG 107, Office of the Secretary of War, Office Administrative, file 383.6, American, B. M. Bryan, brigadier general, assistant provost marshal general, to Vincent A. Carroll, 6 December 1944.

60 NACP, RG 218, Records of the JCS, file CCS 383.6 (13 April 1945), memorandum by the U.S. Chiefs of Staff, C.C.S. 794/3, 24 March 1945. About U.S. casualties after D-Day, see O'Neill, *A Democracy at War*, 322.

61 PRO, CAB122/690, JSM, Washington, to COS, no. 29, 23 March 1945.

62 PRO, FO916/1175, minute by Roberts, 4 April 1945.

63 Ibid.

64 PRO, WO193/349, Bern to FO, no. 686, 4 April 1945; see also Eden's statement in the House of Commons on 11 April 1945: *Hansard, House of Commons*, vol. 409, cols. 1800–1801. Satow and Sée, *The Work of the Prisoners of War Department*, 61–64.

65 PRO, FO916/1174, minute by Roberts, 5 April 1945.

66 PRO, WO193/349, COS to JSM, Washington, April 1945.

67 See below, chap. 8.

CHAPTER SIX

1 PRO, WO208/3247, memorandum on British POWs, 28 September 1939.

2 PRO, FO916/544, memorandum by German Ministry of Foreign Affairs, 28 September 1943. During the same period, of the German POWs in British hands, five had been shot in 1941, six in 1942, and three in the first seven months of 1943. Eight of the fourteen cases had been escape attempts, and three were cases of insubordination. See also *Hansard, House of Commons*, vol. 391, col. 2063, 3 August 1943. For statistics on American prisoners who died in German captivity, see Hasselbring, "American Prisoners of War," 189 n. 3; Carlson, *We Were Each Other's Prisoners*, 66 n. 12.

3 Lochner, *The Goebbels Diaries*, 419; see also Middlebrook, *The Battle of Hamburg*, and Hinsley et al., *British Intelligence in the Second World War*, vol. 3, pt. 1, chap. 397.

4 Kershaw, *Hitler*, 597–98; Kitchen, *Nazi Germany at War*, 87–95.

5 Quoted in Foy, *For You the War Is Over*, 21.

6 Ibid., 21–23; see also MacKenzie, "The Treatment of Prisoners of War in World War II," 494–96.

7 Lochner, *The Goebbels Diaries*, 497.

8 Ibid., 522–23, 25.

9 Ibid., 529. See also Welch, *The Third Reich*, 113–16; Beck, *Under the Bombs*, chap. 5; Murray and Millett, *A War to Be Won*, 319–22; Weinberg, *A World at Arms*, 616–19.

10 On the Kharkov trial, see Kochavi, *Prelude to Nuremberg*, 66–73.

11 NACP, RG 59, GRDS, 740.00116 EW 1939/1204, Harrison to Hull, no. 8085, 23 December 1943, and Winant to Hull, no. 269, 12 January 1944; PRO, FO371/38990, FO to Washington, no. 249, 11 January 1944. See also Kochavi, "The Moscow Declaration, the Kharkov Trial, and the Question of a Policy on Major War Criminals."

12 NACP, RG 59, GRDS, 740.00116 EW1939/1201, Harrison to Hull, no. 8062, 22 December 1943; ibid., 740.00116 EW 1939/1204, Harrison to Hull, no. 8085, 23 December 1943; ibid., 740.00116 EW 1939/1214, Hull to Moscow, 31 December 1943.

13 NACP, RG 165, RWDGSS, ODPO, General Records—Correspondence, Security-Classified General Correspondence, 1942–45, OPD 383.6, sec. 5-B, cases 168–205, memorandum for the president, 29 December 1943.

14 Ibid., memorandum for General Marshall, 10 January 1944.

15 *FRUS*, 1943, 1:434–45, Hull to Harrison, 24 December 1943; *FRUS*, 1944, 4:1198, Hull to Harriman, 1 January 1944.

16 *FRUS*, 1944, 1:1231, Harrison to Hull, 30 March 1944.

17 Rolf, *Prisoners of the Reich*, 142–434; Foy, *For You the War Is Over*, 22–26.

18 PRO, AIR2/10121, Bern to FO, no. 1276, 24 March 1944. About Burckhardt, see Favez, *The Red Cross and the Holocaust*, 284–85.

19 Cf. 1929 Geneva Convention, art. 50: "Escaped prisoners of war who are retaken before being able to rejoin their own army or to leave the territory occupied by the army which captured them shall be liable only to disciplinary punishment." Friedman, *The Law of War*, 1:506. Article 54 stated that "Arrest is the most severe disciplinary punishment which may be imposed on a prisoner of war. The duration of a single punishment may not exceed thirty days." Ibid., 1:510–11.

20 PRO, WO32/15502, Norton to FO, no. 2070, 12 May 1944. Another notorious case was the murder of a group of U.S. Army personnel consisting of two officers and thirteen enlisted men in the vicinity of La Spezia, Italy, the Dostler Case. *Law Reports of Trials of War Criminals*, 1:22–35.

21 PRO, WO32/15502, Norton to FO, no. 2070, 12 May 1944.

22 Ibid., FO to Bern, no. 1556, 16 May 1944.

23 Ibid., FO to Bern, no. 1605, 19 May 1944.

24 PRO, FO916/881, minutes of a meeting of the DPW, 25 May 1944.

25 Ibid., extract from the *Daily Mail*, 24 May 1944, and minute by Roberts, 24 May 1944.

26 PRO, FO916/882, Frederick Orme G. Bovenschen to Sargent, 14 June 1944.

27 PRO, WO32/15502, Bern to FO, no. 2702, 14 June 1944.

28 Ibid.; see also PRO, AIR2/10121, United Nations War Crimes Commission, United Kingdom against German War Criminals, 18 September 1944.

29 PRO, AIR2/10121, Bern to FO, no. 2674, 12 June 1944.

30 PRO, CAB65/42, conclusions of eightieth War Cabinet meeting, 19 June 1944. On foreign labor in Germany, see Homze, *Foreign Labor in Nazi Germany*.

31 *Hansard, House of Commons*, vol. 401, cols. 477–82, 23 June 1944. See also PRO, KV2/172, conversation between General Gottlob Berger and British officer, 8 May 1945; *Trials of War Criminals before the Nuremberg Military Tribunals*, 13:1–32; Brickhill, *The Great Escape*; Gill, *The Great Escape*; Smith, *Mission Escape*; Vance, "The War Behind the Wire," 675–93; Delarue, *The Gestapo*, 277–78.

32 PRO, WO32/15502, *Canadian House of Commons*, 23 June 1944.

33 PRO, FO916/883, note verbale, 21 July 1944.

34 PRO, FO916/891, FO to Bern, no. 2230, 7 July 1944.

35 PRO, AIR2/10121, United Nations War Crimes Commission, United Kingdom Charges against German War Criminals, 18 September 1944; see also Jones, "Nazi Atrocities against Allied Airmen."

36 See also Vourkoutiotis, *Prisoners of War and the German High Command*, 94–101.

37 PRO, FO916/894, report by the JISC, JIC (44) 322, 29 July 1944; see also PRO, PREM3/364/11, JSM, Washington to COS, no. 236, 1 September 1944; Nichol and Rennell, *The Last Escape*, 34–35, 52–58.

38 PRO, AIR40/280, memorandum, "Position of Imperial and American Ps/W on Collapse of Germany," 8 January 1945.

39 Ibid.

40 PRO, PREM3/364/11, memorandum by the secretary of state for war, WP (44) 554, 18 October 1944; see also PRO, WO193/355, Chiefs of Staff Committee, "Court of Enquiry on the Murder of Canadian and British Prisoners of War," 26 July 1944; PRO, FO916/871, FO to Bern, no. 2502, 31 July 1944. Margolian, *Conduct Unbecoming*, chap. 8; Datner, *Crimes against POWs*, 43–46; Russell, *The Scourge of the Swastika*, 39–43; Mason, *Prisoners of War*, 446.

41 PRO, CAB122/684, British embassy, Washington, to the State Department, 19 October 1944.

42 NACP, RG 165, RWDGSS, ODPO, Top Secret "American-British-Canadian," ABC 383.6 (16 June 1943), sec. 1-A, note by the secretaries, JPS, JPS, 554, 6 November 1944, apps. D and E.

43 Ibid.; NACP, RG 59, GRDS, Decimal File, 1945–49, file 740.00114EW/1-2245, DPW, "Protection of Allied Prisoners of War against Acts of Violence Committed by S.S. and Other German Forces," 24 November 1944; see also Nichol and Rennell, *The Last Escape*, 14–15.

44 PRO, AIR20/9162, Headquarters Seventh Army, 15 January 1945, Chief of the Party Chancery, Circular Letter 229/44 Confidential, Subject: "Resistance movement among prisoners of war," 10 September 1944.

45 PRO, WO193/345, Headquarters Seventh Army, 8 January 1945, Chief of the Party Chancery, Circular Letter 288/44, Subject: "Reorganization of the control of prisoners of war," 30 September 1944; see also *Trials of War Criminals before*

the Nuremberg Military Tribunals, 13:32–34; Durand, *Stalag Luft III*, 134–41; Foy, *For You the War Is Over*, 20–30.

46 *Trials of War Criminals before the Nuremberg Military Tribunals*, vol. 13: "The Ministries Case," 60.

47 PRO, WO193/355, Directors of Plans, meeting to be held on 5 December 1944, note on JP (44) 299 (o) Draft; PRO, FO916/881, Bern to FO, no. 1276, 24 March 1944; see also Nichol and Rennell, *The Last Escape*, 325–35.

48 PRO, FO916/879, "Possible Treatment of Prisoners of War by Germany in Final Stages," 15 December 1944.

49 PRO, CAB122/678, memorandum by JCS, CCS 472/6, 3 January 1945.

50 *Trials of War Criminals before the Nuremberg Military Tribunals*, 11:127–28; see also above, chap. 2.

51 *Trials of War Criminals before the Nuremberg Military Tribunals*, 11:73–75.

52 Ibid.; see also Datner, *Crimes against POWs*, chap. 4.

53 NACP, RG 165, RWDGSS, ODPO, Top Secret "American-British-Canadian," ABC 383.6 (16 June 1943), sec. 1-C, note by the secretaries, COS, CCS 792, 9 March 1945, and appendix.

54 Ibid.; see also *Trials of War Criminals before the Nuremberg Military Tribunals*, 11:110–22.

55 PRO, CAB65/44, conclusions of 134th War Cabinet meeting, 9 October 1944.

56 NACP, RG 165, RWDGSS, ODPO, Top Secret "American-British-Canadian," ABC 383.6 (16 June 1943), sec. 1-B, note by the secretary, Joint Intelligence Committee, 13 January 1945. See also PRO, WO208/3244, report compiled by members of Stalag Luft III Escape Organisation, 9 May 1950; PRO, WO208/3242, M.I. 9 Historical Record, August 1945; Foot and Langley, *MI 9 Escape and Evasion*; Durand, *Stalag Luft III*, chaps. 13–14; Levine, *Captivity, Flight, and Survival in World War II*, 91–102, 114–24.

57 Durand, *Stalag Luft III*, 301.

58 PRO, PREM3/364/11, report by the vice chiefs of staff, WP (44) 512, 9 September 1944; NACP, RG 165, RWDGSS, ODPO, Top Secret "American-British-Canadian," ABC 383.6 (16 June 1943), sec. 1-A, report by the JPS, JP (44) 234 (Final), 8 September 1944.

59 PRO, CAB122/684, note by the secretary, COS, "Possible German Threat to Murder Prisoners of War," COS (44) 878 (o), 5 October 1944; On the Quebec meeting, see Dallek, *Franklin D. Roosevelt and American Foreign Policy*, 467–78. Gilbert, *Road to Victory*, chap. 51.

60 NACP, RG 165, RWDGSS, ODPO, Top Secret "American-British-Canadian," ABC 383.6 (16 June 1943), sec. 1-A, note by the secretaries, JPS, JPS, 554, 6 November 1944, enclosure, and apps. A and C; NACP, RG 218, Records of the JCS, file CCS 383.6 (15 January 1944), sec. 2, memorandum by the JCS, CCS 472/4, 23 November 1944, enclosures, A and B; PRO, WO193/351, JSM to COS, no. 389, 24 November 1944.

61 The American draft message to SCAEF reads: "[The CCS] believe plans should be made to drop parachutists or air land troops near German prisoners of war

installations to provide initial security for such prisoners." PRO, PREM3/364/7, JSM to COS, no. 390, 24 November 1944.

62 NACP, RG 218, Records of the JCS, file CCS 383.6 (15 January 1944), sec. 2, memorandum by the representatives of the COS, CCS, 472/5, 15 December 1944, and enclosure; PRO, CAB122/678, COS to JSM, 14 December 1944. The EAC was set up at the suggestion of Foreign Secretary Eden during the Moscow Conference of Foreign Ministers in October 1943 and included representatives of Britain, the United States, and the Soviet Union. Its main aim was to provide a forum to discuss European problems, and its members met for the first time in January 1944. In November 1944, the French were invited to join the EAC. See also Sainsbury, *The Turning Point*, 69–79, 95–97, 99–101, 108–9.

63 NACP, RG 218, Records of the JCS, file CCS 383.6 (15 January 1944), sec. 2, report by the JPS, JCS 1168/1, 28 December 1944.

64 Ibid., memorandum by the JCS, CCS 472/6, 3 January 1945; PRO, PREM3/ 364/ 7, JSM, Washington, to COS, no. 487, 5 January 1945.

65 NACP, RG 218, Records of the JCS, file CCS 383.6 (15 January 44), sec. 2, CCS to Eisenhower and Alexander, no. 43767, 26 February 1945; NACP, RG 165, RWDGSS, ODPO, Top Secret "American-British-Canadian," ABC 383.6 (16 June 1943), sec. 2, note by the secretaries, CCS, CCS 472/8, 27 February 1944; see also PRO, CAB122/666, memorandum for Field Marshal Wilson, 21 February 1945.

66 NACP, RG 59, GRDS, Decimal File, 1945–49, file 740.00114EW/1-2245, DPW, 29 November 1944.

67 PRO, PREM3/384/17, Alexander to War Department, no. 886, 15 March 1945.

68 General George Patton at one point sent a rescue mission into Stalag XIII C to try to extract his son-in-law Colonel John Waters, which ended disastrously. Carlson, *We Were Each Other's Prisoners*, 10–11; Nichol and Rennell, *The Last Escape*, 183–84.

69 PRO, ADM116/5019, Eisenhower to Adjutant General, War Department for CCS, no. 248, 26 March 1945; see also PRO, WO193/351, F. E. Morgan, deputy chief of staff, SHAEF, to undersecretary of state for war, WO, 11 March 1945.

70 NACP, RG 331, AOOH, SHAEF, General Staff, G-4 Division, Executive Section, Decimal File, 1945, file 383.6, POW, Eisenhower to War Department, no. 248, 26 March 1945, and Walter Beddle-Smith to General d'Armee Juin, chief of the general staff for National Defence, January 1945, and Eisenhower to CCS, no. 222, 27 February 1945; see also Nichol and Rennell, *The Last Escape*, 175–82.

71 PRO, WO193/351, report by JISC, JIC (44) 322, 29 July 1944; PRO, CAB122/ 665, chief of staff to SCAEF, COS (44) 668 (0), 3 August 1944; see also PRO, WO193/351, extract from the minutes of the COS (44) 251st meeting, 28 July 1944.

72 PRO, CAB122/684, Eden to Halifax, nos. 9057, 9056, 17 October 1944, and Eden to Moscow, no. 17, October 1944, and communication to the State Department from the British embassy, 10 October 1944; see also ibid., note by secretary, COS, "Possible German Threat to Murder Prisoners of War," COS (44) 878 (0), 5 October 1944.

73 NACP, RG 218, Records of the JCS, file CCS 383.6 (21 October 1944), sec. 1, note by the secretaries, JLC, JLC 208/2, 7 November 1944.

74 On the Malmédy massacre, see *History of the United Nations War Crimes Commission*, 365–66; Weingartner, *Crossroads to Death*; Smith, *The Road to Nuremberg*, 113–18; Dupuy, Bongard, and Anderson, *Hitler's Last Gamble*, app. G: Malmédy: Massacre and Trial; Buscher, *The U.S. War Crimes Trial Program*, 37–39, 167–68; Bower, *Blind Eye to Murder*, chap. 12; Ambrose, *Citizen Soldiers*, 354–56.

75 NACP, RG 165, RWDGSS, ODPO, Top Secret "American-British-Canadian," ABC 383.6 (16 June 1943), sec. 1-B, memorandum by the chief of staff, U.S. Army, JCS 1164/4, 23 January 1945, and memorandum for General Craig, "German Atrocities against Allied Prisoners of War," 26 January 1945. See also NACP, RG 218, Records of the JCS, file CCS 383.6 (21 October 1944), sec. 1, William D. Leahy to Stettinius, 22 December 1944; NACP, RG 218, Records of the JCS, file CCS 383.6 (21 October 1944), sec. 1, note by the secretaries, JLC, JLC 208/2, 7 November 1944.

76 NACP, RG 165, RWDGSS, ODPO, Top Secret "American-British-Canadian," ABC 383.6 (16 June 1943), sec. 1-B, Stimson and Forrestal to Leahy, 8 February 1945, and memorandum for General Craig, "German Atrocities against Allied Prisoners of War," 26 January 1945.

77 Stimson Diaries, reel 9, 30 December 1944, 139.

78 Ibid., 31 December 1944, 144.

79 NACP, RG 165, RWDGSS, ODPO, Top Secret "American-British-Canadian," ABC 383.6 (16 June 1943), sec. 1-B, Stimson and Forrestal to Leahy, 8 February 1945.

80 Stimson and McGeorge, *On Active Service in Peace and War*, 568–83; Kimball, *Swords or Ploughshares*, 25–55; Blum, *Roosevelt and Morgenthau*, 573–87.

81 NACP, RG 165, RWDGSS, ODPO, Top Secret "American-British-Canadian," ABC 383.6 (16 June 1943), sec. 1-B, Stimson and Forrestal to Leahy, 8 February 1945.

82 NACP, RG 107, Office of the Secretary of War, Assistant Secretary of War, Formerly Security-Classified Correspondence of John J. McCloy, 1941–45, file ASW 383.6, American POWs, memorandum for the secretary of war and the secretary of the navy by Fleet Admiral Leahy, 7 March 1945; NACP, RG 165, RWDGSS, ODPO, Top Secret "American-British-Canadian," ABC 383.6 (16 June 1943), sec. 1-B, report by the Joint Strategic Survey Committee, JCS 1164/6, 16 February 1945, and memorandum for General Hull on German atrocities against Allied POWs, 22 February 1945, and memorandum for the secretariat, COS, 2 March 1945.

83 NACP, RG 165, RWDGSS, ODPO, Top Secret "American-British-Canadian," ABC 383.6 (16 June 1943), sec. 1-B, memorandum by Schmidt, 26 February 1945. See also Krammer, *Nazi Prisoners of War in America*; Krammer, "American Treatment of German Generals," 27–46.

84 NACP, RG 165, RWDGS, ODPO, Top Secret "American-British-Canadian," ABC 383.6 (16 June 1943), sec. 1-B, memorandum for the assistant chief of staff, G-1, U.S. Army, "Report on Interviews with German General Officers," 12 April 1945.

85 NACP, RG 218, Records of the JCS, file CCS 383.6 (21 October 1944), sec. 2, memorandum by the JCS, U.S. Army. JCS 1164/9, 24 April 1945.

86 NACP, RG 107, Office of the Secretary of War, Assistant Secretary of War, Formerly Security-Classified Correspondence of John J. McCloy, 1941–45, file ASW 383.6, American POWs, Stimson and Forrestal to Stettinius, 14 March 1945.

87 PRO, PREM3/364/11, Eden to Churchill, 9, 14 March 1945.

88 PRO, WO193/356, Bern to FO, no. 391, 2 March 1945. In fact, it was Goebbels who had demanded the execution of tens of thousands of Allied POWs in retaliation; Hitler initially had tended to agree but was later convinced by his chief commanders and Ribbentrop to give up the idea. Kershaw, *Hitler*, 779.

89 Richards, *The Hardest Victory*, 269–75; Messenger, *"Bomber" Harris and the Strategic Bombing Offensive*, 184–88; Gilbert, *The Second World War*, 640–42; Beck, *Under the Bomb*, 177–80; Hinsley et al., *British Intelligence in the Second World War*, vol. 3, pt. 2, chap. 58.

90 MR 300, Churchill to Roosevelt, nos. 920, 921, 22 March 1945.

91 Ibid., Roosevelt to Churchill, no. 725, 22 March 1945.

92 NACP, RG 331, AOOH, SHAEF, SSAGD, Executive Section, Decimal File, 1944, file 383.6, Allied POWs, vol. 1, Carlos J. Warner, American embassy, London, to Lieutenant Colonel W. L. Hays, 10 March 1945.

93 NACP, RG 218, Records of the JCS, file CCS 383.6 (21 October 1944), sec. 2, memorandum by the representatives of the COS, CCS 792/2, 26 March 1945, enclosure B; PRO, WO193/359, JSM, Washington, to COS, no. 625, 23 March 1945.

94 PRO, PREM3/364/11, Eden to Churchill, 7 April 1945; PRO, WO193/359, extract from the minute of the COS (47), eighty-seventh meeting, 4 April 1945.

95 NACP, RG 165, RWDGSS, ODPO, Top Secret "American-British-Canadian," ABC 383.6 (16 June 1943), sec. 1-D, report by the JLC, JCS 1164/8, 18 April 1945, annex "A" to app. "B," annex "B" to app. "B"; PRO, WO193/359, JSM, Washington, to COS, no. 717, 20 April 1945.

96 PRO, PREM3/364/11, Feodor Gousev to Alexander Cadogan, 21 April 1945.

97 Ibid., Stettinius to Churchill, no. 2792, 22 April 1945, and Churchill to Halifax, 22 April 1945.

98 Ibid., FO to Moscow, no. 2001, 22 April 1945, and minute by Churchill, 21 April 1945.

99 Among those taken were Lieutenant Lord Lascelles, who was a nephew of King George VI; Captain the Master of Elphinstone, a nephew of the queen; Captain Lord Haig, son of Field Marshal Alexander; Captain Lord Hopetoun, son of Lord Linlithgow, Captain Michael Alexander, a cousin of the field marshal; Lieutenant Duhamel, a relative of Churchill; and a civilian, Giles Romilly, a nephew of Churchill. Two of the prominent non-British POWs were John Winant, a son of the American ambassador in London, and the Polish general Tadeusz Bor-Komorowski, who was commander of the Polish Home Army. In addition, a dozen other senior Polish officers had been captured after the suppression of the Warsaw rising. PRO, CAB122/684, FO to Halifax, no. 3954, 20 April 1945. About Oflag IV C, see also PRO, WO208/3288, History of Oflag IV C (Colditz), Army, Navy and Air Force Personnel, November 1940–April 1945; Crawley, *Escape from Germany*, chap. 18; Wood, *Detour*; Nichol and Rennell, *The Last Escape*, 177–78.

100 *FRUS*, 1945, 3:709, press release issued by the White House, 23 April 1945. A last-minute suggestion by Churchill was not included. It read: "On the other hand, those who help to preserve the lives of prisoners of war, deported citizens and internees of the United Nations at risk to themselves may be sure that their services will be taken into full consideration by the Allied Powers." Not only were the Americans unable to agree to the additional sentence, but the Foreign Office itself was not enthusiastic. Sargent told the prime minister that the Foreign Office had earlier considered, and rejected, the idea of offering an inducement in the warning. In any case, some days would have to elapse before the issue could be cleared with Washington and Moscow: "To drop a third edition in three or four nights time would be something of an anti-climax and, if the substantial differences in the text are agreed, considerable comment may be aroused." Under the circumstances, Sargent suggested that Churchill forgo the amendment. The prime minister gave in and also left the message out of a speech he made in the House of Commons on 26 April; NACP, RG 107, Office of the Secretary of War, Assistant Secretary of War, Formerly Security-Classified Correspondence of John J. McCloy, 1941–45, file ASW 383.6, General, Eden to Stettinius, 23 April 1945; PRO, PREM3/364/11, Sargent to Eden, 24 April 1945, and Grew to Stimson, 24 April 1945; *Hansard, House of Commons*, vol. 410, cols. 989–990, 26 April 1945; *FRUS*, 1945, 3:709–710, Winant to Stettinius, 26 April 1945.

101 PRO, PREM 3/364/1, Sargent to Churchill, 24 April 1945, and Halifax to FO, no. 2813, 23 April 1945.

102 Stimson Diaries, reel 9, 25 January 1945, 74.

103 Bird, *American POWs of World War II*, 141; Foy, *For You the War Is Over*, 156; Carlson, *We Were Each Other's Prisoners*, 66, note 12.

104 About Germany's attitude toward the United States and Britain and its racist ideology, see Weinberg, *Hitler's Second Book*, chap. 14; Weinberg, *Germany, Hitler, and World War II*, chap. 14; Weinberg, *World in the Balance*, 53–95; Diner, *America in the Eyes of the Germans*, 81–103; Herzstein, *Roosevelt and Hitler*, 18–21; Friedländer, *Prelude to Downfall*, 1–26, 307–9; Wegner, *The Waffen-SS*, 20–25, 47–57; Kershaw, *Hitler*, 150–51, 246, 275; Fischer, *Nazi Germany*, 166–71, 383–91, 475–76.

105 Trevor-Roper, *The Diaries of Joseph Goebbels*, 184–85, 193–94; Kershaw, *Hitler*, 762–64, 770–71, 778, 800, 807, 816–19, 826; Bauer, *Jews for Sale?*, 241–55; Woodward, *British Foreign Policy in the Second World War*, 5:388–90.

106 Stimson Diaries, reel 9, 2 March 1945, 153.

CHAPTER SEVEN

1 PRO, FO916/1183, C. E. King, SHAEF, Political Office, British, to PWD, 30 May 1945.

2 Clark, *Barbarossa*, chap. 21; Overy, *Russia's War*, 255–57; Weinberg, *A World at Arms*, 757–60, 799–801.

3 PRO, FO916/1156, Bern to FO, no. 216, 1 February 1945. About British POWs at E 715, see White, " 'Even in Auschwitz,' " 266–95.

4 PRO, CAB122/694, Bern to FO, no. 292, 17 February 1945. About Dr. Marti's activities before the outbreak of World War II and in other countries, see Moorehead, *Dunant's Dream*, 324–27, 377–78, 397–98, 417–18, 423.

5 NACP, RG 165, RWDGSS, OCOS, Security-Classified General Correspondence, 1942–1947, file 383.6, sec. 3, cases 81–135, military attaché, London, to ETOUSA TC G-2, no. 94335z/177, 11 February 1945; see also Nichol and Rennell, *The Last Escape*, 84–87.

6 NACP, RG 331, Allied Operational and Occupation Headquarters, World War II, SHAEF, Special Staff Adjutant General's Division, Executive Section, Decimal File, 1944, 383.6 to 383.6-19, file 383.6-9#2, Strengths of Prisoner of War Camps in Germany as Known to PWX-SHAEF at 1 December 1944.

7 See above, chap. 6.

8 PRO, AIR40/1489, report on the forced evacuation of Allied officers and other rank prisoners of war from Stalag Luft III, Sagan, Germany—January, February 1945, 20 February 1945.

9 Ibid.

10 Ibid.

11 Durand, *Stalag Luft III*, chap. 16; Crawley, *Escape from Germany*, chap. 33; Nichol and Rennell, *The Last Escape*, chap. 3.

12 PRO, WO311/221, report on the transfer of group of POWs from Stalag 344 Lamsdorff to West Germany, 12 April 1945.

13 Ibid.

14 PRO, WO311/221, affidavit by Turner McLardey, 24 August 1945. See also ibid., affidavit by Private J. Noel, 31 July 1945.

15 PRO, WO311/221, special report on marching conditions from Stalag VIII A Goerlitz to Stalag IX A Ziegnhain, no. 746, 3 April 1945.

16 PRO, WO311/221, UNWCC, United Kingdom Charges against German War Criminals.

17 PRO, WO311/195, UNWCC, United Kingdom Charges against German War Criminals, 23 November 1945.

18 PRO, WO309/648, In the Matter of a War Crime, 1 June 1945. See also PRO, WO208/4680, United Nations War Crimes Commission, affidavit of Alexander McCaskill on a march from Görlitz to Duderstadt from 15 February to 14 March 1945. For a diary written by the squadron leader of the Royal Air Force, C. A. Room, during his march, see Unpublished Memoirs, Department of Documents, Imperial War Museum, London, 88/60/1; John D. White also marched from Upper Silesia to Moosburg; on his recollections, see Neillands, *The Conquest of the Reich*, 247–49; see also Foy, *For You the War Is Over*, chap. 13, and Bard, *Forgotten Victims*, chap. 9; for an account by a German officer who participated in one of the forced marches, see PRO, WO208/4644, Voluntary Declaration by PW Captain Arno Terry, 25 September 1945. For testimonies of American POWs who participated in the marches, see Carlson, *We Were Each Other's Prisoners*, 13–15, 93–94, 123–25. For testimonies of Canadian POWs, see Dancocks, *In Enemy Hands*, chap. 12; see also Nichol and Rennell, *The Last Escape*, chaps. 5–7, 10–11.

19 NACP, RG 165, RWDGSS, OCOS, Security-Classified General Correspondence,

1942–47, file 383.6, sec. 3, cases 81–135, WO to SHAEF, no. 67298, 19 February 1945.

20 NACP, RG 59, GRDS, Decimal File, 1945–49, file 740.00114EW/2-1345—2—2485, DPW, IPWC, Sub-Committee A, 15 February 1945.

21 PRO, FO916/1179, minute by Roberts, 16 February 1945.

22 PRO, WO219/1460, Barker to COS, 17 February 1945.

23 Article 9: "Prisoners of war may be interned in a town, fortress, or other place, and bound not to go beyond certain fixed limits. They may also be interned in enclosed camps; they may not be confined or imprisoned except as an indispensable measure of safety or sanitation, and only while the circumstances which necessitate the measure continue to exist. Prisoners captured in unhealthful regions, or where the climate is injurious for prisoners coming from temperate regions, shall be transported, as soon as possible, to a more favorable climate. Belligerents shall, so far as possible, avoid assembling in a single camp prisoners of different races or nationalities. No prisoner may, at any time, be sent into a region where he might be exposed to the fire of the combat zone, nor used to give protection from bombardment to certain points or certain regions by his presence." Friedman, *The Law of War*, 1:495–96.

24 NACP, RG 107, Office of the Secretary of War, Administrative Assistant to the Secretary of War, file 383.6, American, Eisenhower to CCS, no. S-79573, 18 February 1945; PRO, FO916/38, minute by Roberts, 22 February 1945.

25 Stimson Diaries, reel 9, 19 February 1945, 122.

26 NACP, RG 165, RWDGSS, ODPO, Top Secret "American-British-Canadian," ABC 383.6 (16 June 1943), sec. 1-B, memorandum by the JCS, CCS 781, 20 February 1945, and note by the secretaries JCOS, JCS 1246, 20 February 1945. On British and U.S. military missions in Moscow, see below, chaps. 7 and 8.

27 PRO, FO916/1179, Sargent to Major General L. C. Hollis, War Cabinet Offices, February 1945; PRO, FO916/1180, minute by Roberts, 22 February 1945.

28 See, e.g., NACP, RG 218, Records of the JCS, file CCS 383.6 (18 February 1945), memorandum by the representatives of the COS, CCS 781/1, 21 February 1945.

29 Ibid.

30 PRO, FO916/1179, COS to No. 30 Mission, Moscow, no. 1236, 21 February 1945; NACP, RG 331, AOOH, SHAEF, General Staff, G-4 Division, Executive Section, Decimal File, 1945, file 383.6, POW, JCOS to Deane, no. 41313, 21 February 1945.

31 NACP, RG 107, Office of the Secretary of War, Administrative Assistant to the Secretary of War, file 383.6, American, General Deane to War Department, no. 22965, 28 February 1945; PRO, FO916/1182, Molotov to Clark Kerr, 27 February 1945.

32 NACP, RG 107, Office of the Secretary of War, Administrative Assistant to the Secretary of War, file 383.6, American, Eisenhower to War Department, 2 March 1945.

33 Ibid., Deane to Marshall, 2 March 1945.

34 Ibid., memorandum for the president, 3 March 1945.

35 See below, chap. 9.

36 NACP, RG 389, ROPMG, American POW Information Bureau, Records Branch,

Decimal File, 1942–45, 387.7 to 704, file 383.6, American P/W #5, American legation, Bern, to Hull, no. 1311, 28 February 1945.

37 Ibid., SHAEF, General Staff, G-1 Division, Prisoners of War Branch, Decimal File, 1944–45, file 383.6, POW, Harrison to the State Department, 28 February 1945; see also PRO, AIR14/1239, Bern to FO, no. 427, 7 March 1945.

38 Stalags II B (Hammerstein) and II D (Stargard), Stalag Luft IV (Burzlaff), Stalag XXB (Marienburg) and the military prison at Graudenz, Stalags III B (Fürsten-burg) and III C (Altdrewitz), Stalags Luft III (Sagan) and VII (Bankau), Stalags VIII A (Görlitz), VIII B (Teschen), VIII C (Kunan), and 344 (Lamsdorff), and work detachments and hospitals in the areas.

39 PRO, WO163/582, memorandum by the WO to the IPWC, 7 March 1945.

40 PRO, CAB122/694, JSM to War Cabinet Offices, no. 447, 21 February 1945.

41 PRO, FO916/1179, Bern to FO, no. 336, 24 February 1945.

42 PRO, FO916/1181, PWD to British embassy, Paris, 16 March 1945; Roberts to Victor Mallet, Stockholm, 14 March 1945; and Mallet to FO, no. 426, 14 March 1945. See also above, chap. 2.

43 *Hansard, House of Commons*, vol. 408, cols. 1391–94, 28 February 1945.

44 Ibid., vol. 409, cols. 636–37, 20 March 1945, and vol. 408, cols. 2391–93, 9 March 1945.

45 PRO, FO916/1208, Bern to FO, no. 745, 11 April 1945; NACP, RG 218, Records of the JCS, file CCS 383.6 (13 April 1945), Brigadier A. T. Cornwall-Jones to General McFarland, 13 April 1945.

46 PRO, FO916/1208, minute by Roberts, 12 April 1945.

47 Ibid., conclusions of forty-third War Cabinet meeting, 12 April 1945; *FRUS*, 1945, 3:711, Winant to Hull, 13 April 1945.

48 PRO, CAB122/684, Eden to Halifax, no. 3588, 13 April 1945.

49 Ibid., Halifax to FO, nos. 2505, 2506, 13 April 1945.

50 PRO, WO193/349, Eden to Halifax, no. 3657, 14 April 1945.

51 *Hansard, House of Commons*, vol. 410, cols. 10–11, 17 April 1945, and cols. 1004–5, 26 April 1945.

52 PRO, FO916/1208, Halifax to FO, no. 2700, 19 April 1945.

53 NACP, RG 331, AOOH, SHAEF, General Staff, G-1 Division, Administrative Section, Decimal File, 1944–45, file 383.6-15, Marshall to Eisenhower, no. 70557, 20 April 1945.

54 PRO, FO916/1208, Bern to FO, no. 905, 28 April 1945.

55 *Hansard, House of Commons*, vol. 410, cols. 1220–21, 1 May 1945.

56 PRO, FO916/1209, Department of State, press release, 1 May 1945.

57 PRO, WO311/134, UNWCC, affidavit by Frank Norbury, 13 August 1945.

58 Bauer, "The Death-Marches," 9:491–511; Blatman, "The Death Marches," 475–89; Goldhagen, *Hitler's Willing Executioners*, chaps. 13–14.

CHAPTER EIGHT

1 See, e.g., Sainsbury, *The Turning Point*, chap. 7; Harbutt, *The Iron Curtain*, 53–60.

2 PRO, PREM3/364/8, extract from conclusions of ninety-first War Cabinet meeting, 17 July 1944; PRO, FO916/892, Grigg to Eden, 19 July 1944.

3 PRO, PREM3/364/8, Eden to the Soviet ambassador, 20 July 1944, Annex 1 in memorandum by the secretary of state for foreign affairs, W.P. (44) 492, 3 September 1944.

4 PRO, FO916/892, minute by Warner, 21 July 1944.

5 PRO, PREM3/364/8, memorandum for the prime minister, "Russians Taken Prisoner in France," 25 July 1944. Murphy, "SOE and Repatriation," 313–15.

6 PRO, PREM3/364/8, Eden to Churchill, 2 August 1944.

7 Ibid.; PRO, WO32/11139, Eden to Grigg, 13 August 1944; PRO, FO916/892, Grigg to Eden, 19 July 1944. See also Tolstoy, *The Secret Betrayal*, 51–61.

8 PRO, CAB122/665, Eden to Halifax, no. 7355, 19 August 1944.

9 PRO, PREM3/364/8, Soviet embassy to Eden, 23 August 1944, Annex 2 in memorandum by the secretary of state for foreign affairs, W.P. (44) 492, 3 September 1944.

10 Quoted in Bethell, *The Last Secret*, 10.

11 PRO, PREM3/364/8, memorandum by the secretary of state for foreign affairs, W.P. (44) 492, 3 September 1944; see also Bethell, *The Last Secret*, 8–13; Tolstoy, *The Secret Betrayal*, 54–61; Woodward, *British Foreign Policy*, 3:124.

12 PRO, CAB65/43, conclusions of 115th War Cabinet meeting, 4 September 1944.

13 PRO, FO916/892, FO to Moscow, no. 3186, 25 September 1944.

14 Ibid.; see also Tolstoy, *The Secret Betrayal*, 68–69.

15 See, e.g., Dennett and Johnson, *Negotiating with the Russians*, chaps. 1–4; Kochavi, "From Cautiousness to Decisiveness," 481–509.

16 PRO, FO916/892, FO to Washington, no. 8712, 3 October 1944, and minute by Roberts, 29 September 1944.

17 Ciechanowski, *The Warsaw Rising of 1944*; Hanson, *The Civilian Population and the Warsaw Uprising*; Kitchen, *British Policy toward the Soviet Union*, 220–32; Woodward, *British Foreign Policy*, 202–24; Kacewicz, *Great Britain, the Soviet Union and the Polish Government in Exile*, chap 9; on the conference, see Gilbert, *Road to Victory*, chaps. 53–54.

18 PRO, FO916/892, Tolstoy (Eden) to FO (Sargent), no. 60, 12 October 1944; Eden, *The Eden Memoirs*, 484–85; PRO, PREM3/364/8, extract from COS (44) 338th meeting, 13 October 1944; Moscow to FO, no. 2993, 16 October 1944; extract from COS (44) 332nd meeting, 9 October 1944; and Moscow to FO, no. 2563, 14 October 1944.

19 PRO, PREM3/364/8, Moscow to FO, no. 3016, 17 October 1944; see also PRO WO32/11139, Moscow to FO, no. 2809, 11 October 1944; Tolstoy, *The Secret Betrayal*, 72–76.

20 PRO, PREM3/364/8, Moscow to FO, no. 3018, 17 October 1944.

21 Kitchen, *British Policy toward the Soviet Union*, 233–35, 238–39; Ross, *The Foreign Office and the Kremlin*, 175–83; Tsakaloyannis, "The Moscow Puzzle," 37–55; Stalin, *The Great Patriotic War*, 138.

22 PRO, FO916/893, British embassy, Moscow, to the People's Commissariat for Foreign Affairs, 11 December 1944, and FO to Moscow, no. 4385, 21 November 1944.

23 PRO, FO1079/12, memorandum by Strang, 14 December 1944.

24 Ibid., memorandum by Strang, 20 December 1944.

25 PRO, WO193/348, Moscow to FO, nos. 238, 239, 23 January 1945.

26 PRO, FO916/1186, memorandum by Eden, W.P. (45) 68, 29 January 1945; minute by Sargent, 27 January 1945; and Bovenschen to Sargent, 27 January 1945.

27 PRO, CAB65/49, conclusions of 13th War Cabinet meeting, 31 January 1945.

28 *FRUS*, 1945, The Conferences at Malta and Yalta, 691–92, Eden to Stettinius, 5 February 1945.

29 Ibid., 693–94, Eden to Molotov, 5 February 1945; Bethell, *The Last Secret*, 31–34; Tolstoy, *The Secret Betrayal*, 94–98.

30 See below, chap. 9.

31 PRO, PREM3/364/9, Eden to Churchill, 7 February 1945, and ARGONAUT (Eden) to COS (FO), no. 185, 7 February 1945, and Eden to Churchill, 8, 9 February 1945.

32 PRO, WO32/11139, Moscow to FO, no. 413, 8 February 1945.

33 PRO, PREM3/364/9, Eden to Churchill, 9 February 1945.

34 PRO, FO916/1190, record of conversation between the prime minister and Marshal Stalin, 10 February 1945.

35 PRO, FO1079/12, "Agreement Relating to Prisoners of War and Civilians Liberated by Forces Operating under Soviet Command and Forces Operating under British Command," 11 February 1945.

36 Ibid.

37 PRO, CAB122/687, Eden to Halifax, no. 1388, 12 February 1945.

38 See above, chap. 2.

39 See, e.g., Kochavi, *Post-Holocaust Politics*, 18–19, 28–29.

40 Stalin's lack of care about Soviet POWs was demonstrated when his son Jacob Djugashvili, an artillery captain, was captured by the Germans and Stalin refused to negotiate exchanging him for a German commander; Ulam, *Stalin*, 548–49.

41 PRO, WO224/227, BMM to WO, no. 2337, 13 February 1945; PRO, WO32/11139, record of meeting at Otdel, 15 February 1945.

42 PRO, FO916/1190, 30 M.M., Moscow to the WO, no. 2357, 18 February 1945. See also PRO, WO224/227, Gepp to C. F. G. Warner, FO, 15 January 1945, and FO to Moscow, no. 337, 21 January 1945.

43 PRO, AIR20/9167, FO to Moscow, no. 763, 19 February 1945; PREM3/364/9, extract from conclusions of twenty-first War Cabinet meeting, 19 February 1945.

44 PRO, AIR20/9167, Moscow to FO, no. 500, 20 February 1945; PRO, FO181/ 994/6, Andrei Vyshinski to Clark Kerr, 21 February 1945.

45 PRO, FO916/1189, Moscow to FO, no. 535, 22 February 1945.

46 PRO, FO916/1190, Grigg to Eden, 22 February 1945.

47 Ibid., *House of Commons*, 22 February 1945.

48 PRO, FO181/1005/5, Sargent to Clark Kerr, no. 844, 23 February 1945; on Marshal Koniev, see Bialer, *Stalin and His Generals*, 633; Sydnor, *Soldiers of Destruction*, 296–98.

49 PRO, WO193/342, Moscow to FO, no. 559, 24 February 1945.

50 PRO, FO916/1190, Molotov to Eden, 24 February 1945.

51 See also Foregger, "Soviet Rails to Odessa," 844–60.

52 PRO, WO224/227, 30 M.M., Moscow to WO, no. 2569, 13 March 1945; PRO,

WO32/11139, 30 M.M., Moscow to COS, no. 2555, 13 March 1945; PRO, FO916/
1190, report on British POWs formerly in camps in eastern Germany, 13 March
1945; PRO, PREM3/364/11, 30 M.M., Moscow to COS, no. 2445, 4 March 1945.

53 PRO, WO32/11139, Moscow to FO, no. 805, 15 March 1945; see also PRO, FO181/
1003/8, Archer to Golubev, 5 March 1945, and Archer to Golubev, 9 March 1945.

54 PRO, WO32/11139, Moscow to FO, no. 806, 15 March 1945; on the same day, the
British embassy also reported that a train taking liberated British POWs from the
front line to Odessa was involved in an accident, west of Cracow, in which eight
men were killed and thirty-one injured, twenty-two of them seriously; the Soviets
had buried the dead, hospitalized the seriously wounded, and sent the slightly
injured on to Odessa; PRO, WO32/11139, Moscow to FO, no. 826, 15 March 1945.

55 *FRUS*, The Conferences at Malta and Yalta, 973, communiqué issued at the end of
the conference, 11 February 1945; Woodward, *British Foreign Policy*, 3:252–77;
Gilbert, *Road to Victory*, chap. 62; Churchill, *Triumph and Tragedy*, chap. 3; Eden,
The Eden Memoirs, 516.

56 *Correspondence between the Chairman of the Council of Ministers of the U.S.S.R.
and the Presidents of the U.S.A. and the Prime Ministers of Great Britain*, 1:292,
Stalin to Churchill, 1 January 1945; see also Coutouvidis and Reynolds, *Poland*,
chaps. 5–6; Rozek, *Allied Wartime Diplomacy*, chap. 6; and below, chap. 9.

57 Ross, *The Foreign Office and the Kremlin*, doc. 34, 193–99; Kacewicz, *Great Britain, the Soviet Union and the Polish Government in Exile*; Rothwell, *Britain and the
Cold War*, 136–50; Woodward, *British Foreign Policy*, 3:490–99; Churchill, *Triumph and Tragedy*, chap. 6.

58 PRO, FO916/1191, Moscow to FO, no. 835, 16 March 1945.

59 PRO, WO32/1139, FO to Moscow, no. 1325, 17 March 1945; on Clark Kerr's proposal, see ibid., Moscow to FO, no. 807, 15 March 1945.

60 Making it through recently Russian-occupied territory on his way to freedom,
David Wild recounts (*Prisoner of Hope*, 261) how he had asked a Russian major
what was being done "to repatriate British prisoners. He proudly presented me
with a poster in three languages (Russian, French and English) which he said was
being posted in every town and village. . . . This is the English version:

ANNOUNCEMENT

Officers and soldiers of the allied armies freed from the German captivity by
the troops of the Soviet Army and citizens of the Allied States which were
interned by the enemy, have to call on the next military commandant of town,
common or country, and direct themselves by his order to the camps of recollection.

Besides they can march to the camp of recollection in the town of Wrzesnia and
beginning from the 25th February, 1945 also in towns of Lodz, Praga and Lublin.
Recording to that the further itineraries are designed by the representatives of
the Allied Governments and that the further travelling to this points will be
arranged by these camps of recollection, it is DEFENDED to omit them to continue desorderly the route.

THE COMMAND OF THE FRONT

61 PRO, WO32/11139, Moscow to FO, no. 864, 19 March 1945.

62 Ross, *The Foreign Office and the Kremlin*, doc. 34, Clark Kerr on Soviet policy, 27 March 1945, 199; see also Warner, "From Ally to Enemy," 221–43.

63 PRO, WO32/11139, Moscow to FO, no. 917, 22 March 1945; see also below, chap. 9.

64 PRO, WO32/11139, FO to Moscow, no. 1397, 21 March 1945.

65 PRO, PREM3/364/9, Churchill to Stalin, no. 312/5, 21 March 1945.

66 Ibid., Stalin to Churchill, no. 346/5, 23 March 1945.

67 PRO, WO32/11139, Molotov to Eden, 23 March 1945.

68 PRO, FO916/1152, minute by Sargent, 29 March 1945; see also PRO, FO181/1003/8, 30 M.M. to Troopers, 22 March 1945.

69 Churchill, *Triumph and Tragedy*, 418, 422.

70 See also Gilbert, *Road to Victory*, chaps. 64–65; Kitchen, *British Policy toward the Soviet Union*, 251–53; Woodward, *British Foreign Policy*, 3:492, 494, 498.

71 PRO, FO371/47944/N3610, minute, 30 March 1945; PRO, FO916/1192, report of an interview with Captain W. D. H. Allen and Captain N. Maclean, 19 March 1945; PRO, WO193/351, report of an interview with Warrant Officer Nevins, RAF; Regimental Quartermaster Sergeant Primrose; and six RAF NCOs, 21 March 1945.

72 Wild, *Prisoner of Hope*, 257.

73 Ibid., 259.

74 Ibid., 262.

75 PRO, WO32/11139, Moscow to FO, no. 11173, 8 April 1945; PRO, FO916/1194, 30 M.M., Moscow to WO, no. 2802, 9 April 1945; PRO, FO916/1157, daily report on position of British POWs in Germany, no. 41, 12 April 1945.

76 PRO, FO916/1196, Clark Kerr to Molotov, 18 April 1945; NACP, RG 334, RIAUSMMM, Subject File: October 1943–October 1945, file POWs 27 March–24 April 1945, Golubev to Archer, 13 April 1945.

77 PRO, FO916/1195, Moscow to FO, no. 1439, 20 April 1945.

78 PRO, FO916/1194, minutes by Roberts, 13, 17 April 1945; PRO, FO371/47792, FO to Moscow, no. 1922, 18 April 1945; PRO, FO916/1207, Grigg to Eden, 12 April 1945.

79 PRO, FO916/1194, minutes by Wilson and Dean, 18 April 1945.

80 PRO, FO916/1195, FO to Moscow, no. 1958, 20 April 1945.

81 Ibid., FO to Washington, no. 3936, 20 April 1945.

82 Kitchen, *British Policy toward the Soviet Union*, 253.

83 *Correspondence between the Chairman of the Council of Ministers of the U.S.S.R. and the Presidents of the U.S.A. and the Prime Ministers of Great Britain*, 1:330, Stalin to Churchill, 24 April 1945.

84 Ibid., 348, Stalin to Churchill, 4 May 1945; see also Churchill, *Triumph and Tragedy*, bk. 2, chap. 10; Coutouvidis and Reynolds, *Poland*, 172–75.

85 In his memoirs, General Deane, head of the U.S. Military Mission in Moscow, described Golikov as follows: "He must have been seven feet tall and was almost as wide. Unfortunately his mental stature did not conform to the size of his body." Deane, *The Strange Alliance*, 188.

86 PRO, WO32/11139, Moscow to FO, no. 1624, 30 April 1945.

87 *Hansard, House of Commons*, vol. 410, cols. 1388–90, 2 May 1945; see also PRO, WO32/11139, FO to Moscow, no. 3210, 10 June 1945.

88 PRO, PREM3/364/17, United Kingdom Delegation, San Francisco, to FO, no. 290, 13 May 1945.

89 PRO, WO32/11139, FO to Moscow, no. 2440, 5 May 1945.

90 *Hansard, House of Commons*, vol. 410, cols. 1878–79, 9 May 1945.

91 PRO, PREM3/364/17, United Kingdom Delegation, San Francisco, to FO, no. 290, 13 May 1945.

92 PRO, FO916/1198, Moscow to FO, no. 2225, 3 June 1945.

93 PRO, WO193/349, Moscow to FO, no. 1633, 30 April 1945.

94 PRO, WO32/11139, FO to Moscow, no. 2440, 5 May 1945; PRO, FO916/1196, FO to Moscow, no. 2375, 3 May 1945; PRO, WO219/1465, SCAEF to Twelve Army Group, May 1945, and Admiral Archer to Admiralty, no. 161701B, 17 May 1945; see also below, chap. 9.

95 See, e.g., PRO, FO916/1201, Moscow to FO, no. 32, 28 August 1945, and Roberts to V. G. Dekanozov, 1 August 1945.

96 PRO, WO32/11139, FO to Moscow, no. 3342, 15 June 1945; FO to Moscow, no. 3107, 6 June 1945; and Moscow to FO, no. 2226, 2 June 1945.

97 PRO, FO371/47792, Moscow to FO, no. 3384, 1 August 1945.

98 PRO, FO916/1211, Parliamentary Questions, 19, 27 November 1945.

99 Ibid., Cavendish Bentinck to FO, no. 1036, 30 November 1945; *Sunday Times*, 9 December 1945, "Poland's 'No' to Search Parties"; on complicated British-Soviet relations after the war, including on Poland, see Kochavi, *Post-Holocaust Politics*, pt. 3.

100 PRO, FO916/1211, Political Adviser to the Commander in Chief, Germany to FO, no. 491, 14 December 1945, and *News Chronicle*, 14 December 1945.

CHAPTER NINE

1 Deane, *The Strange Alliance*, 182.

2 Bethell, *The Last Secret*, 1–4; Tolstoy, *The Secret Betrayal*, 36–41; Elliott, *Pawns of Yalta*, chap. 1; Murphy, "SOE and Repatriation," 309–13.

3 The seven camps were Stalag Luft VI (Heydekrug), with 2,411 USAAF enlisted men; Stalag Luft III (Sagan), with 3,300 USAAF officers; Stalag Luft IV (Gross Tychow), with 350 USAAF enlisted personnel; Stalag Luft VII (Bankau), personnel strength unknown; Oflag 64 (Schubin), with 513 U.S. Army Ground Force officers; Stalag II B (Hammerstein), with 4,800 enlisted personnel; and Stalag 344 (Lamsdorf), with 252 enlisted personnel, mostly in hospital.

4 NACP, RG 334, RIAUSMMM, Subject File: October 1943–October 1945, file POWs 24 June–31 December 1944, Walsh to Slavin, 1 August 1944.

5 PRO, FO916/893, Harriman to Molotov, 30 August 1944; NACP, RG 331, AOOH, SHAEF, G-1 Division, Decimal Correspondence File, 1944–45, file SHAEF, G-1 383.6 Allied POWs, North African Theater of Operations, U.S. Army, to SHAEF, no. 92068, 4 September 1944, and Bedell-Smith to Russ Deane, 16 August 1944.

6 *FRUS*, 1944, 4:1246, Gromyko to Stettinius, 9 September 1944.

7 Ibid., 1247, memorandum of conversation by Stettinius, 12 September 1944. On

Gromyko's assessment of Soviet-American relations, see Perlmutter, *FDR and Stalin*, app. 3.

8 *FRUS*, 1944, 4:1252–53, Gromyko to Hull, 23 September 1944.

9 Ibid., 1251, memorandum of conversation by Stettinius, 24 September 1944.

10 NACP, RG 331, AOOH, SHAEF, OCOS, Secretary, General Staff, Decimal File, May 1943–August 1945, file 383.6/7, vol. 1 (of 2), Eisenhower to Deane, no. 65269, 3 November 1944.

11 Ibid., SSAGD, Executive Section, Decimal File, 1944, file 383.6-9 #2, Deane to Bedell-Smith, no. 21613, 4 November 1944; see also *FRUS*, 1944, 4:1251, Hull to Harriman, 21 September 1944.

12 Deane, *The Strange Alliance*, 186.

13 NACP, RG 331, AOOH, SHAEF, SSAGD, Executive Section, Decimal File, 1944, file 383.6-9 #2, Deane to Bedell-Smith, no. 21627, 6 November 1944.

14 PRO, WO32/11139, Kennan to Molotov, 6 November 1944; see also Falls, "American POWs in Romania," 37–44.

15 *FRUS*, 1944, 4:1262–63, Stettinius to Gromyko, 8 November 1944.

16 Ibid., 1264, Kennan to Stettinius, 11 November 1944.

17 Ibid. Moscow's determination to return its citizens was also demonstrated by sending a team of forty Soviet officers to France, Belgium, Holland, and Luxembourg to identify and repatriate Soviet citizens. PRO, CAB122/686, Gromyko to Stettinius, 20 November 1944; PRO, CAB119/95, JSM, Washington, to COS, no. 398, 27 November 1944; MR 300, JCS to SHAEF, no. 6958, 28 November 1944. See also Volkogonov, *Stalin*, 491–92.

18 PRO, WO32/11139, Molotov to Kennan, 25 November 1944; NACP, RG 59, GRDS, 740.00114EW/12-544, Moscow to Stettinius, no. 4526, 27 November 1944.

19 Deane, *The Strange Alliance*, 188.

20 *FRUS*, 1945, The Conferences at Malta and Yalta, 415, Harriman to Stettinius, 29 December 1944; *FRUS*, 1944, 4:1271, Stettinius to Gromyko, 13 December 1944.

21 Ibid., 1272, Stettinius to Kirk, 20 December 1944, and 1270–71, Kirk to Stettinius, 10 December 1944.

22 Ibid., 1272–73, memorandum of telephone conversation, 29 December 1944.

23 *FRUS*, 1945, The Conferences at Malta and Yalta, 416, Stettinius to Harriman, 3 January 1945.

24 Stimson Diaries, reel 9, 16 January 1945, 48; see also Elliott, *Pawns of Yalta*, 36–37.

25 *FRUS*, 1945, The Conferences at Malta and Yalta, 450–55, Harriman to Stettinius, 10 January 1945.

26 NACP, RG 331, AOOH, SHAEF, OCOS, Secretary, General Staff, Decimal File, May 1943–August 1945, Deane to Marshall, no. 22423, 21 January 1945.

27 NACP, RG 331, AOOH, SHAEF, General Staff, G-1 Division Administrative Section, Decimal File, 1944–45, file GAP 383.6, 092.2, Deane to Marshall, no. 22453, 23 January 1945; Deane to Marshall, no. 22423, 21 January 1945; Eisenhower to SHAEF, no. 76547, 25 January 1945; and Bedell-Smith to Marshall, no. 15473, 26 January 1945; also, MR 300, Sweeny to McFarland (ARGONAUT), no. 42, 28 January 1945. See also above, chap. 8.

28 MR 300, JCOS to ARGONAUT, no. 28993, 29 January 1945; see also Elliott, "The United States and Forced Repatriation of Soviet Citizens," 263–69.

29 Article 1 of a decree of the Presidium of the Supreme Soviet, dated 7 September 1940, read as follows: "In accordance with Article 1 of the law 'Concerning Citizenship of the U.S.S.R.' of August 19, 1938, it is established that citizens of Lithuanian, Latvian and Estonian Soviet Socialist Republics are citizens of the U.S.S.R. from the day of the acceptance of these republics into the U.S.S.R." NACP, RG 59, GRDS, 740.00114EW/3-345, Grew to London, 24 March 1945.

30 Kochavi, "Britain, the Soviet Union, and the Question of the Baltic States in 1943," 173–82.

31 NACP, RG 59, GRDS, 740.00114EW/2-345, Grew to American embassy, Moscow, no. 240, 3 February 1945.

32 Ibid.; Bethell, *The Last Secret*, 24–30; Tolstoy, *The Secret Betrayal*, 82–94.

33 PRO, FO916/1187, COS to ARGONAUT, no. 100, 3 February 1945.

34 Quoted in Bethell, *The Last Secret*, 26.

35 *FRUS*, 1945, The Conferences at Malta and Yalta, 691–92, Eden to Stettinius, 5 February 1945; see also above, chap. 8.

36 *FRUS*, 1944, 4:1262 n. 82; Elliott, *Pawns of Yalta*, 43–49.

37 *FRUS*, 1945, The Conferences at Malta and Yalta, 756–57, Stettinius to Grew, 9 February 1945; 754–56, draft reciprocal agreement on POWs as approved by the CCS, 8 February 1945; and 697, Grew to Stettinius, 7 February 1945. On Stettinius's perspective of the Yalta Conference, see Stettinius, *Roosevelt and the Russians*, pt. 2.

38 NACP, RG 331, AOOH, SHAEF, General Staff, G-3 Division, PHPS, Decimal File, 1943–45, file 383.2, Allied POWs during Post Hostilities, ARGONAUT to AGWAR, no. 150, 11 February 1945; see also Marrus, *The Unwanted*, 315, and above, chap. 8.

39 Deane, *The Strange Alliance*, 189.

40 See, e.g., *FRUS*, 1944, 4:1264, Kennan to Stettinius, 11 November 1944.

41 Harriman and Abel, *Special Envoy to Churchill and Stalin*, 416.

42 NACP, RG 331, AOOH, SHAEF, General Staff, G-3 Division, PHPS, Decimal File, 1943–45, file 383.2, Allied POWs during Post Hostilities, Deane to Marshall, no. 22792, 19 February 1945, and Deane and Archer to CCS, no. 22960, 28 February 1945; NACP, RG 334, RIAUSMMM, Subject File: October 1943–October 1945, file POWs 1 January–28 February 1945, meeting in Moscow of American and Soviet teams, 17 February 1945.

43 MR 330, Deane to Marshall, no. 23022, 3 March 1945.

44 NACP, RG 107, Office of the Secretary of War, Administrative Assistant to the Secretary of War, file 383.6, American, memorandum for the president by Stimson, 3 March 1945; NACP, RG 165, RWDGSS, OCOS, Top-Secret General Correspondence, 1944–1945, file 383.6, Deane to Marshall, 2 March 1945; Stimson Diaries, reel 9, 2 March 1945, 152–54.

45 NACP, RG 334, RIAUSMMM, Subject File: October 1943–October 1945, file POWs 1 January–28 February 1945, meeting at Moscow between Deane and his team and General Golubev, 3 March 1945. See also Buhite, "Soviet American Relations and the Repatriation of Prisoners of War."

46 NACP, RG 334, RIAUSMMM, Subject File: October 1943–October 1945, file POWs 1 March–12 March 1945, Harriman to Molotov, 4 March 1945; Kimball, *Churchill and Roosevelt*, 3:542.

47 For Stalin's reply to the British, see above, chap. 8.

48 NACP, RG 218, Records of the JCS, file CCS 383.6 (28 February 1945), Stalin to Roosevelt, 5 March 1945.

49 MR 330, Harriman to Roosevelt, no. 23119, 8 March 1945. About Polish aid to the POWs, see Wadley, *Even One Is Too Many*, 35, 37–38, 46.

50 MR 330, Harriman to Roosevelt, n. 23119, 8 March 1945.

51 To illustrate this point, Hall listed the daily menu supplied by the Soviets to the officer camp in Odessa (italicized items were supplied by the Americans): break-fast—fish, cabbage, *creamed chicken*, coffee; dinner—soup, kasha, hamburger, coffee; supper—*string beans*, kasha, *chili*, *peaches*, *coffee*. Bread was served at all meals. In the enlisted men's camp, the menu included soup and *coffee* for break-fast; soup, *crackers*, kasha, and bread for dinner; and *beef stew*, *coffee*, and *one cookie* for supper. The Soviets attempted to supply a limited amount of clothing on a replacement basis to those sorely in need of it. Soviet-made underwear had been supplied to all POWs (after they had been given a hot shower on arrival in Odessa).

52 NACP, RG 334, RIAUSMMM, Subject File: October 1943–October 1945, file POWs 1 March–12 March 1945, interim report on transit camp, 5 and 8 March 1945.

53 On the trip to Odessa, see Foregger, "Soviet Rails to Odessa," 846–52.

54 MR 330, Harriman to Roosevelt, no. 23119, 8 March 1945; see also NACP, RG 331, AOOH, SHAEF, Entry 6, G-1 Division, Decimal Correspondence File, 1944–45, file 383.6-15, Interim Report on Russian Transit Camp for Liberated POWs at Odessa, 14 March 1945.

55 NACP, RG 334, RIAUSMMM, Subject File: October 1943–October 1945, file POWs 1 March–12 March 1945, Dean to U.S. Army Forces in the Middle East, Cairo, 5 March 1945.

56 Ibid., notes on the official meeting between General Deane and General Golubev on POWs, 7 March 1945.

57 MR 330, Harriman to Roosevelt, no. 23174, 12 March 1945; NACP, RG 334, RIAUSMMM, Subject File: October 1943–October 1945, file POWs 1 March–12 March 1945, meeting at Moscow between Deane and his team and General Golubev, 6 March 1945; NACP, RG 59, GRDS, Decimal File, 1945–49, file 740.00114EW/3-345, Harriman to Stettinius, no. 738, 14 March 1945; see also Nolan, "Americans in the Gulag," 525–29.

58 NACP, RG 334, RIAUSMMM, Subject File: October 1943–October 1945, file POWs 1 March–12 March 1945, Deane to Wilmeth, 10 March 1945. About Wilmeth's mission, see Wadley, *Even One Is Too Many*, chap. 3.

59 Deane, "Negotiating on Military Assistance," 16–17; PRO, WO32/11139, FO to Moscow, no. 1396, 21 March 1945; see also above, chap. 8.

60 NACP, RG 334, RIAUSMMM, Subject File: October 1943–October 1945, file POWs 13 March–26 March 1945, meeting at Moscow between Harriman and Molotov,

13 March 1945. See also Kimball, *The Juggler*, 159–83; Harbutt, *The Iron Curtain*, 82–99.

61 NACP, RG 59, GRDS, Decimal File, 1945–49, file 740.00114EW/3-345, Harriman to Stettinius, no. 738, 14 March 1945; NACP, RG 334, RIAUSMMM, Subject File: October 1943–October 1945, file POWs 13 March–26 March 1945, Harriman to Molotov, 14 March 1945.

62 NACP, RG 59, GRDS, Decimal File, 1945–49, file 740.00114EW/3-345, Harriman to Stettinius, no. 738, 14 March 1945; see also Herring, *Aid to Russia*, chap. 7.

63 Clemens, "Averell Harriman, John Deane, the Joint Chiefs of Staff," 277–306; Bland, "Averell Harriman," 403–16; Stoler, *Allies and Adversaries*, chap. 11; Yergin, *Shattered Peace*, 74–77.

64 NACP, RG 165, RWDGSS, ODPO, Top Secret "American-British-Canadian," ABC 383.6 (16 June 1943), sec. 1-C, memorandum for General Lincoln, 16 March 1945.

65 MR 330, Roosevelt to Stalin, no. 209, 17 March 1945; Stimson Diaries, reel 9, 16 March 1945, 194–95.

66 *Correspondence between the Chairman of the Council of Ministers of the U.S.S.R. and the Presidents of the U.S.A. and the Prime Ministers of Great Britain*, 2:196–97, Stalin to Roosevelt, 22 March 1945.

67 MR 330, Harriman to Roosevelt, no. 23408, 24 March 1945.

68 Ibid.

69 Ibid., Roosevelt to Harriman, no. 216, 26 March 1945; NACP, RG 165, RWDGSS, ODPO, Top Secret "American-British-Canadian," ABC 383.6 (16 June 1943), sec. 1-C, memorandum for record: "Repatriation of Russian Prisoners of War," 4 April 1945.

70 Quoted in Clemens, "Averell Harriman, John Deane, the Joint Chiefs of Staff," 280.

71 Loewenheim, Langley, and Jonas, *Roosevelt and Churchill*, 709.

72 *Correspondence between the Chairman of the Council of Ministers of the U.S.S.R. and the Presidents of the U.S.A. and the Prime Ministers of Great Britain*, 2:201–4, Roosevelt to Stalin, received on 1 April 1945; 211–13, Stalin to Roosevelt, 7 April 1945; 215–17, Truman and Churchill to Stalin, 18 April 1945; and 219–20, Stalin to Roosevelt, 24 April 1945. See also Gromyko, *Memoirs*, 85–93; Bohlen, *Witness to History*, 187–92, 207–8; Yergin, *Shattered Peace*, 63–64; Dallek, *Franklin D. Roosevelt and American Foreign Policy*, 513–16.

73 Sherwood, *Roosevelt and Hopkins*, 898–901, 905–10; Bohlen, *Witness to History*, 217–19; Harbutt, *The Iron Curtain*, 105–9; Rozek, *Allied Wartime Diplomacy*, 180–86; Stoler, *Allies and Adversaries*, 231–39.

74 Deane, *The Strange Alliance*, 190.

75 NACP, RG 165, Records of the War Department, General and Special Staffs, ODPO, General Records—Correspondence, Security-Classified General Correspondence, 1942–45, file OPD 383.6, sec. 15, cases 410–451, statements of liberated POWs regarding treatment while in Russian hands, 11 April 1945. In a meeting between American and Soviet teams on 25 April 1945, Colonel James Crockett, who had just returned from a visit to Odessa, Lwow, and Volkvysk,

stated that conditions in all three reception camps were satisfactory. NACP, RG 334, RIAUSMMM, Subject File: October 1943–October 1945, file POWs 26 April–15 June 1945, meeting at Repatriation Commission Headquarters, Moscow, 25 April 1945; Kimball, *Churchill and Roosevelt*, vol. 3, 634.

76 Foregger, "Soviet Rails to Odessa," 844; Elliott, *Pawns of Yalta*, 62. According to Wadley, 5,159 POWs had been removed to Odessa. Wadley, *Even One Is Too Many*, 48.

77 Analysis and assessment of the data furnished by 1,500 U.S. POWs who had arrived in the United States via Russia established the following conclusion: "In general the attitude of the Russians was exemplified by an air of preoccupation and indifference. No concerted effort was made to transport the recovered prisoners of war to concentration point for further evacuation to the rear. The food supplied was, for the most part, inadequate and the American personnel experienced considerable difficulty 'living off the land' as appears to be the custom of the Russians. There were many reports of watches, rings, overcoats, shoes and other valuables being stolen by Russian soldiers and officers by violence or threat of bodily harm. Little or no clothing was supplied and sanitary conditions were bad. It is believed that no plan of procedures was established prior to the recovery of large numbers of prisoners of war, which may account for much of the delay and discomfort encountered by the repatriates. Russian troops in a number of instances could not identify recovered prisoners as Americans and great difficulty was experienced in establishing proper identity." NACP, RG 334, RIUSMMM, Subject File: October 1943–October 1945, file POWs (Personnel evacuated through Odessa), memorandum for commanding general, U.S. Military Mission in Moscow, by Brigadier General R. W. Berry, 21 April 1945.

78 Loewenheim, Langley, and Jonas, *Roosevelt and Churchill*, 709. About the Bern incident, see *Correspondence between the Chairman of the Council of Ministers of the U.S.S.R. and the Presidents of the U.S.A. and the Prime Ministers of Great Britain*, 2:297; 197, Roosevelt to Stalin, 25 March 1945; 204–5, Roosevelt to Stalin, 1 April 1945; 205–6, Stalin to Roosevelt, 3 April 1945; 207–8, Roosevelt to Stalin, 5 April 1945; 208–10, Stalin to Roosevelt, 7 April 1945; and 214, Roosevelt to Stalin, received on 13 April 1945; Gilbert, *Road to Victory*, 1279–81; Mayers, *The Ambassadors and America's Soviet Policy*, 154. See also Kimball, *Forged In War*, 321–26; Kimball, *Churchill and Roosevelt*, 3:586–87.

79 *FRUS*, 1945, 5:1075–77, memorandum by the chairman of the State-War-Navy Coordinating Committee, James C. Dunn, to Stettinius, 9 March 1945; NACP, RG 59, GRDS, Decimal File, 1945–49, file 740.00114EW/3-145—3—145, memorandum for Bernard Gufler, Special War Problems Division, 2 March 1945; MR 300, JCOS to McNarney, no. 63626, 4 April 1945.

80 NACP, RG 338, Theaters of War, World War II, ETO, sec. G-1, Decimal file, 1943–46, 381–383.6, file 383.6, POWs, Eisenhower to Normandy Base Section, no. 21518, 16 March 1945, and file 383.6, Foreign Nationals, Brigadier General R. G. Lovett to Commanding Generals, 27 April 1945.

81 NACP, RG 59, GRDS, Decimal File, 1945–49, file 740.00114EW/2-1345—2—2485, Grew to Gromyko, 23 March 1945.

82 *FRUS*, 1945, 5:1090–91, Gromyko to Grew, 10 April 1945.

83 Ibid. Charles E. Bohlen, State Department adviser on eastern Europe, recommended Stettinius telling Molotov that the United States "had no intention of holding Soviet citizens after the collapse of Germany regardless of whether they desire to return to the Soviet Union or not." Ibid., 832–37, memorandum by Bohlen to Stettinius, 19 April 1945.

84 Ibid., 1086–88, Harriman to Stettinius, 2 April 1945; NACP, RG 331, AOOH, SHAEF, SSAGD, Decimal File, 1945, 383.6-4 to 383.6-8, file 383.6-5, Deane to Eisenhower, no. 23950, 18 April 1945; NACP, RG 331, AOOH, WWII, SHAEF, SSAGD, Decimal File, 1945, 383.6-4 to 383.6-8, file 383.6-5, SHAEF to Deane, no. 85820, 22 April 1945. On the Soviet response, see NACP, RG 59, GRDS, Decimal File, 1945–49, file 740.00114EW/5-3045, Soviet embassy to the State Department, 30 May 1945.

85 NACP, RG59, GRDS, Decimal File, 1945–49, file 740.00114EW/4-3045, Kennan to Stettinius, no. 1423, 30 April 1945; Mosley, "Some Soviet Techniques of Negotiation," 272–74; see also Kochavi, *Prelude to Nuremberg*, 68–70, and above, chap. 8.

86 NACP, RG 59, GRDS, Decimal File, 1945–49, file 740.00114EW/5-145-3145, press release, no. 410, 3 May 1945; NACP, 165, RWDGSS, ODPO, Top Secret "American-British-Canadian," ABC 383.6 (16 June 1943), sec. 1-D, memorandum for the president, 2 May 1945.

87 Ibid., file 740.00114EW/4-3045, Kennan to Stettinius, 2 May 1945.

88 NACP, RG 331, AOOH, SHAEF, G-1 Division, Decimal Correspondence File, 1944–45, file SHAEF, G-1 383.6 Allied POWs, Eisenhower to Deane, no. 87705, 11 May 1945; NACP, RG 59, GRDS, Decimal File, 1945–49, file 740.00114EW/5-1545, Murphy to Stettinius, no. 15 May 1945.

89 NACP, RG 59, GRDS, Decimal File, 1945–49, file 740.00114EW/5-1545, Paris to Stettinius, no. 2625, 15 May 1945.

90 NACP, RG 334, RIAUSMMM, Subject File: October 1943–October 1945, file POWs 26 April–15 June 1945, plan for delivery through the army lines of former POWs and civilians liberated by the Red Army and the Allied forces, 22 May 1945.

91 Ibid. NACP, RG 59, GRDS, Decimal File, 1945–49, file 740.00114EW/6-145, Donald R. Heath, deputy U.S. political adviser, to Stettinius, no. 449, 1 June 1945, and Murphy to Stettinius, no. 2936, 24 May 1945; Proudfoot, *European Refugees*, 207–10; Ziemke, *The U.S. Army in the Occupation of Germany*, 289–90.

92 NACP, RG 59, GRDS, Decimal File, 1945–49, file 740.00114EW/5-2445, Murphy to Stettinius, no. 2936, 24 May 1945.

93 NACP, RG 331, AOOH, SHAEF, G-1 Division, Decimal Correspondence File, 1944–45, file SHAEF, G-1 383.6 Allied POWs, Eisenhower to AGWAR, no. 23059, June 1945, and Deane to Marshall, no. 24524, 31 May 1945.

94 *FRUS*, 1945, V: 1105, Byrnes to Murphy, 29 August 1945. Between April 1942 and September 1945, 291 American airmen landed in the Soviet Union. After the Soviet Union joined the war with the Japanese, they liberated approximately 1,300 American POWs held by the Japanese. Nenninger, "United States Prisoners of War and the Red Army," 763–65. On Allied POWs held by the Japanese, see Daws, *Prisoners of the Japanese*; Roland, *Long Night's Journey*.

95 *FRUS*, 1945, V: 1106–7, Dean Acheson, acting secretary of state, to Byrnes, 29 September 1945; see also NACP, RG 59, GRDS, Decimal File 1945–1949, file 740.00114EW/6-1145, Flitt, State Department, Special War Problems Division to Matthews, 27 June 1945, and file 740.00114EW/6-145-6-3045, Flournoy to Herrick and Durbrow, 22 June 1945; *FRUS*, 1945, V: 1103, Kirk to the Secretary of State, 7 August 1945; Elliott, *Pawns of Yalta*, 86–90, chap. 5; Bethell, *The Last Secret*, chap. 7.

96 *FRUS*, 1945, V: 1098–99, Grigg to Murphy, 11 July 1945; see also Bethell, *The Last Secret*, chaps. 4–6; Tolstoy, *The Secret Betrayal*, chaps. 7–13; and Booker, *A Looking-Glass Tragedy*.

97 *FRUS*, 1945, V: 1108–9, memorandum by the State-War-Navy Coordinating Committee, 21 December 1945.

98 Ibid.; see also Proudfoot, *European Refugees*, 207–20; Tolstoy, *The Secret Betrayal*, particularly 408–9; Elliott, "The United States and Forced Repatriation of Soviet Citizens," 269–73.

CONCLUSION

1 PRO, WO208/3247, memorandum on British POWs, 28 September 1939.

2 Hitler, *Mein Kampf*, 260.

3 Kershaw, *Hitler*, 826.

4 Churchill, *Triumph and Tragedy*, 366.

5 Wild, *Prisoner of Hope*, 271.

6 Quoted in Nichol and Rennell, *The Last Escape*, 388.

BIBLIOGRAPHY

ARCHIVES AND MANUSCRIPT COLLECTIONS

United Kingdom

British Red Cross Archive, London
  The Prisoner of War
Imperial War Museum, London
  Department of Documents, Unpublished Memoirs
Public Record Office, Kew
  Admiralty
    ADM 116 Admiralty and Secretariat Papers
  Air Ministry
    AIR 2 Air Ministry, Registered Files
    AIR 14 Bomber Command
    AIR 20 Unregistered Papers
    AIR 40 Directorate of Intelligence and Other Intelligence Papers
  Cabinet Records
    CAB 65 War Cabinet Minutes
    CAB 66 War Cabinet Memoranda WP and CP Series
    CAB 119 Joint Planning Staff
    CAB 122 British Joint Staff Mission: Washington Office Files
  Colonial Office
    CO 980 Prisoners of War and Civilian Internees Department
  Foreign Office
    FO 115 Embassy and Consular Archives: United States of American
      Correspondence
    FO 181 Embassy and Consular Archives: Russia Correspondence
    FO 369 General Correspondence: Consular
    FO 370 General Correspondence: Library
    FO 371 Foreign Office: General Correspondence: Political
    FO 916 War of 1939 to 1945: Consular (War) Department: Prisoners of War
      and Internees
    FO 1049 Control Commission for Germany (British element): Hansestadt
      Hamburg
    FO 1079 European Advisory Commission
  Ministry of Information
    INF 1 Files of Correspondence
  Prime Minister Private Office
    PREM 3 Operational Papers
    PREM 4 Confidential Papers

Records of the Security Service, 1905–53
    KV2 Personal Files
Treasury Solicitor
    TS 26 Treasury Solicitor and HM Procurator General: War Crimes Papers
War Office
    WO 32 Registered Files: General Series
    WO 163 War Office Council and Army Council Records
    WO 193 Directorate of Military Operations: Collation Files
    WO 208 Directorate of Military Intelligence
    WO 219 War of 1939 to 1945, Military Headquarters Papers: SHAEF
    WO 222 War of 1939 to 1945: Medical Historian Papers
    WO 224 War of 1939 to 1945: Enemy Prisoners of War Camps: Reports of
        International Red Cross and Protecting Powers
    WO 309 War of 1939 to 1945: HQ BAOR: War Crimes Group (NEW): Files
    WO 311 War of 1939 to 1945: Military Deputy, Judge Advocate General: War
        Crimes Files
    WO 366 War Office: Department of the Permanent Under Secretary of State:
        C3 Branch: Branch Memoranda on Historical Monographs
United States
Franklin D. Roosevelt Library, Hyde Park, New York
    Map Room Files
National Archives, College Park, Maryland
    RG 18 Army Air Process, Central Decimal Files, October 1942–May 1944
    RG 59 General Records of the Department of State, American Prisoners of War in
        Germany
    RG 59 Records of the Special War Problems Division Policy Books, 1939–45
    RG 107 Assistant Secretary of War, Correspondence of John J. McCloy, 1941–45
    RG 160 Army Service Forces, Office of the Commanding General Control
        Division, Historical File, 1941–46
    RG 165 Records of the War Department General and Special Staffs, Office of the
        Chief of Staffs, Security-Classified General Correspondence, 1942–47
    RG 218 Records of the United States Joint Chiefs of Staff
    RG 331 Records of Allied Operational and Occupation Headquarters, WWII,
        SHAEF
    RG 338 Records of United States Army Commands, 1942–, European Theater of
        Operations
    RG 389 Records of the Office of Provost Marshal General, American POW
        Information Bureau
    RG 407 Record of the Adjutant General's Office
Yale University Library, New Haven, Connecticut
    Henry L. Stimson Diaries, 1944–45

NEWSPAPERS
Prisoners of War Bulletin
The Prisoner of War

PUBLISHED PRIMARY SOURCES

Cambray, P. G., and G. G. B. Briggs, eds. *Red Cross and St. John War Organisation, 1939–1947*. London: Sumfield and Day, 1949.

Cantwell, John D. *The Second World War: A Guide to Documents in the Public Record Office*. London: Public Record Office, 1993.

Correspondence between the Chairman of the Council of Ministers of the U.S.S.R. and the Presidents of the U.S.A. and the Prime Ministers of Great Britain during the Great Patriotic War of 1941–1945. Vol. 1. Moscow: Foreign Languages Public House, 1945.

Correspondence between the Chairman of the Council of Ministers of the U.S.S.R. and the Presidents of the U.S.A. and the Prime Ministers of Great Britain during the Great Patriotic War of 1941–1945. Vol. 2. Moscow: Foreign Languages Public House, 1957.

Friedman, Leon. *The Law of War: A Documentary History*. Vol. 1. New York: Random House, 1993.

History of the United Nations War Crimes Commission and the Development of the Laws of War. London: HMSO, 1948.

Hitler, Adolf. *Mein Kampf*. London: Hutchinson, 1988.

Kimball, Warren F., ed. *Churchill and Roosevelt: The Complete Correspondence*. Vols. 2, 3. Princeton, N.J.: Princeton University Press, 1984.

Law Reports of Trials of War Criminals. Selected and prepared by the United Nations War Crimes Commission. Vol. 1. Buffalo, N.Y.: William S. Hein and Co., 1997.

Levie, Howard S., ed. *Documents on Prisoners of War*. Newport, R.I.: Naval War College, 1979.

Loewenheim, Francis L., Harold D. Langley, and Manfred Jonas. *Roosevelt and Churchill: Their Secret Wartime Correspondence*. New York: Saturday Review Press, E. P. Dutton and Co., 1975.

Red Cross and St. John War Organisation 1939–1947: Official Record. Eastbourne, Sussex, England: Sumfield and Aday, n.d.

Report by the Supreme Commander to the Combined Chiefs of Staff on the Operations in Europe of the Allied Expeditionary Force 6 June 1944 to 8 May 1945. London: HMSO, 1946.

Report of the International Committee of the Red Cross on Its Activities during the Second World War (September 1, 1939–June 30, 1947). Vols. 1, 2. Geneva: Red Cross, 1948.

Rosenman, Samuel I. *The Public Papers and Addresses of Franklin D. Roosevelt: The Call of Battle Stations*. New York: Random House, 1969.

Ross, Graham. *The Foreign Office and the Kremlin: British Documents on Anglo-Soviet Relations, 1941–1945*. Cambridge: Cambridge University Press, 1984.

Satow, Harold, and M. J. Sée. *The Work of the Prisoners of War Department during the Second World War*. London: Foreign Office, 1950.

The Strategic Air War against Germany, 1939–1945: Report of the British Bombing Survey Unit. London: Survey Unit, 1998.

Trials of War Criminals before the Nuremberg Military Tribunals under Control Council

Law No. 10, Nuremberg, October 1946–April 1949. Vols. 11, 13. Washington, D.C.: GPO, 1952.

United Kingdom. *House of Commons Debates* (1939–45).

U.S. Congress. *Congressional Record, Proceedings and Debates of the 78th Congress, Second Session*, 10 January 1944 to 19 December 1944. Microfiche. Washington, D.C.: GPO, 1978–79.

——. *Congressional Record, Proceedings and Debates of the 79th Congress, First Session*, 3 January 1945 to 21 December 1945. Microfiche. Washington, D.C.: GPO, 1978–79.

U.S. Congress. House. *Report of Proceedings, Hearing Held before Special Committee of the Committee on Military Affairs, Treatment of Prisoners of War*, 30 April 1945. Washington, D.C., 1945.

U.S. Department of State. *Foreign Relations of the United States: Diplomatic Papers*. 1943, vol. 1; 1944, vols. 1, 3, 4; 1945, vols. 3, 5, The Conferences at Malta and Yalta. Washington, D.C.: GPO, 1955–67.

Weinberg, Gerhard L., ed. *Hitler's Second Book: The Unpublished Sequel to Mein Kampf*. New York: Enigma Books, 2003.

Woodward, Llewellyn. *British Foreign Policy in the Second World War*. Vol. 3. London: HMSO, 1971.

DIARIES AND MEMOIRS

Arnold, H. H. *Global Mission*. London: Hutchinson, 1951.

Bernadotte, Folke. *Instead of Arms: Autobiographical Notes*. Stockholm: Bonniers, 1948.

Bird, Tom. *American POWs of World War II: Forgotten Men Tell Their Stories*. Westport, Conn.: Praeger, 1992.

Bohlen, Charles E. *Witness to History, 1929–1969*. New York: Norton, 1973.

Carlson, Lewis H. *We Were Each Other's Prisoners: An Oral History of World War II American and German Prisoners of War*. New York: Basic Books, 1997.

Churchill, Winston S. *Closing the Ring*. Boston: Houghton Mifflin, 1951.

——. *The Grand Alliance*. Boston: Houghton Mifflin, 1950.

——. *The Hinge of Fate*. Boston: Houghton Mifflin, 1950.

——*Their Finest Hour*. Boston: Houghton Mifflin, 1949.

——. *Triumph and Tragedy*. Boston: Houghton Mifflin, 1953.

Crawley, Aidan. *Escape from Germany*. New York: Dorset Press, 1985.

Dancocks, Daniel G. *In Enemy Hands: Canadian Prisoners of War, 1939–1945*. Edmonton, Canada: Hurtig Publishers, 1983.

Deane, John R. *The Strange Alliance: The Story of American Efforts at Wartime Co-operation with Russia*. London: J. Murray, 1947.

Eden, Anthony. *The Eden Memoirs: The Reckoning*. London: Cassell, 1965.

Eisenhower, Dwight D. *Crusade in Europe*. London: Heinemann, 1948.

Gromyko, Andrei. *Memoirs*. New York: Doubleday, 1989.

Harriman, Averell W., and Elie Abel. *Special Envoy to Churchill and Stalin, 1941–1946*. New York: Random House, 1975.

Hull, Cordell. *The Memoirs of Cordell Hull*. Vol. 2. London: Macmillan, 1948.

Junod, Marcel. *Warrior without Weapons*. New York: Macmillan, 1951.

Lochner, Louis P., ed. *The Goebbels Diaries: 1942–1943*. New York: Doubleday, 1948.

McKibbin, M. N. *Barbed Wire: Memories of Stalag 383*. New York: Staples Press, n.d.

The Memoirs of General the Lord Ismay. London: Heinemann, 1960.

Montgomery, Bernard Law. *The Memoirs of Field-Marshal the Viscount Montgomery of Alamein*. Cleveland: World Publishing Co., 1958.

North, John, ed. *The Alexander Memoirs, 1940–1945*. London: Cassell, 1962.

Sherwood, Robert E. *Roosevelt and Hopkins: An Intimate History*. New York: Grosset and Dunlap, 1948.

Spiller, Harry. *Prisoners of Nazis: Accounts by American POWs in World War II*. Jefferson, N.C.: MacFarland, 1998.

Stalin, Joseph. *The Great Patriotic War of the Soviet Union*. New York: Greenwood Press, 1969.

Stettinius, Edward R., Jr. *Roosevelt and the Russians: The Yalta Conference*. New York: Doubleday, 1949.

Stimson, Henry L., and Bundy McGeorge. *On Active Service in Peace and War*. New York: Harper, 1948.

Swedberg, Claire. *In Enemy Hands: Personal Accounts of Those Taken Prisoner in World War II*. Mechanicburg, Pa.: Stackpole Books, 1997.

Toliver, Raymond F. *The Interrogator: The Story of Hans-Joachim Scharff, Master Interrogator of the Luftwaffe*. Atglen, Pa.: Schiffer, 1997.

Trevor-Roper, Hugh, ed. *Final Entries 1945: The Diaries of Joseph Goebbels*. New York: Avon Books, 1978.

Vietor, John A. *Time Out*. Fallbrook, Calif.: Aero Publishers, 1951.

Wild, David. *Prisoner of Hope*. Sussex, England: Book Guild, 1992.

Williams, Elvet. *Arbeitskommando*. London: Victor Gollancz, 1975.

Winograd, Leonard. "Double Jeopardy: What an American Officer, a Jew, Remembers of Prison Life in Germany." *American Jewish Archives* 28 (1976): 3–17.

Wood, J. E. R., ed. *Detour: The Story of Oflag IV C*. London: Falcon Press, 1946.

SECONDARY SOURCES

Ambrose, Stephen E. *Citizen Soldiers: The U.S. Army from the Normandy Beaches to the Bulge to the Surrender of Germany, June 7, 1944–May 7, 1945*. New York: Simon and Schuster, 1997.

Atkin, Ronald. *Pillar of Fire: Dunkirk, 1940*. Edinburgh: Birlinn, 1990.

Baldwin, Hanson. *Battles Lost and Won: Great Campaigns of World War II*. London: Robson Books, 2000.

Barber, Noel. *Prisoner of War: The Story of British Prisoners Held by the Enemy*. London: George G. Harrap, 1944.

Bard, Mitchell G. *Forgotten Victims: The Abandonment of Americans in Hitler's Camp*. Boulder, Colo.: Westview Press, 1994.

Barker, A. J. *Behind Barbed Wire*. London: B. T. Batsford, 1974.

Bartov, Omer. *The Eastern Front: German Troops and the Barbarisation of Warfare*. Oxford: Macmillan, 1985.

———. *Hitler's Army: Soldiers, Nazis, and War in the Third Reich*. New York: Oxford University Press, 1991.

Bauer, Yehuda. "The Death-Marches, January–May 1945." In *The Nazi Holocaust: Historical Articles on the Destruction of European Jews*, edited by Michael R. Marrus, 9:491–511. Westport, Conn.: Meckler, 1989.

———. *Jews for Sale? Nazi-Jewish Negotiations, 1933–1945*. New Haven, Conn.: Yale University Press, 1994.

Beaumont, Joan. "Rank, Privilege and Prisoners of War." *War and Society* 1 (May 1983): 67–94.

Beck, Earl R. *Under the Bombs: The German Home Front, 1942–1945*. Lexington: University Press of Kentucky, 1986.

Berkhoff, Karel C. "The 'Russian' Prisoners of War in Nazi-Ruled Ukraine as Victims of Genocidal Massacre." *Holocaust and Genocide Studies* 15 (Spring 2001): 1–32.

Bethell, Nicholas. *The Last Secret: The Delivery to Stalin of Over Two Million Russians by Britain and the United States*. London: Deutsch, 1974.

Bialer, Seweryn, ed. *Stalin and His Generals: Soviet Military Memoirs of World War II*. Boulder, Colo.: Westview Press, 1984.

Bischof, Günther. "Einige Thesen zu einer Mentalitätsgeschichte deutscher Kriegsgefangenschaft in amerikanischem Gewahrsam." In *Kriegsgefangenschaft im Zweiten Weltkrieg: Eine vergleichende Perspektive*, edited by Günter Bischof and Rüdiger Overmans, 175–212. Ternitz-Pottschach, Austria: Verlag Gerhard Höller, 1999.

Bischof, Günter, and Stephen E. Ambrose, eds. *Eisenhower and the German POWs: Facts against Falsehood*. Baton Rouge: Louisiana State University Press, 1992.

Bischof, Günter, and Rüdiger Overmans, eds. *Kriegsgefangenschaft im Zweiten Weltkrieg: Eine vergleichende Perspektive*. Ternitz-Pottschach, Austria: Verlag Gerhard Höller, 1999.

Bland, Larry I. "Averell Harriman, the Russians and the Origins of the Cold War in Europe, 1943–1945." *Australian Journal of Politics and History* 23 (December 1977): 403–16.

Blatman, Daniel. "The Death Marches (January–May 1945): Who Was Responsible for What?" *Yad Vashem Studies* 28 (Fall 2000): 155–201.

Blum, John Morton. *Roosevelt and Morgenthau*. Boston: Houghton Mifflin, 1970.

Böhme, Kurt W. *Die deutschen Kriegsgefangenen in amerikanischer Hand: Europa*. Vol. 10, pt. 2. Bielefeld, Germany: Gieseking, 1973.

Booker, Christopher. *A Looking-Glass Tragedy: The Controversy over the Repatriations from Austria in 1945*. London: Duckworth, 1997.

Bower, Tom. *Blind Eye to Murder: Britain, America and the Purging of Nazi Germany—A Pledge Betrayed*. London: Deutsch, 1981.

Brickhill, Paul. *The Great Escape*. New York: Norton, 1950.

Buhite, Russell D. "Soviet American Relations and the Repatriation of Prisoners of War, 1945." *Historian* 35 (August 1973): 384–97.

Burns, James MacGregor. *Roosevelt: The Soldier of Freedom, 1940–1945*. New York: Harcourt Brace Jovanovich, 1970.

Buscher, Frank M. *The U.S. War Crimes Trial Program in Germany, 1946–1955*. New York: Greenwood Press, 1989.

Canning, Paul. *British Policy towards Ireland, 1921–1941*. Oxford: Clarendon Press, 1985.

Carlgren, Wilhelm M. *Swedish Foreign Policy during the Second World War*. London: E. Benn, 1977.

Ciechanowski, Jan M. *The Warsaw Rising of 1944*. London: Cambridge University Press, 1974.

Clark, Alan. *Barbarossa: The Russian-German Conflict, 1941–1945*. London: Phoenix Giant, 1995.

Clemens, Diane S. "Averell Harriman, John Deane, the Joint Chiefs of Staff, and the 'Reversal of Co-operation' in April 1945." *International History Review* 14 (May 1992): 277–306.

Coakley, Robert W., and Richard M. Leighton. *Global Logistics and Strategy, 1943–1945*. Washington, D.C.: Office of the Chief of Military History, Department of the Army, 1968.

Coutouvidis, John, and Jamie Reynolds. *Poland, 1939–1947*. Leicester, England: Leicester University Press, 1986.

Cowdrey, Albert E. "Die medizinische Versorgung von amerikanischen Kriegsgefangenen im Zweiten Weltkrieg." In *Kriegsgefangenschaft im Zweiten Weltkrieg: Eine vergleichende Perspektive*, edited by Günter Bischof and Rüdiger Overmans, 165–73. Ternitz-Pottschach, Austria: Verlag Gerhard Höller, 1999.

Dallek, Robert. *Franklin D. Roosevelt and American Foreign Policy, 1932–1945*. New York: Oxford University Press, 1979.

Datner, Szymon. *Crimes against POWs: Responsibility of the Wehrmacht*. Warsaw: Zachodnia Agencja Prasowa, 1964.

Davis, Gerald H. "Prisoners of War in Twentieth-Century War Economies." *Journal of Contemporary History* 12 (October 1977): 623–34.

Daws, Gavan. *Prisoners of the Japanese: POWs of World War II in the Pacific—The Powerful Untold Story*. New York: W. Morrow, 1994.

Deane, John R. "Negotiating on Military Assistance, 1943–1945." In *Negotiating with the Russians*, edited by Raymond Dennett and Joseph E. Johnson, 3–30. Boston: World Peace Foundation, 1951.

Delarue, Jacques. *The Gestapo: A History of Horror*. New York: Paragon, 1987.

Dennett, Raymond, and Joseph E. Johnson, eds. *Negotiating with the Russians*. Boston: World Peace Foundation, 1951.

Diner, Dan. *America in the Eyes of the Germans: An Essay on Anti-Americanism*. Princeton, N.J.: M. Wiener Publishers, 1996.

Dupuy, Trevor N., David L. Bongard, and Richard C. Anderson Jr. *Hitler's Last Gamble: The Battle of the Bulge, December 1944–January 1945*. New York: HarperCollins, 1994.

Durand, André. *History of the International Committee of the Red Cross: From Sarajevo to Hiroshima*. Geneva: Henry Dunant Institute, 1978.

Durand, Arthur A. *Stalag Luft III: The Secret Story*. Baton Rouge: Louisiana State University Press, 1988.

Dwyer, Ryle T. *De Valera: The Man and the Myths*. Dublin: Poolbeg, 1991.

Elliott, Mark R. *Pawns of Yalta: Soviet Refugees and America's Role in Their Repatriation*. Urbana: University of Illinois Press, 1982.

——. "The United States and Forced Repatriation of Soviet Citizens, 1944–47." *Political Science Quarterly* 88 (June 1973): 253–75.

Ellis, John. *World War II: A Statistical Survey*. New York: Facts on File, 1993.

Engdahl, B. E., W. F. Page, and T. W. Miller. "Age, Education, Maltreatment, and Social Support as Predictors of Chronic Depression in Former Prisoners of War." *Social Psychiatry and Psychiatric Epidemiology* 26, 2 (Spring 1991): 63–67.

Falls, Donald R. "American POWs in Romania." *Air Power History* 37 (Spring 1990): 37–44.

Favez, Jean-Claude. *The Red Cross and the Holocaust*. Cambridge: Cambridge University Press, 1999.

Fedorowich, Kent. "Axis Prisoners of War as Sources for British Military Intelligence, 1939–1942." *Intelligence and National Security* 14 (Summer 1999): 156–78.

——. "Propaganda and Political Warfare: The Foreign Office, Italian POWs and the Free Italy Movement, 1949–3." In *Prisoners of War and Their Captors in World War II*, edited by Bob Moore and Kent Fedorowich, 119–48. Oxford: Berg, 1996.

Fedorowich, Kent, and Bob Moore. "Co-Belligerency and Prisoners of War: Britain and Italy, 1943–1945." *International History Review* 18 (February 1996): 28–47.

Fischer, Klaus P. *Nazi Germany: A New History*. New York: Continuum, 1995.

Foot, M. R. D., and J. M. Langley. *MI 9 Escape and Evasion, 1939–1945*. Boston: Little, Brown, 1980.

Foregger, Richard. "Soviet Rails to Odessa, British Ships to Freedom." *Journal of Slavic Military Studies* 8 (December 1995): 844–60.

Foreman, John. *Battle of Britain: The Forgotten Months, November and December 1940*. New Molden, Surrey, England: Air Research Publications, 1988.

Förster, Jörgen. "The German Army and the Ideological War against the Soviet Union." In *The Politics of Genocide*, edited by Gerhardt Hirschfeld, 15–29. Boston: Allan and Unwin, 1986.

Foy, David A. *For You the War Is Over: American Prisoners of War in Nazi Germany*. New York: Stein and Day, 1984.

Fried, John H. "The Fate of Soviet POWs in World War II." *Simon Wiesenthal Center Annual* 5 (1988): 203–25.

Friedländer, Saul. *Prelude to Downfall: Hitler and the United States, 1929–1941*. London: Chatto and Windus, 1967.

Gelber, Yoav. *Jewish Palestinian Volunteering in the British Army during the Second World War*. Jerusalem: Yad Izhak Ben-Zvi Publication, 1984 (Hebrew).

Gilbert, Martin. *Road to Victory: Winston S. Churchill, 1941–1945*. London: Heinemann, 1986.

——. *The Second World War: A Complete History*. New York: Henry Holt, 1989.

Gill, Anton. *The Great Escape: The Full Dramatic Story with Contributions from Survivors and Their Families*. London: Review, 2002.

Goldhagen, Daniel Jonah. *Hitler's Willing Executioners: Ordinary Germans and the Holocaust*. New York: Alfred Knopf, 1996.

Hanson, Joanna K. M. *The Civilian Population and the Warsaw Uprising of 1944.* Cambridge: Cambridge University Press, 1982.

Harbutt, Fraser J. *The Iron Curtain: Churchill, America, and the Origins of the Cold War.* New York: Oxford University Press, 1986.

Hasselbring, Andrew Strieter. "American Prisoners of War in the Third Reich." Ph.D. diss., Temple University, 1991.

Hately-Broad, Barbara. "Prisoner of War Families and the British Government during the Second World War." Ph.D. diss., Sheffield University, 2002.

Herren, Madeleine. " 'Neither This Way nor Any Other': Swiss Internationalism during the Second World War." In *Switzerland and the Second World War*, edited by Georg Kreis, 171–93. London: F. Cass, 2000.

Herring, George C., Jr. *Aid to Russia, 1941–1946: Strategy, Diplomacy, the Origins of the Cold War.* New York: Columbia University Press, 1973.

Herzstein, Robert E. *Roosevelt and Hitler: Prelude to War.* New York: Paragon, 1989.

Hinsley, F. H., E. E. Thomas, C. F. G. Ransom, and R. C. Knight. *British Intelligence in the Second World War.* Vol. 3, pts. 1 and 2. London: HMSO, 1984, 1988.

Homze, Edward L. *Foreign Labor in Nazi Germany.* Princeton, N.J.: Princeton University Press, 1967.

Jackson, Robert. *The Prisoners, 1914–1918.* London: Routledge, 1989.

Jackson, W. G. F. *The North African Campaign, 1940–1943.* London: B. T. Batsford, 1975.

James, T. C. G. *The Battle of Britain.* London: F. Cass, 2000.

Jones, Priscilla Dale. "Nazi Atrocities against Allied Airmen: Stalag Luft III and the End of British War Crimes Trials." *Historical Journal* 41, 2 (June 1998): 543–65.

Jung, Hermann. *Die deutschen Kriegsgefangenen in amerikanischer Hand: USA.* Vol. 10, pt. 1. Bielefeld, Germany, Gieseking, 1972.

Kacewicz, George V. *Great Britain, the Soviet Union and the Polish Government in Exile (1939–1945).* The Hague: Martinus Nijhoff, 1979.

Kershaw, Ian. *Hitler, 1889–1936: Hubris.* London: Penguin Books, 1998.

———. *Hitler, 1936–1945: Nemesis.* New York: Norton, 2000.

Kimball, Warren F. *Forged in War: Churchill, Roosevelt and the Second World War.* New York: W. Morrow, 1997.

———. *The Juggler: Franklin Roosevelt as Wartime Statesman.* Princeton, N.J.: Princeton University Press, 1991.

———. *Swords or Ploughshares? The Morgenthau Plan for Defeated Nazi Germany, 1943–1946.* Philadelphia: Lippincott, 1976.

Kitchen, Martin. *British Policy toward the Soviet Union during the Second World War.* Basingstoke, Hampshire, England: Macmillan, 1986.

———. *Nazi Germany at War.* London: Longman, 1995.

Kochavi, Arieh J. "Britain, the Soviet Union, and the Question of the Baltic States in 1943." *Journal of Baltic Studies* 22 (Summer 1991): 173–82.

———. "Britain, the United States and Irish Neutrality." *European History Quarterly* 25 (January 1995): 93–115.

———. "Britain's Attitude towards the Swedish Position on War Criminals, 1943–1945." *Scandinavian Journal of History* 18, 4 (1993): 291–306.

——. "From Cautiousness to Decisiveness: Changes in Soviet Negotiation Tactics toward the British during World War II." *East European Quarterly* 36 (January 2003): 481–509.

——. "The Moscow Declaration, the Kharkov Trial, and the Question of a Policy on Major War Criminals in the Second World War." *History* 76 (October 1991): 401–17.

——. *Post-Holocaust Politics: Britain, the United States, and Jewish Refugees, 1945–1948*. Chapel Hill: University of North Carolina Press, 2001.

——. *Prelude to Nuremberg: Allied War Crimes Policy and the Question of Punishment*. Chapel Hill: University of North Carolina Press, 1998.

Krakowski, Shmuel. "The Death Marches in the Period of Evacuation of the Camps." In *The Nazi Concentration Camps*, edited by Yisrael Gutman and Avital Saf, 475–89. Jerusalem: Yad Vashem, 1984.

Krammer, Arnold. "American Treatment of German Generals during World War II." *Journal of Military History* 54 (January 1990): 27–46.

——. *Nazi Prisoners of War in America*. New York: Stein and Day, 1979.

Kreis, Georg, ed. *Switzerland and the Second World War*. London: F. Cass, 2000.

Levine, Alan J. *Captivity, Flight, and Survival in World War II*. Westport, Conn.: Praeger, 2000.

Lewis, George L., and Mewha John. *History of Prisoner of War Utilization by the United States Army, 1776–1945*. Washington, D.C.: Department of the Army, 1955.

Lord Russell of Liverpool. *The Scourge of the Swastika: A Short History of Nazi War Crimes*. New York: Ballantine Books, 1954.

Lunden, Walter A. "Captivity Psychoses among Prisoners of War." *Journal of Criminal Law and Criminology of Northwestern University* 30 (March–April 1949): 721–33.

MacKenzie, S. P. "Prisoners of War and Civilian Internees: The European and Mediterranean Theaters." In *World War II in Europe, Africa, and the Americas, with General Sources: A Hand Book of Literature and Research*, edited by Loyd E. Lee, 302–12. Westport, Conn.: Greenwood Press, 1996.

——. "The Shackling Crisis: A Case Study in the Dynamics of Prisoners-of-War Diplomacy in the Second World War." *International History Review* 17 (February 1995): 78–98.

——. "The Treatment of Prisoners of War in World War II." *Journal of Modern History* 66 (September 1994): 487–520.

Maier, Klaus A. "The Battle of Britain." In *Germany and the Second World War*, edited by Research Institution for Military History, Frieburg im Breisgau, Germany, 2:374–407. Oxford: Clarendon Press, 1991.

Margolian, Howard. *Conduct Unbecoming: The Story of the Murder of Canadian Prisoners of War in Normandy*. Toronto: University of Toronto Press, 1998.

Marrus, Michael R. *The Unwanted: European Refugees in the Twentieth Century*. New York: Oxford University Press, 1985.

Maschke, Erich, ed. *Zur Geschichte der deutschen Kriegsgefangenen des Zweitten Weltkrieges*. 22 vols. Bielefeld, Germany: E. und W. Gieseking, 1962–74.

Mason, Wynne W. *Prisoners of War: Official History of New Zealand in the Second*

World War, 1939–1945. Wellington, New Zealand: War History Branch, Department of Internal Affairs, 1954.

Mayers, David A. *The Ambassadors and America's Soviet Policy*. New York: Oxford University Press, 1995.

Messenger, Charles. *"Bomber" Harris and the Strategic Bombing Offensive, 1939–1945*. New York: St. Martin's Press, 1984.

Middlebrook, Martin. *Arnhem, 1944: The Airborne Battle, 17–26 September*. Boulder, Colo.: Westview Press, 1994.

———. *The Battle of Hamburg: Allied Bomber Forces against a German City in 1943*. New York: Scribner, 1980.

Moore, Bob. "Axis Prisoners in Britain during the Second World War: A Comparative Survey." In *Prisoners of War and Their Captors in World War II*, edited by Bob Moore and Kent Fedorowich, 19–46. Oxford: Berg, 1996.

———. "Turning Liabilities into Assets: British Government Policy towards German and Italian Prisoners of War during the Second World War." *Journal of Contemporary History* 32, 1 (January 1997): 117–36.

———. "Unruly Allies: British Problems with the French Treatment of Axis Prisoners of War, 1943–1945." *War in History* 7 (April 2000): 180–98.

Moore, Bob, and Kent Fedorowich. *The British Empire and Its Italian Prisoners of War, 1940–1947*. London: Palgrave, 2002.

———, eds. *Prisoners of War and Their Captors in World War II*. Oxford: Berg, 1996.

Moorehead, Caroline. *Dunant's Dream: War, Switzerland and the History of the Red Cross*. London: HarperCollins, 1998.

Morison, Samuel Eliot. *The Battle of the Atlantic, September 1939–May 1943*. Boston: Little, Brown, 1966.

Mosley, Philip E. "Some Soviet Techniques of Negotiation." In *Negotiating with the Russians*, edited by Raymond Dennett and Joseph E. Johnson, 271–304. Boston: World Peace Foundation, 1951.

Müller, Rolf-Dieter. "Die Behandlung sowjetischer kriegsgefangener durch das Deutsche Reich 1941–1945." In *Kriegsgefangenschaft im Zweiten Weltkrieg: Eine vergleichende Perspektive*, edited by Günter Bischof and Rüdiger Overmans, 283–302. Ternitz-Pottschach, Austria: Verlag Gerhard Höller, 1999.

Murphy, Christopher J. "SOE and Repatriation." *Journal of Contemporary History* 36, 2 (April 2001): 309–23.

Murray, Williamson, and Allan R. Millett. *A War to Be Won: Fighting the Second World War*. Cambridge: Harvard University Press, Belknap Press, 2000.

Neillands, Robin. *The Conquest of the Reich: D-Day to VE-Day: A Soldiers' History*. New York: New York University Press, 1995.

Nenninger, Timothy K. "United States Prisoners of War and the Red Army, 1944–45: Myths and Realities." *Journal of Military History* 66 (July 2002): 761–81.

Nichol, John, and Tony Rennell. *The Last Escape: The Untold Story of Allied Prisoners of War in Germany, 1944–1945*. London: Penguin Books, 2002.

Nolan, Cathal J. "Americans in the Gulag: Detention of U.S. Citizens by Russia and the Onset of the Cold War, 1944–49." *Journal of Contemporary History* 25 (October 1990): 523–45.

O'Halpin, Eunan. "Irish Neutrality in the Second World War." In *European Neutrals and Non-Belligerents during the Second World War*, edited by Neville Wylie, 283–303. Cambridge: Cambridge University Press, 2002.

O'Neill, William L. *A Democracy at War: America's Fight at Home and Abroad in World War II*. New York: Free Press, 1993.

Overy, Richard. *Russia's War*. London: Penguin Books, 1999.

———. *Why the Allies Won*. London: Pimlico, 1995.

Parker, R. A. C. *Struggle for Survival: The History of the Second World War*. Oxford: Oxford University Press, 1989.

Perlmutter, Amos. *FDR and Stalin: A Not So Grand Alliance, 1943–1945*. Columbia: University of Missouri Press, 1993.

Polivy, Janet, Sharon B. Zeitlin, C. Peter Herman, and A. Lynne Beal. "Food Restriction and Binge Eating: A Study of Former Prisoners of War." *Journal of Abnormal Psychology* 103, 2 (February 1994): 409–11.

Prince, Cathryn J. *Shot from the Sky: American POWs in Switzerland*. Annapolis, Md.: Naval Institute Press, 2003.

Proudfoot, Malcolm J. *European Refugees, 1939–1952: A Study in Forced Population Transfer*. Evanston, Ill.: Northwestern University Press, 1956.

Ray, John. *The Night Blitz, 1940–1941*. London: Arms and Armour, 1996.

Richards, Denis. *The Hardest Victory: RAF Bomber Command in the Second World War*. London: Hodder and Stoughton, 1994.

Robin, Ron. *The Barbed-Wire College: Reeducating German POWs in the United States during World War II*. Princeton, N.J.: Princeton University Press, 1995.

Roland, Charles G. *Long Night's Journey into Day: Prisoners of War in Hong Kong and Japan, 1941–1945*. Waterloo, Ontario: Wilfrid Laurier University Press, 2001.

Rolf, David. "'Blind Bureaucracy': The British Government and POWs in German Captivity, 1939–1945." In *Prisoners of War and Their Captors in World War II*, edited by Bob Moore and Kent Fedorowich, 47–68. Oxford: Berg, 1996.

———. "The Education of British Prisoners of War in German Captivity, 1939–1945." *History of Education* 18, 3 (September 1989): 257–65.

———. *Prisoners of the Reich: Germany's Captives, 1939–1945*. London: Leo Cooper, 1988.

Rothwell, Victor. *Britain and the Cold War, 1941–1947*. London: Jonathan Cape, 1982.

Rozek, Edward J. *Allied Wartime Diplomacy: A Pattern in Poland*. Boulder, Colo.: Westview Press, 1989.

Ryan, Cornelius. *A Bridge Too Far*. London: Hamilton, 1974.

Sainsbury, Keith. *The Turning Point: Roosevelt, Stalin, Churchill, and Chiang-Kai-Skek, 1943*. Oxford: Oxford University Press, 1986.

Schulte, Theo J. *The German Army and Nazi Policies in Occupied Russia*. Oxford: Berg, 1989.

Shavit, David. "'The Great Morale Factor Next to the Red Army': Book and Libraries in American and British Prisoners of War Camps in Germany during World War II." *Libraries and Culture* 34 (Spring 1999): 113–34.

Shedd, Clarence Prouty, et al. *History of the World's Alliance of Young Men's Christian Associations*. London: World's Committee of Young Men's Christian Associations, 1955.

Smith, Bradley F. *The Road to Nuremberg*. New York: Basic Books, 1981.

Smith, Sydney. *Mission Escape*. New York: D. McKay, 1969.

Sorge, Martin K. *The Other Price of Hitler's War: German Military and Civilian Losses Resulting from World War II*. New York: Greenwood Press, 1996.

Speed, Richard B., III. *Prisoners, Diplomats, and the Great War: A Study in the Diplomacy of Captivity*. New York: Greenwood Press, 1990.

Sponza, Lucio. "Italian Prisoners of War in Great Britain, 1943–6." In *Prisoners of War and Their Captors in World War II*, edited by Bob Moore and Kent Fedorowich, 205–26. Oxford: Berg, 1996.

Steininger, Rolf. "Some Reflections on the Maschke Commission." In *Eisenhower and the German POWs: Facts against Falsehood*, edited by Günther Bischof and Stephen E. Ambrose, 170–80. Baton Rouge: Louisiana State University Press, 1992.

Stelzl, Barbara. "Im Gewahrsam des 'Dritten Reiches': Aspekte der Kriegsgefangenschaft, dargestellt am Beispiel des Stalag XVII B Krems-Gneixendorf." In *Kriegsgefangenschaft im Zweiten Weltkrieg: Eine vergleichende Perspektive*, edited by Günter Bischof and Rüdiger Overmans, 135–63. Ternitz-Pottschach, Austria: Verlag Gerhard Höller, 1999.

Stoler, Mark A. *Allies and Adversaries: The Joint Chiefs of Staff, the Grand Alliance, and Strategy in World War II*. Chapel Hill: University of North Carolina Press, 2000.

Streim, Alfred. *Die Behandlung sowjetischer Kriegsgefangener im "Fall Barbarrosa": Eine Dokumentation*. Heidelberg, Germany: C. F. Mueller, 1981.

Streit, Christian. *Keine Kameraden: Die Wehrmacht und die sowjetichen Kriegsgefangenen, 1941–1945*. Stuttgart, Germany: Deutsche Verlags-Anstalt, 1978.

Sullivan, Matthew Barry. *Thresholds of Peace: German Prisoners and the People of Britain, 1944–1948*. London: Hamish Hamilton, 1979.

Sutker, Patricia B., and Albert N. Allain. "Psychological Assessment of Aviators Captured in World War II." *Psychological Assessment* 7 (March 1995): 66–68.

Sutker, Patricia B., Albert N. Allain Jr., and Judith L. Johnson. "Clinical Assessment of Long-Term Cognitive and Emotional Sequelae to World War II Prisoners-of-War Confinement: Comparison of Pilot Twins." *Psychological Assessment* 5 (March 1993): 3–10.

Sydnor, Charles W., Jr. *Soldiers of Destruction: The SS Death's Head Division, 1933–1945*. Princeton, N.J.: Princeton University Press, 1990.

Tolstoy, Nikolai. *The Secret Betrayal*. New York: Scribner, 1977.

Tsakaloyannis, Panos. "The Moscow Puzzle." *Journal of Contemporary History* 21 (January 1986): 37–55.

Ulam, Adam. *Stalin: The Man and His Era*. Boston: Beacon Press, 1987.

Umbreit, Hans. "The Battle of Hegemony in Western Europe." In *Germany and the*

Second World War, edited by the Militärgeschichtliches Forschungsamt (Research Institute for Military History), Freiburg im Breisgau, Germany, 2:227–326. Oxford: Clarendon Press, 1991.

Vance, Jonathan F. "Men in Manacles: The Shackling of Prisoners of War, 1942–1943." *Journal of Military History* 59 (July 1995): 483–504.

———. *Objects of Concern: Canadian Prisoners of War through the Twentieth Century*. Vancouver, British Columbia: UBC Press, 1994.

———. "The Politics of Camp Life: The Bargaining Process in Two German Prison Camps." *War and Society* 10 (May 1992): 109–26.

———. "The Trouble with the Allies: Canada and the Negotiation of Prisoners of War Exchanges." In *Prisoners of War and Their Captors in World War II*, edited by Bob Moore and Kent Fedorowich, 69–86. Oxford: Berg, 1996.

———. "The War behind the Wire: The Battle to Escape from a German Prison Camp." *Journal of Contemporary History* 28, 4 (October 1993): 675–93.

Vat, Dan van der. *The Atlantic Campaign: World War II's Great Struggle at Sea*. New York: Harper and Row, 1988.

Volkogonov, Dimitri. *Stalin: Triumph and Tragedy*. New York: Grove Weidenfeld, 1988.

Vourkoutiotis, Vasilis. *Prisoners of War and the German High Command: The British and American Experience*. London: Palgrave Macmillan, 2003.

Wadley, Patricia Louise. *Even One Is Too Many: An Examination of the Soviet Refusal to Repatriate Liberated American World War II Prisoners of War*. <http://www.aiipowmia.com/research/wadley.html>.

Warner, Geoffrey. "From Ally to Enemy: Britain's Relations with the Soviet Union, 1941–1948." In *Diplomacy and World Power: Studies in British Foreign Policy, 1890–1950*, edited by Michael Dockrill and Brian McKercher, 221–43. Cambridge: Cambridge University Press, 1996.

Wasserstein, Bernard. *Britain and the Jews of Europe, 1939–1945*. Oxford: Clarendon Press, 1979.

Waters, Christopher. "Australia, the British Empire and the Second World War." *War and Society* 19 (May 2001): 93–107.

Wegner, Bernd. *The Waffen-SS: Organization, Ideology and Function*. Oxford: B. Blackwell, 1990.

Weinberg, Gerhard L. *Germany, Hitler, and World War II: Essays in Modern German and World History*. Cambridge: Cambridge University Press, 1995.

———. *A World at Arms: A Global History of World War II*. Cambridge: Cambridge University Press, 1994.

———. *World in the Balance: Behind the Scenes of World War II*. Hanover, N.H.: University Press of New England, 1981.

Weingartner, James J. *Crossroads to Death: The Story of the Malmedy Massacre and Trial*. Berkeley: University of California Press, 1979.

Weitz. John. *Joachim Von Ribbentrop: Hitler's Diplomat*. London: Weidenfeld and Nicolson, 1992.

Welch, David. *The Third Reich: Politics and Propaganda*. London: Routledge, 1993.

Werth, Alexander. *Russia at War, 1941–1946*. London: Barrie and Rockliff, 1964.

White, Joseph Robert. " 'Even in Auschwitz . . . Humanity Could Prevail': British
POWs and Jewish Concentration-Camp Inmates at IG Auschwitz, 1943–1949."
Holocaust and Genocide Studies 15 (Fall 2001): 266–95.

Wylie, Neville. " 'Keeping the Swiss Sweet': Intelligence as a Factor in British Policy
towards Switzerland during the Second World War." *Intelligence and National
Security* 11 (July 1996): 442–67.

———. "Pilet-Golaz and the Making of Swiss Foreign Policy: Some Remarks." In
Switzerland and the Second World War, edited by Georg Kreis, 158–70. London:
F. Cass, 2000.

———. "Switzerland: A Neutral of Distinction?" In *European Neutrals and Non-
Belligerents during the Second World War*, edited by Neville Wylie, 331–54.
Cambridge: Cambridge University Press, 2002.

Yergin, Daniel. *Shattered Peace: The Origins of the Cold War*. London: Penguin Books,
1990.

Ziemke, Earl F. *The U.S. Army in the Occupation of Germany, 1944–1946*. Washington,
D.C.: Center of Military History, 1975.

Zweig, Ronald W. "Feeding the Camps: Allied Blockade Policy and the Relief of
Concentration Camps in Germany, 1944–1945." *Historical Journal* 41, 3
(September 1988): 825–51.

INDEX

Adams, Lloyd S., 57
Aitken, Thomas S. C., 212
Alexander, Albert V., 149, 150, 158
Alexander, Harold, 192–93, 194, 278
Alkire, Darr H., 186
Allan, Less, 286
Allied air raids: and German civilians, 3, 53, 172, 182, 283; and sick and wounded POW exchanges, 4–5, 125, 127, 147, 282; and safety of POWs, 160, 171–75, 182, 187, 191, 198, 221, 302 (n. 117); and evacuation of POWs, 218, 284
Allied POWs: number of, 1, 90, 192, 194; and food rations, 26, 97; and Red Army, 161; safety of, 171, 185, 189, 190, 192, 197–98; German policy toward, 182, 185; and tripartite warning, 195–201; and Yalta Conference, 234; Soviet liberation of, 255. *See also* Evacuation of POWs; Safety of POWs; *and specific nationalities*
Allies. *See specific countries*
American embassy personnel, 17–18
American Jews, 202
American POW camps, 135, 271
American POWs: number of, 1, 71, 75, 88–89, 90, 97–98, 153, 192, 303 (n. 4); fear of German retribution toward, 2, 5, 69, 71, 171, 173, 184, 185, 187, 191, 192, 194, 201, 221, 283; evacuation of, 5, 69, 81, 96–97, 145–46, 201, 204, 208, 216, 219, 258, 265–67, 269; mental health of, 55–56, 85; and food rations, 68, 69, 90; and clothing rations, 81; health conditions of, 81–83, 84, 85, 98–99, 266, 269, 270, 271, 282; and Swiss inspectors, 94; lack of preferential treatment of, 102; and sick and wounded POW exchanges, 116–17, 119, 123, 128, 132, 133–35, 146, 147; Jewish POWs, 125; and long-term POW exchanges, 152, 168; safety of, 161, 171, 173–74, 193–94, 198, 262–63, 264, 281; executions of, 185, 195; and Nazi racist ideology, 221, 280; and liberated POW exchanges, 225, 233, 243, 249, 250, 255; and Red Army, 256, 258; and conditions in Poland, 258, 266, 268, 273, 345–46 (n. 75), 346 (n. 77)
American Red Cross, 86, 95, 96–97, 216, 243
Arbeitskommando E 249 (Kriegsdorf), 61
Arbeitskommando E 337 (Freudenthal), 61
Arbeitskommando E 339 (Freudenthal), 60–61
Arbeitskommando E 715 (Auschwitz), 203
Arbeitskommando I (Trattendorf), 78–80
Arbeitskommando 54, 38
Arbeitskommando 81, 38
Arbeitskommando 275, 37
Arbeitskommando 283, 38
Arbeitskommando 1135, 65
Arbeitskommando 1536, 84
Arbeitskommandos (work camps): conditions of, 3, 4, 32–35, 37–38, 39, 58–65, 76–77, 79–80, 306 (n. 45); organization of, 10; and food rations, 27, 29, 30; and health conditions, 27, 34, 84
Archer, E. R., 237, 239–40, 247
Ardennes, 143, 163, 283
Attlee, Clement R., 43, 47, 66–67

Australia, 41, 43, 52, 55, 113, 128
Australian POWs, 36, 43, 53, 177
Austria, 27, 60, 192–93, 194, 248, 278–79
Axis POWs, 41, 116, 119, 256. *See also* German POWs; Italian POWs

Balkans, 229, 230
Baltic countries, 5, 225, 233, 236, 255, 262, 263, 265, 285
Barker, Ray W., 212–13, 276, 277
Battle of Britain, 9, 106
Battle of the Bulge, 91, 97–98, 101, 143
Bedell-Smith, Walter, 256, 257–58
Belgian POWs, 27, 161, 177
Bennet, Clyde M., 77, 78
Berger, Gottlob, 186, 198
Bernadotte, Folk, 138
Betts, Edward C., 139
Bohlen, Charles E., 347 (n. 83)
Booth, E., 45–46, 49–50
Bor-Komorowski, Tadeusz, 332 (n. 99)
Bormann, Martin, 174, 186
Bowers, H. S., 14
Braun, Walter, 87, 88, 309 (n. 75)
Britain: attitudes toward POWs, 1–2; and safety of POWs, 2, 171, 175, 185, 198, 202, 281, 284; and Swiss inspectors, 4, 81; and long-term POW exchanges, 5, 149, 150, 151–52, 153, 159, 160–68, 283; and evacuation of POWs, 5, 212–13, 218–19, 285; and Soviet nationals as German POWs, 5, 229; and government department coordination, 18–19; and food rations, 22, 23; and conditions of German POW camps, 38–39, 55, 69, 71, 102; and shackling issue, 42–43, 45, 47–48, 49, 50, 52, 53; and mental health of British POWs, 58; and support of International Committee of the Red Cross, 96; and sick and wounded POW exchanges, 106–50 passim, 282, 314 (n. 54); and neutrality of Ireland, 107; and Anglo-American repatriation

proposal, 116–22; and tripartite warning, 195–201; and Poland, 226, 245; and Polish government in exile, 226; and reorganization of Polish government, 242–43, 246; and British POWs in Poland, 251, 252; and Polish Provisional Government, 254. *See also* United Kingdom
British Admiralty: and British POWs, 18; and repatriation, 106, 116; and sick and wounded POW exchanges, 127; and long-term POW exchanges, 149, 150, 158, 159, 166; and exchange of merchant seamen, 150, 151; and evacuation of POWs, 213, 214
British Air Council, 151
British Air Ministry, 18, 106, 213, 214
British Army Council, 63, 106
British Army Staff, 141
British Chiefs of Staff Committee (COS), 131, 158, 162, 163–64, 167, 190–91, 200, 214
British civilians, 9, 112–14, 234
British Colonial Office, 18
British Combined Repatriation Committee, 237–38
British Directorate of Prisoners of War (DPW), 18, 114, 290 (n. 23)
British Foreign Office: and Axis countries, 18; and criticism of food and clothing distribution, 21; and Stalag XX B, 38; and shackling issue, 48; and labor conditions in mines, 63, 65; and sick and wounded POW exchanges, 105–8, 110, 112, 113, 118, 120, 126, 127–28, 129, 141; and long-term POW exchanges, 154, 155, 166; and evacuation of POWs, 214, 218; and Soviet repatriation issues, 229, 239–40, 263; and treatment of British POWs in Poland, 246, 248–49, 251, 252–53; and definition of Soviet nationals, 263; and safety of POWs, 333 (n. 100)
British Joint Intelligence Sub-Committee (JISC), 182–84

Dulag Luft interrogation camp, 10, 71–74

Duncan, James Alexander Lawson, 252

Dunkirk, 3, 9, 10, 47, 67, 71, 102, 105, 117, 147, 281, 283, 289 (n. 7)

Dutch POWs, 161

Eden, Anthony: and Red Cross parcels, 20–21; and condition of British POWs in Germany, 22; and shackling issue, 45, 47, 50, 51–52; and sick and wounded POW exchanges, 110, 115–18, 119, 129; and long-term POW exchanges, 153–54, 157, 158; and safety of POWs, 177, 179, 181, 182, 198, 200; and evacuation of POWs, 219; and Soviet repatriation issues, 225, 226, 227–32, 236, 237, 238; and liberation of British POWs, 233–34, 241; and British-Soviet repatriation agreement, 236, 237, 238, 240, 241, 243, 244, 245, 249, 257, 263–64; and condition of British POWs in Soviet Union, 252

Egypt, 113, 160, 250

Eisenhower, Dwight D.: and sick and wounded POW repatriation, 120, 131; and safety of POWs, 188, 192, 193–94, 199–200; and evacuation of POWs, 213, 215, 217; and repatriation of liberated British POWs, 248; and American POWs under Soviet supervision, 256, 264; and treatment of Soviet POWs, 272, 274; and repatriation of liberated American POWs, 276

Engstrom, Bob, 101

Escapes: punishment for, 16, 61, 85, 88, 175, 177, 181–82, 189, 327 (n. 19); and German POWs, 41, 181–82, 187; and mental health, 57; from Stalag Luft III, 88, 175, 177–78, 179, 181, 185, 186–87, 189, 204; and Switzerland, 152; and executions of POWs, 171, 179, 181, 183, 188–89, 214, 326 (n. 2); and interrogation, 177–78, 179; and location of German POW camps, 203; and evacua-

tion of POWs, 205, 207, 214; from Axis POW camps, 256

Estonia, 261, 273, 274

European Advisory Commission (EAC), 191, 231, 330 (n. 62)

European Theater of Operations, U.S. Army, 139, 192, 278

Evacuation of POWs: and American POWs, 5, 69, 81, 96–97, 145–46, 201, 204, 208, 216, 219, 258, 266–67, 269; and British POWs, 5, 69, 81, 201, 203, 204, 208, 216–17, 219, 230–31; conditions of, 5, 203–12, 213, 284; and Red Army, 81, 98, 99, 145–46, 203, 212–15, 221; and German POW camp authorities, 97; and food rations, 99, 203, 204; and health conditions, 99–100, 146, 207, 208, 209, 210, 212, 216, 217, 219; and transportation, 203, 204, 209, 217; and execution of POWs, 208, 212; halting of, 218–21, 285; long-term effects of, 220–21

Evans, R. E., 32

Farr, Walter, 177

Food rations: distribution of, 5, 19–21, 25, 68–69, 89–91; and evacuation of POWs, 5, 99, 203, 204, 205, 206, 207, 208, 209, 210, 216, 217, 218, 219, 221, 284; and German POW camp conditions, 15, 16, 17, 21, 22–23, 25, 26, 27, 29, 31, 34, 37, 39, 55, 84, 87–88, 91, 95, 101, 204, 282, 289 (n. 17), 292 (nn. 46, 56), 293 (n. 68); and Geneva Convention, 15, 16, 19, 23, 289 (n. 15); and health conditions, 15, 27, 28, 68, 69, 71, 89, 91, 94, 99, 310 (n. 97); of German POWs, 25; and Red Cross parcels, 26, 31, 33, 36, 37, 72, 78, 80, 84, 87, 89; and Arbeitskommandos, 32, 61, 65, 79, 80, 84; and accumulation of food reserves, 36, 66, 67, 89–90, 95, 217, 282; and interrogation, 73, 74; and German POW camps, 76, 78, 304 (n. 17); and punishment, 85, 88; and

Swiss inspections, 90; and Gestapo, 179; and escapes, 182; and safety of POWs, 193, 194; and repatriation of liberated American POWs, 267, 268, 344 (n. 51); and condition of American POWs in Poland, 272, 346 (n. 77)

Forced marches. *See* Evacuation of POWs

Forrestal, James V., 92, 196–97, 198

Fort XIV, 11

France: fall of, 3, 9; Dieppe port raid, 40; British POWs in, 53; and sick and wounded POW exchanges, 106, 107, 108, 131; invasion of (Operation Overlord), 129, 131; and German POWs, 136, 140, 164, 226, 227; and safety of POWs, 184; and repatriation of United Nations POWs, 231; and Soviet nationals as German POWs, 256; and conditions of Soviet POWs, 258

Free French, 123, 158

French POWs, 27, 90, 161, 164, 177

Friedrich, M., 35

Fuel rations, 55, 78, 81, 90, 209

Geneva Convention: and treatment of POWs, 2, 9; and inspection of camps, 3–4, 30; and food rations, 15, 16, 19, 23, 289 (n. 15); and Directorate of Prisoners of War, 18; and clothing rations, 23, 292 (n. 48); and health conditions, 27, 30; and German POW camps, 39, 102, 171; and shackling issue, 40, 41, 43, 46–47, 48, 294–95 (n. 3), 297 (n. 45); and labor of POWs, 59, 63, 64, 65, 76, 79–80; and work camps, 59–60, 76; U.S. as signatory of, 71; and punitive measures, 73; U.S. protests concerning, 86; and POWs saluting officers, 89; and heating, 91; and Swiss inspectors, 92; and mixed medical commissions, 105, 312 (n. 2); and sick and wounded POW exchanges, 106–19 passim, 124, 125, 128, 139, 141, 311–12 (n. 1); and medical personnel,

142, 143; and long-term POW exchanges, 148, 154, 323 (n. 2); and active military service of repatriated POWs, 151, 154, 157, 162; and mental health, 153; and safety of POWs, 172, 174–75, 187; and escapes, 182, 327 (n. 19); and tripartite warning, 196; and evacuation of POWs, 210, 213, 335 (n. 23); and Soviet nationals as German POWs, 260, 262, 274; and representative agents, 289 (n. 13)

Gepp, E. C., 18, 114, 124, 138–39, 140, 290 (n. 23)

German air force. *See* Luftwaffe

German civilians: and Allied air raids, 3, 53, 172, 182, 283; and food rations, 15, 22, 23, 26, 27, 37, 84, 87; attitude toward British POWs, 56; and work camps, 60, 63–64, 65, 79, 80, 83; and sick and wounded POW exchanges, 105, 109, 110, 111, 112–14, 115, 137, 140; number of, in United Kingdom, 113; casualties among, 160; and fear of SS and Gestapo, 184; and safety of POWs, 185, 186, 190; and evacuation of POWs, 206, 208

German concentration camps, 200, 221, 284–85

German depot troops: and rations, 15, 21, 22, 23, 26, 55

German Foreign Ministry: and food rations, 22; and shackling issue, 46, 49, 52; and labor conditions, 64; and repatriation, 105, 108, 110, 111; and sick and wounded POW exchanges, 138, 139; and safety of Allied POWs, 171; and execution of POWs, 178, 182; and evacuation of POWs, 218

German High Command. *See* Oberkommando der Wehrmacht

German Naval Command (Kriegsmarine), 10, 106, 107, 149–50

German POW camp authorities: and condition of camps, 3, 86–87, 99; and relations with British POWs, 25; and relations with American POWs, 77–80, 83–84, 89; and food waste, 87–88; and punishment, 88, 89; and heating, 90–91; and Swiss inspectors, 94, 99; and evacuation marches, 97; and health conditions, 100–101

German POW camp conditions: deterioration of, 3, 5, 69, 90, 97–102; and overcrowding, 3, 16, 25, 36, 39, 55, 66, 88, 98; and camp authorities, 3, 86–87, 99; and reports from repatriated prisoners, 4, 54–55, 81, 84, 85, 246; and inspections, 9, 14, 22–23; and mail, 14, 16, 17, 31–32, 39, 55, 83, 88, 105, 307 (n. 54); and recreation, 14, 16, 17, 45, 46, 56, 57, 83, 182, 204, 300 (n. 80); and food rations, 15, 16, 17, 21–31 passim, 34, 37, 39, 55, 71, 84, 87–88, 91, 95, 101, 204, 282, 289 (n. 17), 292 (nn. 46, 56), 293 (n. 68); and clothing, 16, 17, 25–26, 31–34, 36, 37, 39, 91; health conditions, 27–30, 34, 54, 61, 62, 64–65, 68, 69, 81–83, 84, 85, 98–101; adequacy of, 38–39; and mental health, 54, 55–58, 101; British influence on, 65; and interrogation, 72–73; and heating, 90–91, 99; and evacuation of POWs, 98; and reports from escapees, 289 (n. 3). *See also specific camps*

German POW camps: capacity of, 3, 10, 33, 54, 55, 66, 77, 88, 98, 101, 161, 199, 282; inspection of, 3–4, 9, 11, 14, 17–18, 22–23, 27–32; types of, 4, 10; location of, 4, 189, 193–94, 203; Gestapo in charge of, 5, 186, 187, 199, 280, 282, 283, 286; organization of, 10–11, 28; administration of, 27, 186–87; and Geneva Convention, 39, 102, 171; and shackling issue, 49, 51, 52, 298 (n. 63); and separation of nationalities, 72, 75, 98; information forms required by, 73, 304 (n. 9); security measures of, 186, 194; and Red Army, 212–15, 216, 233, 256. *See also specific camps*

German POWs: and parcel shipments, 23; food rations of, 25; and Dieppe port raid, 40; shackling of, 40, 41, 44, 45; number of, 41, 51, 106, 107–8, 116, 154, 174; and escapes, 41, 181–82, 187; execution of, 41, 187; conditions of, 46, 86; and North Africa invasion, 50–51, 122, 136, 143; and labor conditions, 64; and sick and wounded POW exchanges, 106, 107, 108–10, 117, 119, 123, 132–46 passim; long-term POW exchanges, 150, 151, 154, 160; safety of, 171, 326 (n. 2); and safety of Allied POWs, 197–98; nationality of, 225, 226. *See also* Soviet nationals as German POWs

German-Soviet relations, 183

Germany: and Geneva Convention, 2, 27, 30, 39, 43, 92, 171, 187, 197, 202, 281; collapse of, 2, 182–84, 185, 186, 198, 201, 221, 269, 284; camp condition protests in, 4, 38–39; invasion of Poland, 9, 226; and food rations, 26, 90; and shackling issue, 44, 47, 48–49, 52, 53, 297 (n. 45); and sick and wounded POW exchanges, 58, 105–47 passim, 281, 282; transportation problems in, 89, 90, 91, 95, 97, 101, 203; and Swiss inspectors, 92, 93; and mixed medical commissions, 105; Allied invasion of, 159, 166; and long-term POW exchanges, 159–61, 162, 167, 283; deterioration of conditions in, 166, 192; and execution of British POWs, 178–79; and tripartite warning, 195–201; and safety of POWs, 198; and evacuation of POWs, 218–21, 285

Gestapo: and responsibility for POW camps, 5, 186, 187, 199, 280, 282, 283, 286; and relations with American POWs, 89; and execution of POWs, 175, 179–89 passim, 283; and interrogations, 177–78, 179; and treatment of POWs, 183, 184, 190, 194, 201; and tripartite warning, 195

Inter-Governmental Prisoners of War
Committee, 18–19
International Committee of the Red
Cross (ICRC): and Geneva Convention, 2; and inspection of camps, 3–4,
24, 76, 77, 78, 81; and British Red Cross
Society, 20, 21, 22, 26, 35, 67–68; staff
of, 24–25; criticism of, 26, 93, 94, 95;
and shackling issue, 48; and sick and
wounded POW exchanges, 54–55, 148,
150; and American Red Cross, 92; and
mixed medical commission, 105; and
repatriation, 106; and long-term POW
exchanges, 148, 150; and safety of
POWs, 187; and overrunning of Ger-
man POW camps, 220; and British
POWs in Poland, 248; and American
POWs in Poland, 269. *See also* Red
Cross parcels; Swiss inspectors
Interrogations, 46, 73–74, 177, 179, 184
Ireland, 106, 107, 108, 109, 110, 113
Iron Curtain, 255
Irvins, Fred, 156
Italian POW camps, 51
Italian POWs, 41, 51, 114, 118
Italy: and British POWs, 41, 53–54; and
sick and wounded POW exchanges,
114, 115, 118, 125, 144, 314 (n. 54); and
German POWs, 136; and Soviet
nationals as German POWs, 256

Japan, 43, 189, 196, 278, 347 (n. 94)
Jewish POWs, 125
Jews, 125, 202, 221, 280
Johnson, Herschell, 23
Jones, Garro, 24

Kadler, Albert A., 79, 98, 101, 210, 212
Kalway, William, 80, 98, 101
Kasserine Pass, battle of, 80, 123
Keitel, Wilhelm, 52, 172
Kennan, George F., 258–60, 275–76
Kharkov trial, 173, 174
King, William L. Mackenzie, 42, 45, 181–
82

Knox, Alfred, 19–20, 22, 24, 47, 151, 153,
219, 239, 291 (n. 34)
Knox, Gordon, 15, 16
Konev, Ivan S., 239
Kordt, Dector, 112

Lascelles, Lord, 332 (n. 99)
Latvia, 261, 273, 274
Law, Richard, 25, 124, 151, 251–52, 290
(n. 27)
Lazarette (military hospitals), 10, 27, 28,
29, 72, 74, 99, 216, 220, 299 (n. 78)
Leahy, William D., 119
Leathers, Lord, 149
Lee, A. W., 163
Lehner, Otto, 35
Liberated POW exchanges: and British-
Soviet agreement, 5, 69, 158, 168, 225,
234, 235–36, 238, 239, 240, 241, 245,
248–51, 252–53, 263; and U.S.-Soviet
negotiations, 5, 69, 216, 225, 233, 243,
249, 250, 255, 258, 264, 265, 266–76;
and British POWs, 5, 69, 220, 227,
228–29, 230, 232–33, 238, 239–40,
241, 250, 252, 254, 278, 339 (nn. 54,
60); and American POWs, 225, 233,
243, 249, 250, 255; and access to British POWs in Poland, 225, 236–49 passim, 254; and access to American
POWs in Poland, 225, 267, 268, 269,
270, 271, 273; and Soviet nationals as
German POWs, 225–34, 237, 238, 245,
254–65 passim, 274–76, 278–79, 285;
and Soviet POWs, 250, 251, 253, 254,
256, 257
Lithuania, 261, 273, 274
Lithuanian POWs, 177
Long-term POW exchanges: and British
policy, 148–52; British proposals for,
152–59, 160, 166–67, 168, 225, 283;
and British-U.S. relations, 154, 155,
158, 161–66, 167, 168, 282; German
proposals for, 159–61, 167; failure of
negotiations, 167–68
Low Countries, 9

Lublin Government, 242
Lucas, Jocelyn, 155
Luftwaffe, 5, 9, 10, 19, 162

Malmédy massacre, 195, 196, 283
Malmquist, Folke, 34
Margesson, H. David R., 21–22, 24, 26, 31–32, 106, 111, 112
Marlag Milag Nord, 10, 298 (n. 63)
Marshall, George C., 119–20, 165–66, 167, 173–74, 198, 217, 264
Marti, Roland, 77, 204
Massey, H. M., 179, 181
Matthews, G. B., 56
May, Andrew J., 102
Mayer, Eric, 77
McCloy, John J., 91–92
McGrath, John V., 186
McLardey, Turner, 212
McNarney, Joseph T., 119, 273
Medical personnel: and sick and wounded POW exchanges, 107, 109–10, 114, 116, 117, 120, 135, 137, 141, 142, 143; and activation for German combat duty, 140–41, 142; and evacuation of POWs, 207; and access to British POWs in Poland, 244; and American POWs under Soviet supervision, 256, 267
Meier, M., 78, 79
Members of Parliament (MPs): and criticism of British policy on POWs, 19, 22, 24, 66, 67, 236, 239, 281; and Red Cross parcels, 25, 35, 36; and conditions of German POW camps, 39, 94; and shackling issue, 47, 50; and long-term POW exchanges, 154, 155; and repatriation of liberated British POWs, 239; and repatriation of Soviet POWs, 251–52; and Soviet zone of occupation, 254
Men of confidence (MOC), 11, 34, 76, 77, 78–80, 83, 84, 101, 109
Mental health: and German POW camp conditions, 54, 55–58, 101; causes

of problems with, 56–57, 58; and Stalag Luft III, 57, 204; and sick and wounded POW exchanges, 58, 117, 155; and long-term POW exchanges, 151, 152, 156, 157, 162; and Geneva Convention, 153
Merchant seamen: and repatriation, 115, 116, 136, 144, 149, 150–51, 152, 160; as POWs, 154, 167, 323–24 (n. 7)
Mickelson, Stanley R., 276
Middle East, 1, 41, 121, 122, 128, 144, 154, 157–59, 227
Miller, Philip B., 58, 91
Mining camps, 31, 61–65
Mixed medical commission (MMC): and Geneva Convention, 105, 312 (n. 2); and sick and wounded POW exchanges, 106, 107, 108–9, 114, 117, 118, 124–40 passim, 145; and long-term POW exchanges, 153
Molotov, Vycheslav: and evacuation of POWs, 215; and British-Soviet relations, 229, 233, 237, 238, 240–46, 247, 252, 260; and U.S.-Soviet relations, 255–56, 258, 260, 269, 270, 347 (n. 83)
Morgenthau, Henry, Jr., 197
Morris-Jones, Henry, 24
Moscow Commission, 241–42
Moscow Conference of Foreign Ministers, 230, 233, 257, 330 (n. 62)
Murphy, Robert, 278
Murray, Vance B., 27–30, 293 (n. 68)

Naville, Gabriel, 34, 54, 60–62, 65, 160, 161, 175, 177, 178, 199
Nazi leadership: and treatment of POWs, 2, 174, 183, 184, 185, 187, 199, 202; and racist ideology, 2, 221, 280, 284; pragmatism of, 5; and shackling issue, 50; and sick and wounded POW exchanges, 125; and long-term POW exchanges, 154, 162; and safety of POWs, 197, 201, 202; and fear of capture by Soviets, 284
Nazi Redoubts, 192

Sales, A., 62–63

Sanderson, Frank, 47

Sargent, Orme, 214, 239, 245, 333 (n. 100)

Sark Island raid (Operation Basalt), 40–41, 42, 187

Schirmer, Robert, 76, 83, 216

Schmidt, Paul Karl, 173

Schutzstaffel (SS): and responsibility for POW camps, 5, 65, 187, 198–99, 201, 282, 283, 286; and long-term POW exchanges, 162; and treatment of POWs, 183, 184, 194, 199, 201; and execution of POWs, 183, 184–85, 188, 195, 196; and Austria, 193; and tripartite warning, 195; and evacuation of POWs, 212

Selborne, Lord, 226–27

Senior American officers (SAOs), 11, 74, 185–86, 205

Senior British officers (SBOs), 11, 14, 18, 178, 179, 184, 204, 205–6, 207, 289 (n. 13)

Shackling issue: and Dieppe port raid, 40; and British POWs, 40–52 passim; and Geneva Convention, 40, 41, 43, 46–47, 48, 294–95 (n. 3), 297 (n. 45); and Sark Island raid, 40–41; Churchill's handling of, 41–53 passim; and Dominion governments, 42–43, 44, 51, 52, 53, 281, 295 (n. 13); and mental health, 55; and sick and wounded POW exchanges, 115; and safety of POWs, 171; and reciprocity, 281

Sick and wounded POW exchanges: and reports of POWs' condition, 4, 81, 84, 184; negotiations for, 4–5, 110–13, 114, 118, 160; and shackling issue, 52; and reciprocity, 53; and International Committee of the Red Cross, 54–55; and mental health, 58, 155; and long-term POWs, 66, 148, 150, 155, 157; and transportation, 105, 106, 117, 126–27, 128, 129–30, 131, 145, 146; and Geneva Convention, 106–19 passim, 124, 125,

128, 139, 141, 311–12 (n. 1); and compromises, 111–16; and Anglo-American proposal, 116–22; and first exchanges, 122–25; and second Barcelona exchange, 125–32; and strategic concerns, 129, 131, 132, 140, 144–45; and second Gothenburg exchange, 132–40; and final exchange, 140–44; and last attempts, 144–46; and liberated POWs, 158

Slavin, N. V., 256, 261

Smuts, J. C., 44–45

Soldiers, Sailors and Air Force Families Association, 31

Somerville, Annesley, 22

South Africa, 43, 45

South African POWs, 177

Southern Rhodesian POWs, 53

Soviet civilians, 231–32, 236, 256, 260, 274

Soviet Foreign Office, 258

Soviet High Command, 237

Soviet Military Mission in London, 228

Soviet nationals: serving in German Army, 225, 227, 255–57, 260, 275; definition of, 256, 259, 260–62, 263, 265, 273–74, 276, 343 (n. 29)

Soviet nationals as German POWs: and British-Soviet relations, 225–34, 237, 245, 254, 285; and Yalta Conference, 234–35; and U.S.-Soviet relations, 255, 256, 260, 261, 262, 263, 265, 274–76, 278–79, 285

Soviet POWs: German treatment of, 44, 231, 251, 257, 280, 281; number of, 90, 192; and safety of POWs, 190; location of, 203; evacuation of, 230–31; and liberated POW exchanges, 250, 251, 253, 254, 256, 257; treatment in France, 258; and Soviet nationals as German POWs, 261; American treatment of, 271

Soviet Repatriation Committee, 250, 261, 266, 278

Soviet Union: Hitler's attack of, 3, 5, 26,

113; invasion of Germany, 5, 68, 69, 193–94, 203, 204; and retaliation, 44; and long-term POW exchanges, 154–55, 158, 162, 164; and Kharkov trial, 173, 174; and safety of POWs, 193; and tripartite warning, 195, 198, 200; and evacuation of POWs, 213, 214, 215, 219, 220; geopolitical interests of, 225; and execution of Soviet nationals as German POWs, 225, 227, 260, 264, 285; and repatriation of United Nations POWs, 231; and reorganization of Polish government, 242, 246, 270, 272, 285; propaganda hostile to, 257, 259; and Nazi racist ideology, 280. *See also* British-Soviet relations; Red Army; U.S.-Soviet relations

Soviet zone of occupation (Germany), 190, 192, 194, 254

Soviet zone of occupation (Japan), 278

Spain, 107, 108, 117

SS. *See* Schutzstaffel

Stalag II B (Hammerstein), 81–86, 90, 306 (n. 45), 341 (n. 3)

Stalag II D (Stargard), 27

Stalag III A (Luckenwalde), 72, 98

Stalag III B (Fürstenberg), 75–81, 90, 96, 99, 101, 186

Stalag III C (Alt Drewitz), 90–91

Stalag IV A (Hohnstein), 64

Stalag IV D/Z (Annaburg), 91

Stalag IV F (Hartmansdorf), 65

Stalag IX B (Hessen-Nassau), 25

Stalag IX C (Bad Sulza), 30, 45, 49, 298 (nn. 63, 73)

Stalag 344 (Lamsdorf), 156, 203, 204, 210, 212, 341 (n. 3)

Stalag 383 (Hohenfels), 298 (nn. 63, 73), 299 (n. 78)

Stalag Luft I (Barth), 57, 86–89, 90, 91, 98, 307 (n. 54)

Stalag Luft III (Sagan): conditions of, 55, 56, 299–300 (n. 80); and mental health, 57, 204; and number of American POWs, 72, 90, 341 (n. 3); escapes

from, 88, 175, 177–78, 181, 185, 186–87, 189, 204; and long-term POW exchanges, 152, 156; and executions of POWs, 175–82, 185, 189, 199, 204, 283; and safety of POWs, 186; and evacuation of POWs, 204–10; and number of British POWs, 298 (n. 73)

Stalag Luft IV (Gross Tychow), 90, 341 (n. 3)

Stalag Luft VI (Heydekrug), 256, 299 (n. 78), 341 (n. 3)

Stalag Luft VII (Bankau), 341 (n. 3)

Stalag VII A (Moosburg), 68, 90, 98

Stalag VII B (Memmingen), 55

Stalag VIII A (G"rlitz), 204

Stalag VIII B (Lamsdorf): and number of British POWs, 30, 33, 60, 298 (n. 73); conditions of, 31–36, 54; and shackling issue, 49, 298 (n. 63); and working parties, 60–61; and number of American POWs, 72; and evacuation of POWs, 204

Stalag VIII B (Teschen), 62, 65, 203

Stalag VIII C (Kunau), 212

Stalag XII A (Limburg), 90

Stalag XIII C (Hammelburg), 94, 101, 330 (n. 68)

Stalag XIII D (Nuremberg), 101

Stalag XVII B (Gneixendorf), 65, 86, 90, 185

Stalag XVIII A (Wolfsberg, Austria), 30, 298 (n. 73)

Stalag XVIII D, 30, 293 (n. 72)

Stalag XX A (Thorn Podgorz), 11, 14, 60, 293 (n. 70), 298 (n. 73)

Stalag XX B (Marienburg), 30, 36–38, 298 (n. 73)

Stalag XXI D (Posen), 30

Stalags: as type of German POW camp, 10; organization of, 11, 68; and food rations, 27, 29, 293 (n. 68); conditions of, 55; and punishment, 85, 89

Stalags Luft, 10

Stalin, Josef: and Kharkov trial, 173; and safety of POWs, 198, 199, 200–201,

Arieh J. Kochavi is professor of modern history and chair of the history department at the University of Haifa. He is author of *Post-Holocaust Politics: Britain, the United States, and Jewish Refugees, 1945–1948* and *Prelude to Nuremberg: Allied War Crimes Policy and the Question of Punishment.*